A REVOLUTIONARY HISTORY OF INTERWAR INDIA

KAMA MACLEAN

A Revolutionary History
of Interwar India

Violence, Image, Voice and Text

OXFORD
UNIVERSITY PRESS

OXFORD
UNIVERSITY PRESS

Oxford University Press is a department of the
University of Oxford. It furthers the University's objective
of excellence in research, scholarship, and education
by publishing worldwide.

Oxford   New York
Auckland   Cape Town   Dar es Salaam   Hong Kong   Karachi
Kuala Lumpur   Madrid   Melbourne   Mexico City   Nairobi
New Delhi   Shanghai   Taipei   Toronto

With offices in
Argentina   Austria   Brazil   Chile   Czech Republic   France   Greece
Guatemala   Hungary   Italy   Japan   Poland   Portugal   Singapore
South Korea   Switzerland   Thailand   Turkey   Ukraine   Vietnam

Oxford is a registered trade mark of Oxford University Press
in the UK and certain other countries.

Published in the United States of America by
Oxford University Press
198 Madison Avenue, New York, NY 10016

Library of Congress Cataloging-in-Publication Data is available
Maclean, Kama.
A Revolutionary History of Interwar India
ISBN 978-0-19-021715-0 paperback
978-0-19-939611-5 hardback

Printed in India on acid-free paper

CONTENTS

CONTENTS

ACKNOWLEDGEMENTS

I visited Amritsar while on sabbatical in 2007 and couldn't help noticing pictures of Bhagat Singh everywhere in the town's bazaars. *Rang de Basanti* had recently been released, and Bhagat Singh was on my mind; I had shown parts of the film, despite its ahistoricity, to my class. One student became so enthused that she approached me to write her paper on the way in which the revolutionaries had impacted on the mainstream nationalist movement. Sure, I said. She soon returned, disappointed, reporting that there was simply not enough scholarship to support her thesis. Of course, this gap had been noticed several years earlier by Christopher Pinney in his engaging book, *'Photos of the Gods'*. That is how this project was born.

Much of the initial archival research was completed while I was employed as Professorial Research Fellow at the University of the United Arab Emirates in 2009. I remain grateful to the university and my colleagues in Al Ain for their support while I was in India, researching; or in absentia, writing; in particular to Rory Hume and Don Baker for their staunch support for the project. From 2010–2013, the project was furthered back at UNSW in Sydney. I am especially thankful for the encouragement of Dipesh Chakrabarty, Christopher Pinney and Michael Dwyer, each of whom insisted that I draw together the material as a book; Chris kindly provided the poster on the cover.

I have accrued many other debts to readers, mentors and friends, and am especially grateful to those who generously pored over and commented on drafts of the manuscript: Sekhar Bandyopadhyay, Geoffrey Batchen, Dipesh Chakrabarty, Ian Copland, Robin Jeffrey, Tom Weber and Ben Zachariah. For their feedback on ideas, individual chapters and papers, I wish to thank Vinayak Chaturvedi, Frank Conlon, Assa Doron, Sandria Freitag, Charu Gupta, Max Harcourt, Philip Lutgendorf, Jim Masselos, Christopher Pinney, Ira Raja, Anupama Roy and Ujjwal Kumar Singh. I will always be grateful to the anonymous readers who provided helpful feedback along the way, as I published early chapters and various other fragments as articles. Audiences at workshops (Georg-August-Universität, Göttingen;

ACKNOWLEDGEMENTS

La Trobe University; the Australian National University) at conferences (the AHA, AAS, ECSAS, ASAA, and the South Asia Conference at the University of Wisconsin, Madison) and at seminars (at the University of Chicago, Northwestern University, the University of Sydney, Flinders University and the University of New South Wales) were also constructive.

I am grateful for discussions about politics and pictures—real time and virtual—with David Arnold, Greg Bailey, Chris Bayly, Adam Bowles, Harald Fischer-Tiné, Peter Friedlander, Durba Ghosh, Kajri Jain, Shruti Kapila, Chaman Lal, Rochona Majumdar, the late S. L. Manchanda, Anil Nauriya, A. G. Noorani, Ursula Rao, Sanjay Seth and Ian Tyrrell, which provided food for thought. The final stages of this project were happily invigorated by exchanges with friends and colleagues who took part in the 'Reading the Revolutionaries' workshop and double-panel at the Annual South Asia Conference at the University of Wisconsin-Madison in October 2012, partly published as a Special Issue of *Postcolonial Studies* in 2013. Special thanks must go to Daniel Elam and Chris Moffat for their engaged and thoughtful insights. And I am very thankful to Hurst's anonymous readers, whose astute comments made this book (I hope) so much better, and to Hurst's editorial team—particularly Rob Pinney, Alasdair Craig and Jon de Peyer—for assistance with copyediting, permissions and other niceties that bring a book to publication.

While thanking all of the above, I also must duly indemnify them: the interpretation herein is mine.

This research could not have be completed without the assistance and enthusiasm of the dedicated archivists at Teen Murti, particularly Shashi Anand and Sanjeev Gautam; Jaya Ravindran and Rajmani Srivastava at the National Archives of India; Rajesh Prasad, Curator at the Supreme Court of India Museum; Richard Bingle and Antonia Moon at the British Library; Kevin Greenbank at Cambridge University's Centre for South Asian Studies; and Jim Nye at the Regenstein Library, University of Chicago. I am also grateful for periodic research assistance by Aparajita Mukhopadhyay, Amit Sarwal, Reema Sarwal, and Aarti Rastogi; translations from Panjabi by Gurmeet Kaur, from Awadhi by Amit Ranjan, from French by Rachel Routley, interpretations of colonial legislation from Graham Greenleaf and generally helpful orientations from Pradip Krishen, and the hospitality of the whole Raja family. I am obliged to my colleagues in the Faculty of Arts and Social Sciences at UNSW, particularly Paul Brown, Ian Tyrrell, Ursula Rao, Duncan McDuie-Ra, Kristy Muir and Sally Pearson; as well as Glenn Forbes and Julie Nolan in the University Library. And it goes without saying that the support of my family, Michael and Clodagh, has been crucial throughout the project.

This book is a testament to the generosity and inspiration of friends, and it is to those friends that it is dedicated.

Early or partial versions of the chapters herein have been published as:

ACKNOWLEDGEMENTS

'Imagining the Nationalist Movement: Revolutionary Images of the Freedom Struggle', *Journal of Material Culture*, Vol. 19, 1, 2014, pp. 7–34 (a small section of Chapter Five is elaborated on in substantial depth in this article, which stresses the multivocality of imagery).

'What Durga Bhabhi Did Next: Or, Was there a Gendered Agenda in Revolutionary Circles?', *South Asian History and Culture*, 4(2), 2013 pp. 176–195 (Chapter Three).

'The History of a Legend: Accounting for Popular Histories of Revolutionary Nationalism', *Modern Asian Studies*, 46(6), 2012, pp. 1540–1571 (part of the introduction and some of Chapter One).

'The Portrait's Journey: The Image, Social Communication and Martyr-Making in India', *Journal of Asian Studies*, 70(4), November 2011, pp. 1051–1082 (an early version of Chapter Two; the argument in this book is extended substantially—the article now strikes me as too tentative).

A NOTE ON SPELLING

I have not attempted to override diverse spellings across various sources, nor to arrive at a uniform method of spelling words transliterated from the vernacular, and I refrain from using '[sic]' to flag slippages. I have kept the spellings consistent with the source from which they are drawn, embracing the disparities and variations that arise, reflecting the fluidity of everyday and/or historical usage (for example, Jawahar/Jowahir; Verma/Varma; Kapoor/Kapur; Bejoy/Vijay; Gadar/Ghadar; Kitchlew/Kichlu/Kitchloo; Cawnpore/Kanpur; Punjab/Panjab; and so on). As with the spelling of place names, there are political implications embedded in the spelling of 'non-violence'. While in colonial documents 'non-violence' is fairly standard, increasingly the accepted usage is without the hyphen. Contemporary Gandhians prefer the latter, as it confers 'a positive quality that is not well expressed by the simple negation, non-violence'.[1]

ACRONYMS

AICC	All-India Congress Committee
CID	Criminal Intelligence Department
CSAS	Center of South Asian Studies, Cambridge University
CWC	Congress Working Committee
CWMG	Collected Works of Mahatma Gandhi
DIB	Director, Intelligence Bureau
EINC	Encyclopedia of the Indian National Congress
GOI	Government of India
HP	Home Political
HRA	Hindustan Republican Army
HSRA	Hindustan Socialist Republican Association/Army
INC	Indian National Congress
IOR	India Office Records, British Library
IPI	Indian Political Intelligence
NAI	National Archives of India
NMML	Nehru Memorial Museum and Library
NCO	Non-Cooperation Movement
OHC	Oral History Collection
OHT	Oral History Transcript
PCC	Provincial Congress Committee
SWJN	Selected Works of Jawaharlal Nehru
SWMN	Selected Works of Motilal Nehru

GLOSSARY

Anna	Coin
Bhabhi	Elder brother's wife (sister-in-law)
Bhadralok	Middle class
Bhaiya	Elder brother
Bhangra	Panjabi celebratory dance
Chaprasi	Peon
Devas	Gods
Dhobi	Washerman
Didi	Elder sister
Filmi	Cinematic
Hartal	Strike, especially the closure of shops
Holi	Celebratory Hindu festival featuring the throwing of colours
Inquilab	Revolution
Jalebi	A sticky, syrupy sweet
Kalapani	'Black waters', commonly associated with the remote cellular prison on the Andamans Islands
Khaddar	Homespun cloth
Lathi	Truncheon
Leela	Play or sport
Panda	Hindu religious functionary
Prabhat pheri	Singing party, in this context akin to political street theatre
Puja	Worship
Purna swaraj	Complete Independence
Rakshasi	Demonic, evil
Ramnami angochha	Prayer shawl
Shaheed/shahid/ amar shaheed	Martyr, eternal martyr

GLOSSARY

Shraddha	Hindu ritual performed to honour the dead
Sola topi	Pith helmet, favoured by imperialists
Tika	Auspicious forehead marking
Tonga	Horse cart
Zindabad	An exhortation used in sloganeering, meaning 'Long live', as in *Inquilab Zindabad!* (Long Live the Revolution!)

LIST OF ILLUSTRATIONS

LIST OF ILLUSTRATIONS

LIST OF ILLUSTRATIONS

INTRODUCTION

VIOLENCE AND ANTICOLONIALISM IN INDIA

Historians have generally accounted for the centrality of nonviolence in the anti-colonial movement with reference to the influence and determination of one extraordinary individual: Mohandas Karamchand Gandhi, also known as Mahatma, Great Soul. From as early as 1909, when he wrote *Hind Swaraj*, much of Gandhi's thinking about nonviolence was framed as a dialogue with activists who favoured violence as a means of political redress for the oppression of colonialism.[1] However by the early 1920s, Gandhi had withdrawn from agitational politics, dismayed and disillusioned by the violent outbreaks that attended the Non-Cooperation Movement. From this point it was not clear whether Gandhi would continue to command nationalist action, or even be in a position to continue to steer the Indian National Congress within nonviolent parameters. As the Gandhian conscience of Britain, C. F. Andrews, remarked sagely in his introduction to Horace Alexander's book *The Indian Ferment*,

The one question which perplexes the soul of Young India to-day is not at all whether freedom is immediately to be achieved or not. Already that has been decided in the affirmative by every Indian who has thought over the matter. The burning question to-day is this: whether freedom is to be obtained by violent means or by non-violent means.[2]

Narratives of the Indian freedom struggle have been predominantly framed as a triumph for the Gandhian ideology of nonviolence, but there is much evidence to suggest that the interwar years were marked by urgent discussions questioning its viability. The contribution that this book makes to the scholarship of this era is both epistemological and methodological. It aims to reconsider the impact of the revolutionaries on nationalist agitation; to deploy oral histories and factor in other 'un-archived' materials such as satire, hearsay and rumour in reconstructing a history of nationalism in the interwar period;[3] and to lean on visual cultural artifacts to open a window onto debates about the anti-imperial struggle in British India.

The Revolutionaries[4]

The rather tight timeframe of the book is conveniently encapsulated by the term 'interwar', 'a transitional moment' in India, as elsewhere.[5] This book closely examines the politics of Indian nationalism from its moment of acceleration in 1928, with the agitation launched against the all-British Simon Commission on constitutional reform, to the withdrawal of the first wave of civil disobedience in 1931, with some spillover on either side. This was a formative time for the Congress, as it struggled with several new political developments: the injection of youth radicalised by nationalist colleges; the formation of a discrete but divided left in India; the emergence of women in nationalist agitation; and the rise of caste politics and an escalation of communal violence. These challenges pressured and changed the Congress from a loose movement to a more disciplined organisation.[6]

In revisiting this period, my aim is to factor in the political impact of the north Indian revolutionaries—the votaries of violence who coordinated attacks on colonial interests in an attempt to undermine British confidence and expedite decolonisation—on the broader nationalist movement. Focusing on the activities of one organisation in particular, the Hindustan Socialist Republican Army (HSRA), formed by Chandrashekhar Azad and Bhagat Singh, this book draws on new evidence to deliver a fresh perspective on the ambitions, ideologies and practices of this short-lived but influential party. I argue that it was no coincidence that the Civil Disobedience Movement—often thought of as the second great campaign directed by Gandhi and the Congress, after the Non-Cooperation Movement—substantially overlapped with the wave of revolutionary action unleashed by the HSRA.

As the party's moniker suggests, the revolutionaries of the HSRA were motivated by socialist ideologies and methodologies of dissent in Russia and Ireland; they aspired to free India from foreign domination as the first step towards the larger goal of creating an equitable society. As such they were deeply engaged in the nationalist enterprise even as they embraced different strategies and had their eye on a larger goal. In some ways, there were striking commonalities between Gandhi and the revolutionaries: both were prepared to face the violence of the state, and indeed, as Faisal Devji has recently reminded us, 'Gandhi's politics might not simply have been about independence' either.[7] Too frequently, however, the revolutionaries' well-known critique of Gandhian nonviolence is presumed to have rhetorically positioned them in perpetual opposition to the Congress as a whole. This conjecture has precluded a nuanced understanding of how the revolutionaries interacted with the mainstream organisation and its members on an individual basis.

The revolutionaries of the HSRA have long been marginalised in the academic historiography of nationalism, despite their extraordinary popularity in popular culture—in colonial India, this was most evident in proscribed literature and posters, and in contemporary India, in film, posters, comics and bazaar histories.[8] Yet it is demonstrable that the presence of the revolutionaries on the political landscape during these crucial interwar years strengthened the anticolonial front, even as they tested and ultimately redefined the policy of nonviolence. The dynamic between members of the Congress and the HSRA was far less antagonistic than is frequently imagined. Oral traditions whisper compelling stories of surreptitious connections between Congress leaders and revolutionaries, which have been largely dismissed by historians as unsubstantiated hearsay. This book demonstrates the important role that the revolutionaries played in influencing Congress policy and provoking colonial responses, in the process bringing India closer to independence.

While the importance of the revolutionaries has long been cemented in memory and popular culture, an overly rigid violence/nonviolence dichotomy, inferring a strict either/or choice between two opposing strategies to wrest power from the British, has towered over the historiography of Indian nationalism. Occasional moments of anticolonial violence are noted, but they are portrayed as deplorable exceptions to the nonviolent rule. Chauri Chaura, the town where twenty-two policemen were murdered in February 1922 by peasants raising the slogan 'Mahatma Gandhi ki Jai!', has come to stand as a powerful metaphor for the dangerous consequences of untrammelled peasant violence.[9] Gandhi responded to the indiscipline at Chauri Chaura by suspending the Non-Cooperation Movement, to the dismay of his Congress colleagues.

In the event, as many historians have argued, the pedagogical imperative that informed Gandhi's unilateral suspension of non-cooperation backfired. Indeed the suspension of the agitation in 1922 has been widely cited as the moment when a coterie of revolutionary organisations across north India came into existence, pledging to work to remove the British, using violence as necessary.[10] Moreover, the extraordinary popularity of revolutionary figures such as Bhagat Singh even during the first wave of civil disobedience in 1930–31 would suggest that support for nonviolence was far from unanimous or unambiguous during these years.[11] And while a debate might be had as to whether Bhagat Singh's popularity was predicated on his willingness to use violence to address the insults of colonialism,[12] it is evident from the speeches and resolutions made by Congress leaders straining against the dominance of the Mahatma in these key years that many nationalists believed violent action could not be precluded.[13]

The Mahatma and the Martyrs

What I wish to underscore in the following pages is the manner in which nonviolence was thrown into stark relief by the actions of the revolutionaries. The degree to which Gandhi struggled to gain acceptance of nonviolence as Congress policy has already been stressed by Judith Brown, among others.[14] More recently Perry

Anderson, pointing to Gandhi's early involvement in auxiliary services in British wars and his much later statements as colonialism was teetering on the point of collapse, has suggested that 'contrary to legend, his attitude to violence had always been—and would remain—contingent and ambivalent'.[15] Applied to his interactions with the revolutionaries, I would say, rather, that the Mahatma's approach to nonviolence was tempered by a pragmatism honed by his awareness of the popularity of retributive violence—even among Congress leaders—which frequently compelled him to make seemingly ambivalent statements.

By the late 1920s, a small but powerful canon of martial heroes and nationalist martyrs had been established, which provided a framework within which dissidents could aspire to challenge the Raj. At the top of a rather rudimentary list of such heroes would be the Chapekar brothers, hanged for assassinating the Bombay Plague Commissioner, Walter Rand, and his assistant, Lieutenant Ayerst in 1897; and Khudiram Bose, hanged in 1908 for bombing a carriage he thought to contain Douglas Kingsford, the presidency magistrate of Calcutta, instead killing two English women. Each attempted assassination inspired the next; the Plague murders inspired the formation of underground societies such as the Mitra Mela, and later the Abhinava Bharat Society by V. D. Savarkar in the opening years of the twentieth century.[16] A dialectic between one act of revolutionary violence and the next was soon established. In 1909, Madanlal Dhingra was executed for the murder of Sir Curzon Wylie in London, which he had plotted partly in response to the government of India's determination in hanging the teenaged Khudiram. In Bengal, Sir Charles Tegart (a policeman renown for his dogged attempts to arrest and punish revolutionaries) became the target of several assassins, including Gopinath Saha, who in 1924 shot Ernest Day, mistaking him for Sir Charles.[17] Assassinations proceeded despite their perpetrators knowing that they were destined for the gallows, and their final, defiant exhortations to their countrymen at the point of death became legendary. Their executions were celebrated as martyrdoms, high points in a genealogy of rebellion that reached back to the insurgencies of 1857. Gandhi was alert to this, and his convoluted statements on 'brave but deluded patriots' indicate that he was wary of the consequences of demeaning their sacrifices.[18]

One of the many outcomes of the revolutionaries' explosion onto the political landscape was that Gandhi was coaxed back into political activity in late 1928, to take part in the Calcutta session in December. The challenge of revolutionary violence forced him into an extremely difficult position. By 1931, it had become customary for Congress members admiring the sacrifice of the revolutionaries in political discourse to echo the ambiguous disclaimer which Gandhi incorporated in *Hind Swaraj*, disapproving of political violence while acknowledging Madanlal Dhingra as a 'patriot, but his love was blind'.[19] This was repeated in 1924 when the Bengal Provincial Congress, presided over by C. R. Das, passed a motion paying homage to the patriotism of Gopinath Saha, convicted of the murder of Day. From Sabarmati Ashram, Gandhi gave an interview to the *Times of India*, conceding that 'I would call murderers like Gopinath Saha patriots, but not without that indispensable adjective, namely, "misleading".[20] Gandhi later insisted the disclaimer be inserted into the Congress resolution.

But the executions of Bhagat Singh, Rajguru and Sukhdev in March of 1931 threw the Congress into a quandary, for the public commemorations of the deaths of the revolutionaries as martyrs had the potential to overwhelm the fragile truce just concluded between Gandhi and the Viceroy, Lord Irwin. At the party's Karachi session, held barely a week after the executions, Gandhi and the Congress leadership were forced to try to balance the popularity of the revolutionaries, notably Bhagat Singh, by reaffirming the Congress's stated ideology of nonviolence. The situation, Gandhi explained to a European correspondent who wrote to protest,

is very delicate. There is a romance around the life of Bhagat Singh. He was no coward. From all enquiries made by me he was a man of spotless character and of great daring. He exercised a great influence on some young men. … The only thing therefore that was possible and that the Congress was bound to do was to pass a resolution condemning murderous deeds as also the execution and at the same time appreciating the bravery and sacrifice underlying such deeds.[21]

However a wave of political assassinations that followed Bhagat Singh's execution prompted a much less cautious line from the Mahatma, which had the effect of perpetually alienating many of the revolutionaries' supporters.

A Politics of Impatience

The appeal of Bhagat Singh and his fellow revolutionaries to the inchoate body referred to as 'the youth movement' stemmed largely from their growing alienation. Radicalised in nationalist colleges, largely averse to joining the ranks of government, provoked by the deliberations and the hubris of the Simon Commission, and finding the Congress organisation dominated by staid and moderate elders, an underemployed and impatient body of young men began seeking alternative outlets through which to channel their politics. Other youths, too, were driven to commit to the revolutionary path during the 1920s, incensed by the humiliations of colonialism and their anger at the increasingly violent conduct of a colonial regime weakened by the Great War, the steady challenge of liberalism, the international growth of communism, and the effects of global depression.[22]

Enter the revolutionaries of the HSRA. The subcontinental usage of 'revolutionary' is rather particular.[23] While the stalwarts of the HSRA intended the moniker to signal their socialist inspiration and aspiration, in popular contemporary discourse this element of meaning was, and is, frequently dropped. As Maia Ramnath has argued, a reductive conflation of anticolonialism and nationalism has under-mined attempts to understand leftist currents in groups such as the HSRA.[24] Yet it is important to bear in mind that in the late 1920s, these ideologies were difficult to disentangle.[25] Thus Bipan Chandra describes Bhagat Singh as 'not only one of India's greatest freedom fighters and revolutionary socialists, but also one of its early Marxist thinkers and ideologues'.[26]

In the late 1920s, as the HSRA readied itself to challenge the British with a string of violent actions, the left in India and the Indian left abroad were far from united, with several 'contrasting opinions about the meaning of Indian commu-nism and its relation to national struggle'.[27] These did not promptly dissolve after the Comintern's ruling in 1928 that communists in colonial countries should break with bourgeois nationalists such as the Indian National Congress.[28] The HSRA and its front organisation, the Naujawan Bharat Sabha (NJBS, translated as the Indian Youth Association, or Young India Association), were as strongly attuned to insur-rectionary nationalist precedents—from Ghadr to the Babbar Akalis in Punjab, and to the earlier revolutionary movement in Bengal—as they were engaged in contem-porary trade union politics.[29] While the HSRA does not appear to have had close connections to the Comintern in the late 1920s, it might be understood as one of the leftist organisations that Mridula Mukherjee describes as having 'too strong a nationalist orientation to follow [the Comintern line] the whole hog'.[30] Having said that, this position altered once they were imprisoned, had time to read and reflect on communist literature smuggled into the jail, and observed the unfolding of civil disobedience around them.[31] Writing to Sukhdev, Bhagat Singh reflected that 'in jail, and in jail alone, can a person get the occasion to study empirically the great social subjects'.[32] Bhagat Singh's final ruminations are infused with commu-nist discourse and a sense of alienation from bourgeois nationalism, no doubt informed by his disappointment with the Gandhi–Irwin Pact.[33]

The HSRA lost some of its closest supporters in the Kirti Group (later the Workers and Peasants Party), when Sohan Singh 'Josh', Kedarnath Sehgal and M. A. Majid were arrested and tried in the Meerut Conspiracy Case in 1929.[34] The members of the HSRA were grasping for leftist literature at a time when the British government was beginning to seize it and arrest anyone guilty of affiliations with the international communist movement. The legislation crafted for this purpose—the Public Safety and Trade Dispute Bills—forced the HSRA's hand in April 1929, sending Bhagat Singh and B. K. Dutt to the Legislative Assembly in Delhi to throw bombs into the chamber as the Bills were read. Their subsequent battle in court became so closely connected to Congress politics that the construction of the revo-lutionaries as irate young nationalists has never quite dissipated.

Accordingly, 'revolutionary' is generally understood in contemporary discourse to denote actors who were willing to exert violence against the British in order to free the country of imperialism.[35] That said, it is clear that compared to the more deliberative Congress, revolutionaries *were* impatient, determined to effect a brisk if bloody transition to independence, and largely indifferent to the constructive nationalist programs which aimed first at building a disciplined citizenry before proceeding in an orderly fashion to nonviolent nationhood. The revolutionaries' use of the word 'action' to denote their decisive attacks on strategic targets is perhaps most indicative of their emphasis on urgent achievement. Unlike the mainstream evolutionary nationalists, the revolutionaries were willing to deploy weapons and bombs, and engage in acts of political assassination, with a view to altering the political landscape.

Despite their very different modalities of action, separating the revolutionaries of the HSRA from the rubric of the nationalist movement is a difficult task. The revolutionaries were deeply engaged with the Congress movement, even as they attempted to radicalise it through critique and polemic, but also through what can best be described as collegial interaction. Many histories of nationalism have noted in passing the connections and complementarities between the Congress and revolutionary movements,[36] particularly in the case of the province of Bengal.[37] At the risk of sounding overly theatrical, a British analyst declared that Bengal was 'the Hamlet in the drama of terrorism', cheered on by leaders of the Provincial Congress and political notables such as C.R. Das and Sarat Bose.[38] While the efforts of these lawyer-nationalists were mostly confined to urging revolutionary groups to take part in constitutional politics, or defending the revolutionaries in court, Congress organisation in the districts, 'especially in eastern Bengal, as well as the provincial committee, continued to be dominated by leaders with "terrorist" links right up to independence.'[39]

Much less is known about how the north Indian revolutionaries of the HSRA interacted with the All-India Congress leadership, although revolutionary pressure on politics is frequently noted in passing in many seminal studies of the period. Judith Brown, for instance, suggests that Gandhi's return to the political stage at the Calcutta Congress in December 1928 might have been influenced by the HSRA's assassination of a British policeman, John Poyantz Saunders, in Lahore a mere ten days earlier, reflecting that the Mahatma 'must have wondered whether the time was immanent for renewed satyagraha in order to "sterilise" the violence visible in public life'.[40] Similarly, D. A. Low describes how, by the end of 1929, Gandhi became 'exceedingly worried that violence might be taking control of his movement', implying that this pressed him closer towards confrontation with the British in the form of civil disobedience.[41] Significantly, before setting off on his march to Dandi to make illegal salt, Gandhi conceded that this *satyagraha* was, in part, intended as a 'safety valve' to divert 'the reign of terrorism that has just begun to overwhelm India'.[42]

Yet such arguments imply that the reluctant acknowledgement of violence on the political spectrum was the extent of revolutionary–Congress interactions. It was not. As I will argue, the revolutionaries of the HSRA demonstrably influenced Congress machinations by closely interacting with Congress leaders as individuals. While a few scholars of revolutionary history have long contended that such a dynamic existed, the detailed nature of this collaboration has not been fully demonstrated, and a close analysis of it has remained elusive.[43] There are good reasons for this.

Archival, Oral and Visual Evidence

The revolutionaries, as I elaborate in Chapter One, operated largely in secrecy, careful to avoid colonial surveillance. As a result, the colonial archive is of limited use in revealing revolutionary praxis. Besides this, the files of the Indian Political Intelligence unit held in the British Library were not available to scholars until very recently.[44] Reams of lengthy intelligence reports were released in 1996, when 'a large number' of them were placed in the India Office Records Division, in 'the only known instance of a British intelligence organisation's archives being opened to the public for research'.[45] With the majority of the seminal accounts of the operations of the Indian National Congress being drafted by scholars from the 1960s, the injection of Indian Political Intelligence files—constituting '21,660 volumes/files and 224 boxes' of data—to the archival pool cannot but transform our understandings of the conduct of the nationalist movement, even if some files have still been withheld, as the above quote seems to imply. While similar—in some instances, duplicate—files have been available in Delhi's National Archives, their absence in London until 1996 partially accounts for Western academic inattention to the topic of the revolutionary movement, given the reliance on materials of the India Office Library.

However, it is also evident that some historians have adopted Gandhian sensibilities to the extent that, like the Mahatma, they are dismissive of revolutionary actions.[46] Passive and often rather amorphous references in the historiography to 'the violence movement' reflect that posture as much as the condemnatory censure of the state. Gandhi was adamant that violent 'outrages' were detrimental to the freedom struggle, on several occasions engaging the revolutionaries in polemical exchanges.[47] Significantly, and often less discernibly, the colonial habitus implied by the term 'outrage' shaped the articulations of Congress members who learned to keep their sympathies for the revolutionaries muted.

As oral history methodologies began to gain broader acceptance as potential windows on the past in the late 1960s, projects such as those commissioned by the Nehru Memorial Museum and Library (NMML) and the University of Cambridge's Centre of South Asian Studies began to systematically record the testimonies of former freedom fighters.[48] Surprisingly, these have been under-used by historians, but the trend should soon be reversed, as the latter collection is in the process of being digitised and is available on the Centre's website.[49] Apart from the beauty of its free accessibility, the Cambridge collection is distinguished by the provision of not only a printed transcript, but the actual sound files of the interviewees, whose invariably elderly voices inject the transcripts, so dutifully typed out in staid courier font and overlaid with marginalia for absolute accuracy, with an animated and exciting interpretive layer.

Many of these accounts reveal important elements of the previously clandestine operations of the revolutionaries, including their dealings with the Congress. Similarly, revolutionary memoirs written since 1947 have been generally quite candid, relieved as they were of the threat of sedition that had silenced them before. Still, other pressures operating in independent India continued to constrain some testimonies. For instance, Bhikshu Chaman Lal, an ideologically agile nationalist who in the late 1920s and early 1930s worked closely with Gandhi and the HSRA simultaneously, curiously neglected to mention his revolutionary dealings in 1969, when interviewed by Hari Dev Sharma of the NMML. Yet he was far more outspoken six years later, in 1975, when speaking to Cambridge University's oral historian Uma Shankar, revealing much detail about revolutionary organisation.[50]

Chaman Lal's willingness to unburden himself only in the later interview might be explained in two ways. Firstly, it took some time for post-colonial governments to acknowledge the revolutionaries as part of the freedom struggle. The immediate security challenges facing the new government of India were such that it was reluctant to embrace those who had deployed violence against the state.[51] This remained a source of bitterness to many families of revolutionaries, especially those who had died on the gallows and those who were excluded from state welfare benefits that recognised 'Freedom Fighters' and their families were entitled to.[52] Again, while a number of former revolutionaries were absorbed into the Congress after independence, becoming party members and in some cases office-holders,[53] many more were drawn into the communist movement, and might be seen as transitioning from one form of anti-state discourse to another—an ethos embedded in some revolutionary memoirs.[54] And the government's stand on revolutionary violence hardened further after the Mahatma's murder in 1948.

These imperatives were reflected in 'history'. When the independent nation state set about crafting the history of the freedom struggle, it was the Gandhian narrative that took centre stage. Reacting to the mammoth state-sponsored project *The Collected Works of Mahatma Gandhi*, Manmathnath Gupta, a former member of the Hindustan Republican Association (HRA—the precursor of the HSRA), went so far as to label this as a 'conspiracy' forged by the 'hired historians' of the government, who in his view sought to downplay the revolutionary contribution to the struggle for independence.[55] Over time, the pendulum would swing; nevertheless, the electoral dominance of the Congress for much of the post-independence period has informed a party-centric teleology in history-writing.[56] This explains why some of the most detailed accounts of revolutionary history have been crafted not by academics, but by journalists.[57] Durba Ghosh has recounted how, when she began her research on *bhadralok* revolutionaries in colonial Bengal, archivists in India 'full-heartedly embraced this new project, telling me that the subject had been long ignored by "professional" historians'.[58]

In the mid-1960s, a change in the attitudes towards revolutionaries was discernible, with government projects formally recognising revolutionary contributions.[59] This shift was no doubt influenced by the popularity of the Bhagat Singh biopic, which by 1965 was in its third incarnation.[60] Bhagat Singh's mother, Srimati Vidyavati, was publicly honoured as 'Mother of the Punjab' in the 1970s, and was given a state funeral after her death. A number of statues were erected remembering the executed revolutionaries Bhagat Singh, Rajguru and Sukhdev, such as the Shaheed Smarak (Martyrs' Memorial) in Husainiwala, and in 1981, to celebrate the fiftieth anniversary of the hangings, the government of India issued a 'Homage to Martyrs' stamp, and the Punjab government issued a series of commemoration volumes.[61] Indira Gandhi was personally involved in some of these initiatives, entertaining former revolutionaries at her home in Delhi, and climbing ladders to unveil and garland statues of revolutionaries, including of Bhagat Singh in his ancestral village, Khatkarkalan, on the anniversary of his death in 1973.[62] When Chaman Lal was first interviewed in 1969, the prevailing *zeitgeist* that privileged nonviolence was only just beginning to shift; it was much more accommodating to revolutionary narratives six years later.

The second reason for Chaman Lal's disclosures in 1975 relates to the agendas and imperatives of his different interviewers. Oral history interviewers are in a commanding position when interacting with all but the most curmudgeonly subject. The desire of an interviewer to pursue narratives contrary to nationalist historiography was a powerful inducement for interviewees to relate previously unknown stories. Shyam Lal Manchanda, who conducted interviews for the NMML's oral history unit in the 1970s, was personally animated by revolutionary narratives, relishing revolutionary history so heartily that he 'could eat it!'.[63] He keenly pursued former revolutionaries and their supporters as his interview subjects, frequently cross-checking their narratives for accuracy—indeed, researchers attempting to piece together revolutionary histories owe much to his enthusiasm and dedication to his task. But the other primary interviewer in the early days of the NMML oral history unit, Hari Dev Sharma, was much more interested in Congress nationalism. When he interviewed Chaman Lal in 1969, he pressed him to reflect on his Gandhian encounters, and did not feed his interviewee any open-ended questions that would lead into anything but nonviolent territory. Sharma was of the opinion that the revolutionaries had failed to attract the masses, a claim which Manmathnath Gupta strenuously refuted when Sharma blithely presented the idea to him in 1969,[64]

Some historians continue to be wary of handling oral history—I was admonished by one scholar, early on in this project, for not providing an adequate disclaimer in a paper based on testimonies. Yet to continue to eschew popular narratives and memories in historiographical practice is to risk replicating or endorsing colonial knowledge formations. Naturally, some oral testimonies are clearly more reliable than others, yet we would do well to remember that this is also the case with colonial records, infused, as Ranajit Guha famously put it, with 'the prose of counter-insurgency'.[65] As an exasperated Motilal Nehru pointed out to Gandhi, the government's minutes of their crucial meeting with the Viceroy on 23 December 1929—just hours after an attempt by HSRA members to assassinate Irwin by bombing his train—'produce an entirely wrong impression of what you said'.[66] I have identified several incomplete or inaccurate colonial accounts in the course of this project alone. Oral histories, Mahua Sarkar recently reminded us, are 'an invaluable tool that can help raise necessary, if inconvenient, questions about what historical records foreground and what they marginalise'.[67] Mindful of the problems that beset all primary sources, I have drawn on multiple accounts—and have left aside tantalising allegations which I have not been able to corroborate—to reconstruct and understand the revolutionary pressures on the Congress Working Committee from 1928 into the early 1930s. There are disagreements and inconsistencies that arise between revolutionary memories; I have chosen to note these discrepancies in my text, rather than discount revolutionary voices.

In general, though, there is sufficient agreement between the former revolutionaries' oral testimonies and other sources to confirm those accounts. The respective testimonies of fellow travellers Shiv Verma and Jaidev Kapoor, for example, independently recorded two years apart, agree on all substantial aspects; indeed Verma's narrative of his own arrest in his interview closely mirrors the account recorded by the police.[68] Verma was a stickler for accuracy, challenging the post-colonial memoirs of some revolutionaries who sought to inscribe their own agency into a narrative dominated by Bhagat Singh, which he argued were written to satisfy a popular demand for the 'stories of heroic deeds of our martyrs, their sufferings, their exploits, their death-defying courage, their will to sacrifice everything for the sake of the country and its people'.[69] The discrepancies that are discernible in many oral histories tend to be minor, relating to issues over precise agency, as many historical actors vied to remember their role in a narrative that has been posthumously largely ascribed to Bhagat Singh.

Discursive Terrors and Gandhian Legacies

Perhaps the most powerful indictment of revolutionary politics was the imperial allegation that their resort to violence was illegitimate. From the British perspective, their tactics were 'terrorist' and therefore dismissed from the domain of rationality and legitimacy; there was no need to entertain any justifications or excuses. Of course, as governments do, the British viewed the nationalist recourse to violence as fundamentally different to their own. Aware of the derogatory deployment of the discourse of 'terrorism' by the government, the HSRA issued several manifestoes and documents qualifying their use of violence.[70] Moreover, post 9/11, 7/7 and 26/11, the term 'terrorism' has become so hopelessly embroiled in global politics that its use has come to take on an inflated and rather contorted meaning from its usage in the early twentieth century. In some ways, the word operated discursively then as it does now: to excise violent actions from the circle of reason and justifiability, and to enable the full brunt of state violence to be unilaterally unleashed, regardless of legal niceties.[71]

In the case of the revolutionaries of the HSRA, dismissing them as 'terrorists' gave the British the pretext to expunge and ignore their elaborate arguments in court that attempted to explain and justify their resort to violence. In his memoirs, Sohan Singh 'Josh' contended that the persistent use of 'terrorist' terminology served to defame the revolutionaries 'in the eyes of the Indian people'.[72] That this was successful to some degree is evident in the almost apologetic tone with which Balshastri Hardas introduced a chapter on the HSRA, translated into English from Marathi in 1958,

Citizens of Free Bharat! We now take you to the site of that battle fought by your predecessors as the result of whose struggle, you have the fortune to enjoy your present freedom. We beseech you, if you cannot appreciate their efforts, at least do not despise or deprecate them. For which of you can honestly come forward to assert that any one of those brave sacrificers had any other motives in their violent actions except the freedom of our Mother and the happiness of her children?[73]

In their rejection of revolutionary methods, the British received great comfort from Gandhi's disapproval of the revolutionary resort to violence. Gandhi implied that the revolutionaries were random and irrational, arguing that revolutionary praxis was underpinned by a philosophy of 'mad revenge and impotent rage'.[74] This was true, to a point: the HSRA themselves declared that Saunders' murder was to avenge the death of Lala Lajpat Rai. Nonetheless, the HSRA was a well-disciplined organisation—albeit one liable to youthful innovations and last-minute changes of plan. Terms such as 'mad' do insufficient justice to their strategic choice of targets and their consistent attempts to prevent harm to bystanders.[75]

It is also true that revolutionary errors were made despite well-laid plans.[76] Jai Gopal, the HSRA member deputed to identify the organisation's target, Superintendent of Police Jock Scott, in Lahore on 17 December 1928, failed to do so correctly, with the result that a junior policeman, Saunders, was killed instead (the revolutionaries regretted this, but reasoned that this outcome still met their objectives). However, it is important to note that the revolutionaries of the HSRA were not out to exert damage on just any target, and that many actions were suspended when plans went awry. In 1929, an action in Delhi was aborted at the last minute when the intended target, the Viceroy, failed to attend.[77] Likewise, when he went to bomb the Legislative Assembly, Bhagat Singh identified but renounced an opportunity to shoot Sir John Simon (leader of the infamous all-white parliamentary commission) who was seated in the visitors' gallery next to the brother of the Speaker, Vithalbhai Patel. Bhagat Singh later stated to the police that he did not shoot at Simon because 'it was feared that if the shot missed Sir John it would kill the brother of Mr Patel'.[78] This reluctance to take advantage of any situation was interpreted by David Petrie, the Director of the Intelligence Bureau, as 'abnormal' behavior for someone they were determined to construe as a unilaterally dangerous terrorist.[79] Constructing the revolutionaries as dangerous to all and sundry was an important strategy in the government's management of political violence, and vital to maintaining the morale of its increasingly Indianised police force.

The revolutionaries operated within ideological constraints and, for the most part, observed organisational processes that regulated their actions. In late 1929, Yashpal was dismayed when he was approached with an invitation to assassinate Mohammad Ali Jinnah, a plan which would have greatly inflamed communal tensions, and which suggested that the revolutionaries were seen as bloodthirsty mercenaries, looking for any opportunity to wield their weapons.[80] In an HSRA plot in late 1930, Hari Kishen shot at (but failed to kill) the Punjab Governor, Sir Geoffrey de Montmorency, at a university convocation ceremony. As his wounded target fled for the door, Kishen hurriedly explained to one eminent onlooker, Dr Radhakrishnan, that he missed his target because 'he had been instructed to see that not a hair of Dr Radhakrishnan's head was touched'.[81] The future president of India would be eternally grateful for such scruples,[82] although it struck the Governor as curious that Radhakrishnan could be so publicly favoured by the revolutionaries and still qualify, as he did in July 1931, for a knighthood.[83] In the same vein, posters issued by the party after Saunders' murder gave a sense of the procedural, in the enunciation that 'Under the rules and regulations of the HSRA (Rule 10th B & C), it is hereby notified that this was a retaliatory action of none but a direct political nature' (Figure 1).[84] Another poster twice expressed remorse for taking human life, pleading that in Saunders they saw 'the representative of an institution which is so cruel, lowly and so base that it must be abolished'.[85]

Oral history interviews with surviving revolutionaries emphasise that they were actuated by their analysis of the injustice of colonialism, which made a distinction between the evils of British rule and the British as individuals. Gajanand Potdar recalled that Azad had cautioned him against indulging in personal hatred: 'we don't want to be governed by them. But we should not hate them'.[86] Potdar further recalled that Azad reasoned that in killing selected British targets, the revolutionaries were sending a message to the government which might prevent future state

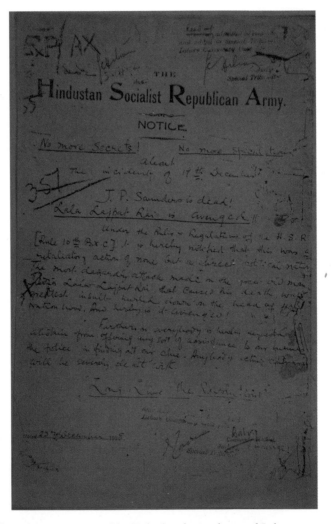

Figure 1: The HSRA notice signed by 'Balraj' and pasted around Lahore, accepting responsibility for Saunders' death, requests readers to 'abstain from offering any sort of assistance to our enemies the police in finding any clue'. (Courtesy of the Supreme Court of India Museum)

excesses, such as Jallianwalla Bagh or the *lathi* attack on Lala Lajpat Rai, from recurring.[87] In a similar vein, Jaidev Gupta, Bhagat Singh's firm childhood friend, submitted a recollection that while Bhagat Singh was in jail:

European or British ladies and children of the officials at times used to come to see this brave man of India. He would meet them just as his own family members had come. No malice against them for their being European or British. And when some European or British officer came to see him as a representative of the imperialist power he was very cold and hard towards him and even would not greet him. His fight was against the capitalist and imperialist system and not against any individuals. Such was the nature which can be felt and experienced and not explained. Had you the fortune of seeing him, you would have never forgotten the broad charming smile and pleasing manners with which he would have received you.[88]

Such extraordinarily personable details are difficult to reconcile with the social profile accorded to a terrorist, which the British government so energetically tried to press onto Bhagat Singh.

A credulous reliance on the colonial sources that framed the revolutionaries in such unambiguous terms has delivered a body of scholarship ill-equipped to engage with political violence as a phenomenon which posed a challenge to mainstream political thought. The need to evade the disparaging discourses enmeshed in colonial records calls for fresh ways of drawing out the revolutionaries' secrets; this is where images, as a popular commodity and a vehicle for the articulation and communication of revolutionary ideals, enter the historiographical picture.

Picturing Interwar Anticolonialism

While there has for some time been an eye for visuality in South Asian Studies,[89] anthropology has led the way in scoping out the analysis of images as a research methodology.[90] It was the path-breaking interventions of the visual anthropologist Christopher Pinney that first drew my attention to the question of a Congress-revolutionary nexus in the interwar years. In the course of his explorations into Indian visual culture, Pinney noted that images of Bhagat Singh are more prevalent than those of Mahatma Gandhi, in both contemporary India and in chromolithographs of the pre-independence era.[91] This, Pinney suggests, is a stunning anomaly, given the dominance of the Mahatma in narratives of the nationalist movement. 'Official history', Pinney concludes, 'has diverged so fundamentally from the popular narrative that it has left us with few tools with which to understand a figure such as Bhagat Singh.'[92]

In search of a corrective, Pinney has provocatively explored the possibility of a visual Indian history—'that is a history constituted by the visual in which the visual was something other than simply a reflection of something already established "by other means", to recall Carlo Ginzburg's phrase'.[93] Sumathi Ramaswamy has extended this, appealing to historians to 'work with pictures in all their denseness and resistant otherness, and fight the urge to immediately translate them into the recognisable certitudes of a (textual) history'.[94] Partha Chatterjee has contended that 'it is too early to pronounce on Pinney's specific hypotheses', but he has emphasised that the visual must constitute an 'appropriate source for the study of popular politics, especially in a country where most people do not read'.[95]

In Part I of this book, I draw attention to the importance of imagery in revolutionary strategy, and in Part II, I extend this by applying Pinney's hypothesis—using the images as evidence—by allowing them to both lead and corroborate written and spoken narratives. Here I build on my earlier explorations of this method to argue, in Chapters Two, Five and Six in particular, how a critical analysis of images can answer—sometimes even autonomously—important historical questions.[96]

The images that I draw on as evidence are of a particular nature. They are not, for the most part, photographs, but they do establish a close relationship with the photographic medium by referencing studio portraits of the revolutionaries, some of which were initially disseminated in newspapers. Herein lies their efficacy. Photography theory has deeply engaged with photography's alleged indexicality to a known (if past) presence before the camera. In 1930s India, a time when studio portraiture was growing as a social practice, the revolutionaries sought to enmesh themselves as martyrs in the public consciousness through photography.[97] Yashpal writes that it was standard practice for HSRA members embarking on missions in which death was a distinct possibility to have their photographs taken as mementoes.[98] Yashpal's own photograph featured him dressed in military uniform complete with the HSRA logo, although it seems to have fallen into British hands (as indeed did Yashpal, captured in 1932 after a gunfight in Allahabad) before it was ever disseminated through revolutionary channels. Other studio portraits, such as those of Bhagat Singh, B.K. Dutt and Chandrashekhar Azad, were taken strategically to illustrate the revolutionary struggle and were instrumental in gaining extraordinary public support for their actions, as I demonstrate in Chapter Two.

Images of Bhagat Singh and Chandrashekhar Azad—both handsome young men who died violently—powerfully captured the romance of revolutionary life. Their photographs underscored the tragedy of their sacrifices to their contemporaries, and they continue to do so today. Both portraits incorporated distinctive elements, which are famous symbols in contemporary India—Bhagat Singh's hat (Figure 8) and Azad's deliberative, moustache-twirling gesture (Figure 20) lent their portraits an enduring recognisability and a certain rakish style. These characteristic elements were replicated enthusiastically by artists, enabling the mass dissemination of their images across a range of media, predominantly in posters. Bhagat Singh's particularly dashing mien no doubt encouraged the replication of his portrait in the press in early 1929 to illustrate the major news event that was the HSRA's bombing of the Legislative Assembly, and enabled an abiding public recognition of him as the face of the revolutionary movement.

There is a considerable collection of revolutionary posters from this period, in both public collections in the UK (particularly in the India Office Collection, where they were sent to form a bank of proscribed materials, a *kalapani* of sorts) and in India, as well as in private collections. In these posters, the artists' replication of revolutionary portraiture establishes a link to reality that is implied by the photographic medium. In the Indian context, the implied nexus to reality is even more powerful, as in conversational usage, *foto* is part of the vernacular and is used interchangeably for 'poster', implying that no distinction is made between the two mediums. Indeed, it was this quirk of usage which partially inspired Pinney's anthropological forays in visual culture.[99] Likewise, in her analysis of Anand Patwardhan's documentary on Rup Kanwar's *sati*, Kajri Jain quotes an exchange between Patwardhan and Godavari, a Rajput cook, in which the former invites Godavari to acknowledge that a poster commemorating the *sati* (incorporating a photo-portrait of the doomed young widow) has been graphically embellished to include god (*bhagwan*). This is *not* a photo, Patwardhan suggests to her. But Godavari is insistent, according extraordinary power to the camera; of course we can't see god, 'but he'll definitely come in the photo'.[100] Similar comments have been made to me in the course of travelling and researching in north India. In the late 1990s I was emphatically assured by a vendor that a pilgrimage poster of Allahabad's holy sites was a *foto*.[101] As a representation of Allahabad's topography incorporating, by its own admission, *asli aur naqli* (real and imagined, in this context perhaps translatable as 'real and religious') attractions, including a constellation of gods and goddesses, the poster of Allahabad certainly represented a pilgrim reality.

In his other work, Pinney has demonstrated the ways in which photography's indexicality was engaged to challenge colonialism.[101] As a colonially-imported technology, photography—along with other elements of what Pinney describes as the 'xeno-real'—brought to India a 'form of colonially authorised realism that circulates outside its framework of origination'.[102] The interstice between photography and posters, in this instance the migration of portraits of the revolutionaries to poster art, creates a medium in which the seductive 'reality' of the photograph can be enlisted to establish challenging scenarios. This xeno-reality becomes even more powerful when the images are drawn from newspapers, as were Bhagat Singh and B.K. Dutt's (Figures 13, 22, 32).

There is a case for reading many of these poster-images as montages (even though they do not conform to the artistic definition, which implies a cut-and-paste methodology) to underscore the carriage of photography into them. By adapting replications of the photographic medium from the newspapers of the day, these extraordinary tableaux challenge contemporary readers to slot them into the certitudes of news and history. Figure 2, for example, which depicts the parents of the martyrs (Figure 32) delivering their sons' heads to *Bharat Mata* (Mother India), here the custodian of a transcendent reality, might be read as a semi-secular narrative of martyrology, tracing the posthumous trajectory of the executed revolutionaries. As Sumathi Ramaswamy has pointed out, the trope of decapitation overrules any pedantry over their precise mode of death—the knowledge that the trio were hanged is subverted to invoke a range of established conventions of sacrifice and martyrology in both Sikhism and Hinduism.[104] There is a large range of such martyrology images, some of which are more religiously-inspired than others in their depiction of a heaven officiated by gods or the divine *Bharat Mata*, perhaps emphasising the difficulty in imagining death outside of religious and cultural parameters.

Not all of these images are amenable to analysis; for each image a number of readings is possible and some images are deliberately slippery.[105] However, it is

"HEROES SACRIFICE"

Printed at The Janki Printing Press, old mewa mandi, Lahore.   Published by Krishna Picture House Lohari Gate, LAHORE.

Figure 2: 'Heroes Sacrifice', Lahore: Krishna Picture House, c. 1931. (British Library, PP HIN F 72)

possible to discern a preferred reading in the images by factoring 'the institutional/ political/ideological order imprinted on them'.[106] While the political context of the images will be unfurled in the following pages, the analysis of some images is hampered by the frequency with which some archives crop them, in doing so shearing off the text with their publication details. Much more can be gleaned from images whose provenance has not been excised, whether by archivists or by the artists and publishers themselves, who thought it better not to identify themselves with their subversive content.

What are we to make of composite pictures such as *Shesh Shayi* (Figure 3)? The styling of Gandhi as Vishnu (the controller, at rest on Sheshnag) certainly aligns with scholarly acknowledgement of the Mahatma as the dominant force in the nationalist movement.[107] However, the implication of a united front of nationalist agitation challenges the bifurcation of nationalist historiography into rival moderate and extremist camps. In *Shesh Shayi*, two Allahabadi moderates, Madan Mohan Malaviya and Motilal Nehru, and two revolutionaries, Bhagat Singh and B.K. Dutt, stand unproblematically shoulder-to-shoulder, accompanied by Jawaharlal Nehru, Vallabhbhai Patel and Subhas Chandra Bose. Leaving aside the well-known conflict of ideas between Malaviya and Motilal,[108] such popular images might reveal a general lack of engagement or concern with the high politics of the Congress at the time, or indicate a desire for unified purpose in the face of factional infighting.

We might dismiss such pictures as purely aspirational decoupages that compel unlikely personalities to share the same frame. However I will return to *Shesh Shayi* in Chapter Six to suggest that images might speak as productively as oral history interviewees as guides to historical inquiry.

A substantial body of these poster-montages were produced by presses in Kanpur and Lahore, both important bases of HSRA activity. Their referencing of revolutionary portraits (which, with the exception of Bhagat Singh and B.K Dutt's, were only circulated underground), and their apparent knowledge of revolutionary praxis belie an active sympathy, if not actual liaisons, with subversive organisations. In this, their highly coded enunciations in allegory and culturally dense tropes allude to a politics pushed underground. Thus these images echo contemporary narratives and theories—of which there were many in the 1930s—about politics in general and imperial perfidy in particular. Such images murmur hints about what transpired in nationalist circles and in imperial schemes, and how the two came together in a clash; they speak of legal travesty, nationalist imbrications, secret pacts, and implicitly understood strategies devised to challenge the empire. They act to plug the vacuum of evidence of revolutionary activity and provide an index to the popular debates about them in the interwar period.

The government threw considerable effort into banning political posters bearing revolutionary subjects. This speaks of their capacity to communicate a pro-revolu-

अत्याचारी शासन से पीड़ित होकर भारतमाता की पुकार

ग्रेष-शायी

Copy right No. 6.

प्रकाशक —श्यामसुन्दरलाल
पिक्चर मर्चेन्ट चौक कानपुर

Lakshmibilas Press Ltd. Calcutta.

Published by
SHYAM SUNDER LAL
Picture Merchant
Chowk Cawnpur.

Figure 3: Ramshankar Trivedi, 'Shesh Shayi: Mother India, overcome by oppression, appeals for help', Kanpur: Shyam Sunder Lal, c. 1930. (Author's collection)

tionary politics. Sandria Freitag has pointed out that a 'visual vocabulary works, at least in part, because it bridges the divide between literacy and illiteracy, crosses linguistic boundaries, and possesses sufficient ambiguity to appeal to people in various socio-economic and power positions'.[109] As vectors of anti-imperialism and targets of the censorship regime, these revolutionary poster-montages deserve to be read as evidence, and be interpreted as critically as any other document.

The Revolutionaries and the Congress

The core argument of this book is that the presence of the revolutionaries on the political landscape during the crucial interwar years served to radicalise the

INTRODUCTION

Congress which, in turn, injected a fresh urgency into the slow British project of constitutional reform. The book is therefore both a history of the north Indian revolutionaries in the interwar period, and a history that is revolutionary, in that it details the important role that the revolutionaries played in influencing the Congress, and thus bringing India closer to independence. In this, I extend the foundational work of S. Irfan Habib, S.K. Mittal and Bipan Chandra.[110] At the same time, outbreaks of political violence orchestrated by the revolutionaries served to reinforce conceptions of India's perpetual state of unreadiness for the responsibilities of enlightened citizenship. The revolutionaries' apparent distance from the Congress allowed the British to surmise that the revolutionaries were a marginal phenomenon that ought not to be taken into consideration in matters of constitutional reform. Tellingly, once the revolutionary moment had somewhat abated in the mid-1930s, more liberal British statesmen tended to view the extension of political representation to Indians as a way of precluding exasperated activists from resorting to violence.

Drawing on largely untapped oral history interviews, memoirs, pictures and colonial archives, I have assembled a story about the intersections between the HSRA, the Congress and the government of India. But this story does not follow a neat linear narrative; indeed it is necessarily messy at times because the legacies of secrecy are such that not all of the questions raised by this vexed tripartite exchange can be easily answered. Partly for this reason, the argument is elaborated thematically, in three parts. Part I examines the interwar period from the perspective of the revolutionaries themselves, drawing on a range of oral history testimonies to bring revolutionary voices to the fore, highlighting revolutionary politics and objectives which thus far have been obscured not only by necessarily stealthy practices, but by a strong hagiographical tradition in popular histories. Chapters One and Two explore key issues of revolutionary strategy and ideology, with attention to their objectives, planning, and operations. Chapter Three focuses on the life of one revolutionary in particular—Durga Devi Vohra—whose role in assisting Bhagat Singh's escape from Lahore has been celebrated in popular cinema, comics and bazaar histories (although many extraordinary details of her story remain entirely unknown). Additionally, this chapter provides a window into the politics of gender in the revolutionary movement, and an illustration of the level to which revolutionary narratives have been popular yet somewhat rudimentary.

Taking a different tack, Part II concentrates on the ways in which revolutionary politics overlapped and interacted—sometimes intimately and mostly clandestinely—with the Congress. Chapter Four traces the various intersections through which the Congress and the HSRA came together in three key sites of activity: Lahore, Delhi and Kanpur. Chapter Five demonstrates, through a more sustained analysis of revolutionary imagery, some of these interstices, before looking in detail, in Chapter Six, at revolutionary politics leading up to the all-important Lahore Congress in 1929. In this narrative, the focus falls upon the Nehrus—Motilal and Jawaharlal—who were at the front and centre of nationalist events, with father and son serving as Congress presidents in 1928 and 1929 respectively. Radicalism was to be expected of the young Jawaharlal, whose 'history sheet', compiled by Scotland Yard in 1927, noted his 'unenviable record in Indian revolutionary [as in leftist] affairs' in India and on the continent, a record marked by his meetings with an array of extremists and exiles, his support for the convicts of the Kakori Conspiracy Case and for 'suspect bodies' such as the League Against Imperialism.[111] In the 1920s, B. R. Nanda observed, Jawaharlal 'seemed to have outgrown the ideological framework of the Indian National Congress' and was straining against it.[112] But for Motilal Nehru, the formidable elder statesman who for decades led the moderate charge of the Congress, forming the Swarajya Party to critique British imperialism in legal and legislative terms, details of his revolutionary linkages reveal an unappreciated aspect of what would turn out to be the final years of his long and distinguished anticolonial career.

Part III considers the challenge of revolutionary violence to Gandhism, the British, and ultimately the revolutionaries themselves. Gandhi's conviction that nonviolent action was the only acceptable method of resistance was informed by his own belief in the immorality of violence. In the 1920s, Gandhi found himself pleading for the acceptance of nonviolence even if for reasons of expedience and pragmatism, on the basis that India was ill-equipped for an armed struggle.[113] Recent debates between scholars of nonviolence around pragmatic and conscientious approaches have seen these as very different conceptualisations of nonviolence.[114] Others have suggested that these typologies might be productively seen as different phases in the development of a political program, in which pragmatism eventually gives way to a contentious conviction of the immorality of violence.[115]

Pragmatism is by definition contextual. Provoked by stories of both prosaic and outrageous acts of imperial violence—among which we might include, on an escalating scale, the sight of British police flicking off *satyagrahis'* Gandhi caps, the whipping of young boys for shouting slogans, and giving orders to open fire on protestors in Sholapur—so many nationalist leaders accommodated revolutionary sympathies and Congress membership in the years 1928–1931 without extensive ideological dilemma. In 1931, in the aftermath of the Gandhi–Irwin Pact and the Karachi Congress which ratified it, it fell to Gandhi to insist upon tightening Congress organisation and to redefine nonviolence in utterly unambiguous terms. This is described in Chapter Seven.

While much debate on this period has been focused on Gandhi's apparent failure to save Bhagat Singh, Sukhdev and Rajguru from their fate by negotiating clemency, I draw attention to the dynamics generated by the British expatriate community in India as they responded to the rise in political violence, even as debates in British politics moved towards conceding the need for political reform in India. The politics of the 1930s spelled the beginning of the end of empire. This was becoming glaringly evident to all but the most strident apologists at home, exemplified by Churchill's well-known and oft-cited anti-Gandhian outbursts.

Most of the revolutionaries of the HSRA involved in the Lahore Conspiracy Case were arrested in 1929. The Central Committee of the organisation was re-formed, and a small number of actions were performed between 1929–1931 by a skeleton staff headed by Chandrashekhar Azad (who evaded capture to his death), although not all of these actions were necessarily directed or condoned by him. Despite the tenure of key HSRA members in jail, political violence escalated during these years. Sympathetic organisations styled themselves on the HSRA, and many individuals, excited by the surge of revolutionary action, took up self-appointed roles in a mélange of assassinations, bombings and other violent or disruptive activities that the government aggregated under the rubric of 'outrages'. It is telling that it was not until 1932 that the revolutionary wave in north India subsided, after the government unleashed a range of measures aimed at limiting the capacity for revolutionaries to organise. Chapter Eight draws together these measures, while demonstrating that a change in the revolutionaries themselves is as important in explaining the demise of the revolutionary activity, as was the weight of governmental repression and the withdrawal of Congress support.

The story told in the following pages is far from complete. There are oral history collections that I have not been able to consult, police records that I have not been able to access, and images in unseen collections that will add layers and twists to the narrative pieced together here, to say nothing of the sorts of 'un-archived' and un-archivable sources that Gyanendra Pandey has gestured towards.[116] The knowledge that other scholars are engaged in exciting revolutionary projects—recovering legal histories, tracing international networks, closely analysing the literary works of revolutionary actors, recovering historical memories and reading revolutionary literature—indicates that this book represents only the beginning of a larger, collective project of understanding revolutionary history, from a range of post-subaltern and postcolonial scholarly perspectives.[117]

PART I

THE REVOLUTIONARIES OF THE HINDUSTAN SOCIALIST REPUBLICAN ARMY

HISTORIES, ACTIONS, ACTIVISTS

1

OF HISTORY AND LEGEND

REVOLUTIONARY ACTIONS IN NORTH INDIA, 1928–31

The Hindustan Socialist Republican Association (HSRA), or Army, as it was variously called, emerged in north India in the late 1920s at a time when Congress organisation was relatively dormant. Historians acknowledge that during the Non-Cooperation Movement revolutionary organisations, largely based in Bengal but also Maharashtra, adjourned their operations at the behest of Congress leaders such as Gandhi and C. R. Das.[1] However, when non-cooperation was suspended in 1922, revolutionary organisations began to regroup, and, inspired by global precedents such as the Russian Revolution and Sinn Fein in Ireland, began to focus on strategic acts of violence in order to undermine the British.[2] By the early 1930s, they had made a substantial impression on nationalist politics, with the most prominent activists attaining legendary status.

Bipan Chandra identifies two discrete strands of revolutionary organisation that developed at this time: one in north India, the other in Bengal.[3] This reflects governmental attempts to understand political violence, which adhered to a rather basic Bengali/non-Bengali ordering principle. In 1933, for example, the government produced 'A Note on Terrorism in India (except Bengal)', with a comparably-sized volume detailing political violence in Bengal from 1905.[4] Such a division did not acknowledge that the north Indian-based Hindustan Republican Army (HRA) in its formative stages owed much to Bengali activists based in the United Provinces, particularly to fringe members of the Anushilan group.[5] There were several elements of cross-fertilisation between activists in Bengal and north India, such as in the sharing of bomb-making techniques and periodic, if informal, consultations on strategy.

The HRA's constitution, written in 1924 by Sachindranath Sanyal, declared its aim to be the establishment of a 'Federated Republic of the United States of India by an organised and armed revolution.'[6] Based in Banaras, Sanyal and Jogesh Chandra Chatterjee led the HRA, of which 'about 100 members were acknowledged'.[7] The HRA was scarcely able to move beyond the stage of fundraising, mostly in the form of dacoities, the most bold of which was an attack on a train transporting a cache of government funds in Kakori (near Lucknow) on August 9, 1925, in which Rs. 4,500 was stolen and a passenger on the train killed. The prosecution of the case took two years, and in 1927, four members were condemned to hang (Ashfaqallah Khan, Ramprasad Bismil, Roshan Singh and Rajendra Lahiri), five were transported for life, and a further eleven awarded jail terms. The deaths on the gallows of the Kakori prisoners served as the inspiration to the next generation of revolutionaries, led by Chandrashekhar Azad and Bhagat Singh, as did the writings of Sanyal, in particular *Bandi Jeevan* (*A Jailed Life*).

Following the prosecution of the Kakori Conspiracy Case, Bhagat Singh, who had established contacts with members of the HRA in Kanpur in 1923–4, aimed to re-organise revolutionaries across India, calling for a meeting of representatives from different provinces in Delhi at Ferozeshah Kotla on 8–9 September 1928.[8] Representatives of organisations from Bihar, Uttar Pradesh, Rajasthan and Punjab attended and agreed to form one organisation, and, motivated by the growing influences of trade unionism and communism, determined to undermine the British and work towards the establishment of socialism, renaming the organisation the Hindustan Socialist Republican Army.[9] Bengali revolutionary organisations were invited to attend but did not.[10] The contemporary Bengali organisations, most notably the Jugantar and Anushilan groups, had established a pattern of working independently, which neither was prepared to renounce.[11] More significantly, the HSRA constituted an ideological departure from Bengali revolutionary groups, which had from the late 1910s been strongly affiliated 'with caste and communal categories', both of which the new organisation sought to override.[12] Nonetheless, there were many Bengali activists in the HSRA, most notably Jatindranath Das who died following a hunger-strike in jail in 1929, and B.K. Dutt, born in Kanpur but with roots in Burdwan, who would be arrested with Bhagat Singh in April 1929.

The exact number of members of the HSRA at any given time in the late 1920s until its demise in the early 1930s cannot be reliably established, a deliberate and necessary result of the secretive nature of revolutionary organisations. The organisation floated across India's northern provinces, mostly based in Kanpur, Agra, Delhi and Lahore, although they had satellite hideouts in places as far-flung as Calcutta, Jhansi and Banaras. The organisation formed a Central Committee which allocated positions (Bhagat Singh was General Secretary; Bhagwati Charan Vohra was

Propaganda Minister; and so on)[13] to its most distinguished and dedicated members, and allocated leaders to each geographical region (for example, Azad was the All-India coordinator; Virabhadra Tiwari and Kailashpati were in charge of UP and Delhi, respectively).[14] Only the leadership was aware of the true nature, infrastructure and extent of the organisation. It is telling, for example, that once Sukhdev, the Punjab Commander, was arrested in May 1929, none of the absconding Lahori revolutionaries knew how to make contact with Azad, who rotated between hide-outs in Delhi, Kanpur, Agra and Jhansi.[15] This inner circle of HSRA operatives became the chief instigators of the two main conspiracies that they were charged with in 1929, namely the Assembly Bomb Case and the Lahore Conspiracy Case.

It is difficult to authoritatively name who was in the party's inner circle, partly because some of these would 'turn approver' and bear witness against their friends in court, in doing so fundamentally re-inscribing their relationship to the party.[16] Additionally, membership of the inner party circle continually morphed and adapted as key members were eliminated from active participation through arrest, internal politics or untimely death, and as fields of action shifted from Delhi to Kanpur, Lahore and Bombay. However, based on the list of those prosecuted for or absconding in the Lahore Conspiracy Case, members of the inner circle in 1928 would include Chandrashekhar Azad, Bhagat Singh, Sukhdev, Shiv Verma, Jaidev Kapoor, Bejoy Kumar Sinha, Gaya Prasad and Bhagwati Charan Vohra.[17] Yashpal emerges as a key figure slightly later,[18] taking a major role in the Delhi Conspiracy Case (revolving around the attempt to blow up the Viceroy's train in 1929), but also because he was one of the first of the surviving revolutionaries to write about his life, in the three-volume *Singhavalokan* (*The Lion Looks Back*). Additionally, members with particular skills were drawn on in order to carry out actions, among which were Rajguru, Jatindranath Das, B.K. Dutt and Durga Devi Vohra.

Yet of all of these activists the most celebrated has been Bhagat Singh; he has emerged as the chief character around which biographies, biopics, visual culture and histories of the revolutionaries cohere. Oral history sources relating to the revolutionaries, collected in the late 1960s and 1970s (at a time when Bhagat Singh's iconicity and popularity had been re-inscribed by Manoj Kumar's career-defining performance in *Shaheed* in 1965), name Bhagat Singh more than any other character, and his prominence in contemporary poster art and bazaar literature is equally impressive (Figure 4). This legacy of primary sources naturally skews this study, and while I will seek explanations of Bhagat Singh's enduring popularity in the following chapter, for the remainder of this chapter I will organise the narrative of revolutionary history around its central character, whose name has become synonymous with anti-imperialism. My aim below is to provide a rather skeletal chronology of revolutionary history with particular reference to historiographical challenges (rather than a comprehensive account of revolutionary activity in north India), which will form the matrix upon which successive chapters are overlaid.

Figure 4: 'Freedom Fighters', New Delhi: Subhash Calendar Co., c. 1960s. Portraits of Subhas Chandra Bose, Chandrashekhar Azad and Bhagat Singh, gathered around the memorial to Jallianwala Bagh. (Author's collection)

A Short History of Bhagat Singh

Born in 1907 into a family renowned for sedition—his uncle Ajit Singh was a peasant organiser and the founder of the Bharat Mata Society, who spent most of his life in exile, and his father Kishan Singh was a Congress worker who also spent time in jail—Bhagat Singh was under British surveillance from a relatively young age.[19] By his late teenage years he was, in police parlance, 'a well-known suspect' on his own account, as a result of his connections with the HRA in Kanpur, and his activities in the Punjabi youth organization, Naujawan Bharat Sabha.[20] The Criminal Intelligence Department (CID) had, in 1926, thought it necessary to place on the record that he was of 'medium height; thin oval face; fair complexion; slightly pock-pitted; aquiline nose; bright eyes; small beard and moustache; wears khaddar.'[21]

Using this description, police tracked and arrested Bhagat Singh in 1927, suspecting him of complicity in the bombing of a crowd celebrating Dussehra in Lahore. He was innocent of this, but the police alleged otherwise, charging him with testing a bomb to use in an elaborate plot to free HRA members accused in the Kakori Conspiracy Case.[22] After about a month of imprisonment, investigators were still unable to implicate him, and so he was released on the payment of a bond. He continued his organisational activities undeterred, forming the HSRA. The party began to look for openings in the Indian political landscape to make a positive impact on public opinion, and it was not long before they found them. 'Actions', as they called their strategic attacks on select public officials and targets, were carefully calculated and planned with clear propaganda objectives in mind.

The first of these actions took place in December 1928, although its genesis lay in events connected to the Congress-led protests against the Simon Commission, the all-white parliamentary delegation that had come to determine India's suitability for legislative reforms a month earlier. In a nonviolent demonstration against the Simon Commission in Lahore on 7 November, J.A. Scott, the Senior Superintendent of Police in Lahore, had ordered a *lathi* (baton) charge against protestors, in the course of which the aged Punjabi Congress leader Lala Lajpat Rai was gravely injured. He died ten days later and was publicly mourned. In a condolence speech, Basanti Debi, the wife of the late Bengali Congressite C.R. Das, issued a challenge: "I, a woman of India, ask the youth of India; What are you going to do about It?"[23] The members of the HSRA saw this as their opportunity to respond, and make a decisive impact. They began to plot to avenge Lajpat Rai's death.[24]

So it happened, on 17 December 1928, that Bhagat Singh and Rajguru, the party's marksman, gunned down J.P. Saunders, a twenty-one year old assistant superintendent of police, and as the pair made their escape, Chandrashekhar Azad shot an Indian constable, Channan Singh, who gave chase.[25] Saunders had taken part in the *lathi* charge on Lajpat Rai, so the party was satisfied that they had achieved their objective, and they placed posters with the HSRA letterhead around Lahore to make their point clear: 'Saunders is dead. Lalaji has been avenged'.[26] The HSRA dispersed, and Bhagat Singh, disguised, boarded a train for Calcutta. By February the HSRA had regrouped in Agra, where they set up a bomb factory. They began to plot further actions, including one on the Simon Commission in Delhi (which never came to fruition),[27] and another on the Legislative Assembly, where Bhagat Singh was arrested on 8 April 1929, along with his friend and co-conspirator, Bhatukeshwar Dutt.

From an elevated position in the Visitor's Gallery, on the speaker's right, the pair threw two low-intensity bombs, fired two shots from a pistol, and scattered HSRA propaganda leaflets into the legislative chamber below, before offering themselves for arrest. In doing so, they interrupted the passing of twin Bills that had been the subject of much debate and criticism in nationalist media circles. The Bills were aimed at smothering growing labor unrest and banning members of any Communist Party from coming to India in the interests of 'Public Safety'. By throwing the bombs as the ruling of the second of these Bills was introduced, the pair registered their protest at the imperial order. Their primary aim, according to their leaflets, was 'to make a loud noise'.

During a long drawn out trial, Bhagat Singh skillfully managed to turn Indian media opinion, which had initially condemned the attack on parliament as an 'outrage' committed by 'lunatics', in his favor.[28] Within days of his detention, he was linked to Saunders' murder, as he knew he would be.[29] Arrests in Lahore of key party members on 16 April 1929 led to more arrests, and eventually most of the inner circle of the HSRA was sent to trial. Bhagat Singh conducted the court case with considerable nous, inviting extraordinary suffering, undertaking several hunger-strikes and withstanding police abuse in the courtroom. In the twenty-three months it took for the imperial justice system to take him to the gallows, Bhagat Singh became a household name.

Recent scholarship makes it clear that, since 1929 when he first came to public prominence after his arrest and trial, Bhagat Singh's story has become deeply enmeshed with popular narratives and genres. A discernible body of Bhagat Singh scholarship exists, mainly in the form of biographies, and tends to inhabit the margins of mainstream nationalist historiography, but curiously has had little impact in the western academy.[30] It is only relatively recently that scholarship has begun to position Bhagat Singh and the HSRA within a larger historical framework.[31] Crucial to the problematic of polarised popular and academic histories is understanding why Bhagat Singh's story has for so long been the domain of vibrant popular histories, as opposed to its somewhat dowdy but more authoritative academic counterpart.

While Bhagat Singh's current popularity in India has already been deftly accounted for,[32] I wish to draw attention to the way in which his story was crafted in and shaped by the political ferment of the interwar years. Ishwar Dayal Gaur has written a lengthy account describing how Bhagat Singh is uniquely remembered in vernacular songs and poems as a colorful folk hero 'rooted in the heroic and chivalric traditions of the Punjab'.[33] A large body of Bhagat Singh literature has been produced since the 1930s in both Hindi and Bengali (linguistic regions where he was briefly active during his short life),[34] and writings in regional languages such as Marathi, Gujarati and Tamil, speak of an enduring All-India appeal.[35]

Christopher Pinney argues that Bhagat Singh's extraordinary prominence in Indian visual culture, when measured against his neglect by historians, is 'one of the puzzles of twentieth-century Indian history'.[36] Pinney is struck by the fact that 'official history has diverged so fundamentally from the popular narrative',[37] and he contends that exploration of a visual history has the potential to illuminate popular narratives and unveil histories repressed by the biases of conventional academic methodologies and nationalist history writing.[38] While this is a rich mode of inquiry, and one that I will take up in later chapters, the problem is not simply one of visual versus written histories. Written sources do exist, but they have been relegated to forms of chronicling the past which have until relatively recently have been eschewed by academics. It is true, however, that the vibrant lithographs and colorful calendars featuring Bhagat Singh which populate Indian urban spaces even today are the most visible referent of a broader historiographical problem.

Clandestine Histories

Bhagat Singh's life has necessarily been the preserve of the popular since his death, because several levels of censorship have colluded to frustrate the documentation and retrieval of his story. The first among these was self-censorship. As a key member of several organisations identified as seditious by the government, Bhagat Singh's actions and whereabouts in the years before his arrest were necessarily secretive. Members of the HSRA were informed of actions purely on a need-to-know basis; as a result, only members of the inner circle were informed of party plans or the activities of key members at any given time.[39] The organisation had learned much from the Kakori Conspiracy Case, in which the testimonies of three former members were key in capturing and convicting members of the HRA, effectively depleting it of active members.

Bhagat Singh had been pressured to turn government witness (or 'approver') after his first arrest in May 1927 in connection with the Dussehra Bomb Case in Lahore. He was suspected of involvement not only because he was 'the nephew of the notorious Ajit Singh',[40] but also because of his connection with several leftist youth movements, in particular the Naujawan Bharat Sabha,[41] which had, as the Bureau of Intelligence put it, 'adopted as their ideal the inculcation of revolutionary sentiments and of disloyalty to the government'.[42] Bhagat Singh was contemptuous of the offer of freedom and a reward in return for a statement.[43] Realising the intense pressure that was brought to bear by inquisitors on suspects and under-trial prisoners, the HSRA conducted operations with as much discretion as possible to give interrogated members the benefit of deniability.[44] The statements of approvers could be informative up to a point, but simultaneously frustrating in their inability to provide a complete picture of events. Jai Gopal, whose testimony was used to convict Bhagat Singh and his comrades in the Lahore Conspiracy Case, made frequent reference to the fact that Sukhdev 'used to keep all the facts concealed' from him, additionally forbidding him explicitly from 'divulging any secret of the society to Pandit Yashpal', who himself was a party member.[45] More than one attempt to prosecute members of the HSRA failed on the basis of weak or inconclusive evidence squeezed out of approvers.

Similarly, the extensive use of multiple aliases in the party served to confuse investigators. Sukhdev was identified by investigators as 'Sukhdev alias Dayal alias Swami alias Villager', but many of Bhagat Singh's identities remained uncompromised.[46] In the late 1920s, Bhagat Singh was known to many as Balwant, and he used several adjectival pen-names when he wrote for newspapers and periodicals, among which were *Vidrohi* (rebel), *Agyat* (unknown) and *Sainik* (soldier).[47] The soon-to-be knighted David Petrie, Director of Intelligence in Delhi (and himself a former Senior Superintendent of Lahore, whose experience in India would one day qualify him to serve as director-general of MI5),[48] declared that the evidence was 'incontrovertible' that Bhagat Singh was 'Balraj, Chief of the Hindustan Socialist Republican Army', the signatory of the manifesto showered on the Assembly and the author of posters fixed in public places throughout Lahore after Saunders' murder.[49] This was contradicted decades later by a member of the HSRA's inner circle, Shiv Verma, who disclosed that Balraj was actually Chandrashekhar Azad.[50] The use of coded language among party members requires, today as then, an inner party member to decipher the meaning of party communications. Few would guess that a letter requesting the recipient to observe a *shraddha* ceremony on a given date was in fact an invitation to attend a provincial HRA council session, as Sohan Singh 'Josh' revealed in an interview with Max Harcourt in the 1960s.[51]

The shadowy movements of absconding HSRA members have established a somewhat unstable narrative, which allows for contention and some speculation. HSRA members adopted different disguises as a means of passing through the various towns in which they operated undetected. CID investigators had detailed physical descriptions of key party members, in which sartorial choices, including regional styles, were often noted.[52] Bhagat Singh, according to a 1926 CID description, reliably wore khaddar.[53] It was to spoil assumptions such as this that he abandoned his usual kurta-pyjama and styled himself as a Gujarati businessman, donning a dhoti and coat, and on another occasion, dressed in the conspicuous style of a Delhi-wallah.[54] According to Shiv Verma, Bhagat Singh was the hardest of all party members to disguise, because by the late 1920s he was well known to police, and besides, he 'was a handsome figure—amongst hundreds of people, obviously, he would be spotted'.[55]

It is thought that Bhagat Singh attended the Calcutta Congress in disguise in the weeks overlapping late December 1928 and early January 1929, after he fled Lahore following Saunders' murder.[56] Durga Devi Vohra denied this in an interview she gave in 1972, remembering that while in Calcutta Bhagat Singh stayed indoors during the day to avoid detection, feigning illness and supping on *rotis* dipped in ghee, only going out at night in disguise.[57] Sohan Singh 'Josh' recalled

meeting Bhagat Singh on 24 December 1928 in Calcutta at an unlikely location—
a shaving saloon: 'Just think! Josh entering a shaving saloon in Calcutta with a
flowing beard and all the Sikh paraphernalia about him, and the CID shadowing
him and hunting everywhere for Bhagat Singh.'[58] Chhabil Das, Bhagat Singh's
former teacher from Lahore, reported catching a fleeting glimpse of Bhagat Singh
in the Calcutta home of Chajju Ram, a Panjabi merchant. Das presumed that
Bhagat Singh was attending sessions of the Congress meeting.[59] This was not an
altogether unreasonable assumption, given that Bhagat Singh had attended earlier
Congress sessions,[60] the interest he had in Congress politics, and the institutional
porousness that existed at the time between the Congress, particularly its emergent
left, and the Naujawan Bharat Sabha.[61]

Moreover, as was well known by the CID, it was 'consistent practice of revolutionaries from various parts of India to take advantage of the annual sessions of the
Congress in order to discuss their plans in secret, and to interchange their views',
and this almost certainly accounts for Bhagat Singh's activities in Calcutta.[62] David
M. Laushey has emphasised the prominence of Bengali revolutionaries among the
volunteer corps for the Calcutta Congress, who 'in the presence of national leaders,
attempted to merge the efforts of all Bengal terrorist parties in a [short-lived] show
of unity'.[63] Surviving revolutionaries confirm that Bhagat Singh established contacts
with Bengali organisations, including the Anushilan Samiti, during this period, as
the HSRA oriented its focus to bomb-making.[64] By early 1929, the HSRA had
refocused its activities in the United Provinces, with its headquarters based in Agra,
while maintaining several satellite operations. Lalit Kumar Mukherji, in an approver
testimony, claimed to have met a *Sardar* using the name of Ranjit—another alias
that Bhagat Singh used—in Allahabad in January 1929, at a secret meeting in
which they discussed assassinating CID officers.[65] HSRA member Gajanand Potdar
remembered Bhagat Singh and Sukhdev hiding in a safe house in the princely state
of Gwalior in early 1929, where they felt they would be safer from the reach of the
CID.[66] The Intelligence Bureau had registered that Bhagat Singh was 'wandering
about India in a most suspicious manner during the past few months' but did not
seem to be able to capture him, nor did they seem to have sufficient evidence
against him.[67] Disguises, codes, and aliases combined to create the protective layers
of secrecy that kept Bhagat Singh out of custody until 8 April 1929, but also allow
for a certain amount of flexibility in the narrative of his revolutionary life.

Proscribed Histories

A related element in the repression of information on the activities of revolutionaries
was the censorship that the government applied to all seditious literature. The inher-
ently subversive nature of revolutionary organisations meant that publicising their

aims and objectives—necessary for winning broader public support—was dangerous and risked undermining the entire revolutionary project. Few mainstream newspapers, fearful of repressive press legislation that could levy punitive fines and briskly bring financial ruin on a publisher, were willing to print revolutionary material. Whenever the HSRA managed to raise enough funds to produce their own propaganda, it was quickly labelled seditious and proscribed.[68] They were therefore largely reduced to carrying out their clandestine politics, as contrary as this seems, with minimal publicity, which left an opening for public misunderstanding.

It was frustration at the limitations of publicising their cause that Bhagat Singh's final action, dubbed by the press as 'the Assembly Bomb Case', was devised. Whereas the British read the actual attack on the Assembly as being the moment of subversion, for Bhagat Singh, it was just the beginning.[69] He knew that the trial would be transcribed and duly reported in the press, and that this represented an opportunity to communicate the aims and objectives of the organisation. It was ultimately for this reason that Bhagat Singh, with his talent for oration, was chosen for the action at the Assembly, even though the party knew that he would be connected to Saunders' murder after arrest.[70] He was already a suspect, although 'definite evidence against him was lacking';[71] the pistol he surrendered at his arrest (which Bhagat Singh had probably used in both cases, although ballistic reports in London did not conclusively prove this) would connect him to the two incidents. Besides this, they could not discount the possibility of a death in the Assembly.[72] When he went to carry out the Assembly Bombing with B.K. Dutt, Bhagat Singh and his comrades knew he was walking into a death sentence.[73]

Once the trial began, the magistrate presiding, F.B. Pool, recognised that their lengthy statement was a manifesto devised to evade censorship controls. On 9 June 1929, Pool ruled that sections of Bhagat Singh's statement were to be 'expunged' and that, as such, these portions 'cannot be referred to here, nor, being irrelevant, could they affect the case', despite the fact that the attack on parliament had everything to do with the deleted ideology.[74] Unfortunately for the prosecutors, an abridged version of the testimony had already been published in the press,[75] and would be extensively distributed in revolutionary circles in the months to come and translated into different languages, including Bengali and Gujarati.[76] Nonetheless, the deletion had a great bearing on the case's progression in the courts. In an appeal before the High Court Bench, Bhagat Singh argued that removing the lengthy ideological rationale for the attack on the Assembly from their statement had the effect of reducing the revolutionaries to the status of madmen and fanatics.[77]

The government justified its attempts to curtail activities of radical leftist groups by appealing to the growth of communism in the 1920s in Euro-America, which had particular utility in imperial contexts. Throughout the protracted court case, the accused made their socialist politics clear through their frequent sloganeering, particularly 'Long Live the Revolution', frequently shouted with gusto both in English and in its vernacular equivalent, *Inquilab Zindabad*.[78] In one of the sections deleted from their statement, Bhagat Singh and B. K. Dutt had endeavoured to explain that,

Revolution does not necessarily involve sanguinary strife, nor is there any place in it for individual vendetta. It is not the cult of the bomb and the pistol. By Revolution we mean that the present order of things which is based on manifest injustice must change. The producers or the labourers, in spite of being the most necessary element of society are robbed by their exploiters of the fruits of their labour and deprived of their elementary right. On the one hand the peasant who grows corn for all starves with his family; the weaver who supplies the world market with textile fabrics cannot find enough to cover his own and his childrens' bodies; the masons, smiths and carpenters who rear magnificent palaces, live and perish in slums; and on the other the capitalist exploiters, the parasites of Society squander millions on their whims. These terrible inequalities, and forced disparity of chances are heading towards chaos.[79]

Marxist ideology was more than seditious; its transnational aspirations made it globally subversive, and the government of India was alert to its growing influence.[80] The extent to which leftist networks were watching India would become evident in the movement to challenge the death sentences handed down in October of 1930, when sympathisers and activists in the broader socialist movement mobilised their resources to bring Bhagat Singh's predicament to the world stage. HSRA members corresponded with a Polish student who wrote in support to the Bhagat Singh Defence Committee in Lahore, and who subsequently 'proved a very good propagandist for us in foreign countries.'[81] In San Francisco, the Ghadar Party threatened that if Bhagat Singh were executed, they would assassinate Lord Willingdon, the incoming Viceroy, before he even landed in India.[82]

In March 1931, the Secretariat of the Communist Party of Great Britain issued circulars requesting comrades to organise demonstrations against Bhagat Singh's impending execution, protesting that 'this so-called trial, unparalleled in the history of political persecution, is characterised by the most inhuman and brutal treatment which is the outcome of a frantic desire on the part of the Labour Imperialist Government to strike terror into the hearts of an oppressed people'.[83] Weeks later, the New York-based *Daily Worker* would describe Bhagat Singh's hanging as 'one of the bloodiest deeds ever undertaken by the British Labour Government'.[84] The Ghadar Party in San Francisco issued leaflets lamenting the executions, urging its audience to 'give up this unmanly non-violence, which has caused our nation such great humiliation and loss of life, and has emboldened the British intruders to use the guillotine so freely for the Indian Patriots'.[85] The refrain of 'Congress Keerthanai', a Tamil song added to the proscribed list by the government of Madras in early 1932, was not simply indulging in hyperbole when it valorised Bhagat Singh as 'world renowned'.[86]

Aware that transnational networks were abuzz with criticism of the British legal position as the executions neared, the Home Department was keen to ensure that the government of India's perspective was communicated internationally. Responding to the rumour circulated at the Karachi Congress in April 1931 that Bhagat Singh was innocent, the Home Department wrote to the Commissioner in Sind, requesting that he pull some strings to retard the growth of such an idea in America,

We have made arrangements for England, but American correspondents are at present in Karachi, and we would be very grateful if you could be in personal touch with Mills of Associated Press of America and with Inglis of Christian Science Monitor. You can mention Emerson's name. ... Viceroy will probably mention case in his speech at Chelmsford Club Dinner on Thurs evening and Mills and Inglis may care to work up material now supplied in this connection. They should, of course, not refer to official sources.[87]

While comrades were perhaps the most vehement global supporters of Bhagat Singh, his plight also came to the attention of others. Concerns about the torture and ill treatment of prisoners accused of political violence, including the government's attempts to tailor legislation and ordinances to allow them to hold and prosecute suspects without due process, were widely expressed in the mainstream nationalist press.[88] The Society of Friends delegated Horace Alexander to Delhi in 1930 to research a book, *Political Prisoners In India*. The book was not released until 1937—by which time the HSRA had been effectively suppressed—but the Intelligence Bureau nonetheless viewed the report as an unwelcome intervention, particularly after it failed to influence its findings.[89] '*Rubbish*!' was pencilled in the margins next to the Professor's statement that 'it is often the finest students, men or women of outstanding ability, integrity and courage, who get carried into the revolutionary movement'.[90]

This jotted outburst is indicative of a larger problem in the colonial archive, which has long been the primary repository for scholars piecing together revolutionary history. The bulk of the existing documents relating to the HSRA's activism were authored by a coterie of imperial investigators, administrators and prosecutors whose determination to convict revolutionaries largely inhibited any attempt to dispassionately understand the phenomenon. There is extensive evidence that many revolutionaries of the late 1920s were just as Alexander described, but for servants of the empire to concede this would be to accept that a reasoned critique of imperialism underpinned their recourse to violence. The discourse of condemnation embedded in the various reports, telegrams, and memos that passed between intelligence officers and various provincial authorities, the Home Department and the Viceroy, is pervasive—and provides a stark contrast to nationalist writings that celebrate Bhagat Singh.

Aggrieved Histories

British attempts to control seditious literature were frustrating for the revolutionaries, but have proven to be a boon for historians, as a body of literature that was proscribed is now held in the India Office, and has proven to be an indispensible resource.[91] A smaller collection is housed in the library at the National Archives of India, and a recently published volume brings readers a taste of banned materials about the HSRA.[92] The editor of this volume, Gurdev Singh Sidhu, counted 153 proscribed publications, predominantly in Hindi but also in Tamil, Panjabi, Urdu, Gujarati and Sindhi.[93] The exhaustive lists of freshly proscribed material published in Fortnightly Reports in 1931 suggest that literature memorialising Bhagat Singh in the charged months after his death found wide and receptive audiences.

Most of these writings, predominantly small tracts and booklets, were produced in the immediate aftermath of the executions, constituting a powerful collection of eulogy literature. Given that eulogies compiled in this tumultuous period constitute the first histories of Bhagat Singh's life, this phenomenon is worth considering in some depth. To give an indication of the density of banned material, in one fortnight in Bengal alone, a month after the executions, three booklets (*Desh Bhagat* by Chaudhury Nathulal Jamal, published in Lucknow; *Shahid Bhagat Singh*, by Sambhu Prasad Misra; and *Amar Shahid Bhagat Singh*, published anonymously in Calcutta) were added to the proscribed list, as were three different pictures, each featuring Bhagat Singh, Sukhdev and Rajguru on the scaffold.[94] The eulogy literature captured by the net of British intelligence and registered in Fortnightly Reports, along with the regal but unlikely command that all copies 'be forfeited to his Majesty' forthwith, is not an exhaustive list of what was produced. Many examples of eulogy posters survived the remaining decades of empire to be eventually sold on the collectors' market, and many private collections have tracts unlisted by the British Library.[95]

The intensity and volume of eulogy literature reflected the extraordinary response to the executions, which many hoped would be commuted at the last minute. As will be detailed in the following chapters, several public movements to have the death sentence reduced to transportation for life sprang up after the revolutionaries were sentenced by a Special Tribunal in 1930. While demonstrations by the Naujawan Bharat Sabha in Lahore on 20 March 1931 were to be expected, the protest of the Nationalist Muslim Youth Association in support of the revolutionaries speaks of broader appeal,[96] as does the observance of 'Bhagat Singh Day' in Lahore on 5 March 1931, attended by 'mammoth' crowds and evidenced by three photographs reproduced in the *Tribune* on the following day.[97]

At the beginning of March, no date had been revealed for the executions, leaving followers and family alike pinning their hopes on furtive appeals.[98] The relatives of the three condemned were called for an interview on 4 March, leading to speculation that execution was imminent,[99] sparking a flurry of 'Pray Stay Execution' telegrams to the Viceroy.[100] A number of formal committees and private individuals sent appeals to all levels of government.[101] Subhas Chandra Bose later recalled that the volume of appeals had compelled Lord Irwin to tell Gandhi that he would postpone their execution for the time being and give serious consideration to the matter, but beyond that he did not want to be pressed ... [T]he conclusion which the Mahatma and everybody else drew from this attitude of the Viceroy, was that the execution would be finally cancelled and there was jubilation all over the country.[102]

Yet the trio were hanged on 23 March 1931.

Not only were the executions unexpected, but the manner in which they were carried out added to an overwhelming sense of grievance. By the 1930s, the British had considerable experience in martyr-making, and had come to understand something of the process. The bodies of the Kakori prisoners who were hanged were given over to their families, and post-mortem photographs soon found their way into publications that lamented their deaths.[103] The death of Jatindranath Das, an HSRA member and friend of Bhagat Singh, who had fasted beyond the point of no return in protest at jail conditions in September 1929, had gained the revolutionaries much public sympathy.[104] The prison authorities had handed Das's wasted body over to family members, who, with the support of the Bengal Provincial Congress, repatriated him to Calcutta, where his remains were taken on procession, accompanied by wailing crowds.[105] Keen to avoid such a situation with the hangings of the condemned trio in the Lahore Conspiracy Case, the government of Punjab, which was tasked with carrying out the executions, and the Home Department resorted to subterfuge.

Firstly, the date of the executions was secretly fixed for 23 March at 7pm,[106] instead of the mandated time of 8am,[107] giving prison authorities time before the news was made public on 24 March. Secondly, when the families of Sukhdev and Bhagat Singh arrived for their final interview on the afternoon of 23 March, such a large crowd of extended relatives arrived that the prison authorities refused them entry, stipulating that only immediate family were eligible for interview. Heavily aggrieved, Bhagat Singh's family refused to accept this, instead boycotting the right for a final meeting, in which they were joined by Sukhdev's and Rajguru's families.[108] 'No "Last Interview" with Relations' was widely reported in the nationalist press (Figure 5).[109] Finally, after the killing was done, the bodies were not entrusted to their families; instead, they were secreted out of the prison and 'disposed of according to a pre-arranged plan, being taken at night to the bund of the Sutlej near Ferozepore and cremated with due ceremony'.[110] Sir Henry Craik, the Finance Minister in the Punjab Legislative Council, maintained that this unorthodox night-time cremation was carried out in the presence of representatives of the Hindu, Arya and Sikh faiths;[111] by 5am, the bodies were 'completely burnt' and 'the ashes were thrown midstream in the Sutlej'.[112]

The authorities felt that depriving the families of their sons' bodies would eliminate a focal point for public grieving, which they anticipated would be intense.[113] From his office in the Home Department, Herbert Emerson—a long-serving

Punjab administrator promoted to the capital—had even prevailed upon Gandhi to prevent a public meeting planned in Delhi on 20 March, to be presided over by Subhas Chandra Bose, 'which, if uncontrolled, may have serious consequences'.[114] Gandhi declined.[115] The meeting, convened on Azad Maidan, attracted 25,000 people, who listened to speeches in both English and Hindi.[116]

Prior to the executions, writing in 'strict secrecy' and in cipher, the Home Department had instructed District Magistrates around the country to expect, at some stage in the coming weeks, a simple one-word telegram to signal the impend-

Figure 5: Front page of the *Tribune*, 25 March 1931. (Courtesy of the Supreme Court of India Museum)

ing executions: 'Tomorrow'.[117] This was the signal to put troops on stand by in case of emergency.[118] Once the news of the executions spread, Lahore, Bombay, Kanpur and Madras snapped into *hartal*,[119] and in Calcutta, 'intense excitement prevailed and armed flying squads patrolled the city.'[120]

Jai Dev Gupta, a lifelong friend of Bhagat Singh, was with a crowd of mourners in Lahore who had been tipped off about a cremation late on the night of 23 March on the banks of the Sutlej. Finding a spot where the sand was hot and the smell of kerosene strong, Gupta found a long bone, 'cut in a diagonal form at the wrist', which he suspected was evidence that the bodies had been mutilated.[121] The mourners salvaged what they could, and it was these remains that Sardar Kishan Singh, Bhagat Singh's father, took to the Karachi Congress on 5 April to show the audience that gathered to hear him speak about his son.[122] The *Tribune*'s front page asked 'Was Bhagat Singh's body mutilated?'[123] On 1 April, the Congress Working Committee in Karachi, responding to the 'great public indignation' that the allegations had sparked, undertook an inquiry into the issue, headed by Dr Satyapal.[124] The committee failed to deliver a finding by the appointed date, although Satyapal eventually reported that the evidence was inconclusive.[125] However the idea that the bodies had been maliciously desecrated was already widespread and impossible to retract. Confidence in the government had been greatly eroded, with the Commissioner in Sind reporting from Karachi that the 'local public seem prepared to believe any tale about methods of executions.'[126] Yashpal later reflected that

the people's hearts filled with fierce, helpless hatred toward the foreign government. Consequently they spread stories about the cruelties inflicted on Bhagat Singh and his companions and of their courage as they faced the gallows. To demonstrate their hatred and anger towards the Government and their reverence for the martyrs, the people exaggerated these stories. Whoever heard them added something, and that is how those tales gained currency.[127]

The political environment in which Bhagat Singh was executed was charged, and this was reflected in eulogy literature. The opening months of 1931 were intended to mark a period of rapprochement in British India with the Gandhi–Irwin pact, concluded in early March, following in the wake of the Civil Disobedience Movement and the first Round Table Conference in London. As a result of the pact, Gandhi had called an end to civil disobedience, and the British freed all nonviolent political prisoners who had been arrested during its course. It was in this atmosphere of truce that many hoped that the sentences on Bhagat Singh, Sukhdev and Rajguru would be commuted, and considerable pressure was brought to bear on Gandhi to make it one of the conditions of the pact. Subhas Chandra Bose was of the opinion that 'Gandhi did try his very best' to stay the executions, and so 'it was most painful and unexpected surprise when on March 24th, while we were on our way to Karachi from Calcutta, the news was received that Sardar Bhagat Singh and his comrades had been hanged the night before.'[128]

The announcement that Singh, Rajguru and Sukhdev had been executed was met with devastation. The newspapers were filled with reports of condolence meetings, *hartals*, fasts and mass observances of mourning rituals. In Amritsar's Jallianwala Bagh, thirty police who had been sent to keep the peace at a condolence meeting were stoned, and twenty-three were injured.[129] Terrible violence broke out in Kanpur, where existing tensions were inflamed when Hindu political workers attempted to enforce a Congress-declared *hartal* on their Muslim neighbours. The death toll was placed at approximately 400.[130] A motion for the adjournment of the Legislative Council in Calcutta in protest at the executions failed when put to the vote, but the debate on its desirability 'gave an opportunity for the delivery of a number of speeches from which glorification of murder and eulogy of the Lahore assassins was not absent.'[131]

The executions were widely interpreted as vindictive—in Jawaharlal Nehru's words, 'an act of wanton vengeance and a deliberate flouting of the unanimous demand for commutation'.[132] This perfidy was perhaps best encapsulated in a poster, later proscribed by the government, in which a British officer in a *sola topi* taunts the trio on the scaffold, farewelling them with his handkerchief (Figure 6).

The hangings caused such grief and shock that radical newspapers (some with revolutionary connections) such as *Kirti, Bande Mataram, Milap* and *Tufan*, went to press with direct incitements to violence. One Lahori newspaper, *Zamindar* (landlord), urged its readership to

Give an answer to England with action and not with words. India esteems these three martyrs more than the whole British nation. We cannot fully avenge them even if we kill thousands and lakhs of Englishmen. The revenge can only be complete if you free India. Thus the glory of England will be mixed with dust. O Bhagat Singh, Rajguru, and Sukh Dev! The British are glad that they have murdered you but they are mistaken. They have not murdered you but have supplied a knife to their future. You are alive and will ever remain so.[133]

Literature compiled in this heavily charged atmosphere of grief included plays (a report of one such drama, performed '40 miles from Mangalore in the "far south"', had it that the entire village began to wail when the hanging scene was enacted),[134] poems and songs which drew on images of Bhagat Singh as a brave hero who played *holi* with his own blood.[135]

Many of these writings were biographical in nature, some of it by writers who had known Bhagat Singh.[136] Chandravati Devi knew Bhagat Singh from National College in Lahore. She wrote a 'small booklet of 100 to 150 pages in prattling style and lacking in coherence' about his life, recounting his childhood in fond detail (once, running to get sweets, he fell over, and his nose bled profusely); and sketching early indications of his revolutionary proclivities (he was trained as a cultivator, but

43

Figure 6: 'Rajguru, S. Bhagat Singh and Sukhdev Hanged', Lahore: Rattan Printing Press, artist unknown, c. 1931. (Courtesy of NMML, Kulbir Singh Collection, Album 808, 36515)

planned to open a gun shop when he grew up).[137] Other articles divulged facts and occurrences which revealed that the writers had followed events closely in the press, who either knew of or had heard details from family members of the final days of the condemned. *Watan de Lal* (Rubies of the Nation), for example, included details of a letter Bhagat Singh wrote to his young brother, prompted by Kultar's tears in their final meeting, gently urging him to be brave in the difficult days ahead.[138]

But in the immediate aftermath of the executions many writings purporting to be histories sprang up, some which made questionable claims. Rishabhcharan Jain's 'Hartal', written during the strikes following the executions, made claims to be an *itihas* (history), confirming that Bhagat Singh was 'in fact' innocent of the murder of Saunders.[139] Such an idea might have been formed by Sardar Kishan Singh's five-page petition to the Special Tribunal, written in late 1930,[140] which explained that his son could not possibly have been involved in the murder because he was in Calcutta at the time (Bhagat Singh had responded to this indignantly, contradicting his father in an open letter).[141] Bhagat Singh's mother Vidyawati issued a 'humble petition' to the Viceroy on 19 February 1931, contending that if her son had been given the opportunity to be cross-examined, 'his innocence would have been established'.[142] A telegram reporting on the progress of the Karachi Congress, held days after the hangings, claimed that 'Congress is busy spreading rumours that Bhagat Singh had a complete alibi'.[143] The Punjab government responded to this by releasing to the press an unfinished letter written by Sukhdev that reflected in some detail on the actions the HSRA had taken, and was tantamount to an admission.[144] The *Tribune* greeted the posthumous release of the letter with suspicion— why was such a vital piece of evidence withheld from the court during the many trials, tribunals, and finally in the appeal?[145]

C. S. Venu's *Sirdar Bhagat Singh* also argued that the trio was innocent of Saunders' murder, extending (an admittedly well-founded) scepticism with the imperial justice system by alleging that the police had planted false evidence in order to convict the trio.[146] However other writings, whose authors were disconnected from the events in Lahore, made uncorroborated claims which satisfied a desperate demand for information in the absence of any.[147] Thus one 1931 publication mourned the death of B.K. Dutt, who survived both a long sentence in the Andamans and the British Raj, before succumbing in a Delhi hospital in 1965.[148] But in an atmosphere in which Bhagat Singh loomed large as a martyred hero, to point out such inaccuracies would seem churlish, or worse, to mitigate the oppression of the imperial order.

The Pakistan Disconnection

Location has proven to be a sensitive element in the collation of revolutionary histories. Much of Bhagat Singh's early life and ultimately his death took place in Lahore, now in Pakistan. When researching his book on Bhagat Singh the journalist Kuldip Nayar suspected that the archives of Pakistan might hold the richest sources on his life and death, but attempts to access files on Bhagat Singh were denied on the basis of the sensitivity of 'the Sikh problem'.[149] Similarly, the Pakistani researcher and archivist Ahmad Salim found that some records relating to the trial of the Lahore Conspiracy Case and held by the Lahore High Court are still restricted on the basis that their publication 'might affect the integrity of Pakistan', implying that the postcolonial state might be forced to accept culpability for executions carried out more than fifteen years before its creation.[150] In 2007, a function organised to celebrate the anniversary of the hangings in Lahore was slapped with a Section 144 by the Pakistan government, an ordinance preventing the gathering of more than five people, despite the fact that the planned event had the support of provincial authorities, including the Chief Minister of (Pakistani) Punjab himself.[151] In 2012, Lahore's district government renamed the site of the hangings Bhagat Singh Chowk, under pressure from activists who sought to 'challenge the official historical narrative' of Pakistan, although this was rapidly overturned after protests by Islamist groups.[152]

Some form of diplomatic pressure was exerted upon Pakistan in the 1970s to dispatch documents relevant to the Lahore Conspiracy Case to India. In 1974, the remains of Uddham Singh, who had avenged the Jallianwalla Bagh atrocity by murdering Michael O'Dwyer in London, were repatriated and honoured in the Punjab.[153] This inspired the families of Sukhdev and Bhagat Singh to lobby the Indian government to retrieve the 'personal effects of the martyrs S. Bhagat Singh, Rajguru and Sukhdev, and their last letters which were withheld by the Lahore Central Jail and Authorities, and also the Proceedings book and judgement of the Special Tribunal on the sensational Lahore Conspiracy Case in order to give them place of pride as national monuments'.[154] In his retirement years, the energetic Mathuradas Thapar (who habitually signed his correspondence 'the real younger brother of the martyr Sukhdev') lobbied a range of people from the Ambassador of Pakistan in Delhi to Zail Singh, then Chief Minister of Punjab. Bhagat Singh's brother, Kultar Singh (a Minister in the Uttar Pradesh government in the 1970s), wrote similar requests to the Union Minister for External Affairs, arguing that 'the importance of the last letters and other belongings of the three great martyrs … cannot be over-emphasised. These things are of no use to Pakistan Government but have great value to India.'[155] In 2006, Pakistan's Acting Chief Justice, Judge Rana, made four volumes relating to the trial available to India, where they are held in the National Archives in Delhi.[156]

The contention that the memorabilia relating to the martyrs is 'of no use to Pakistan' speaks of the extent of the partitioning of history. According to the communal logic that delivered a citizen to one side of the border or another in 1947, the Punjabi martyrs were designated Indian, and as such are largely absent from the annals of Pakistani history, which have been chiefly concerned with the progression of the Pakistan movement.[157] The HSRA and Naujawan Bharat Sabha worked on a very different trajectory, eschewing communalism with a strident secularist critique which forbade its members from membership of religious or communal organisations.[158] It was therefore a revelation to many when A.G. Noorani wrote at length in his book of M. A. Jinnah's impassioned defence of Bhagat Singh, Rajguru and Sukhdev in the Legislative Assembly in 1929,[159] objecting to the bill introduced to allow the prisoners of the Lahore Conspiracy Case to be tried in absentia by a Special Tribunal.

In the Grip of Popular Culture

Legends formed in the past cohere in contemporary India with those perpetuated in contemporary popular culture, to inform both quasi-historicist notions of anti-colonialism and national memory. The dramatic story of Bhagat Singh's life and untimely death, redolent with stirring anti-imperial themes and a compelling narrative—what Avinash Kumar has aptly called 'thriller nationalism'[160]—made it eminently translatable to celluloid. Several films have been made on his life since independence, and many television dramas. While the 'Bhagat Singh in Bollywood' phenomenon deserves a study of its own,[161] it is worth noting that frequent remakes of Bhagat Singh's story have strongly influenced public conceptions of historical narrative, even as they have been challenged by various stakeholders for their accuracy. The first film, *Shaheed-e-Azam* (directed by Jagdish Gautam) was released in 1954 and even in production sparked considerable debate about its representation of history. The Central Board of Film Censors was lobbied by the board of editors of a Bhagat Singh Commemoration Volume and the Punjab Congress Committee, including one of Bhagat Singh's brothers, who made submissions about what the film should, and should not, depict. They were successful in appealing to have two cuts made to the film, but were still unhappy with the result.[162]

A second film was made in 1963, starring Shammi Kapoor and directed by Kidarnath Bansil. Two years later, in 1965, came the third and most enduring version, *Shaheed*, starring Manoj Kumar, which established his *filmi* persona as the quintessential patriotic hero. The film's opening scenes carried a disclaimer warning viewers that the film's focus was on the revolutionaries' heroic struggle, in the course of which 'inadvertent deviation from actuality' was likely and indeed, unavoidable (Figure 7).

The influence of Kumar's film has been felt across visual cultures, overseeing the revival of Bhagat Singh as a favorite subject in calendar art from the 1960s. Pinney notes that scenes from Manoj Kumar's film were frequently referenced in popular posters of Bhagat Singh produced by the prolific Meerut-based artist, H. R. Raja, in the 1970s and beyond.[163] In 2002, no less than three Bhagat Singh movies were released: *23 March 1931: Shaheed* (starring Bobby Deol) and—on the same day—*The Legend of Bhagat Singh* (featuring Ajay Devgan in the titular role). Deol's film was publicised with the telling byline: 'Some stories are not written—they write themselves'.[164] Within weeks, *Shaheed-e-Azam* (with Sonu Sood as Bhagat Singh) hit the cinemas.[165] This barrage of films prompted Professor Jagmohan Singh, Bhagat Singh's nephew and General Secretary of the Bhagat Singh Research Committee, to issue a press release protesting that the films were 'distorting Bhagat Singh's legacy'.[166]

None of the 2002 films could be called box office hits, although in 2006, *Rang de Basanti* (directed Rakeysh Omprakash Mehra), which featured Bhagat Singh and his revolutionary colleagues in a subplot which slowly comes to inform and highlight the film's contemporary narrative of Indian youth disillusionment with the state, enjoyed considerable success and was India's official entry in the Academy Awards that year in the Best Foreign Film category. It failed to win, perhaps because Academy judges lacked the historical context necessary to locate the revolutionaries

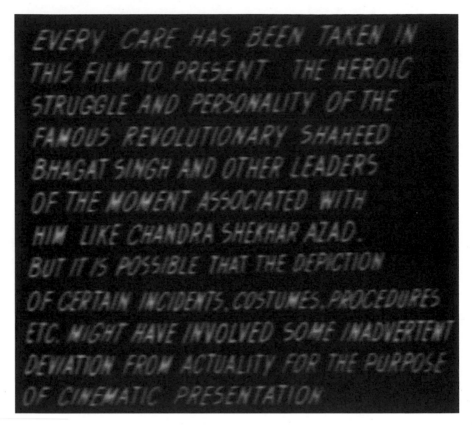

Figure 7: Screen capture of a disclaimer from *Shaheed* (1965).

in an otherwise contemporary narrative. Critics rightly argued that the film divested Bhagat Singh's passion 'of its ideological moorings', presenting his politics as a 'manly antidote' to the abuses of colonialism, rather than as a means of addressing broader societal inequalities.[167] The Bhagat Singh film genre has become a vehicle for articulating the role of violence in the construction or recuperation of nationhood.[168] It is precisely the denial of this narrative that makes Gandhi so revolutionary (to engage a different usage of the term), presenting an ongoing challenge to filmmakers and comic book artists who seek to tell the Mahatma's life story in popular formats notorious for their action and violence.[169]

In recent years, enduring popular cultural commodities such as posters, comics, and bazaar histories featuring Bhagat Singh have been matched by innumerable virtual tributes, particularly on social networking sites, Wikis and blogs. Orkut, now exceeded by Facebook as the most widely used social networking site in India, has hundreds of fan sites. Intense debates about historical accuracy lie concealed under the 'discussion' tab on Wikipedia's 'Bhagat Singh' entry, and the 'history' tab reveals that the page is altered several times a day in 'edit wars'. In 2014, 165 Wikipedia users were registered as 'watchers' of the page, alerted to edits as they are made, allowing for swift attention to revisionist interventions.

Bhagat Singh's popularity has tempted a wide range of groups to claim his legacy, which, given the multiple narratives and uncertainties as indicated above, creates heated contestation.[170] Pritam Singh's tally of such groups spans the political spectrum, counting 'Gandhi-inspired leftists, Hindu nationalists, Sikh nationalists, the parliamentary Left, [and] the pro-armed struggle Naxalite Left'.[171] A particular anxiety—represented by the very existence of a Shaheed Bhagat Singh Research Committee—can be discerned around the need to pare back the accretions of popular tellings of Bhagat Singh's story.

The centenary of Bhagat Singh's birth in 2007 was celebrated by a number of unrelated publications and celebrations, including several central government-sponsored initiatives, among which was the installation of a statue of Bhagat Singh in the parliamentary complex. Many of these publications advocated a return to primary sources: the publication of a multivolume series of historical documents connected to his trial and execution;[172] fresh editions of revolutionary memoirs;[173] an exhibition of historical documents and memorabilia at the Supreme Court Museum in Delhi and at the Nehru Memorial Museum; plans to establish a Bhagat Singh Chair at JNU;[174] and the production of a documentary backed by the Nehru Memorial Museum and Library, specifically aimed as a corrective to the narrative posed in popular Hindi films.[175] This project, *Inquilab*, was aimed at senior school students, featuring interviews with academic historians, and drew on press clippings to illustrate the narrative, unlike a Doordarshan production released in the same year—also called *Inquilab*—which resorted to montages from several of the abovementioned Bollywood films to provide the necessary visuals.[176] Thus the films, which have to a degree drawn on revolutionary portraits to extrapolate their narratives, are increasingly being prioritised over original sources.

Various forms of censor and censure have been the key inhibitors to the establishment of a clear chronicle of Bhagat Singh's life, paving the way for his exciting story to be celebrated predominantly in the relatively unregulated domain of the popular. As Chandravati Devi reflected in 1931, 'in these days is it easy to write the life of Bhagat Singh? Can the Sardar's true life be written in this slave country or if written can it be printed and if printed can it ever be published?'[177] These issues are further beset by the multiple and competing narratives which were born in the charged atmosphere of Bhagat Singh's execution, and the clamour to save him from his fate. These factors, along with a deep suspicion of colonial justice systems and of the clandestine operations of imperial investigators, have left a legacy of accounts which variously challenge the colonial 'terrorist' narrative, including the very accusations that led him to the gallows.

The difficulties in working around the constraints of censor and censure were effectively counteracted by the fact that Bhagat Singh's compelling story combined elements of extraordinary bravery and patriotism with the tragedy of his untimely death. As a result, his story remains the basis of much contemporary popular culture, especially bazaar literature, invariably published unreferenced and predominantly in Indian languages, in which new twists and turns of narrative have been added to the palimpsest that has become his biography. Add to this the phenomenon of the Bhagat Singh 'historical' film—one of which self-consciously celebrates 'the legend' of Bhagat Singh—and the estrangement of popular and academic accounts of a revolutionary life is understandable, perhaps irrevocable. With this caveat in mind, I will now return to the past, to focus on the actions of the HSRA.

2

THAT HAT

INFAMY, STRATEGY AND SOCIAL COMMUNICATION

Bhagat Singh's celebrity, over and above all other revolutionaries who gave their lives to the cause, has been a source of wonderment for some time. In the days after his execution, Jawaharlal Nehru wondered aloud how it was that 'a mere chit of a boy suddenly leapt to fame'.[1] How did Bhagat Singh achieve such extraordinary and enduring popularity? He did not attend the gallows alone; his friends Sukhdev and Rajguru were hanged alongside him. Yet even in the months before his hanging, the condemned trio were frequently referred to in the press as 'Bhagat Singh and others' or 'Bhagat Singh and his comrades', to the point that the two words 'Bhagat Singh' were frequently used as shorthand for the revolutionary movement writ large.[2] How can we explain his prominence over that of his fellow martyrs, or over important members of the HSRA, such as Chandrashekhar Azad? Bhagat Singh's hat portrait, and the extraordinary campaign around it, holds some of the answers to these enduring questions.

The photograph is a fairly conventional studio portrait (Figure 8). The young revolutionary—he was just 21 when he posed for the photograph—stares calmly into the camera, as if to defy the empire and the weighty charges that are about to be brought against him, namely, that he had

been engaged in conspiracy to wage war against his Majesty, the King Emperor, and to deprive him of the Sovereignty of British India, and to overawe by criminal force or show criminal force, the Government established by law in British India and to collect arms and ammunition and men for, or otherwise make preparation for the said object and purpose.[3]

Bhagat Singh knew these charges would inevitably lead to a death sentence, yet he stands cool and poised, a felt hat tipped on his head. The photograph has

51

Figure 8: Bhagat Singh, posing for Ramnath Photographers in Delhi, April 1929. (Courtesy of the Supreme Court of India Museum)

become an icon of defiant nationalism, which continues to be widely referenced in poster art and calendars.[4] It is a regular feature of the contemporary urban landscape in India, readily encountered on cars and hoardings, and in bazaars, on posters and books.

The ubiquity of the image in contemporary Indian popular culture is such that it is frequently compared to Alberto Korda's famous photograph of Che Guevara.[5] Both Bhagat Singh and Che were undeniably photogenic, effectively capturing the romance, idealism and sacrifices demanded of the revolutionary; factors which no doubt make their portraits captivating. Both photographs, too, have been so widely appropriated that they have become disconnected from their historical context. In Bhagat Singh's case, this is partly because there is considerable uncertainty about the nature of his portrait's production. Below, I demonstrate that the photograph was taken with the ethos that it should be as widely distributed as possible and that this was such a success that the origins of the image have been obscured.

THAT HAT: INFAMY, STRATEGY AND SOCIAL COMMUNICATION

Some have assumed that Bhagat Singh's famous photograph was taken to be fixed to a security pass, enabling him to infiltrate and undermine British institutions; others have speculated that the police took the photograph immediately after his arrest in 1929. Neither of these is correct. This chapter traces the genealogy of the photograph and in doing so, situates it within the nationalist politics of interwar India, with particular reference to the late 1920s and early 1930s. During this time the image was, simultaneously, memento, propaganda, evidence and placard.

The story of the portrait's journey contributes to existing theories of social communication vis-à-vis the spread of nationalism in the early twentieth century, providing one answer to the question of how 'political leaders in a poor country with a relatively low rate of general literacy should have been able to create a widely diffused and popular nationalist movement so early'.[6] Sandria Freitag has connected Chris Bayly's conceptualisation of an information order to popular South Asian visual culture as an effective conduit of political ideas, a visual vocabulary acting as an instantaneous vector of anticolonial content.[7] This is evident in the story of the portrait's journey from a studio photograph to a widely reproduced icon, demonstrating how the image travelled and morphed, defying attempts to arrest it and sparking animated debates about empire and resistance.

The Image: A Prelude to a Martyrdom

Bhagat Singh's photo-portrait may appeal to different viewers for any number of reasons. These might include his youthful handsomeness, his engaging, clear, and steady stare, and his rather fashionable hat, set at an angle, just so. But thinking of the photograph in Barthesian terms, 'that element which rises from the scene, shoots out of it like an arrow and pierces me'[8] is the knowledge that the dashing young man who meets our gaze will be hanged—and he knows it. The photograph becomes all the more compelling with the realisation that Bhagat Singh explicitly had it taken as a political tactic, before provoking the government of British India to seal his fate—to hang him by the neck until dead. The portrait therefore can be seen as both a prelude to and a vital ingredient in the widespread acceptance of him as a *shaheed* (martyr). This story is largely unknown and is one worth telling, not least because it amplifies the power of the image.

Besides Bhagat Singh's direct eye contact, perhaps the most arresting feature of the portrait is his stylish but obviously western hat. Bhagat Singh had, in order to wear the said hat, renounced his *kesh* (the uncut hair of a Sikh) and turban when disguising himself became vital to evading capture, in September 1928.[9] After the widespread distribution of the photograph, Bhagat Singh's hat would become his defining attribute.[10] Only relatively recently have images of Bhagat Singh wearing a turban become popular.[11] It is important to note, however, that his Sikh heritage was explicitly acknowledged in the 1930s. He was known as 'Sardarji' among friends and was memorialised as a Sardar in eulogies, although this was not so much a communal designation in pre-partition India, as much as it was a polite, and often affectionate, form of address for a Sikh gentleman.[12]

Scholarly Debates on Bhagat Singh's Fame

In his work on the contemporary visual culture of Bhagat Singh, Christopher Pinney draws attention to and elaborates on observations made by Simeran Gell,[13] suggesting that the power of the Bhagat Singh's portrait lies in its embodiment of that discomforting form of mimicry first described by Homi Bhabha. By posing as a *sahib* in modern, fashionable dress, Bhagat Singh closed the racial gulf between 'Indian' and 'European' which was the basis of the colonial rationale.[14] Pinney describes how the hat photograph recalls an incident in Bhagat Singh's life, popularised across a range of popular cultural formats such as comics and film, in which he disguised himself as an Anglo-Indian to escape Lahore in 1928, after taking part in Saunders' assassination.[15] Therefore the photograph, alongside Bhagat Singh's revolutionary politics, signals a threat to the imperial order, and stands as an icon of what British intelligence rhetorically referred to as the 'violence movement'.

However, historian Neeti Nair negates the idea that Bhagat Singh was popular because he was violent, or that, as Pinney would have it, he represented 'a structural negation of Gandhi's corporeal practices'.[16] Rather, for Nair, Bhagat Singh's popularity stemmed from his hunger-strike in jail, well-documented in newspapers at the time, for a popular cause: the rights of political prisoners. Nair challenges the prevalent idea of the violent Bhagat Singh by drawing attention to ample evidence which points to a clear hesitation on his part to inflict violence to achieve his aims—to remove British rule, and create the conditions for a more equitable society.[17]

Somewhat provocatively, Nair mounts an argument for closing the longstanding ideological ground between Bhagat Singh and Gandhi, suggesting that 'with regard to the strategic use of non-violence and the relationship between means and ends, Bhagat Singh was ideologically closer to the Mahatma than the latter cared to acknowledge'.[18] Thus, according to Nair, Bhagat Singh may be read as a *satyagrahi*, and herein lies his fame. 'The immediate images that flashed across the minds of Punjabis when they thought of Bhagat Singh', she concludes, 'were not of the trilby hat but of the painful ordeal that the young men had undergone for the sake of political prisoners'.[19] Nair draws attention to the often-forgotten support in the Congress (with the important exception of Gandhi) for the hunger strikers. However, if the hunger strike was critical in popularising the revolutionaries, then why is it that the Bengali HSRA member Jatindranath Das (Figure 9), who died a slow and horrible death as a result of his hunger strike, does not eclipse Bhagat Singh, who survived several grueling fasts, before he was delivered to the gallows?

Another rationalisation of Bhagat Singh's fame has been recently offered by Shalini Sharma, who writes that Bhagat Singh 'achieved iconic status because … he was the embodiment of the ideal hero, a brilliant theoretician, a modern man who went to the films, an ardent nationalist and a committed celibate, undistracted by desire in his struggle against the Raj'.[20] While all of Bhagat Singh's surviving associates confirmed these stellar traits in their respective testimonies,[21] it is less

Figure 9: 'Jatindra Nath Das', Martyrdom Portrait, Kanpur: Shyam Sunder Lal c. 1929. (Author's collection)

clear how the details of Bhagat Singh's character were made widely known in the 1930s, given the secretive nature of revolutionary activity. Not many people in the 1930s knew, for example, of Bhagat Singh's extraordinary hunger for reading, his good humour, or for that matter, his penchant for films—his close friends fondly reported his love of cinema, particularly *Uncle Tom's Cabin*, Charlie Chaplin films, and his repeat visits in 1928 to see the silent hit, *Anarkali*.[22]

In this chapter, I want to add further texture to scholarly responses to the question of how Bhagat Singh achieved such notoriety, by drawing attention to the journey of his studio portrait, taken in early April 1929. The power of this arresting image, in concert with the way it was deployed in the media and disseminated widely throughout India in the charged context of his prolonged trial and execution, extends our understanding of how Bhagat Singh became so famous, so quickly. At the same time, tracing the portrait's journey provides a further window on the objectives and strategies of the HSRA as they sought to make a political impact in 1929, determined by Congress elders as 'the year of waiting' to see if the government would respond to the ultimatum delivered at the Calcutta Congress: to accept the demand for dominion status by the close of 1929, or suffer a campaign of civil disobedience under the escalated demand of *purna swaraj* (complete independence). The image of Bhagat Singh was a vital element in a sophisticated media campaign constructed around an 'outrage', which aimed to communicate a revolutionary politics and radicalise nationalist organisation.

The degree to which this was successful is evident in Jawaharlal Nehru's reflection on Bhagat Singh's popularity in the wake of his death:

Bhagat Singh ... became a symbol; the act [of violence] was forgotten, the symbol remained, and within a few months each town and village of the Punjab and to a lesser extent in the rest of northern India, resounded with his name. Innumerable songs grew up around him and the popularity that the man achieved was something amazing.[23]

Nehru, writing in his autobiography some three to four years after Bhagat Singh's death, intimates that Bhagat Singh was popular *despite* his violence. But as Nehru himself was acutely aware, as will become clear in later chapters, in the late 1920s there was no perfect consensus within the Congress movement that violence was inappropriate. Jawaharlal himself had argued, after Bhagat Singh's arrest, that the government had no right to condemn its use when they themselves made ample use of it.[24] In October 1930, after Bhagat Singh was sentenced to death, Nehru pointedly commented that:

the courage of Bhagat Singh is exceedingly rare. If the Viceroy expects us to refrain from admiring this wonderful courage and the high purpose behind it, he is mistaken. Let him ask his own heart what he would have felt if Bhagat Singh had been an Englishman and acted for England.[25]

The widespread dissemination of the portrait in its many guises enabled a predominantly illiterate people to imagine Bhagat Singh independently of imperial allegations that he was a terrorist, and to visualise the legendary stories, songs, poems and sayings that quickly grew up around him.[26] Disseminated widely, initially in the media, the photograph soon began to travel independent of print. Copied and distributed freely by political interest groups, the portrait proliferated and was soon to be found adorning walls and on badges, 'even in villages'.[27]

Received in the intense political context of the late 1920s and early 1930s, a period characterised by ongoing post-war negotiations about political reforms, the hubris of and intense agitation against the Simon Commission, bitter memories of the traumatic imperial violence displayed at Jallianwalla Bagh, and the repression of the Civil Disobedience Movement, Bhagat Singh's gentle gaze served to contradict British charges that he was a cold assassin, feeding rumours that he was innocent. Those who knew of his guilt were able to forget the act of violence, reasoning that he was amply provoked by British oppression: as one Congressite argued in March of 1931, 'however one may disagree with the methods used by violent revolutionaries, hatred of the British rule had gone down so deep in the Indian heart that there are few Indians who do not acclaim Bhagat Singh and others of the same school of thought as heroes'.[28] This too has been an enduring concept; relatively recent images of Bhagat Singh frequently position him in the company of other militant national heroes (including his contemporaries Chandrashekhar Azad and Subhas Chandra Bose), collected around the memorial built in homage to the victims of the Jallianwalla Bagh massacre, the event which serves as their provocation or justification (Figs. 4, 10 and 45).

Memento

The infamous hat photograph was taken a few days prior to the action in the Legislative Assembly, probably around 4 April, in the studios of Ramnath Photographers at Kashmiri Gate in Delhi.[29] Jaidev Kapoor, the HSRA member who did much of the reconnaissance and planning for the attack, arranged for the photograph to be taken. He specifically asked the photographer to make a memento of Bhagat Singh, specifying that 'our friend is going away, so we want a really good photograph of him'.[30] B.K. Dutt was photographed on a separate occasion, but with the same instruction. The first photograph he had taken did not come out, and he had to return for a second sitting which produced a portrait of Dutt gazing contemplatively beyond the frame (Figure 11).

While the photographs were being developed, Bhagat Singh and Dutt were attending the Legislative Assembly on a daily basis, closely observing the debate on the Public Safety Bill; their plan was to throw the bombs at the exact moment the

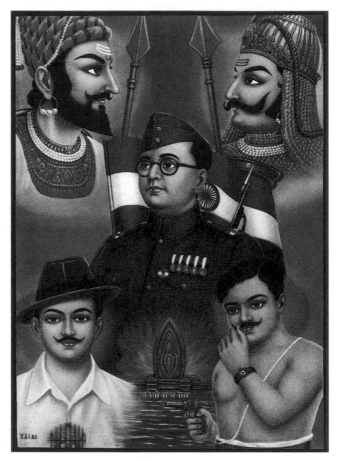

Figure 10: Untitled Poster, featuring Shivaji, Rana Pratap, Subhas Chandra Bose (centre), Bhagat Singh and Chandrashekar Azad. Purchased in Lucknow, 1998. (Courtesy of J. B. Khanna; author's collection)

president of the House moved to give his ruling, which happened on the morning of 8 April. A number of newspaper reporters were present in the Assembly at the time of the bombing, as were many political notables, both Indian and British, which no doubt added to the sense of excitement with which the so-called Assembly Outrage was initially carried in the press.

At Ramnath Photographers, however, production was delayed and Kapoor was unable to collect the photographs before the action took place, as was planned. The revolutionaries did not realise that Ramnath were also contracted to take photographs for the police, and had been summoned to the police station in Old Delhi, where Bhagat Singh was taken after his arrest on 8 April 1929, to photograph

Figure 11: B. K. Dutt, posing for Ramnath Photographers, April 1929. (Courtesy of the Supreme Court of India Museum)

him.[31] These police photographs have not yet surfaced, but were almost certainly used in the early investigation of the 'outrage', as the police 'ransacked all the hotels in Delhi with photographs of the accused'.[32]

The delay in collecting the photographs put the HSRA in a difficult position, as party worker Shiv Verma explained:

Our apprehension was: should we go for the photographs and this fellow is in league with the police, then he may hand us over ... but then we could not check our temptation. We took the risk. And Jaidev—with his finger on the trigger of the revolver standing behind—and I went to the photographer, demanded the photographs. That photographer saw me, smiled and handed over the packet to me. I made the payment. Then he brought the negatives also and said: they are no good for me, you take them also. He did not charge anything for the negatives ... that is how the photographs were procured.[33]

Jaydev Kapoor remembered it slightly differently, eliminating Verma's role in the collection and remembering a less congenial photographer, thus framing himself into a more daring role:

I was afraid that Ramnath had already given information to the police, and that they would be waiting for me. I had all these concerns, but still, I had to get the photographs. So, about three days after the 'action', I went to the shop. At first, he stared at me, but he said nothing. I just threw the money down on the counter and took the photographs. I took the negatives too.[34]

We might see the discrepancy between these two oral accounts as part of an attempt to reinscribe individual agency into a narrative which has become dominated by Bhagat Singh, overlooking the orchestrations of the other HSRA members. In his oral history testimony Kapoor reported that he became depressed whenever he looked at the photographs the following day. Not only was he imagining the interrogation and torture that his friends were being subjected to, but he was aghast at the early media coverage of the action, which had been resoundingly negative.[35]

The Lahore *Tribune*'s editor had at the outset remarked that it was 'inconceivable' that any opinion about the attack could differ from that of the Delhi police—that it was the 'isolated act of mad men'.[36] The *Hindustan Times*, owned by the Moderate Congressite Madan Mohan Malaviya, lectured in an editorial to the perpetrators of the 'diabolical deed' that they were

doing more harm than good ... What India needs to-day is not so much coercion of the Government, as constructive national activity, unity, political education and a strong sanction behind national demands ... once Indians are politically conscious enough to staunchly stand up for their rights, without the raising of a little finger, without the firing of a single bomb, freedom can be attained.[37]

It was the task of HSRA members Shiv Verma, Sukhdev and Kapoor to turn this coverage to their advantage. The photographs would be pivotal to this. Sukhdev left Delhi for Lahore, taking with him the negatives, from which he had multiple positive photographs made.[38]

Media Campaign

As a revolutionary organisation dedicated to the spread of socialism, in which the first object was to undermine and remove the colonial power, the HSRA faced major constraints in publicising its aims and getting the public support necessary to form a mass movement. The party sought innovative ways of publicising its aims and popularising its ideology, and its actions were largely oriented towards propaganda. As Sukhdev later reflected from his jail cell, the Saunders assassination and the Assembly bombing were both calculated 'to fix the revolutionaries in the minds of the people'.[39]

Martyrdom was very much on Bhagat Singh's mind; he had resolved that his struggle against British imperialism would conclude in his early death. Unwilling to leave behind a widow, he had refused to marry, and had secured a solemn promise from a close friend, Jaidev Gupta, to take care of family members in his absence.[40] He had a lucid understanding of how martyrs were made, and his work as a journalist shows that he had a strong appreciation of the utility of photography in bringing texture to a story. In 1926, he had assisted in the compilation of a special issue on the death penalty, *Chand ka Phansi Ank (Chand's Hanging Edition)*.[41] Bhagat Singh had contributed entries on the lives of several revolutionaries, including members of the HRA who went to the gallows,[42] and he took care to see that their photographs accompanied the text.[43] Readers often cut out and saved such images, preserving them in frames, scrapbooks and on walls.[44]

Bhagat Singh's acute awareness of the potency of martyrdom is clear in his writings.[45] Shortly before his execution fellow prisoners passed him a note, asking him if he preferred to live. His response was unambiguous:

My name has become a symbol of Indian revolution. The ideal and the sacrifices of the revolutionary party have elevated me to a height beyond which I will never be able to rise if I live. … If I mount the gallows with a smile, that will inspire Indian mothers and they will aspire that their children should also become Bhagat Singh. Thus the number of persons ready to sacrifice their lives for the freedom of the country will increase enormously. It will then become impossible for imperialism to face the tide of the revolution.[46]

Ramnath Studio's portrait of Bhagat Singh played a major role in the above process, providing a vivid illustration of the legend that he became. At a time when literacy in India was limited,[47] the image of Bhagat Singh was able to circulate independently of any text-based public sphere. His image came to be loaded with a range of interpretations, some of which were inaccurate, but all of which were anti-imperial. In death, Bhagat Singh breathed life into existing religiously-informed traditions of martyrdom to make 'a new category of male patriot', the *shaheed*.[48]

'It was Bhagat Singh's desire', Jaidev Kapoor recalled, 'and mine also, that after the action the pictures would be published and distributed widely'.[49] Kapoor reproduced and arranged for them to be delivered to major Indian-owned newspapers, in the hope that it would influence their reportage of the event. In Delhi, they were hand-delivered to the *Hindustan Times* office by Bimal Prasad Jain, a junior worker in the HSRA. He left the packet addressed to the editor, J. N. Sahni, with a *chaprasi* and disappeared. 'When Mr Sahni opened the envelope, I heard (when I was downstairs because Mr Sahni was sitting on the second floor) him shouting to the

Figure 12: Insert from *Bande Mataram*, 12 April 1929. (Ccourtesy of the National Archives of India. NAI, Home Political, File 391/1930)

peon: "Go and bring that Sahib, that gentleman, who has brought that envelope". But I was nowhere to be seen.'[50]

Fear of being accused of sedition meant that the photographs were not published immediately. Kapoor later 'found out that all the presswallahs were waiting to see who would publish the photograph first'.[51] It was the Lahore-based newspaper *Bande Mataram* that obliged, publishing the photographs on 12 April 1929.[52] The pictures appeared not in the actual pages of the newspaper, but on a loose, one-sided poster issued inside (Figure 12); although the *Bande Mataram* was an Urdu newspaper, the poster was in English. The poster format alone made it clear that the newspaper was sympathetic to the revolutionaries.

THAT HAT: INFAMY, STRATEGY AND SOCIAL COMMUNICATION

The editor of *Bande Mataram*, Lala Feroze Chand, was questioned by police in May after a raid on his home turned up a portrait of Bhagat Singh.[53] Chand conceded that he had agreed to publish the photographs of Bhagat Singh and Dutt, which had been 'left by somebody at my house during my absence'.[54] Called as a prosecution witness, Chand eventually confessed that he knew Sukhdev, and that Sukhdev had worked for him at the *Bande Mataram* office.[55] Chand did not mention that he was a friend of Bhagat Singh and had great admiration for him and his ideology.[56] Decades later, in an oral history testimony, Chand reflected,

That photograph, by the way, became very popular throughout the length and breadth of this country for that was the first glimpse that people had of Bhagat Singh in a new outfit with a felt hat—this young Sikh chap with a felt hat on his head. And that was the photograph of Bhagat Singh that remained in circulation ever after.[57]

By airing the photographs of Bhagat Singh and Dutt, *Bande Mataram* introduced a visual component to a story that was animating people and the press all over north India. The secrecy maintained by police about the investigations, combined with the refusal of the accused to make any statement until they were in court, led to incredible speculation in the capital. The names of the accused had been released, but little more was known about them. An early report ventured 'Bhagat Singh, it is understood, is a graduate of the National University, the son of Sardar Kishen Singh and the nephew of Sardar Ajit Singh of 1907 fame'.[58] This much was correct, but within a week 'bazaar gossip' reported in the *Hindustan Times* had it that Bhagat Singh had escaped the police lock-up and run away;[59] and another report claimed (equally falsely) that one of the pair had become a government witness.[60] A curious man of 'unknown identity' caused a sensation near a Gurudwara in Majnu ka Tila, when he set up ominous placards proclaiming 'Saunders' Murderer is Present'; 'The British Government is going to end, so help it'; and 'My Guru knows all'.[61]

Added to this enigma were the statements of public figures who began to speculate about who was really behind the attack on the Assembly. The *Hindustan Times* observed that the London papers had been 'thrown into a fit of acute hysteria', placing 'the most extreme interpretations' on the incident, linking the perpetrators to Moscow.[62] Diwan Chaman Lal, a Member of the Legislative Assembly, claimed that the CID had orchestrated the bombing, with a view to manufacturing sufficient fear of the red menace that the Public Safety Bill would find easy passage through the house.[63] In yet another editorial, the *Hindustan Times* blamed the government for the attack, claiming that 'their dark record of persistent misdeeds … has given new life to the dying embers of anarchy and revolution in India'.[64] Michael O'Dwyer, the former Governor of the Punjab, intimated to the *Evening News* in London that the attack was clear evidence that 'Indians are beginning to think that we are no longer capable of governing them'. This, he concluded in a report passed on by the *Hindustan Times*, 'is the direct result of the misguided policy of bestowing representative institutions'.[65]

As the investigation proceeded, unsolicited correspondence, some written on the HSRA letterhead and its trademark scarlet paper, began to be sent to various newspapers. The editor of the *Daily Chronicle* opened a letter threatening him for publishing an article that was critical of Bhagat Singh and Dutt.[66] A correspondent claiming to represent 'the Real Hindustan Socialist Republican Army' declared that the organisation was *not* responsible for the Assembly bombing.[67] Lahore's Senior Superintendent of Police, Jock Scott (the intended target of the HSRA's 1928 shooting in Lahore), described by a colleague as 'a dour, gruff Edinburgh Scot who wore a deliberately ferocious expression', had been assigned a bodyguard after Saunders' death.[68] But a death threat on crimson paper inspired him to pack his bags for Bombay, where he set sail on the next steamer for England.[69] A spin-off organisation calling itself the 'Bharatiya Republican Association' posted red handbills around Kanpur, exhorting students to oust the British by force.[70] This barrage of handbills, similarly-named organisations and death threats confused investigators. Writing to his son, Motilal Nehru scoffed at the gullibility of the press and the investigators: these 'so-called "Red Letters"', he opined, 'are clearly the very clumsy handicraft of the CID'.[71] The arrest in June of a police constable in Lahore for the authorship of one such poster proved the elder Nehru right on at least one of these instances.[72]

The day after the *Bande Mataram* went to press with its poster, the *Tribune* published a photograph of Bhagat Singh taken some years prior, cropped from a class photograph at Lahore College (Figure 13). On 18 April, not to be outdone, the *Hindustan Times* finally went to press with Ramnath Studio's photographs of Bhagat Singh and Dutt on its front page, each positioned in an oval frame. This immediately registered in police investigations in Delhi as suspicious. Already the police had taken exception to coverage in the newspaper that betrayed intimate knowledge of the case,[73] and now the paper had published 'excellent photographs'.[74] 'Where did it get them? And when? Bhagat Singh wore a beard last summer in Lahore but the picture which the *Hindustan Times* published shows him clean-shaven except for a small moustache, just as he was on the 8th April.'[75]

The HSRA had close links with personnel working for the *Hindustan Times* which enabled the revolutionaries a reasonable airing, inasmuch as censorship and editorial oversight would allow. Kapoor had sent a copy of the leaflet 'It Takes a Loud Voice' to a socialist contact, Durga Das Vaid, who worked for the paper,[76] which perhaps explains why the *Hindustan Times* had published a facsimile of it on the front page of its edition of 10 April 1929, and a full transcription on the following page for good measure.[77] The police had information that Bhagat Singh and Dutt had visited a residence owned by Tribhuvanath Singh and a Mr Ghosh, who

Figure 13: This portrait of Bhagat Singh, published in the *Tribune*, 13 April 1929, was cropped from a class photograph taken at Lahore Central College in 1924. (Courtesy of the Supreme Court of India Museum)

were 'known trade unionists' on the staff of the *Hindustan Times*, on the day prior to the attack.[78]

So it was that while the newspaper's editorials disapproved of the violence, much of the coverage of the Assembly attack was critical of the government and the investigators. A front-page article mocked the police, caught up in a 'wild goose chase', questioning *dhobis* all around Delhi in the hope that they might identify the laundry mark on a pair of Dutt's khaki knickers.[79] Investigators became so suspicious of the sympathies of Chaman Lal, one of the reporters from the *Hindustan Times*, that he was taken in for questioning after the photographs were published,[80] and although nothing was proven at the time, by June the Commissioner of Delhi had ordered his press pass confiscated.[81] Investigators in 1929 had insufficient evidence to prove whether the knowledge Chaman Lal had of the case arose from his role as a reporter or as a co-conspirator. He later disclosed that he was getting inside information about the case daily from a police inspector, Sardar Chet Singh.[82]

Chaman Lal was in fact a co-conspirator as well; he was secretary of the Naujawan Bharat Sabha's Delhi Branch and 'a very close friend of Bhagat Singh'.[83] The revolutionaries had forewarned him of the action in the Assembly explicitly so he could report on it, and he took his editor, J.N. Sahni, along with him. Chaman Lal pointed out the hatted young man in the visitor's gallery to Sahni: 'Watch him … That is why I am here … It is my scoop'.[84] Here the precise narrative diverges, with Sahni and Lal giving slightly different accounts of what happened next. According to Chaman Lal, he witnessed the bombing and waited around for the police to arrest Bhagat Singh and Dutt, and he even scooped up and pocketed some of the cartridges that Bhagat Singh did not use, while Sahni went back to his office, presumably to write the story.[85] Sahni remembers that Chaman Lal slipped out before the bombing, and waited outside the Assembly while Sahni wrote the scoop, folding it into his hat with a paperweight before tossing it down to Lal from the verandah of the Assembly, who then cycled off to the *Hindustan Times* to lodge his story.[86] A police report favoured Chaman Lal's account, complaining that he had got in the way when Bhagat Singh and Dutt were arrested.[87]

The HSRA had several supporters working for major newspapers. Indeed, some active party members, such as Hansraj Vohra and Comrade Ram Chandra in Lahore, were employed as journalists and were able to leverage a certain amount of positive coverage in the immediate aftermath of the bombing of the Assembly.[88] Once Bhagat Singh and Dutt began to give evidence in court, the media attention picked up a momentum of its own as a compelling narrative began to cohere. HSRA organisers in Punjab and UP, Bhagwati Charan and Yashpal, found that 'in the eyes of the people, the men associated with them suddenly became national heroes', with the result that it was much easier to find financial support and refuge from the public.[89]

Evidence: Exhibit A/4 (Hat On)

After the publication of the photographs in the *Hindustan Times*, Jaidev Kapoor fled Delhi with Shiv Verma, and together they arrived in Saharanpur, the party's new base, established earlier by HSRA member Gaya Prasad. From here the three revolutionaries applied to Azad for permission to attack the Viceroy's hunting party in nearby Dehradun, which Azad granted.[90] While preparing for this, they read in the press that Sukhdev had been arrested in Lahore on 15 April. After Sukhdev's arrest, the police recovered a copy of Bhagat Singh's portrait from a photographer in Anarkali, who had been given the task of replicating it.[91] The presence of photographs in Lahore of the Delhi suspects proved to police long-held suspicions that a broader conspiracy was afoot, and they began to think of the Delhi attack in much larger terms. The second 'Lahore Conspiracy Case' was born.[92]

Kapoor and Verma were arrested in Saharanpur on 12 May 1929. The detailed inventory of items confiscated from their hideout went from the banal (item 70: a pair of 'chequered stockings made of cotton') to the damning: a small cache of bomb shells, identical to those thrown in the Assembly; and a small stack of portraits of Bhagat Singh and B.K. Dutt, which police now realised were taken 'for the express purpose of publication as soon as the deed had been committed'.[93] There was ample evidence that Kapoor and Verma were orchestrating a media campaign: envelopes were found addressed to the editors of the *Leader*, *Pratap*, *Amrita Bazaar Patrika*, *Indian Daily Telegraph*, *Hindustan Times*, *Aj*, and *Indian National Herald*, each with a two-paisa stamp affixed, along with a stack of 875 red sheets bearing 'exactly the same printed heading as the posters put up in Lahore after the Saunders' murder and as the Assembly leaflets'.[94] The investigators recovered nine photographs and three glass negatives, including one of Bhagat Singh's portrait, which was now named 'Exhibit A/4 (Hat On)'.[95]

There were several instances throughout the court case in which it was clear that the portrait of Bhagat Singh was vivid in the minds of many. There was extended, albeit fruitless, cross-examination of witnesses to discern whether Bhagat Singh had been wearing a hat at the exact moment of his arrest in the Legislative Assembly, with the most reliable witness recounting that 'Bhagat Singh asked for his hat which was lying nearby' as he was being led away.[96] Mohammed Ali Jinnah, in a debate in the Assembly about Bhagat Singh's hunger strike over the differential treatment of European and Indian prisoners in Indian jails, referred to a section in the *Punjab Jail Manual* which defined a European as 'every European, Eurasian, and American, and every other person (whether a Native of India or not) whose habits and manner of living, in the opinion of the Superintendent, more nearly approach those of the European than those of the ordinary Native of India.'[97] Jinnah concluded: 'so far as I know, Bhagat Singh and Dutt wear *topees* [hats] … therefore, they ought to be treated as Europeans'.[98] A speech given by a Naujawan Bharat Sabha leader in support of the jailed revolutionaries urged the young men present to 'wear hats and keep pistols'.[99] According to this logic, the rakish but humble hat had assumed the importance of bombs and firearms as an indispensable tool of a revolutionary.

Placard

At the Karachi Congress, days after the executions, Jawaharlal remarked on the omnipresence of Bhagat Singh,

Why is everyone thinking of Bhagat Singh today? Even children in villages know about him. Many before him have made sacrifices and many more are still doing so. But why is the name of Bhagat Singh on every tongue? Why is his picture adorning walls and why are buttons studded with it? There must be some reason for this.[100]

Once the photograph of Bhagat Singh was released in the press, it rapidly began to circulate throughout India. It became a placard, which stood first for Bhagat Singh's own legal struggle against the British, but it subsequently morphed into an emblem of anti-imperialism. It is clear that the Naujawan Bharat Sabha (NJBS) took the initiative in its initial dissemination. Many processions and meetings were held in which the photograph was accorded pride of place,[101] and was liberally distributed (Figure 14), particularly after the revolutionaries' commencement of a hunger strike in protest at jail conditions for political prisoners 'which went on from week to week and created a stir in the country'.[102] Flyers featuring Bhagat Singh and Dutt were circulated freely at meetings, and in at least one case, it was advertised in advance that pictures of them would be distributed, indicating that the opportunity to collect the images was in itself something of an attraction.[103] Reports in late 1930 suggest that the Karachi branch of the NJBS had taken to 'augmenting its funds by selling coupons on which pictures of Bhagat Singh, Dutt and Jatindra Das appeared'.[104] Receipts for donations to the Bhagat Singh Memorial Fund bore his photograph, and, after his execution, mourners in Calcutta rallied around a photo of Bhagat Singh 'held aloft on a pole'.[105]

Many rallies and processions in support of Bhagat Singh and his colleagues were accompanied by widely-observed *hartals*, demonstrating that their appeal had begun to transcend the political spectrum. The Home Department was surprised to learn that Delhi's Anti-Red League (previously thought of as a society of 'loyal merchants') objected to the *hartal* proposed to accompany a planned Bhagat Singh and Dutt Day, but still professed sympathy with the 'misguided youths sentenced in the Assembly Bomb Case'.[106] When it was celebrated in Delhi on 21 July 1929, organised by a freshly-opened branch in Delhi of the NJBS, 'the proceedings met with more public support than was anticipated', with a thousand people attending.[107] The NJBS set about marking the calendar with a series of special-purpose protests including Hunger Striker's Day[108] and several All-India Bhagat Singh Days,[109] most notably on the day of his execution.[110]

Bhagat Singh's example inspired a number of political assassinations. Between 1930 and 1933, violent attacks against British officials increased dramatically, and the Intelligence Bureau discerned a pronounced 'growth in the spirit of violence' in youth movements, including the Congress.[111] In the first three months of 1931 alone, as Bhagat Singh awaited execution, five British officials and three policemen were killed, and there were thirty causalities as a result of 'attempts on the lives of government officials'.[112] Many of these attacks were performed with direct reference

Figure 14: 'Starving to Death for Country's Honour', Anarkali, Lahore: The National Art Press. This handbill was circulated in a celebration of 'Bhagat Singh Day', jointly held by the Amritsar City Congress Committee and the NJBS in July 1929. (Courtesy of the Supreme Court of India Museum)

to Bhagat Singh, his photograph serving as an inspiration or left behind as a calling card. In the weeks before the death sentence was pronounced in October 1930, the home of a prominent police investigator was bombed. 'It is significant', deduced the Director of Intelligence, 'that shortly before the attack, a cyclostyled Urdu leaflet, on which was pasted a photograph of Bhagat Singh, made its appearance in Lahore'.[113]

Vasudev Balwant Gogate recalled that, in 1929, the atmosphere at Pune's Fergusson College was charged with news of the Lahore Conspiracy Case, and that photographs of the accused were widely distributed among students. Their subsequent martyrdom, along with the urging of his mentor V.D. Savarkar, inspired Gogate to shoot Sir Ernest Hotson on 22 July 1931, in protest at the Sholapur Martial Law atrocities, in which several *satyagrahi*s were killed.[114] Hotson survived—Gogate supposed that his target had been wearing a bulletproof vest at the time, indicative of a new wariness among British officials. For G.B. Nawalkar, 'the heroic deeds of the revolutionaries like Chandrashekhar Azad and Bhagat Singh, Batukeshwar Dutt and Sukhdev and Rajguru, they were really thrilling and one, in that impressionable young age, would feel that we should do something for our motherland, like these great revolutionaries'.[115] At least one photography studio offered young men the opportunity to dress up as Bhagat Singh, hat and all, to pose with a revolver for a memento of their own (Figure 15).

Figure 15: Photograph of Alberto Viegas, taken at Lord's Studio, Margao in 1940, captioned 'Posing against a forest backdrop'. (Collection of Savia Viegas)

Bhagat Singh's portrait became photo-mechanically replicated so frequently[116] that, as an image, it began to lose its clarity. By April of 1931, in an effort to retrieve his handsome features, copies of the photograph would be drawn over, narrowing his eyes and redefining his lips, somewhat altering his expression (Figure 16). Using the photograph as a basis, many drawings and paintings were made of Bhagat Singh in the early 1930s, reproduced widely as posters and calendars, adding significantly to the image's mobility. The government instantly proscribed such pictures.[117]

Figure 16: The front cover of *Abhyudaya*'s *Bhagat Singh Ank*, 8 May 1931. From *Amar Shahid ko Naman* (A Homage to Eternal Martyrs), New Delhi: Rashtriya Abhilekhagar, 2002, p. 1.

As Bhagat Singh's image migrated from photograph to poster, the hat became his defining feature, as indeed it is today. Less skilled artists were not troubled by the need to depict his fine features with precision, for they were able to cater to the demand for images of Bhagat Singh by simply referencing the photograph, relying on his distinctive hat to signal his identity. This enabled the circulation of Bhagat Singh's image independently of, even as it cited, the photographic image, enhancing its capacity for dissemination. The photograph's migration to calendar art meant that it could be reproduced in unimaginable ways and apparently dissonant contexts, for example to suggest a secret complicity between the Congress and the revolutionaries (Figure 3).

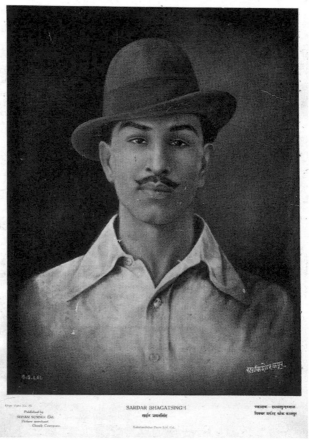

Figure 17: Roop Kishore Kapoor, 'Sardar Bhagat Singh', Kanpur: Shyam Sunder Lal, c. 1931. (Author's collection)

Posters eulogising Bhagat Singh survive in great numbers today, in archives, libraries and in personal collections, mute evidence to their popularity in the 1930s.[118] More rare is evidence of *how* they were interacted with before they were captured. Shiv Verma described an anecdote from some time around 1930 which gives us a sense of how one chance encounter with a poster in Haridwar led to an impromptu public rally, and the softening of a mother's exasperation that her son had chosen the life of a revolutionary. Verma's mother had recently visited her son in jail to implore him to cooperate with the investigation (which he refused to do). On her return from Lahore, accompanied by her brother, she stopped at Haridwar to perform religious rites, officiated by a family *panda*, where,

One calendar, depicting all the photographs of the Lahore Conspiracy Case accused, was hanging on the wall in the room where the Panda had lodged them. My uncle explained to my mother: This is Bhagat Singh, this is Sukhdev, this is Shiv Verma, this is so and so. The Panda was watching them from behind. The Panda asked: how do you know these people? My uncle said, she is the mother of so and so. He kept quiet and lodged them comfortably. Then he took a tonga [horse and cart], went round the city and announced that the mother

Figure 18: 'Lahore Conspiracy Case Decision', Lahore: Arorbans Press. (Courtesy British Library, EPP 1/35)

of so and so, an accused in the Lahore Conspiracy Case, has come and anyone, who wanted to have darshan [see her], come at 4 o'clock to the Har-ki-podi. At 4 o'clock, he asked my mother and uncle to come out. They came out and found thousands of people gathered there shouting slogans. So that is how these people eulogised our relatives and inspired them.[119]

Figure 18 includes the likeness of Shiv Verma and the other Lahore Conspiracy Case convicts who were sentenced to transportation for life, their names listed underneath, on the left. This picture would have been drawn after the sentences were handed down on 8 October 1930. It is not necessarily the image referred to in Verma's vignette, but is indicative of such posters distributed bearing the convicts of the Lahore Conspiracy Case.

Just as Bhagat Singh's portrait was extensively photo-mechanically replicated and copied, subtly changing its physical form to infer innocence or intent, so too the message that accompanied the image was received and reinterpreted in divergent ways. Bhagat Singh became an idea 'thought out and reworked in the popular imagination', not unlike the reception of Gandhi in Gorakhpur in the early 1920s.[120] From the many fragments relating to Bhagat Singh's life in various archives, it becomes clear that his revolutionary agenda was not well understood, and it emerges that in the India of the 1930s, general usage of the term 'revolution' was ambiguous. Indeed, where the term 'revolution' (*inquilab*) came to enter public discourse, usually in the form of sloganeering, it seemed to signal a political revolution rather than the more comprehensive revolution of the proletariat that was at the heart of HSRA ideology.[121] Some people even presumed that the slogan popularised by the revolutionaries in the court room, *Inquilab Zindabad* (Long Live Revolution!) was an exhortation for the longevity of 'another great person in prison'.[122]

Of course a political revolution—removing the British—was the first step to effecting any kind of social program; but removing the British has been popularly presumed to be the sole aim of Bhagat Singh's politics. An examination of the various speeches, tracts and posters produced in the aftermath of Bhagat Singh's execution reveals that the bulk of eulogies did not reflect his program.[123] Thus the portrait of Bhagat Singh has come to symbolise his defiant and heroic anticolonialism, which is not inaccurate, but incomplete. The fact that he inspired a range of political activists—from Gogate, a follower of Savarkar, to the qualified sympathy of the Anti-Red League, to mention just two we have encountered here—is indicative of how broad his appeal came to be.

That a certain concept of Bhagat Singh came to represent the paradigmatic revolutionary is evident from Bejoy Kumar Sinha's 1939 memoirs:

Fantastic are some of the notions prevailing about revolutionary youths amongst a section of our countrymen. I recall a funny incident in this connection. In the year 1931 when I reached Rajahmandri Central Prison in Andhra, I was placed in the midst of my comrades of Civil Disobedience Campaign. To meet me the first day, there was a regular stampede but many of those who met me were visibly disappointed. The reason I was told when I grew familiar with them. I was informed that their expectations were not fulfilled. They had thought that as a northern India revolutionary, a colleague of Bhagat Singh and Azad, I would be a flaming youth of an austere face with red hot eyes, that I would be sullen and silent, would fly at a tangent at the least provocation from the authorities. In short they expected a revolutionary to be an uncommon creature—an object of adoration and respect but inspiring positive fear and awe.[124]

The British played their own role in making Bhagat Singh a martyr; they conducted themselves just as he predicted. They knew that his execution would create ripples all over India, yet they were unwilling to consider a reprieve, and so they obliged, sending him to a death that gave him a perpetual life.[125] The Home Department was acutely aware of the phenomenon of martyr-making unfolding before them, complaining that 'the propaganda to which the youth of the country is being subjected is calculated to inflame their minds to an extent which makes it probable that unbalanced persons will commit sporadic acts of violence in order to earn the martyr's crown which they are constantly urged to attain'.[126]

A close reading of the portrait's journey highlights a number of aspects of revolutionary history in the interwar period. Foremost among these is the extraordinary awareness of visuality that Bhagat Singh demonstrated, at a time when media dissemination was limited by literacy, linguistic divides and censorship regimes. This emerged from his own experience as a voracious reader, writer and keen observer of politics, combined with a genuine desire to communicate as broadly as possible. As Sumathi Ramaswamy has recently argued, 'Pictorial history challenges us to dwell on the overlapping zone between the sayable and the seeable so as to shuttle back and forth between the two. It exhorts us to explore those aspects of the human experience that are unsayable and nonverbalisable, but also correspondingly, to come to terms with those that are unpicturable, even unseeable'.[127] In the 1930s, much was unprintable and unsayable, but much more could be and was inferred by readers of this polysemic image, intended to publicise the revolutionaries' cause.

I have not found anything to suggest that Bhagat Singh deliberately chose the hat as a prop, calculating that it would translate into a powerful tool of self-representation, as it morphed across visual media. It is clear from contemporary advertising and film that the hat was at the time a fashionable accessory,[128] and while the revolutionaries had neither funds nor a penchant for fashion, they did make extensive use of disguises.[129] At the end of 1928, Bhagat Singh had borrowed the hat from a friend, Desraj Bharti,[130] teaming it with a coat and trousers, knowing that the British were looking for a turbaned, khaddar-clad fugitive in the aftermath of Saunder's assassination.[131] A slip in a report in the *Hindustan Times* the day after the Assembly Bombing innocuously noted (for the photographs had not yet been collected) that 'Bhagat Singh, it is understood, was not wearing a hat' at the time of the bombing, from which we might infer that the writer was acquainted with Bhagat Singh, and knew that this was contrary to his habit.[132]

From a series of posters issued by Kanpur's prolific Shyam Sunder Lal Picture Merchant in the early 1930s, it is clear that the inner circle members of the HSRA all had studio photographs taken, which later became the template for eulogy prints for those who died (Figure 19, of Rajguru). None of these achieved the currency of Bhagat Singh's; indeed the centrality of Bhagat Singh's image in 1929 can be said to have detracted attention from absconders. B.K. Dutt's portrait was often reproduced, mostly in concert with Bhagat Singh's, but he survived his jail ordeal. Jatindranath Das' death was covered extensively in the media, and although

Figure 19: 'Rajguru', Martyrdom print, Kanpur: Shyam Sunder Lal, c. 1931. (Author's Collection)

his studio portrait does not seem to have been released to the press at the time (Figure 9), a photograph of his body, laid out in Borstal Jail, was front-page news (Figure 47). His death made a major impact on the Indian body politic, as will be detailed in Chapter Six, but it also provided an important precedent for the crescendo accompanying Bhagat Singh's execution.

While posters referencing the studio portrait of a moustache-twirling Chandrashekhar Azad (Figs. 4, 10, 20, 45, 46) come close to the contemporary currency of Bhagat Singh's hat portrait, this was a somewhat later phenomenon. While this photograph's exact genealogy remains unclear, other than that it was taken by a sympathiser by the name of Rudranarayan while Azad was in hiding in Jhansi,[133] it does not appear to have been in media circulation in the aftermath of Azad's death, in a dramatic police encounter in Allahabad's Alfred Park on 27 February 1931.

Figure 20: Chandrashekhar Azad, studio portrait taken in Jhansi, c. 1930.

With the exception of the posthumous collage *Azad Mandir* (Figure 34), Azad never featured in the poster art of the 1930s. As the only absconder in both the Kakori and Lahore Conspiracy Cases, much less is known about Azad; his final years were spent in hiding and his death was not anticipated in the same way as Bhagat Singh's. Within months of Azad's death, legislation prohibiting the publication of martyrology imagery seemed to limit their production. By contrast, Bhagat Singh's portrait was part of a sophisticated media campaign, carried over a two-year period, illustrating in the media the story of his defiance of the British in the courts. His friend Jaidev Gupta recalled that he 'wanted to be hanged at a time when the country and the whole world might be clamouring for his release', and this he achieved.[134] This made him more prominent and eminently more recognisable than his co-conspirators, even those who were hanged at the same time. A martyrology poster of Sukhdev produced some time in the early 1930s initially confused his identity, evidenced by the scratching out of Rajguru's name in both Hindi and English, and the superimposition of Sukhdev's (Figure 21).

Figure 21: 'Sukhdev', Martyrdom print, Kanpur: Shyam Sunder Lal, c. 1931.

Shortly after his execution, probably during a condolence meeting in Lahore, unknown, upset mourners made a blood sacrifice in the memory of Bhagat Singh. Slicing their thumbs, they let their blood fall onto the front page of the *Tribune* of 25 March 1929 (Figure 22), which had announced Bhagat Singh's death and carried his photograph (Figure 5). In the aftermath of his death, reproduction of his portrait, as with later popular images of martyrs, seemed to 'want', as Sumathi Ramaswamy suggests, 'the devotion and worshipful reverence of the Indian citizen. They want action and sacrifice … on behalf of nation and country; they want martyrs for map and mother'.[135] This was very much the tone of early Naujawan Bharat Sabha conferences, such as one in 1929 when a portrait of Madan Lal Dhingra was unveiled and, in the words of a CID report, 'the audience was asked to follow the example of this great "martyr"… The proceedings of the Conference ended with a lantern display of murderers executed for their "patriotic" services.'[136]

By posing for his photograph, Bhagat Singh was providing a pivotal ingredient for a publicity campaign that created a powerful movement around his pending martyrdom. The campaign began with the print media, but rapidly moved beyond

Figure 22: Copy of a bloodstained *Tribune*, 25 March 1931 (as in Figure 5), as it was exhibited at the Shaheed Bhagat Singh Exhibition, Supreme Court of India Museum in 2007. (Courtesy of the Supreme Court of India Museum)

what was, in the 1930s, a realm of limited reach. The portrait soon circulated independently of text, in the form of reproductions, facsimiles, posters and even badges, in which the hat served to symbolise Bhagat Singh and his imperial challenge. As such, the image became the catalyst of urgent discussions about 'thriller nationalism', with its unpredictable turns of fate; agonising hunger-strikes; intrigues inside court-rooms, plotting from without; and beatings and abuses in squalid jails; countered with tales of enduring camaraderie and astounding bravery. The end, too, was unpredictable, with many believing that the trio would be given clemency at the last minute. By the time Bhagat Singh was executed, he had, through his portrait, become known to many. This explains the extraordinary reaction around India after his death, where many adopted a form of mourning—*cautha*—that they would normally observe for a family member or friend.[137]

3

THE REVOLUTIONARY UNKNOWN

THE SECRET LIFE OF DURGA DEVI VOHRA

While in recent analyses much emphasis has been put on Bhagat Singh's infamous getaway disguise as an Anglo-Indian or a sahib,[1] complete with that hat, it has rarely registered that he was also specifically disguised 'as a married man',[2] a measure intended to confound the police who were on the lookout for unencumbered youths.[3] Being seen in the company of HSRA member Durga Devi Vohra and her young son placed him in an altogether different register, as a family man. Durga Devi, popularly known as Durga *Bhabhi* (sister-in-law, or more precisely, the wife of one's elder brother), is remembered as one of the few women to feature in the machinations of the HSRA. In a scene invariably depicted in comic books, documentary and *filmi* accounts, Durga Devi poses as Bhagat Singh's wife, and with her three-year old son Sachi, the 'family' neatly evades the police cordon set up to capture Saunders' assassin. Yet this was not Durga Devi Vohra's only contribution to the HSRA. Few are aware that she was involved in a range of activities, and even led an action, shooting at a British policeman and his wife in October 1930.

In popular renditions of revolutionary nationalist activities, the roles of women have been largely obscured, with the ongoing use of the epithet *Bhabhi* (generally not an empowered role in the extended family) further reducing her subjectivity. An appreciation of the role of women in the HSRA has been further precluded by conventions which imagine politics to be a male arena of activity,[4] and by history writing practices that read violent responses to colonialism as the product of an ultra-masculine or gendered agenda.[5] However, women were active on the fringes of the inner circle of the HSRA, and both despite and because of prevalent conceptions of femininity in north Indian society at the time, their roles were vital. As the

HSRA was depleted of manpower as inner party members were progressively arrested, women such as Durga Devi began to take more prominent roles in party machinations.

Reconstructing Durga Devi Vohra's revolutionary story is an instructive reminder of how little is known of revolutionary organisation outside the well-loved narratives rehearsed in popular culture. This will necessarily involve a certain amount of narration, as there exists no published account of what she did *after* helping Bhagat Singh escape Lahore. Moreover, much of this narrative is partial; the below has been assembled by drawing on a combination of archival and oral histories, with the latter recorded decades after the events they describe. Foremost among these interviews is one with Durga Devi herself, recorded for the Nehru Memorial Museum and Library's Oral History Project in 1972.[6] At the age of sixty-five, quietly living out her life in Lucknow, when she was approached by the NMML's interviewer, S.L. Manchanda, Vohra was initially reluctant to be interviewed, and her recollections were considerably brief in comparison to many of the other testimonies gathered by the Oral History Project.[7]

This is partially because Durga Devi's interview was not pre-arranged weeks in advance, as was the usual practice for the NMML's oral history project. Manchanda had gone to Lucknow to interview Yashpal, who recommended that he approach Durga Devi who also lived in the town, which Manchanda did at once. Initially, she was reluctant to be interviewed but Manchanda pressed her, and she agreed. As a result, Durga Devi did not have the chance to reflect on what she might talk about in the interview prior to it taking place, nor had she 'practiced' telling her story, like Yashpal, who had extensively written about his revolutionary life in the three-volume *Singhavalokan*. She had given other interviews which impart valuable insights, although most of these were contributions to Bhagat Singh commemoration volumes, in which she had no occasion to reflect on her own revolutionary life.[8] However, when analysed in conjunction with other sources, her testimony represents a vital tool for understanding the role of women in the HSRA, at a time in which mainstream nationalist politics was beginning to accommodate women activists.[9]

Women in the HSRA

It is true that there was, within the inner circle of the HSRA, an ethos that the normative, ideal revolutionary was male; and indeed there was a general policy which urged its male members, particularly those of the party's 'inner circle' who could be called upon at any time to make the ultimate sacrifice, to remain unmarried and therefore celibate. Bhagat Singh set a precedent for this—he famously left Lahore for Kanpur as his parents began to arrange his marriage, reasoning that he was destined to die young, and was unwilling to leave behind a young widow.[10]

This sensibility was most likely a product of his direct experience of the solitude of his aunt, Harnam Kaur, the wife of Ajit Singh, the founder of the Bharat Mata Society who was exiled from India as a result of his political activities. Alone and unable to bear children of her own, Harnam Kaur had been given the responsibility of raising Bhagat Singh.[11]

Additionally, it was generally felt within the HSRA that being married was a distraction to revolutionary activity, or as Manmathnath Gupta put it, being married for a revolutionary was 'not exactly convenient'.[12] Chhabil Das, Bhagat Singh's teacher and an activist involved in leftist politics in Lahore, recalled:

When Bhagat Singh heard that I was going to be married, he approached me and asked me if it was true? I replied in the affirmative. He insisted that I should not marry. I said, "Bhagat Singh, if I could get a really very good life companion who, instead of retarding my activities, would invigorate me, what would be your view?" In the same breath I quoted three concrete examples of Mrs Sun-Yat Sen, who was private secretary to her husband; Mrs Krupskaya, wife of Lenin; and Jenny Von Westphalen, a companion of Karl Marx. About her, his colleague Engels wrote: "But for cooperation of Mrs Jenny, Karl Marx would not have been Karl Marx". So when I talked like this, Bhagat Singh replied, "Guruji, who can vanquish you in argument!" So he yielded.[13]

While there continued to be many exceptions to the rule, there was also an ethos in the party that family attachments could be the downfall of a revolutionary, and with him the movement. Relying on a general perception of the weakness of women, police and intelligence agents habitually leaned on wives, sisters and mothers to pressure their husbands, brothers and sons to co-operate with police inquiries. To cite two such instances, Jai Gopal, the HSRA member whose testimony was used to convict Bhagat Singh, Sukhdev and Rajguru, fell victim to his mother's weeping and 'vomited out everything';[14] and Phanindranath Ghosh also became a government witness after his wife and parents had been brought to prison to plead with him to do so, appealing to his family responsibilities.[15]

Importantly, there were women who refused to be swayed, who inverted these appeals to the strength of the family unit, using them more deftly than did the authorities. Shiv Verma described how one HSRA member in custody, Brahma Dutt Mishra, had given a statement and become an approver. Mishra's wife told her mother-in-law:

You go and see him, tell him that your wife has become a widow; a man who cannot be honest and sincere to his friends cannot be sincere to his wife also. [She then] went and saw her son: I have come to tell you that your wife has become a widow and I have lost my son. You have defamed my name.[16]

The threat of being disowned by the women in his family was so powerful that Mishra withdrew his statement.[17]

It is clear that cultural concepts of celibacy influenced HSRA understandings of the ideal male political activist. Many party members met in Dayanand Anglo-Vedic (DAV) College in Lahore or Kanpur, where they were exposed to an Arya Samaji education, which stressed brahmacarin-style ideals. However, it should be remembered that the emphasis on celibacy and singlehood as character-building was not unique to the revolutionaries of the HSRA, but was common to a number of significant associations and social movements operative in the early twentieth century.[18]

The HSRA's leader, Chandrashekhar Azad, was described by fellow revolutionary Jaidev Kapoor as being highly influenced by the concept of brahmacharya.[19] The HSRA went through turmoil in 1929 after one of its members, Yashpal, chose to marry, and in doing so explicitly flouted Azad's objections. As a result, Azad ordered Durga Das Khanna to shoot Yashpal.[20] Yashpal discovered the plan, averting death by going into hiding, while working to convince the HSRA of his sincerity as a party worker. Yashpal's translator explained, 'falling in love and marrying were a kind of self-indulgence which betrayed a lack of self-control inconsistent with the conduct of a revolutionary'.[21]

It has been extrapolated that this episode indicates how strongly Azad felt about women in the HSRA. However, it is far more likely to indicate Azad's relationship with Yashpal, which several sources indicate was strained.[22] Sridevi Musaddi, who with her husband harboured Azad shortly before he was gunned down in February 1931, stated that while Azad was reluctant to place women in the path of danger, he showed women working in the movement the greatest respect.[23] This is evident in his dealings with Durga Devi Vohra. As Manmathnath Gupta recalled, Azad's appreciation for Durga Devi's work led him to revise his reservations about women in the revolutionary movement on the basis that they faced 'a double danger from the police. So, for some time it was resisted, but ultimately, because of the good work that Bhagwati Charan's wife, Bhabhi, and Susheelaji of Delhi had done, girls began to be taken into the revolutionary party'.[24]

In 1932 intelligence authorities discovered a lengthy HSRA manifesto which they attributed to Bhagat Singh.[25] It contained extensive ideological ruminations, including an incisive Marxist analysis of the state of colonialism in India.[26] The document mapped out opportunities for the revolutionaries to intervene in the Congress-dominated political landscape, and while disclaiming that 'no artificial barrier is recognised between men and women', it also noted that there was, practically speaking, less scope for women to undertake military training.[27] However, it explicitly included roles for women in the party, particularly in intelligence-gathering, fundraising and espionage. The particular utility of women in these roles becomes apparent in Durga Devi's story.

THE REVOLUTIONARY UNKNOWN

Durga Devi Vohra

Durga Devi Vohra was the only child of a Gujarati Brahmin couple settled in Allahabad.[28] Her mother died when she was young and her father took vows of *sannyas*, leaving her to be brought up by her aunt. She studied up to Class V, and married when she was eleven.[29] She first came into contact with the revolutionaries in Lahore through her husband, Bhagwati Charan Vohra (1903–1930), the son of a wealthy Gujarati, Shiv Charan Das, who worked for the railways and was honoured with the title of Rai Sahib.[30] Bhagwati Charan studied at National College, Lahore,[31] where he met Bhagat Singh, who became a frequent visitor to the family home, as did Yashpal and Sukhdev.[32] Bhagwati Charan was involved in student politics, becoming an active member of the Naujawan Bharat Sabha, which functioned (among other things) as a recruiting ground for HSRA members.[33] Bhagwati Charan was relatively wealthy and was able to dedicate much time and money to social and political work.[34] Additionally, he had no family opposition to his politics; his father had died in the early 1920s, and his mother when he was a child.[35] On account of his wealth, party members regarded his initial interest in the HSRA with suspicion, and it took some time to refute allegations that he was not a CID informer.[36] By late 1928, he and Durga Devi were incorporated into the party and he became one of the primary ideologues of the HSRA, officially serving as the Propaganda Secretary, writing a history of the revolutionary movement, and treatises such as 'The Philosophy of the Bomb', which was drafted as a riposte to Gandhi's 1929 critique of the revolutionaries, 'The Cult of the Bomb'.[37]

Durga Devi gave birth to a son, Sachinanda, in 1925, but she remained committed to teaching and continued to work in a girls' college in Lahore until she was forced to go underground in 1929.[38] In a studio photograph from around 1927, she is well turned out, elegant in a silk sari gathered at her shoulder with a brooch. She appears relaxed, confident, with Sachi sidled up to her, clasping something precious to his chest (Figure 23).

Bhagwati Charan's radical political activities brought him to the attention of the CID, and the couple were aware of being monitored, suspecting that their driver was a plant. In 1928, Bhagwati Charan rented a property at the behest of Sukhdev, the mastermind of the Lahore Conspiracy Case, to be used for party activities—including the manufacture of bombs. Durga Devi supported her husband's political activities and, according to Kumari Lajjawati, 'her one motive was to do whatever her husband did ... she said, "I'll do whatever Bhagwati Charan says"'.[39] Her thoughts on being a revolutionary were to develop as she was increasingly drawn into the party. A photograph—interesting because it is not taken in a studio, but in a nondescript urban setting—shows the young family together. Durga Devi appears pensive, her face gaunt and blouse loose, as though she had recently lost weight. Sachi, bigger and a little chubbier, his gaze fixated on something outside

Figure 23: Durga Devi Vohra and her son Sachi, c. 1927. (Courtesy of the National Archives of India, Comrade Ram Chandra photograph collection, S. No. 190, 12)

the frame, is propped up on his father's arm, as though it was the only way to restrain him for long enough for a family portrait to be clicked (Figure 24). These images, donated to the National Archives of India by Comrade Ram Chandra, a friend of Bhagwati Charan's from college, inscribe the small family as a unit, just as Figure 23 frames Durga Devi as a mother; but these were private photographs, not for release to the media or to be deployed in martyrology. There are single portraits of both revolutionaries which seem to have been taken for this purpose, although Durga Devi's was never released, nor did any photograph of her ever fall into the hands of imperial surveillance.[40]

In early December, Bhagwati Charan left Lahore to attend the annual meeting of the Indian National Congress in Calcutta, leaving a large sum of money with his wife in case of emergency—four or five thousand rupees, as she recalled.[41] After Saunders' assassination, Sukhdev and Bhagat Singh came to Durga Devi for help,

Figure 24: The Vohra Family: Bhagwati Charan, Durga Devi and Sachinanda, c. 1928. (Courtesy of the National Archives of India, Comrade Ram Chandra photograph collection, S. No. 190, 11)

bringing with them Rajguru. She had heard of the murder—all of Lahore was abuzz with the news, following the HSRA posters that boldly claimed responsibility. She implicitly knew that Bhagat Singh was involved, yet consistent with party protocol, she did not ask any questions, presuming that Rajguru, whom she had never seen before, was a servant.[42]

As is memorialised in *filmi* accounts, she readily gave over the sum of money her husband had left, and rather daringly, given social conventions of the time that constrained contact between men and women who were not married, agreed to pose as Bhagat Singh's wife in order to help him escape Lahore. Taking Sachi, and accompanied by Rajguru (pretending to be the young family's servant) they passed unencumbered though a police cordon and boarded a first class train carriage for Lucknow, where they changed trains for Calcutta.[43] Azad also escaped Lahore in the company of women. Disguised as a *panda* and wearing a *ramnami angochha* shawl, Azad travelled with Sukhdev's mother and sister, as though he was escorting them on a pilgrimage.[44]

From Lucknow, Bhagat Singh sent a telegram to Bhagwati Charan, informing him that he was coming to Calcutta with 'Durgawati'. Bhagwati Charan received this with great surprise: 'Who is this Durgawati?'[45] The party arrived at Calcutta, where Bhagwati Charan was staying with his sister, Sushila, who was also to become a prominent woman revolutionary.[46] It was with an element of surprise that Bhagwati Charan learned of his wife's role in helping Bhagat Singh and Rajguru escape: 'he was very happy. Then he complimented his wife; I have not recognised you until now; today I can understand that I have got a revolutionary wife'.[47]

After attending some sessions of the Calcutta Congress, Durga Devi returned to Lahore with her son.[48] Bhagwati Charan, who had learned how to make bombs from revolutionaries in Calcutta, was drawn into the preparations to launch the attack on the Legislative Assembly. In early April 1929, Durga Devi was summoned by her husband to Delhi to bid farewell to Bhagat Singh.[49] Travelling with Sushila, she arrived in Delhi to meet her husband, Azad and Bhagat Singh in Qudsia Park, where they picnicked, feeding Bhagat Singh his favorite foods, sweets and oranges. Again, no words were spoken of the plan to bomb the Assembly; it was simply understood that he was going to perform some action, and that he may not survive it. Sushila made an incision in her thumb, and gave Bhagat Singh a protective *tika* of her blood.[50] When Bhagat Singh left the picnic, he went directly to the Assembly, where with B. K. Dutt he set in motion the events that would lead to his execution. Azad slipped away, and the remainder of the party—Bhagwati Charan, Durga Devi and Sushila—hired a *tonga*, and began to circle the Assembly, anticipating the drama unfolding within. As the police were taking Bhagat Singh away, young Sachi recognised him and impulsively called out *Lamba Chacha!* (Tall Uncle!) to Bhagat Singh, who 'could not stop himself, he looked up, but the police were in a great hurry', and so missed an opportunity to arrest his accomplices.[51]

In the following months, police began to close in on the revolutionaries. In Lahore, investigators discovered the HSRA's bomb factory in Kashmir House, rented out in Bhagwati Charan's name, arresting Sukhdev, Jai Gopal and Kishori Lal. Bhagwati Charan was not on site at the time of the raid, and went into hiding.[52] Durga Devi was forced to engage a lawyer in an attempt to forestall police attempts to seize the family home on the basis that her husband was an absconder in the Lahore Conspiracy Case.[53] Comrade Ram Chandra, a family friend and fellow traveller, noted that during this period she continued to support the families of revolutionaries in Lahore, and acted as a 'post box', receiving mail for absconding revolutionaries.[54] She was also involved in the procurement of weapons for the party around this time. In early 1930, J.N. Sahni, the editor of the *Hindustan Times*, saw her in a secret meeting in Delhi with pistols sourced from the North-Western Frontier Province, which she kept concealed under her clothes.[55]

In 1929, Bhagwati Charan plotted and carried out an attempt to bomb the Viceroy's train with Yashpal.[56] Subsequently he became involved in a plot with Azad, Yashpal, Vaishampayan, Sukhdevraj, Sushila and Durga Devi to free Bhagat Singh from prison, by raiding a police van during his transfer from Borstal to Central Jail in Lahore. On 28 May 1930, Bhagwati Charan died. He was testing a bomb in woodland near the Ravi when it exploded prematurely in his hand.[57] His accomplices went for help, but by the time they returned to collect him it was too late.[58] His body was later discovered by police in a shallow grave nearby.[59] Durga Devi was now a widow, and it is here that her role in revolutionary politics is often thought to have ended.[60] She bore her widowhood, according to Kumari Lajjawati, with mute bravery. Restrained by the need to remain silent in their Lahore hideout, she didn't even shed a tear when she was told the news.[61] She summed up what she did next in her interview:

I fled after that. I sent the boy to someone in Allahabad. There was a warrant against me so I threw myself fully into my work. I was not a born revolutionary, but one who becomes a revolutionary with the maturity of ideas. More and more, an individual thinks, understands, reads and writes, his ideas change, they become stronger, it's not about being emotional. The first phase *is* emotional. And I believe that 99 per cent of our comrades were those who had come from an emotional phase, educated themselves, and then became genuine revolutionaries. Of course there are exceptions, such as my husband. Such as Chandrashekhar Azad. I told Azad that I wanted my full share of revolutionary work.[62]

Following Bhagwati Charan's death, Durga Devi stayed with Kewal Kishan Engineer,[63] before moving with her sister-in-law Sushila to the home of Rana Jang Bahadur Singh, a journalist for the *Tribune* in Lahore, where she hid for three weeks.[64] Shortly after, Durga Devi left Lahore, disguised in a *burqa*. She went to stay with Sridevi Musaddi and her husband, and remained there for a month, at the same time as Azad.[65] Her activities and whereabouts following this are somewhat unclear, other than that she was constantly on the move, staying one step ahead of police.[66] In July 1929 she was seen back in Lahore, holding a placard with Bhagat Singh's photograph and leading a procession on 'Bhagat Singh and Dutt Day', and weeks later she was named as a member of the ladies' procession mourning Jatindranath Das.[67]

The Lamington Road Outrage: What Durga Bhabhi Did Next

At midnight on 8 October 1930, Durga Devi shot at a European couple standing outside the police station in Lamington Road, a prominent thoroughfare in South Bombay, in what would later be described as 'the first instance in which a woman figured prominently in a terrorist outrage'.[68] The *Times of India* recorded that this was an ominous development, 'the first outrage of its kind in Bombay in recent years, and is reminiscent of the anarchist outrages of Bengal'.[69]

The victims of the shooting, it turned out, happened to be a police sergeant and his wife. They 'had a miraculous escape'; Sergeant Taylor had a bullet pass through his hand, and Mrs Taylor suffered three wounds on her leg.[70] The shots were fired by more than one weapon from a passing car, with witnesses reporting that they saw three assailants. A trace on the car's license plate quickly led the police to the driver, J. B. Bapat, who after five days of intense questioning gave the 'startling revelation' that one of the assailants was 'a Gujarati woman disguised in male attire'.[71] The police went on to make suppositions that 'with her in the car was her husband and her 8 year old son', which was of course incorrect. This began a search for a suspect described as a 'young, fair, goodlooking' woman, dressed in khaddar, who went by the name of Sharda Devi.[72]

Durga Devi, Prithvi Singh and Sukhdevraj had hastily conceived of the action at Lamington Road to commemorate the death sentence of Bhagat Singh, Sukhdev and Rajguru, handed down the previous day. Technically, the action was in contravention to party policy which stipulated that permission for actions could only be granted by Azad. Because they felt the need to act quickly, so that the authorities would interpret the attack as a distinct response to the death sentences, Azad's permission was not sought.[73] Prithvi Singh and Durga Devi had set off in a car driven by Bapat in the early evening. Their initial target was the Governor of the Punjab, Sir Geoffrey de Montmorency; however security around the house where he was staying in Malabar was such that they could not approach it.[74] Frustrated, they decided to target a police station instead, and finally saw 'two Britishers' standing near the police station on Lamington Road. According to Durga Devi, as the car crept past the pair, Prithvi Singh cried 'Shoot!' and together they leaned out of the windows and opened fire; she recalled firing three or four times.[75]

Following the successful precedent that had convicted Bhagat Singh and his comrades in the Lahore Conspiracy Case, the prosecutors of the Lamington Road Outrage decided to argue that it was a part of a broader conspiracy in the Punjab and UP. While there was reason to suppose this was true, there was insufficient evidence to prove it in court, with only the testimony of one approver. This confession was judged unstable and the 'attempt to make a gigantic superstructure on the flimsiest grounds' failed.[76] There were no convictions; those arrested were released. Meanwhile, Durga Devi had escaped capture, able to use the days it took for the police to realise that a woman had been an assailant to slip out of Bombay undetected.

The Party as Family

From this incident it is clear that gendered roles ascribed to Durga Devi as a mother, wife and later a widow gave her a unique disguise. The mandarins in Indian Political Intelligence had connected 'the violence movement' with young, unencumbered and energetic bachelors. Because this was largely true of inner circle members, the strategic use of the wives of married party members could lend subversive operations a sheen of respectability. Women were the perfect front.[77]

Relations between party members were generally close; indeed many revolutionaries broke ties with their families in order to join the HSRA, which became a surrogate family.[78] Consistent with firm subcontinental friendships, these relationships were marked by the affectionate usage of familial terms. Numerous oral history testimonies reveal that party members addressed both Bhagat Singh and Azad as *bhaiya* (brother), among other names; Bhagwati Charan's sister Sushila was known to all as *didi* (older sister), and Durga Devi was respectfully known as *bhabhi* (sister-in-law). Following Bhagwati Charan's death, this metaphorical relationship was extended. Azad drew Durga Devi closer into party activities than before, telling her: 'You are like a mother-sister to us. And this boy is the property of the party. He would take an *anna* out of his pocket or he would order *jalebis* for my son in the morning, whenever I stayed with him.'[79]

While Durga Devi's motherhood of a small child might have been thought to preclude her from revolutionary activities, in fact it provided a foil for them. On the day of the Lamington Road attack, she had left Sachi with Babarao Savarkar—the brother of Vinayak Damodar Savarkar—with instructions that if anything untoward happened he should be sent to an HSRA member in Punjab, Dhanvantari. When Savarkar read about the action in the newspapers the following day, he panicked— he was engaged at the time in secretly printing copies of his brother's banned book, *The War of Indian Independence*, and was naturally keen to avoid attention.[80] He sent Sachi to the home of Bapat, the driver in the action, who had already been arrested; the boy was then redirected to Vaishampayan's residence; he too had been arrested. Durga Devi began to frantically search for her son, and 'by fate or whatever you want to call it', she finally found him on the street near Prithvi Singh's *akhara* [gymnasium], holding the hand of one of Prithvi Singh's friends.[81] Durga Devi gratefully swept him up and caught a train to Kanpur, where Azad was based at the time. He was angry that party protocols had not been followed, but soon calmed down as she explained their haste.[82] As the case went to trial in February 1931, the prosecutors were still trying to pin down the exact identity of the 'mysterious person with long hair'.[83] It was not until the very end of the court case that the wanted woman was identified as 'Durga Devi of the Lahore Case'.[84]

Durga Devi's widowhood did not drive her into melancholy seclusion; if anything, she became more active than before. By failing to behave in a culturally conscribed manner befitting a mother, wife and later a widow, she confused the intelligence and police networks who sought to anticipate and capture her. As the newspaper coverage of the Lamington Road Outrage demonstrates, the investigators presumed the gunmen were men; and when witnesses' statements suggested otherwise, they guessed that the woman must necessarily be married to one of the men in the car. This too was flawed and informed a search for a fugitive 'couple', which was ultimately fruitless.[85] A daring lone woman, let alone one with a young child, was simply unimaginable.

In the final months of Bhagat Singh's life, Durga Devi became a prominent member of the Bhagat Singh Defence Committee, formed to lobby for legal and financial support; to collect signatures to appeal the death penalty; and ultimately, to take his case to the Privy Council.[86] Interestingly, this was largely organised by women, headed by a dedicated Peshawar-born Congress worker, Lajjawati. Perhaps this was a strategy to render the Defence Committee, whose activities were subsequently construed as illegal, immune to policing attempts. As Durba Ghosh has argued in the case of *bhadralok* women involved in the revolutionary movement in Bengal, as a rule women were much harder to incarcerate than men; they were fiercely protected by their families, with the result that authorities were reluctant to 'raid the houses of prominent Bengalis for their daughters and their wives'.[87]

Durga Devi's activities supporting Bhagat Singh in jail were enabled by her capacity to manipulate gendered forms of anonymity that provided, literally, the perfect cover for revolutionary work. By wearing a black veil and assuming the persona of a lady in purdah, she was able to attend court proceedings and visit Bhagat Singh in jail, which she continued to do even while he was on death row, confidently gliding past jailors to deliver him letters, books and foodstuffs.[88] Several other girls who were trusted by the revolutionaries 'posed as sisters or nieces of the accused men and visited them regularly carrying messages to and from them'.[89] No male absconder would dare to do this.[90] Little wonder that by 1933, the 'wearing of disguises was made a criminal offence, so that men and women ... could not evade police detection by dressing as women and men, respectively, and Hindu men and women were prohibited from masquerading as Muslims.'[91]

Women as Intermediaries

Being generally held above suspicion, women were the ideal conduits between the revolutionaries and the Congress movement. While the two movements were discrete, many of the north Indian revolutionaries had been active Congress members in the early 1920s, as I shall demonstrate in the next chapter. Bhagwati Charan was still a paid-up Congress member in 1929.[92] In a meeting organised by a Delhi Congress leader, Raghunandan Saran, Durga Devi called upon Mahatma Gandhi, who was staying at the home of Dr Ansari in Delhi during the Gandhi–Irwin talks in February 1931.[93] Attended by Sushila, she first was introduced to Jawaharlal Nehru, who by his own account was excited to meet them.[94] Their subsequent meeting with Gandhi, to appeal to him to include a clause in the pact with Irwin to save the condemned trio, did not fare so well. Gandhi had presumed that, tired of living the life of an absconder, she had come to surrender herself to him and he advised her to do so; she refused, made her case to Gandhi, and left.[95]

The early 1930s in general marked an increase in the politicisation of women, especially with the onset of civil disobedience.[96] The large numbers of women taking part served, among other things, to make the work of the police 'particularly unpleasant'.[97] When Bhagat Singh, Sukhdev and Rajguru were executed on 23 March 1931, mass protests across India included an unprecedented and unexpected number of women, even in areas known for conservative restrictions on women's movement. 'Small and excited processions marched about the city all the morning', noted one fortnightly report from the North Western Frontier, where 'large processions of men and (a novel feature for Peshawar) of women marched from cantonments into the city.'[98] Even larger crowds choked the streets in Lahore, and captions accompanying photographs reproduced in the *Tribune* marveled at the number of 'lady mourners'.[99] Women seemed to have been particularly moved by the executions, perhaps because Bhagat Singh had become the subject of a great many songs, poems and ballads which stressed his loving familial relations and his marriageable age.[100] Many students in Lahore Government College for Women continued to hold black dupatta demonstrations in their classes.[101] Months later, in Jhang District in Punjab, it was reported that on 2 July 1931, a procession of women Congress workers from Lyallpur

sang political songs and shouted slogans of the type of 'Indian Napoleon Bhagat Singh zindabad'. At one point they tore the foreign clothes of Hindu ladies whom they met. In the songs, which were led by Durga Devi, feeling references were made to Bhagat Singh, Rajguru and Sukh Dev, and it was said that the women had now come out in the field, and were prepared to make all sorts of sacrifices. In a poem Indians were asked to produce young men like Bhagat Singh, Rajguru and Sukhdev if they wanted to annihilate the British. They were also exhorted to create a mutiny like that of 1857 in India. These songs were sung by Durga Devi and they were repeated by the other women after her.[102]

It is not absolutely clear that this was Durga Devi Vohra, although Lyallpur was not far from her stamping ground, and this protest seems very much in character for her. Because women were difficult for the police to arrest, they were able to push the boundaries further than their male counterparts in their demonstrations. 'A procession of nine women on July the 20th was not interfered with', according to a report on the Naujawan Bharat Sabha from 1930, 'but six more persons, who attempted to defy the order on the 21st, were arrested'.[103] In the immediate aftermath of Bhagat Singh's execution, some of these scruples were waived, such as when police in the central Indian district of Ratlam, where 'thousands of people all over the place' joined a mourning procession with black flags, police lathi-charged them and arrested eight women, including one Kashidevi Panchal.[104] The police demanded that she apologise, Kashidevi recalled, 'and I said I could not do such a thing. I said that even if he beat me or put me into jail I would not apologise.'[105]

Durga Devi was eventually arrested in Lahore on 14 September 1932, and although she did not much elaborate on this in her testimony, Ram Chandra records that she actually invited the police to arrest her, writing a letter to them alerting them to her address.[106] Manmohini Zutshi recalled the excitement when Durga Devi was delivered to the Lahore jail where she was being held as a *satyagrahi*, surmising that with many of her comrades dead or in jail, Durga Devi had simply lost heart: 'she was not very communicative, though we all tried to engage her in conversation'.[107]

A *Political Who's Who* compiled by the government of the United Provinces noted that Durga Devi was 'detained in jail for two months under the Special Powers Ordinance from 28-9-1932; [then] released and restricted to Lahore' for a further twelve months under an Act which allowed for preventative detention of suspects.[108] By 1935, she had returned to her studies and matriculated, and in 1936 began to work as a teacher in the Pyare Lal Girls School, Ghaziabad,[109] after an amnesty was extended to political prisoners, and charges against her 'were dropped or had expired'.[110]

With the revolutionary movement largely suppressed, Durga Devi Vohra began to take part in Congress politics. She served as president of the Delhi Congress Committee in 1937–8, and assisted in organising a reception for the freed prisoners of the Kakori Conspiracy Case.[111] She was arrested again, this time in her capacity as a Congress worker for her involvement in a *hartal* in 1938, and was imprisoned for a week.[112] In 1940, she set up and dedicated all her energies to a Montessori school in Lucknow, and she was still engaged in this when she was interviewed in 1972. When she died in 1999 her funeral rites were performed by Sachi on the banks of Hindon river, celebrated with full state honours.[113]

Revolutionary Women

That women took up revolutionary roles at all was frequently construed in the 1930s as an indication of how oppressive the government had become, that they were willing to flout or depart from their expected roles. 'Who could imagine', wrote the journalist-agitator Chaman Lal, 'that those quiet and humble goddesses of piety and sweetness would turn out to be real warriors in the cause of their country'?[114] It is evident from contemporary sources that revolutionary actions were frequently goaded by appeals to masculinity, or laments of its deprivation under colonial rule. A proscribed tract written by K. Kutralam Pillai of Madurai, for example, lamented: 'If we say that we are men, have we no moustache on our face? When our brethren whose faces we have not seen die, can we live happily? … Is the male person in our country a female person?'.[115] Perhaps it is worth repeating that it was the widow of C. R. Das, Basanti Debi, who set in motion the assassination that took Bhagat Singh to the gallows, when in the aftermath of Lala Lajpat Rai's death she set the challenge: 'I, a woman of India, ask the youth of India: What are you going to do about it?'[116]

Inciting men to violence was one thing; but taking it up, as did Durga Devi in the Lamington Road Outrage, was another. British intelligence networks struggled to understand the phenomenon of women joining the revolutionary movement, reasoning that it was an outcome of the growing trend towards co-education, particularly in Bengal.[117] As Purnima Bose has noted, the phenomenon of Indian women committing acts of violence against European men challenged and complicated understandings of Indian women as 'backward and submissive in comparison with their European counterparts'.[118]

It was, however, a willingness to manipulate such suppositions that ensured that activism by women such as Durga Devi Vohra became an indispensable element of clandestine revolutionary operations. Moreover, it is evident that revolutionary organisations conceded this, even as they were a product of a society where conservative views on the roles of women were in a state of flux, as women and girls began to take up roles in the broader nationalist movement. It was with an element of surprise that British observers noted that during the Civil Disobedience movement 'unexpected assistance' came from women. 'Thousands of them—many being of good family and high educational attainments—suddenly emerged from the seclusion of their homes, and in some instances actually from purdah, in order to join Congress demonstrations'.[119] But as Tanika Sarkar concluded, in Bengal, 'Gandhian radical nationalist and terrorist leaders alike consistently harped on the supreme relevance of traditional roles and values for modern Indians',[120] in which there was little room for feminist sensibilities.

In the case of the HSRA, reservations about the roles of women in the inner party circle existed, but were negotiated, with women such as Durga 'Bhabhi' and Sushila 'Didi' being absorbed into the familial party structure. Nonetheless, Durga Devi paid a price for her politics. Neighbours in Lahore, unappreciative of her personal and social radicalism, primly observed her interactions with the other male revolutionaries and, according to Yashpal, gossiped about her.[121] Peripheral party members made assumptions about her failure to live the life of a widow,[122] and published scandalous allegations about her, which she strenuously denied.[123] In her interview with Manchanda, she made pointed and angry references to her name being used by advertisers after independence to sell cosmetics.[124] Her testimony was defensive, and she abruptly concluded her interview after again refuting allegations that Bhagwati Charan was an informer, adding that it was Bhagat Singh who in the end convinced Azad of her husband's dedication to the revolutionary cause.[125]

The HSRA came to a position of recognising 'no artificial barrier between men and women', with Bhagat Singh urging from jail the formation of a women's committee whose primary duty would be 'to revolutionise the womenfolk and select from them active members for direct service'.[126] Initial reservations about women's participation gave way to a pragmatism towards meeting larger goals. The revolutionaries found that defying gender conventions was an effective means of operating below the radar of the disciplinary machinery of the state, and extended these opportunities to women who wanted them. These women simultaneously defied and appropriated norms and ideals around contemporary concepts of womanhood and it was precisely this that made them such useful operatives.

Practical difficulties around mobilising women nonetheless limited the numbers who were active in the party. As the wife of a party member whose parents had both passed away, and later as a widow, Durga Devi was unhampered by many of the familial restrictions that constrained many women and girls.[127] As one example, the HSRA had initially recruited a young woman to shoot the Governor of Punjab in late 1930, but difficulties in getting her out of her home to train for and complete the mission proved to be insurmountable, and a youth from the Northwestern Frontier Province, Hari Kishen, instead took on the task.[128]

Many other women were drawn into the activities of the revolutionary movement in north India. Intelligence files describe the shady activities of several women involved in the Naujawan Bharat Sabha, including Nikko Devi of Peshawar, 'the mother of terrorists', whose work included supplying bombs and arms to unnamed persons in Karachi and Lahore.[129] Other examples include Suhasini Nambiar, who presided over the 1929 Naujawan Bharat Sabha meeting in Lahore, held alongside the Congress;[130] and a sari-wearing, Urdu-speaking woman of Irish birth, who adopted the name Savitri Devi (also known as Mrs Jaffar Ali and Alyce Nisbet Wright), known to be working with Yashpal engaged in writing party propaganda.[131]

Suruchi Thapar-Bjorkert's research makes it clear that a number of women supported their revolutionary husbands, not simply by keeping their homes, but through illegal activities such as procuring and hiding guns and ammunition.[132] The extent to which women participated in the revolutionary movement, particularly in supportive roles (meaning those who 'provided shelter, food and cover, carried messages or arms, or instilled a passion to "serve the country" among their children, telling them about the "heroes" and "martyrs" who had sacrificed their lives for the country's freedom'),[133] is ultimately unquantifiable. Many women shrouded their actions in supporting the revolutionary movement with silence, as they 'feared that their activities would be associated with "terrorism"', which continued to be stigmatised in the aftermath of independence.[134]

Durga Devi was the most celebrated of these women, made infamous as Durga 'Bhabhi' in Bhagat Singh films, documentaries and comics. And yet, as one newspaper wrote in her obituary, 'while her earlier life reads like a thriller, her later years were spent in exclusion and relative anonymity'.[135] It is telling that many of her surviving male colleagues wrote and published memoirs about their revolutionary lives, some more than one, but she did not.[136] Coaxed to record her testimony by the oral historian Manchanda, it becomes clear that the level of her involvement as a revolutionary has been vastly under-appreciated. That the twists and turns of her story are still largely unknown is a reminder that popular depictions of the revolutionaries have become hegemonic. An immersion in the archives, drawing on governmental, oral and proscribed visual sources, shapes a much more detailed and often complex narrative.

PART II

POROUS POLITICS

THE CONGRESS AND THE REVOLUTIONARIES, 1928–1931

4

INTERMEDIARIES, THE REVOLUTIONARIES
AND THE CONGRESS

On 12 April 1931, a conference of India's martyrs was held in Paradise. We know this because the proceedings were published in the Lahori Urdu newspaper *Vir Bharat* the following week. An English translation of it lies in a file, held in the National Archives of India in New Delhi. This witty yet poignant report of an imagined conference is a rich and revealing fragment, well worth the indulgence of an extended quote (the full version can be found in the Appendix):

To-day a conference of all the India's martyrs was held in Paradise. Hundreds of holy souls who had shed their blood for Indian liberty were adorning the conference in their respective seats. The names of Khudi Ram Bose, Mr Ram Parshad Bismil, Mr Ishfaqullah, Mr Hari Bhai Balmukand, martyr Khushi Ram etc are worthy of note among those who occupied higher places. The Martyrs of Jallianwallah Bagh looked smart in bloody uniforms. The enthusiasm of the Sholapur martyrs was also worthy of note. A high place was vacant for martyr Jatindra Nath Das, Chairman of the Reception Committee, Sardar Bhagat Singh President of the Conference, and his comrades Messers Rajguru and Sukhdev. The arrival of those young men who had to arrive from the Mother country after attaining martyrdom was being anxiously awaited. About this time conches were blown, the gods began to shower flowers and Sardar Bhagat Singh, Mr Rajguru and Shriyut Sukhdev came to the conference amidst such shouts as these: 'Mukammal azadi zindabad' (Long live complete independence), 'Shahidon ki jai' (victory to the martyrs), 'Bartania ka khuni insaf murdabad' (May England's bloody justice be dead). ... Sardar Bhagat Singh rose from his seat and greeting the martyrs said 'A country where bridegrooms are so brutally murdered, cannot remain a slave for much longer'. Poems entitled 'Shahidon ka Tahara' and Ram Parshad Bismil's well known poem 'Ham abhi se kiya batain kiya hamare dil mein hai' were recited. ...

At this moment Jesus Christ arrived. Sardar Bhagat Singh said: 'India's martyrs greet the martyr of Jerusalem'. Voices were raised by the Jallianwala Bagh martyrs: 'Accept our saluta-

101

tion O peaceful shepherd of bloodthirsty sheep'. The Sholapur men said: 'Turn your wolves into sheep again'. In short the welcin [welcome] resounded with shouts like the above. Jesus met every one cordially and after kissing the Cross he said: 'An innocent man's blood never goes in vain'. 'Dyer is to-day being burnt in hell fire. He is crying to me for intercession but can I intercede on the behalf of executioners, murderers, and assassins? I swear by this sacred Cross that there is absolutely no nearness between me and these white people whose hearts have become black with the blood of oppressed people. They will get their desserts and no heavenly power can save them from the wrath of my Holy Father. Rest assured, God will never forgive your murderers.'

After having made the above remarks Jesus patted Sardar Bhagat Singh and gave benedictions to all the martyrs.

In the course of his presidential address, Sardar Bhagat Singh is reported to have said: 'I have merely done my duty. I want to sacrifice myself for the sake of my country's freedom by taking several births. Before putting the hangman's rope around my neck I kissed it. Our dust is flying not only on the banks of the Sutlej but in all corners of India, so that it might enter the eyes of those rulers who have become blind through their setting store by their power and authority and they might become absolutely incapable of seeing the truth. It is in this way that a tyrannical Government can come to an end. ... Those who bathe in the blood of martyrs are cowards. No resolution should therefore be passed respecting them. You are lions. You gave up your lives like lions. It is an insult to us to censure cowards. Their own high priest, their own Prophet, their own Apostle has refused to intercede for them. There could be no greater humiliation than this.'

The idea of passing a resolution of censure was therefore given up.[1]

These fantastic proceedings reveal volumes about the political debates that followed in the wake of the Lahore executions in March 1931. We do not know the identity of the author, but we do know that this vignette was one of many articles published by *Vir Bharat* to register in British intelligence circles as objectionable. For earlier provocations, the offices of *Vir Bharat* were raided,[2] but its editor was apparently undeterred, going to press with these conference minutes, and days later, another provocative article which challenged the administration in Punjab which had carried out the death sentences: 'Everyone feels that Sardar Bhagat Singh and his comrades were hanged in a very barbarous manner. If truth must be told, the bureaucracy forgot at the moment that it was necessary for the rulers to be human. Its agents murdered Sardar Bhagat Singh like ferocious dacoits.'[3]

In the early 1930s, the scenario of departed nationalists congregating in paradise alongside divinities was a recurrent theme in martyrdom imagery (Figures 2, 25, 30, 41 and 43). The minutes might be seen as a textual interpretation of these images, sharing several striking elements with visual constructions of the posthumous life of the revolutionaries. First and foremost is the foregrounding of the violence of the state, either implied or direct, as in the case of hanging pictures (Figures 6, 27, 31 and 36). These images collectively underscored the calculating nature of the colonial killing machine, upheld by questionable notions of justice, which created a quorum of martyr-delegates. Iconic moments of colonial brutality—most notably Jallianwalla Bagh, a mere twelve years prior—are invoked, alongside the deaths-by-execution of revolutionaries from the Kakori and First Lahore Conspiracy Cases. There is a nod to the All-India composition of the martyrs, with cameo appearances of delegates hailing from Delhi, Maharashtra and Bengal. Perhaps the most powerful twist of all is the richly religious and even ecumenical aspects of the conference, taking place in a heaven of sorts and so graciously attended by Jesus Christ, 'the martyr of Jerusalem', who is welcomed enthusiastically by all. It is Christ's wholehearted denunciation of Dyer and Bhagat Singh's executioners that restores an element of balance and justice to a political order that in April 1931 seemed so dramatically skewed.

At the martyrs' conference in Paradise, the lofty principles underpinning the British Empire are exposed as a sham by the attendees, bloodied but unbroken in their anticolonial resolve. The violence visited upon the delegates implicitly justifies more of the same; nonviolence is dismissed, for a 'peaceful man like Mahatma Gandhi cannot quarrel with anyone'; and the freedom struggle is likened to a Mahabharata, or a perverse *leela*, to be concluded when Krishna 'eats the bones' of the *rakshasi* Raj. Sections of the minutes have been underlined in pencil by a nervous official—it is unclear whether they are in Lahore or Delhi, perhaps the former, given the particular insecurity of Punjab-based Englishmen in 1931—to emphasise to their superiors the dangerous intent lurking behind the speeches at the conference, with the aim of re-instituting controls on the press.

Beyond the significance of the themes of struggle, retribution and deliverance that are discussed with such passion at the conference, however, is the actual format of the meeting—in its medium is a message. The highly structured and formal nature of the conference—the appointment of a reception committee, the welcoming of the president, who delivers a rousing address, followed by voting and a discussion about the practicality of a motion of censure—closely mirrors the institutional niceties ritually observed at contemporaneous meetings of the Congress. The martyrs' meeting in Paradise on 12 April 1931, I venture to suggest, is the work of someone well acquainted with the workings of the Congress, and it represents a desired outcome—an honouring of revolutionary sacrifice, along with a tacit reassessment of the validity of violence in the freedom struggle—which had been explicitly overruled in the actual, the *lokik*, annual Congress in Karachi, the fortnight before. I will discuss the Karachi Congress in detail in Part III.

Many other nationalist organisations came to adopt the basic format of the annual Congress meeting. This was partially an outcome of a certain amount of institutional fluidity in nationalist mobilisation in the early twentieth century, a time when considerable differences within the Congress were accommodated by a range of factional alignments, party mechanisms and subgroups which operated

Figure 25: Jatindranath Das is elevated to heaven, where he is received by C. R. Das, Tilak, Lala Lajpat Rai and Dadabhai Naoroji. Title and artist unknown, although the moths (*parwana*) are identified in the NMML photo library register as Bhagat Singh, B.K. Dutt, Kedarnath Sehgal (upper left) and Chaudhury Sher Jang (upper right). Lahore: Krishna Printing House, c. 1929. (Courtesy of NMML, Kulbir Singh Collection, Album 808, 36516)

within and across the Congress.[4] The Naujawan Bharat Sabha also modelled its meetings on the organisational structure of the annual Congress, and, as I detail in this chapter and the next, it had many close dealings with the Congress before their relationship irretrievably soured in April 1931. The religious content of the minutes would suggest, however, that the author of the Paradise proceedings was not from the Naujawan Bharat Sabha (NJBS), which was ideologically anti-communal and stridently secular, even tending to the overtly irreligious, in its outlook.[5] Yet the minutes of the martyrs' conference in Paradise displays political sympathies that in

April 1931 were shared by many in the Congress and the NJBS, and this is precisely the point. The politics of the period were more porous than partisan.

This chapter explains the close linkages between the HSRA's revolutionary networks, the NJBS, and the broader Congress movement, with particular attention to localities and personalities. I will focus in particular on the key colonial cities of Lahore, where the relative weakness of the Congress created a political stratosphere of contestation and ferment; Delhi, as the capital a magnet for political machinations and conspiracies; and Kanpur, a town noted for its leftist activism, nestled in the political 'heartland' of the United Provinces.[6] I will introduce the primary individuals who acted as conduits between the All-India Congress Committee and the revolutionaries, as the latter inserted themselves into the politics of the escalating movement for *purna swaraj*, in particular Saifuddin Kitchlew and Dr Satyapal in Lahore; Chaman Lal in Delhi; and in Kanpur, Ganesh Shankar Vidyarthi. This overview of people and place provides the backstory to the developments in revolutionary and nationalist politics which fed into the *purna swaraj* decision in late December 1929, committing the Congress to civil disobedience in 1930.

Gandhi and the Congress

Gandhi's dominance in Indian politics from 1920 onwards was frequently contested, leading to the creation of what may be described as a 'Gandhi versus' genre which animated political debates of the time.[7] The establishment of an antagonistic 'Gandhi versus Bhagat Singh' discourse, in which Bhagat Singh is construed as the Mahatma's Other, particularly in the aftermath of the March executions, has precluded a nuanced understanding of the relationship between the Congress movement and the HSRA. It is vital to set this debate to one side in order to map out the dynamics of the nationalist movement in north India from 1928 to 1931, a period when many prominent Congress workers were ambivalent and divided over the best way to negotiate and conduct the movement. It is evident that many Congress workers did not see the role of violence in the national struggle in terms of the unambiguous disavowal that it has come to acquire in nationalist historiography. After decades of 'knowing' the centrality of nonviolence to the anticolonial struggle in the early twentieth century, perhaps the time has come to pull apart the violence-nonviolence dialectic, which was questioned and tested during these crucial years.

The marginalisation of the revolutionary movement from Congress-centric nationalist historiography has fed a backlash of sorts, in which surviving revolutionaries and their supporters have written their accounts of the events of the period, which tend to be reactive and critical of the Congress.[8] This has only exacerbated the alienation between the two. Admittedly, the fact that Gandhi stood for nonviolence and Bhagat Singh was willing to use violence makes the attempt at de-pairing them seem counterintuitive. However, a careful consideration of the ways in which Bhagat Singh and his colleagues understood the Congress programme and conducted their actions challenges us to think of them in less adversarial terms. This project certainly becomes complicated by the events of March 1931. However, momentarily setting aside the teleology that leads Bhagat Singh, Sukhdev and Rajguru to the gallows enables us to see the vital period of anticolonial activity in 1928–1930 in a new light.

To be sure, this manoeuvre is complicated by the fact that the NJBS, an organisation which frequently brokered the Congress-revolutionary nexus, was at times critical of Congress methodology, openly and often harshly criticising it as overly timid and even pointless. However it is clear that this is not how Bhagat Singh, who formed the NJBS in 1926, conceived of the broader Congress movement.[9] There is much evidence to suggest that the revolutionaries co-opted elements of the mainstream movement to suit their own ends—for example, a lengthy and considered manifesto drafted by Bhagat Singh in prison prescribed that 'the Congress platform is to be availed of' for revolutionary purposes.[10] Yet there is also much to suggest that the revolutionaries reciprocated, encouraging Congress leaders to make strategic use of their actions in their negotiations with the British, as we shall see in the following chapters.

Moments of cooperation and convergence between the HSRA and the Congress movement have already been alluded to by scholars drawing on government intelligence reports.[11] However the necessarily clandestine nature of the collaboration between the two was such that supporting evidence has been elusive. Both parties were careful to not leave evidence of their interactions, and many Congress members who subsequently 'became the Raj' in post-colonial India bowed to the pressure of statesmanship and were actively reticent about their connections with revolutionaries.[12] While some surviving revolutionaries were frustrated by this, as late as the 1970s there were former HSRA members who still declined the opportunity to furnish the names of Congress members who quietly donated money to them.[13] One HSRA member, Gaya Prasad, went to great lengths to destroy a register of Congress donors when he was arrested in 1930, swallowing the list so hurriedly that he nearly choked. Such a hasty action, noted Yashpal, saved two eminent nationalists—he named Chandrabanu Gupta and Mohanlal Saksena—from a prison spell and the enduring suspicion of the CID.[14]

While the Congress operated largely on its own (admittedly broad) trajectory, since its inception in 1928 the HSRA had been keenly attuned to developments in the political mainstream. Almost all HSRA members had been Congress workers in the early 1920s and had taken part in the Non-Cooperation Movement, and it is widely acknowledged that Gandhi's reaction to the violence at Chauri Chaura provided the greatest fillip to revolutionary organisation.[15] However even after the formation of the HSRA, its members continued to attend annual Congress meetings, not only to liaise with sympathisers, but to calibrate their own activism accordingly, as we saw in earlier chapters at the 1928 Calcutta Congress. Like other satellite organisations that held their own 'miniature Congresses' alongside meetings of the Indian National Congress, the NJBS organised its annual conferences to coincide with those of the Congress from 1928 until 1931.[16]

Several eminent Punjabi Congress leaders have remarked upon their personal connections to Bhagat Singh in interviews. Lala Jagat Narain, for many years the editor of *Punjab Kesari* and a minister in post-Independence Punjab before he was assassinated in 1981, commented that 'Bhagat Singh used to come to our press regularly. He was a very intelligent boy and from his talk I could infer that one day he would shine in India.'[17] Sardar Mangal Singh, a Gandhian Congress leader from Amritsar, knew Bhagat Singh well through his father; this connection would, on one occasion, lead the CID to presume that Bhagat Singh, spotted sitting next to Mangal Singh in a train carriage, was just another 'ordinary Congressman who believes in non-violence'.[18] Ram Kishan, who served as Chief Minister of Punjab in the 1960s, did not acknowledge an acquaintance with Bhagat Singh in his testimony, but recalled the assassination of Saunders as one of the formative political experiences of young men in colleges, as it empowered them to imagine that they had 'some part for achieving the independence of the country'.[19] These linkages and affinities substantially coloured the politics of the late 1920s, as the Congress was propelled towards Civil Disobedience.

The Naujawan Bharat Sabha in Lahore, 1926–1931

Frustrated with Congress organisation in Punjab, in 1926 a group of student activists in Lahore led by Bhagat Singh formed the Naujawan Bharat Sabha. Intelligence reports deduced that the inspiration for the NJBS came from HRA member Sachindranath Sanyal, who was hopeful that it would 'prove a fruitful ground for young revolutionaries'.[20] Primarily a political and social youth movement, the NJBS began to draft a formal program of organising youth and peasants along leftist lines.[21] Covertly, Comrade Ram Chandra established tentative links between the NJBS and the international communist movement through Shapurji Saklatwala in 1927, however Saklatwala is said to have judged them too nationalist in orientation to work with the Comintern.[22] The appeal of the NJBS in Punjab seems to have been largely in urban areas, in particular college students in Lahore and Amritsar, although its mobilisation was geared towards peasants and labourers. In early 1928, the CID named the NJBS as 'the most dangerous' of the 'youth organisations formed in India in the past few years', with connections to the Lahore

Students Union, the Kirti Kisan party, the Shiromani Akali Dal and the Communist Party of India.[23] The NJBS was immediately implicated in the murder of Saunders in December 1928, and many of its members arrested, although the majority of them were released due to a lack of evidence.[24]

Consistent with Congress policy at the time, it was possible to hold dual memberships of and leadership positions in both the NJBS and the Congress.[25] There were a number of key individuals who acted as mediators between the Congress, the NJBS, and by extension the HSRA, or as British intelligence later saw it, who had 'a foot in each of the Congress and terrorist camps'.[26] The most prominent person in this group in Punjab was Dr Satyapal, a left-leaning Punjabi Congressite who in the mid-1920s had an eye on the leadership of the provincial Congress, which had been dominated by Lala Lajpat Rai. Satyapal played a significant role in the formation of the NJBS in Punjab, to the extent that some intelligence reports claimed that it was formed at his instigation.[27]

Many of the revolutionaries had established enduring friendships with Congress workers from the days of non-cooperation.[28] In Punjab and especially in Lahore, many HSRA and NJBS members had spent their formative years of schooling in National College, established by Lajpat Rai for students boycotting British institutions.[29] Additionally, Bhagat Singh—who from all accounts emerges as tremendously charismatic, regarded affectionately by peers and seniors alike—enjoyed a number of personal friendships with Congressites.[30] Many of these were initially brokered through his father Kishan Singh, a Congress worker who in 1921 had started an ashram in Amritsar with Saifuddin Kitchlew, later to become a leader in the Punjabi Provincial Congress.[31] Other known contacts in the Punjab Congress include Kumari Lajjawati (who organised the women volunteers at the Lahore Congress to great acclaim) and Lala Feroze Chand (the editor of *Bande Mataram*), both of whom would take up leading roles in the Bhagat Singh Defence Committee in late 1930.

From its inception, the NJBS was an overtly anti-communal organisation which enunciated an unambiguous critique of religion in politics.[32] Intelligence reports were dismissive of the NJBS in its early days, reasoning that its strident secularism and its anti-establishment rhetoric would lose it more supporters than it gained. At an early meeting of the NJBS in September 1926, one report recounted, Kedar Nath Sehgal made a 'bitter attack' on Lajpat Rai which 'alienated a number of possible sympathisers among the Congress party and Lahore Hindus generally, and caused rifts in the solidarity of the executive of the NJBS itself.'[33] Subsequently, Sohan Singh 'Josh' recalled a NJBS conference in 1927 in which a heated topic of debate was whether it should accept in its ranks members who belonged to 'religious-communal organisations', such as the Akali and Ahrar groups, which was defeated.[34]

Not long after the NJBS's formation the government placed restrictions on its ability to access and recruit students in its colleges, which undermined its capacity to expand and confined it to non-governmental institutions.[35] In April 1928, the reinvigoration of public action as a result of the Simon Commission agitation in Punjab, as well as the Young Men's Conference in Lahore, along with National Week and Jallianwallah Martyrs' Day celebrations, led to a resuscitation of the group's activities.[36] NJBS campaigns were based around issues such as the non-payment of land revenue and water rates; dissuading people from joining the British Indian army; and disseminating propaganda leaflets, such as one authored by Chhabil Das, which accused the government of exploiting the country, 'keeping the inhabitants impoverished and uneducated', and institutionalising racial distinctions through the administration of justice.[37] Analysts in the provincial government downplayed the growth of the NJBS in Punjab, noting in May 1929 that it had 'only' established branches in Lahore, Amritsar, Ludhiana, Jalandhar, Montgomery and Gujranwala.[38]

The NJBS's progress in Punjab was related to a crisis in Congress politics. In the 1920s, the Congress had limited support in the province, with nationalist organisation largely reflecting communal divides between Hindu, Muslim and Sikh communities.[39] In such a political climate the secularism of the NJBS, which became less antagonistic as its mobilisation became more focused on breaching communal divides rather than critiquing religious belief, had discrete appeal to nationalist, college-going youth.[40] Despite the impediments placed on the NJBS by surveillance, it was a more light-footed organisation than the Punjabi Congress; in the late 1920s it was unrestrained by leadership intrigues and able to mobilise recruits on the ground. Additionally, 'unlike the Congress, the NJBS had a definite aim and a clear ideology' in its focus on socialism, secularism and complete independence.[41]

With that said, there were many elements of the NJBS's platform that overlapped with and appealed to the emergent Congress left. In her research on the NJBS, Shalini Sharma has underlined its communist leanings, describing it as a movement which sought to define 'itself as an alternative to Gandhi and his Congress representatives in Punjab'.[42] This emphasis obscures the convergence of interests between Punjab Provincial Congress and the NJBS, particularly in the crucial years of 1929 and 1930. At a time when the effects of the global depression converged with a bad season in the Punjab, putting pressure on the price of grain and creating an ideal market for the NJBS's pro-peasant rhetoric, the organisation grew. The NJBS lent their support to the Congress-led mobilisation against the Simon Commission,[43] and indeed NJBS members claim to have organised—certainly many were present at—the demonstration in Lahore at which Lala Lajpat Rai was wounded, catalysing the HSRA's assassination of Saunders.[44]

However—as is evident from Ram Chandra's account—coordination of the NJBS was a somewhat haphazard affair.[45] Its revolving-door leadership, compelled by the frequent incarceration of key members, accounts for a degree of inconsistency in the NJBS's relationship with the Congress.[46] Additionally, there was a degree of fluidity between the many youth organisations at the time: Bhagat Singh was counted as both a member of the Kirti group and the NJBS,[47] and Abdul Majid Khan, a leader of the Lahore Students Union, was deemed a NJBS member by both British intelligence and even by other NJBS members, although in his testimony decades later, he denied this.[48] The banning of the NJBS in most provinces in 1930 failed to close it down, but it did undermine its cohesiveness. In 1931 there were still many branches across India, each imparting a slightly different emphasis of action. According to 'Notes on Terrorism' assembled in 1931, in the United Provinces the NJBS advocated membership of rifle clubs to its members; in Bombay presidency and in Sind the emphasis was along communistic organisation of workers and peasants; in the Central Provinces NJBS activities were focused on picketing cloth and liquor shops; and in Rajputana and Bengal, a nonviolent creed combined with communist elements was advocated. Madras and the North-West Frontier also had branches of the NJBS, although its stronghold remained in Punjab.[49]

Interactions between the NJBS and the Congress in Punjab were therefore complex and unstable, tending to oscillate between opportunistic and formal, but apparently compelled by the willingness of the latter to borrow the energies and sometimes the agendas of the former. At a time when the left wing of the Congress mounted a considerable challenge to Gandhi and his circle,[50] both provincially and nationally, the NJBS represented a bridging organisation, a more viable leftist alternative than more stridently communist organisations. Co-opting the energies of the NJBS in an attempt to preclude a split in nationalist organisation became a political priority for the Congress leadership, both in Punjab, and at an All-India level. As Vinay Bahl demonstrates in other provinces, in 1928–9 there were many instances where Congress leaders were inexorably pressed towards 'a more militant stance in order to neutralise the Communist hold'.[51]

These tensions became visible in the factions that emerged in the Punjab Provincial Congress in the mid-1920s. Satyapal had initially formed a breakaway clique in response to Lajpat Rai's dominance of the Punjabi Congress, and as a critique of the latter's willingness to bring religion to nationalist mobilisation.[52] Following Lajpat Rai's death in late 1928, leadership of Punjab Congress fell to Dr Gopi Chand Bhargava, supported by Kitchlew, with Satyapal resolutely maintaining leadership of a breakaway group. By this stage, the differences had become personal, rather than ideological.[53] British reports reveal that by August 1929 the inter-party conflict in Punjab was so unbecoming that All-India leaders were summoned 'to compose Lahore rivalries', but even the personal interventions of Jawaharlal Nehru and Gandhi failed.[54]

Both intelligence reports and Satyapal's contemporaries indicate that he brought the institutional resources of the NJBS to bear against his political rivals.[55] In the context of the hardening factionalism within Punjabi Provincial Congress, the NJBS represented an energetic mobilising resource. Unlike the Congress, whose divisiveness over whether to lobby for Dominion Status or *purna swaraj* could only be resolved by nominating 1929 as a year of 'wait and see', the NJBS was relatively unhampered by institutional conventions or the reservations of a conservative leadership. It wanted urgent action. As one observer remarked, 'they were in a great hurry',[56] and it began to gain popularity,[57] with British authorities reasoning that the success of the NJBS in Punjab was attributable to 'the virile character of the population and the rapidity with which they are apt to translate words into action'.[58] Thus while the Congress was divided at both national and provincial levels, revolutionary activities were much less ambiguous, representing, as Gyanendra Pandey has suggested, 'a nobler struggle'.[59] As the revolutionaries of the HSRA began their series of violent actions across north India, the NJBS increasingly advocated for the role taken up in the political spectrum by the revolutionaries.

In 1928, differences of opinion within the Congress on the issue of its means and ends was beginning to be articulated in terms of a fundamental generational divide, with a younger generation of nationalists such as Jawaharlal Nehru eager for a confrontation with the British. NJBS leader Comrade Ram Chandra recalled that Jawaharlal Nehru had approached the NJBS in early 1928, requesting that they merge with his Independence for India League, which NJBS members rejected, for fear of losing their distinct identity and autonomy.[60] Jawaharlal did, however, speak at the NJBS's first annual conference in April 1928, addressing the audience on the evils of industrialism, capitalism, imperialism and religion, in the course of which he criticised the Qur'an, apparently upsetting Muslims in the audience.[61]

Jawaharlal was subsequently invited to preside over the NJBS's second annual session in February 1929 in Lahore, which he declined. Sohan Singh 'Josh' presided over the conference instead, at which the demand for Dominion Status was 'ruthlessly criticised'; although according to a CID observer, 'a disingenuous attempt was made to retain the support of the Congress', by passing a condolence motion for Lala Lajpat Rai.[62] The ambiguous relationship between the NJBS and the Congress at the time was such that sections of the press accused the former of 'defection from the national program of the Congress', indicating that it had been mistaken for an offshoot of the political mainstream.[63]

Had the all-important 1929 Congress not been brought to Lahore in a homage to the late Lajpat Rai, perhaps none of this would have had any All India implications. However as the Lahore Congress loomed and the NJBS grew in popularity, the Punjabi Congress led by Dr Kitchlew—who had been appointed as a compromise candidate in the Satyapal–Bhargava standoff, although he in fact aligned with the latter—edged closer to the NJBS, partly out of political necessity; partly due to commonalities in ideology;[64] and partly as an extension of his own friendships with

NJBS members, including Bhagat Singh.[65] When the decision was made by Congress leaders in December 1928 to hold the next Congress in Lahore, they could not have predicted how quickly the radicalised youth in Punjab would consolidate in the coming year, with the NJBS working in concert with the Lahore Students Union and the Kirti Kisan Party.

Nor could the leadership have predicted that by late 1929 the revolutionaries would have made a significant impact on provincial and national politics by coordinating a hunger-strike campaign from prison. The All-India Congress Committee had set targets for provincial recruitment, which were endorsed by the Punjab Provincial Conference in early 1929. Based on the population of the Punjab, this set a target of 51,718 members and 2,000 volunteers to be enlisted in the province by the end of the year.[66] This was an ambitious aim given the historically low subscription for the Congress in the province, but no doubt one spurred on by the desire to host a memorable annual meeting at the end of the year. Chhabil Das, Bhagat Singh's former teacher and a NJBS sympathiser, was a member of a three-man committee charged with meeting the enlistment quota.[67] The urgency of meeting this target provided the context in which any Congressites who might have had reservations about NJBS policy were able to set these aside in order to grow the organisation and work towards the larger goal of escalating the Congress demand to Complete Independence, as we shall see in the next chapter.

Delhi and the Incorrigible Chaman Lal

Networks matter. They create capacity, stretch abilities and bring together diverse characters. In Delhi, Chaman Lal, the newspaper reporter we encountered in Chapter Two, played the role of an intermediary between Congress leaders and revolutionaries, substantially extending the influence of the latter. The revolutionaries were oriented towards the capital for a number of reasons, not least to be proximate to high-level targets, such as the Legislative Assembly, and the Viceroy.[68] Delhi briefly served as a base for the HSRA in 1929–1930, with organisation of party activities there variously falling to Yashpal, Bhagwati Charan, Kailashpati, Dhanwantari, B. P. Jain, Durga Devi Vohra, Sushila 'Didi', and N. K. Nigam, a lecturer at Hindu College.[69] Chandrashekhar Azad, known in the party as 'Quicksilver' for his capacity to flit between HSRA bases in places as far flung as Jhansi, Allahabad, Agra and Kanpur undetected, frequently came to stay in Delhi to coordinate actions.[70] These included an ambitious plan to save Bhagat Singh and Dutt from jail in Lahore in 1930; carrying out 'money-actions' for fundraising; ordering retributive attacks on approvers; and the attempt to bomb the Viceroy's train in December 1929.[71] In September 1930 there were a sweep of arrests, with Dhanwantari apprehended by police in Chandni Chowk, and Nigam and Kailashpati captured shortly afterwards.[72] Kailashpati made a full confession and became an approver in the subsequent Delhi Conspiracy Case, although the case was never successfully prosecuted. The secretary for the Defence Committee for the Delhi Conspiracy Case, which organised for legal representation for the accused, was one Chaman Lal.[73]

There were three Chaman Lals active in the early 1930s whose politics intersected with the revolutionaries. Firstly, there was Diwan Chaman Lal, a Member of the Legislative Assembly who had earned himself a history sheet at Scotland Yard, which reveals that he had been mixing in communist circles since his time at Oxford in 1918.[74] On his return to India he became involved in trade union activity, edited the *Nation*, and was elected to the Legislative Assembly in 1924, resisting the call to boycott legislatures until 1931, when he resigned.[75] In independent India he would become a prominent figure in Punjabi politics, joining forces with Satyapal in 1948, and was nominated for the leadership of the party against the latter's ever-enduring rival, Bhargava.[76] Diwan Chaman Lal was only very peripherally involved in the Lahore Conspiracy Case, at first alleging that the Assembly Bomb Case was a government conspiracy to create fear of the red menace, before revising this to say that the attack was 'a disgrace'.[77] Later, however, he defended the revolutionaries during their hunger strikes by raising questions about their treatment in the Assembly.[78]

Secondly, there was Chaman Lal Azad, a member of the NJBS based in Mardan, in the North Western Frontier Provinces, where the NJBS was robust.[79] This Chaman Lal's connections were used to procure weapons from across the Afghanistan border, and into revolutionary hands.[80] Chaman Lal Azad was a cousin of Hari Kishen, who in December 1930 attempted to assassinate the Governor of Punjab at a convocation ceremony in Lahore in a plot hatched by Durga Das Khanna, Ranbhir Singh and Virendra. Chaman Lal's role was to conduct Kishen to Lahore to carry out the shooting.[81] Early on in the investigation, the police linked Chaman Lal Azad to the conspiracy,[82] and he was arrested, tried, and found guilty. A government report on terrorism has it that Chaman Lal and his accomplices were sentenced to death.[83] However they successfully appealed this sentence and were acquitted, as Hari Kishen had confessed and claimed in the trial that he had acted alone.[84] Chaman Lal Azad was freed, although he was externed from Delhi in 1931, and re-arrested in 1933 under Regulation III of 1818, which allowed for preventative detention on the basis of being a member of a revolutionary party and 'a danger to the state', after the CID intercepted incriminating letters.[85]

The more interesting Chaman Lal, for the purposes of this story, defies easy categorisation. A tireless journalist for the *Hindustan Times*, Chaman Lal's ideological versatility was such that he balanced what he claimed was a close relationship with Gandhi, even as he served as secretary to a branch of the NJBS in Delhi. He covertly took up a role in organising the HSRA conspiracy to bomb Viceroy Irwin's train in 1929, and in 1931 led a public meeting in Delhi honouring Chandrashekhar Azad's death. In between, he paused to take part in the Delhi Salt Satyagraha, and was imprisoned with Devdas Gandhi.[86] In retrospect, given the dominance of moderate and extremist polarities of nationalist action in historiography, Chaman Lal's political fluidity seems extraordinary, seamlessly spanning a variety of fields of anticolonial action.

Originally from Sargodha in undivided Punjab (now Pakistan), and educated in Amritsar, our third Chaman Lal first met Gandhi when he was deputed to serve him during his visit to Sargodha. He left his studies following Gandhi's call to boycott colonial educational institutions, and subsequently moved to Sabarmati Ashram.[87] After a formative period there, he returned to Punjab, joining the ashram established in Amritsar by Kitchlew and Sardar Kishan Singh. There he became friends with a teenage Bhagat Singh, four years his junior. Following this, Chaman Lal worked with Lala Feroze Chand to establish Congress Committees in Lahore in the early 1920s. To subvert the *Seditious Meetings Act*, he convened political gatherings in temples and gurdwaras. The abstemious young bachelor spent so much time inside temples and gurdwaras that he lost four pairs of shoes to thieves in quick succession, before renouncing the idea of shoes altogether.[88]

His career in journalism began in 1923. He briefly worked for the Swarajist newspaper *Darpan*, before being lured by Lajpat Rai to work for *Bande Mataram* with Feroze Chand. In 1925, he accepted an offer to work for K. M. Pannikar at the *Hindustan Times* in Delhi, which had just been acquired by Madan Mohan Malaviya.[89] In 1926, he founded a branch of the NJBS in Delhi, with his sister-in-law Satyavati and Pandit Indra, a Delhi Congress leader. At the time, the *Hindustan Times* was an evening newspaper; once it had gone to press Lal was free to spend afternoons and evenings in political work. He would announce meetings by beating a drum and address those that gathered.[90] According to Lal, nationalist organisation was in a torpor in Delhi, with public disillusionment with the Congress high in the aftermath of communal rioting in the capital, leaving an opening for the NJBS to mobilise.[91]

His networking with notables of the nationalist movement in his capacity as a journalist was extensive. According to his editor, J.N. Sahni, Chaman Lal was 'incorrigible'. He 'had the devil's energy and an insatiable curiosity for news. As a local reporter he had few equals. He had intimate contacts with leaders of political and social organisations.'[92] When Lala Lajpat Rai died in December 1928, he scrambled to 'rush all over India' to get statements from Mahatma Gandhi, Motilal Nehru, Jawaharlal Nehru and other leaders.[93] Through interactions of this sort he built trusted relationships with the Congress 'High Command', which would later enable him to effectively serve as a mediator between revolutionary and All-India Congress leaders.

An uncompromising nationalist armed with spades of derring-do, Chaman Lal was arrested in 1928 following an episode in the Legislative Assembly when he hurled a suitcase from the press gallery onto the unsuspecting head of the Finance Minister, Sir Basil Blackett.[94] Charged with criminal assault, he happily admitted his guilt and invited the judge to punish him, explaining that this was his protest at the Simon Commisssion. Motilal Nehru intervened, engaging Rafi Ahmed Kidwai and Yusuf Imem to plea that he 'was a young man of 23 and had yet to attain balance in his mind', and he was released with a fine of Rs 250.[95] He was nominally dismissed from the *Hindustan Times*, but he continued to work, even reporting on his own trial for assaulting Sir Basil with the by-line 'ex-Chief Reporter'.[96] Deprived of his press pass lest he fling any more missiles, he used to enter and report on the proceedings in the Legislative Assembly from the visitors' gallery, from where he watched as Bhagat Singh and Dutt hurled two bombs into the chamber below on 8 April 1929.

A few days prior to the attack, Chaman Lal had lunched with Bhagat Singh at a hotel in Delhi where 'it cost only two annas for a whole meal', during which Bhagat Singh warned him of the impending action in the Assembly, so that he might report on it.[97] After the attack was performed, while Bhagat Singh and Dutt were waiting to be arrested, Chaman Lal came to the attention of police when he 'butted in officiously';[98] but it wasn't until later in the investigation that Lal was identified as one of Bhagat Singh's associates.[99] As we saw in Chapter Two, Chaman Lal reported daily on the Assembly Bomb Case, publishing in the *Hindustan Times* inside information he had gleaned from a police contact. Eventually, Sahni received a warning from police that Lal's arrest was imminent, and he was sent away to Simla, where CID agents continually shadowed him.[100] In the lead-up to the Lahore Congress he even accepted an assignment to shoot the Viceroy in Delhi; but the scheme was exposed to Sahni, who apparently forbade him from proceeding.[101]

In April 1930, Lal was arrested after taking part in the Salt Satyagraha in Delhi, a somewhat difficult operation, as no natural salt deposits existed there.[102] He was released in late December and with little ado threw himself back into politics. After Hari Kishen's execution in July 1931, Chaman Lal gave a speech congratulating him on his martyrdom; he was arrested and charged under new legislation banning such plaudits and sentenced to a year's imprisonment, but was released on payment of a surety by Maulana Azad.[103] Following marriage and the birth of his first child in 1933, he was deemed sufficiently responsible to be granted a passport, and he travelled to England for the first time to attend the World Economic Conference, held the same year. Sir Basil Blackett heard that he had arrived in London, and rather sportingly invited him to lunch; 'he was a man of high character, you know'.[104] Chaman Lal went on to author a book in 1937, *The Vanishing Empire*, in which he sagely predicted that the British Empire would collapse within ten years. In a more unpredictable vein, after independence he took Buddhist vows, donning robes and prefixing his name with the title Bhikshu.

Chaman Lal's interventions at the fringes of the Assembly Bomb Case made a substantial impact on the reporting of the event, ensuring that it was given significant coverage in the nationalist press, turning initial construction of the 'outrage' into a principled 'propaganda by deed'.[105] He was an invaluable character in the nationalist drama of the late 1920s and early 1930s, moving seamlessly between the political polarities of violent and nonviolent action, and assiduously networking with a range of political actors and parties, including Motilal Nehru, Bhagat Singh, the NJBS and the revolutionaries of the HSRA. He also represented a tenuous and fragile link between Gandhi and the revolutionaries.

Kanpur Connections, 1923–1933

Kanpur was a key site of revolutionary activity from the mid-1920s. As an industrial town with a large, exploited workforce spread across a number of cotton mills, in which British interests had invested heavily, it was a hub of trade union organisation in the early twentieth century.[106] Communist influences were strong in the town, the site of the so-called Cawnpore 'Bolshevik' Conspiracy Case in 1924, which attracted a number of revolutionary-minded activists,[107] including many of the members of the HRA.[108] Of the HSRA members who were arrested in the Lahore Conspiracy Case, twenty-four were from the United Provinces, and of these, eight were former students of DAV College in Kanpur, including the inner party members, Shiv Verma, Jaidev Kapoor and Bejoy Kumar Sinha.[109] By 1930, Kanpur had established a reputation for being a 'volatile' city, home to a large population of immigrant workers and a concomitant gender imbalance, prone to strikes and outbreaks of communal violence.[110]

Described by intelligence reports as a 'center of terrorist activity', Kanpur was the site of several bomb blasts in 1930–1932, and of several retributive attacks on approvers and suspected informants.[111] Recounting a scenario from June 1930, intelligence officers noted that revolutionary sympathies in Kanpur had 'infected' the Congress. While pursuing 'a terrorist suspect, two injured [Indian] police appealed to a certain Dr Bhalla, a member of the Congress in Cawnpore' for help. He declined, instead rebuking the wounded constables as 'traitors to the country'.[112] A subsequent inquiry into the doctor's failure to render assistance by the United Provinces Medical Council upheld his right to refuse to give treatment, and he was released from the inquiry 'with honour unscathed.'[113] The town's revolutionary sympathies were perhaps most noticeable in March 1931, when the Viceroy received a petition of mercy from the citizens of Kanpur with no less than 39,605 signatories.[114] When Bhagat Singh was executed, Congress workers in Kanpur attempted to enforce a *hartal* on Muslim traders so vehemently that it exacerbated communal tensions, instigating a riot in which hundreds died.[115]

Ganesh Shankar Vidyarthi was an important political activist in Kanpur, and a key figure in the formation of the Cawnpore Mazdoor Sabha in 1919.[116] He was the editor of the nationalist newspaper *Pratap* from 1920 which, by 1930, was the most widely circulated periodical in the United Provinces, out-numbering both the English-owned *Pioneer* and Malaviya's *Leader*.[117] Through *Pratap*, which drew upon its own 'network of local stringers' to create a news imbued with local concerns instead of relying on English news agency releases,[118] Vidyarthi 'came to guide the minds of numerous men and women'.[119] He was also a leading member of the U.P. Provincial Congress, serving as the secretary of the Reception Committee for the 1925 Kanpur Congress. In 1926, Vidyarthi was encouraged to run as a candidate for the Swarajya Party by Motilal Nehru and did so, winning convincingly against strong competition from Malaviya's Nationalist Party. He served as Member of the Legislative Assembly, until he withdrew in 1929, following the call to boycott legislatures.[120]

Vidyarthi's reputation as a trade unionist attracted a number of revolutionaries to Kanpur in the early 1920s.[121] When Bhagat Singh fled Lahore to evade plans for his marriage in 1923, he went to Vidyarthi with a letter of introduction from his teacher in Lahore, Jai Chandra Vidyalankar.[122] Bhagat Singh began to work with Vidyarthi, writing articles for *Pratap* and generally assisting in his press. It is clear that Vidyarthi's influence on the revolutionaries in their formative stages was decisive. His offices operated as a base for revolutionaries to meet and network, and Shiv Verma credited him for turning them 'towards the masses', drawing them into his activities aimed at the uplift of Kanpur's industrial workers.[123] According to his biographer, it was Vidyarthi who introduced Azad, who was a close associate, to Bhagat Singh.[124] Vidyarthi urged the revolutionaries to read and study, contracting Bhagat Singh to translate into Hindi the Irish Republican Army leader Dan Breen's *My Fight for Irish Freedom*,[125] a 'manual for rebellion' which would influence revolutionaries across India.[126] Vidyarthi facilitated the revolutionaries' publication endeavors, lending them the blocks to print sections of *Chand ka Phansi Ank*, edited by Chatur Sen Shastri, and published to popular acclaim and official censure in late 1928.[127] Vidyarthi also published a manuscript by the condemned HRA convict, Ram Prasad Bismil, that Shiv Verma had smuggled out of jail.[128]

It is clear from a range of oral history testimonies that Vidyarthi's friendship with the revolutionaries was marked with mutual respect and affection, transcending political views on the viable means of attaining Swaraj.[129] Shiv Verma reflected that Vidyarthi 'helped us in every possible way', for he

was of the view that anyone who is working for the liberation of the country, no matter what methods or means he adopted, should be helped. Of course, he himself believed in Gandhiji and his non-violence. At the same time he was of the firm opinion that those who believed in violence should not be condemned.[130]

This was echoed by Gaya Prasad, who described Vidyarthi as a Gandhian, but 'not to the point that he was always discerning between violence and nonviolence, therefore everyone loved him and trusted him'.[131] In May 1930, *Pratap* was forced to close after Vidyarthi published an article, 'The Sacrifice of Sardar Bhagat Singh', which led to the forfeit of the newspaper's Rs 3000 security deposit.[132] As such, Vidyarthi joined the unofficial ranks of the agitators Satyapal and Chaman Lal, who were simultaneously enmeshed in Congress networks at the highest level, and had the confidence of and (particularly in Vidyarthi's case) some influence with the revolutionaries.

The intermediary activists described above are indicative of a loose alliance of forces that existed within the nationalist movement at the time,[133] which was over-ridden by the introduction of electoral competition following the government of India Act of 1935. Additionally, the mutual imbrication of such ideologically diverse alliances has been annulled by the supposition that violent and nonviolent anticolonialism operated entirely separately, and that the supporters of each 'camp' held a mutual disregard, if not abhorrence, for the other. Many interactions between Congressites and the revolutionaries were highly amicable. The revolutionaries did not operate in opposition to, or in isolation from, the mainstream Congress. Gandhi's domination of the Congress from the early 1920s and his insistence on a policy of nonviolence has obscured an important history of interactions between the broader Congress and the HSRA. The Mahatma's adherence to nonviolence as a moral and political policy to underpin all nationalist resistance has too often been extrapolated to extend to the Congress as a whole.[134] This view obscures important instances of demurral and dissent. In a letter to C.R. Das, for example, Motilal Nehru confessed in the 1920s that 'Mahatmaji's Non-violence is carried on a very much higher plane than what I have agreed to adopt'.[135] And yet the Congress–Revolutionary dichotomy was, in part, initiated and perpetuated by Congress members themselves as a discursive gesture that allowed them deniability of the workings of the revolutionary movement.

As Ravinder Kumar noted in his assessment of the period, the activities of the revolutionaries 'complemented the non-violent campaign of civil disobedience; and their effect upon popular consciousness was no less decisive than the effect of the satyagraha movement'.[136] Several other historians have noted this dynamic, but the actual interface and mechanisms by which the revolutionaries intersected with the Congress has not been well understood. The following chapters will elaborate on these, beginning with the way in which the interstices of politics were visualised in popular posters of the period.

5

THE REVOLUTIONARY PICTURE

IMAGES AND THE DYNAMICS OF ANTICOLONIALISM

In his path-breaking work on visual culture in colonial north India, Christopher Pinney has argued that political posters of the interwar period throw into 'question the relationship between what we might term "official" and "unofficial" nationalism. Images commonly suggested the indebtedness of official nationalism to revolutionary terrorism.'[1] The most flagrant example of this is what Pinney appropriately describes as an 'astonishing' image of Gandhi, who has cast down his staff to tear open his chest, revealing Bhagat Singh, Rajguru and Sukhdev in the cavity of his chest (Figure 53).[2] While I will discuss this particular picture in more detail in Chapter Seven, here I wish to examine, inasmuch as possible, the production and the politics of the anticolonial images scattered through this book, which are intended to function as much as footnotes as illustrations of my argument.

Images of the revolutionaries made in the late 1920s and early 1930s seem to be overwhelmingly made in either Kanpur or Lahore, both centres of revolutionary activity. There were certainly posters made in other places—Figure 41 hails from Ferozepur—but both Kanpur and Lahore, as we saw in the previous chapter, had residents who were heavily invested in producing and preserving these images. Even so, posters that were discovered and proscribed seem to come primarily from these two towns, although from different presses. Lahori pictures come from a number of established picture houses known for their production of religious imagery, such as Punjab Dharmic Pictures and the Krishna Picture House. Kanpur images were mostly published by or in collaboration with Shyam Sunder Lal Picture Merchant, renowned for its political posters featuring a range of leaders, including Gandhi (Figure 26). It is in these Kanpur images in particular that the connections between revolutionary networks and the Congress movement can be read, while the Lahori posters give us valuable insights into the very localised knowledge of revolutionary actors, as well as a glimpse into the imaginaires provoked by revolutionary politics.

As Sumathi Ramaswamy has shown, there was a vast body of pro-revolutionary art produced in the early 1930s, especially after the killing of Bhagat Singh, Rajguru and Sukhdev, which firmly placed the executions in the discourse of martyrdom.[3] Much of this art drew liberally on Indian visual conventions and religious conceptions of death—rich, graphic and readily available resources for imagining and depicting the mortality of the revolutionaries. Thus Krishna appears promi-

Figure 26: Roop Kishore Kapoor, 'Swarajya Mandir ki Yatra' (Journey to the Temple of Independence), Kanpur: Shyam Sunder Lal Picture Merchant, 1930. (Author's collection)

nently in some of these posters (Figures 18, 27, 35), as he does in eulogy prose; and Bharat Mata makes regular appearances (Figures 2, 3, 18, 25, 27, 33, 40–3, 49). While hanging imagery is quite prominent, the influence of religiously infused concepts of the glorious death, particularly drawing from Sikh visual culture, is evident in posters which show the revolutionaries decapitated, trickles of blood pooling at their feet (see Figures 18, 43, 49). Images that incorporate winged angels and Jesus (Figures 25, 30, 41; all Panjabi-made pictures), reveal an exposure to Christian symbolism.

The influence of *Chand ka Phansi Ank*—as a homage to martyrdom achieved through the death penalty—is glaringly evident in many of the pictorial compositions drawn of the gallows in the aftermath of the hangings (Figure 28). The titular

Figure 27: Raju Lal,'Prominent Knights on whom the Bharat's Eye is Fixed', Lahore, Krishna Picture House, c. 1931. (Courtesy of the Nehru Memorial Museum and Library, Kulbir Singh Collection, Album 808, 36507.)

image of Chand's Phansi Ank depicts an unrecognisable revolutionary suspended from the gallows. Another, freshly hanged by two rather beefy jailors, lies in the foreground, with the functionaries of the Raj—a magistrate and a padre accompanied by generic *sola topi*-wearing armed policemen—triumphantly observing the proceedings. The white men are etched in dark silhouette, as though undeserving of the artists' attention (a dismissive visual effect repeated in a later picture by Roop Kishore Kapoor, Figure 26). The presence of such functionaries—mandated by

Figure 28: R. Banerjee, Title Page of Chatursen (ed), *Chand ka Phansi Ank* (Chand's Hanging Special), 1926. South Asia Microform Project, Reel 15, No. 1.

prison regulations in most provinces—would become a regular feature of hanging images, including a much later one of Khudi Ram Bose (Figure 29). Another sub-genre of images imagine, as did the minutes of the Conference in Paradise, the revolutionaries' reception in heaven by an ecumenical cohort of nationalists who are no more, in one notable example presided over in a suitably grand fashion by a messianic Motilal Nehru (Figure 30).

Proscribed images of the revolutionaries held in the Nehru Memorial Museum and Library's Photography Collection largely come from a collection donated by one of Bhagat Singh's younger brothers, Kulbir Singh. Many of these images were

Figure 29: 'Khudi Ram Phansi' (Khudi Ram's Hanging), Sivakasi Image, c. 1960s–70s. (Author's collection)

Figure 30: 'Bhagat Singh & his Companions being carried to Paradise'. Bhagat Singh, Rajguru and Sukhdev are hanged and welcomed into Paradise by Motilal Nehru, Hari Kishen[?], Jatindranath Das, Lala Lajpat Rai, Maulana Mohamed Ali, and Bhagwati Charan. Artist unknown. Lahore: Punjab Dharmic Pictures/Arorbans Press, c. 1931. (Courtesy of the British Library, PIB 8/31 B)

produced in Lahore's Anarkali bazaar, where HSRA and NJBS members had much of their own printing done. Sukhdev, for example, took the negatives of Bhagat Singh and B.K. Dutt to Anarkali to be copied in April 1929 a few days before his arrest,[4] and NJBS workers had their handbills made there (Figure 14). Rattan Printing Press, also in Anarkali, produced a poster which was captured and proscribed in February 1931, anticipating the execution with portraits of several Lahore-based revolutionaries gathered around Bhagat Singh on the scaffold, presided over by those of Gandhi and Jawaharlal Nehru, appealing to its local audience and those acquainted with the accused (Figure 31). As in so many other bazaar images, there is a hierarchy of personalities observed, with Gandhi-cap wearing Congress luminaries at the top of the picture (see also Figure 27, although the Image has been cropped, somewhat obscuring the Congress leaders). 'Heroes Sacrifice' (Figure 2), a Lahori picture that depicts the parents of the deceased revolutionaries delivering their son's heads to the custody of Bharat Mata, seems to draw on photographs aired in the Lahore press of family members (Figure 32), as well as on local familiarity with political workers such as Kishan Singh.

Figure 31: 'Sardar Bhagat Singh on the Scaffold', Lahore: R. L. Behal Talwalud, Rattan Printing Press, c. 1930–31. (Courtesy of the British Library, EPP 1/2)

Figure 32: *Daily Milap*, 22 March 1931. Images of the condemned men and their extended families (and, on the right, Gandhi), published the day before their executions. An HSRA member in Lahore, Ranbir Singh, worked for the *Daily Milap* and was no doubt instrumental in securing these images for publication.[5] Bhagat Singh remains central, favoured over the others with florid frames. (Courtesy of the Supreme Court of India Museum)

A large number of images of the revolutionaries on posters are traceable to Kanpur, and of these, a disproportionately large number appear to have been published by one press: Shyam Sunder Lal (Figs. 3, 17, 19, 21, 33, 34, 35, 36, 38, 39, 49 and 51). The publishers at Shyam Sunder Lal were sufficiently concerned about the circulation of their work that they affixed copyright to their posters, indicating a commitment, at least on the behalf of the press, to eke a profit from the images. The prolific production of images of Bhagat Singh and his colleagues by Shyam Sunder Lal provides an index of the demand for them in the bazaars of Kanpur and beyond.

Most of the Kanpur images pre-date the executions of 23 March 1931, demonstrating an engagement with their politics prior to their mass popularisation. The work of Kanpur poster artists dating from 1929, in tandem with the machinations described in Chapter Two, established a market hungry for visual celebrations of the revolutionaries, into which so many other presses stepped in 1931 with their own martyrdom illustrations. The coverage of earlier events in revolutionary politics,

Figure 33: Chitrashala Kanpur, 'Desh Chintan' (Concern for the Country), Kanpur: Shyam Sunder Lal, 1933. (Author's collection)

however, such as their hunger strikes, and intriguing scenes from their prison ordeal, reveal not only a keen interest in, but at times a secret knowledge of Congress–Revolutionary cooperation. Extending Pinney's perceptive analysis of the extraordinary art of Roop Kishore Kapoor, and measuring his oeuvre against a range of other oral and archival sources, these complicities become glaringly apparent.

More importantly, it is clear that in the political turmoil of 1929–1931, revolutionary sympathies were accommodated into larger nationalist sensibilities, even as the formal program of the Congress emphasised nonviolence. In other words, the hardened conceptualisation of 'violence/nonviolence', or a 'revolutionary versus Congress' dynamic was a slightly later development, boosted considerably in the aftermath of the executions in 1931, when Gandhi made it very clear to members of the Congress that sympathising with those who had perpetrated violence would not do. The most powerful example of this unified nationalist sensibility is visible in the nuanced composition *Desh Chintan* (Concern for the Country, Figure 33).

In *Desh Chintan*, an elegantly dressed woman sits, radiant against the background of a dimly-lit room—a diamond fixed on her nose; expensive, exquisitely crafted bangles of pearl and gold decorate her wrists; a matching enamel pin gathers her brocade and lace sari on her shoulder; a splash of *sindur* and a *bindi* on her forehead confirm her married status. A deep sadness inhabits her eyes, which forlornly gaze beyond the frame. She slumps, despondent, casting aside her spinning, indicative of a nationalist sensibility, a commitment to making (but not actually wearing) *khaddar*, a coarse and heavy fabric which never draped as nicely as her sari does. The poster's title, thoughtfully rendered in both Devanagari and English, reveals an additional layer of meaning: she is worried about the nation, struggling under the weight of colonial rule. An Awadhi couplet at the base of the picture reads:

आव पतंगिनी संग जलें जलत न मोड़े अंग ।

पहिले तो दीपक जले पाछे जले पतंग ॥

(Come, burn with the moth, don't squirm in the fire's wrath;
For first burns the lamp, then burns the moth).[6]

The couplet draws our attention to crucial background detail, which might otherwise be overlooked—a cluster of ordinary household moths hover around the flame of a candle, their immolation immanent. One moth has already died, its wings floating down to meet its incinerated body; three other moths hover dangerously close, undeterred by the fate of their companion. This intriguing image is a parable of the four revolutionaries of the HSRA who died in prison—Bhagat Singh, Sukhdev, Rajguru and Jatindranath Das. The composition is a cleverly masked means of expressing sympathy with the executed young men, who knowingly sacrificed their lives like moths drawn by irresistible desire to fly into the flame to their destruction.[7]

Desh Chintan, unlike some other images produced here, is stamped 'registered', indicating that by 1933 some sort of screening process had been introduced before posters could be published legally. The artist has not signed his name, but a pseudonym, 'Chitrashala Kanpur', is given, indicating that the artist was Roop Kishore Kapoor, as indeed does the distinctive style of the poster.[8] Based on his research in Kanpur, Christopher Pinney found that Kapoor was active in the Congress, but was also considered something of a revolutionary, jailed for producing provocative pictures of Bhagat Singh.[9] Kapoor was a prolific artist with a penchant for politically sensitive themes; as Pinney points out, the proscribed images section of the India Office Records in the British Library holds more images by Kapoor than 'any other named artist'.[10] The bulk of his work features revolutionary subjects, presumably reflecting his own politics, and much of his art betrays a knowledge of and connection with revolutionary affairs.

From his other work, particularly his photomontage *Azad Mandir* (*Temple to Azad*, Figure 34), compiled as a homage to Chandrashekhar Azad, it is apparent that Kapoor had access to the revolutionaries' collection of studio portraits. *Azad Mandir* is a collage of revolutionary pictures, bringing together martyred members of the HRA and HSRA around the central figure of Azad, who was killed in a shootout with police in Allahabad on 27 February 1931. The pictures of the hanged HRA members are drawn from *Chand ka Phansi Ank*, but some elements are fresh. Unlike the iconic images of Bhagat Singh and B. K. Dutt, which were so deftly disseminated to the media by HSRA party members, the central studio portrait of Chandrashekhar Azad (Figure 20) had *not* been leaked to the press, and indeed this would appear to be its first airing. The photograph, taken in a studio in Jhansi, was never released during his lifetime, which was spent in hiding. Maintaining Azad's capacity for incognito was as vital a strategy for the party as was the deliberate circulation of B.K. Dutt and Bhagat Singh's images. And while we do not know who took the photograph beneath the central studio portrait in *Azad Mandir*, of Azad's body in Alfred Park, we do know that it was in the possession of Chaman Lal, who had reproduced and sold copies at a condolence meeting in Delhi shortly after Azad's death, to the chagrin of the Home Department.[11]

It is unlikely that the components of Kapoor's *Azad Mandir* could have been brought together without the active collaboration of an HSRA member or affiliate, of which Kanpur had no shortage. Once the investigators of the Lahore Conspiracy Case apprehended that the images had been taken 'for the express purpose of publication', and realised that their publication could undermine the identification of suspects in court,[12] the government moved to introduce legislation along the lines of the *British Contempt of Court Act (1926)* in India, making the publication of photographs of any accused person illegal. Following this, the release and circulation of revolutionary portraits seems to have been considerably limited to underground channels, largely through poster art.

The image that best illustrates this is the rather spectacular Figure 25, which draws on the moth-and-flame metaphor to illustrate the revolutionaries' hunger strikes of 1929, which culminated in the death of Jatindranath Das. The image draws on known imagery of Bhagat Singh and B.K. Dutt, and on a postmortem photograph of Jatindranath Das, which was published on the front page of the *Tribune* to illustrate an article announcing his death (Figure 47). However the two

Figure 34: Roop Kishore Kapoor, *Azad Mandir* (Temple to Azad), Kanpur: Shyam Sundar Lal Publishers, c. 1931. (Courtesy British Library, PIB 27/37D)

hunger-striking revolutionaries above Bhagat Singh and Dutt are relatively unfamiliar (identified in the caption as Kedarnath Sehgal, one of the Meerut accused; and Chaudhury Sher Jang, a prisoner in Lahore who joined the hunger strike), their likenesses evidently modeled on their portraits. There were a number of posters published around 1931 (Figure 35) which deployed similar moth imagery to depict martyred revolutionaries fluttering heavenward, while survivors bearing the likenesses of B.K. Dutt and Hari Kishen lie at the bottom of the flame, as though girding themselves for a second attempt at hurling into oblivion.

There are several other indications that Roop Kishore Kapoor moved in the same circles as Bhagat Singh and his revolutionary colleagues. Nationalist publishing circles in Kanpur substantially overlapped and many collaborated during this period as they struggled to stay ahead of censorship restrictions.[13] Until he set up his own printing premises, Vidyarthi had published *Pratap* at Kanpur's Coronation

Figure 35: Prabhu Dayal, *Dukhi Mata* (Sad Mother), Kanpur: Shyam Sunder Lal/Bhargava Press, c. 1931. (Author's collection)

Press, which also produced some of Kapoor's early posters, such as *Swatantrata Ki Bhent: Amar Shahid Yatindranath Das* (Figure 49).

Another poster by Kapoor, *Phansi* (*Hanging*, Figure 36), is striking for its departure from the representational conventions of revolutionaries in poster art in the early 1930s, where the recognition of the revolutionaries was predicated on the artists' capacity to replicate, as closely as possible, their studio portraits. In *Hanging*, in order to position Sukhdev and Bhagat Singh in such a fashion that they are able to solemnly witness Rajguru's execution before their own, Kapoor has depicted them in profile. Realising that this will make their identification difficult, the publisher has helpfully named each of the condemned men in a caption below. This image differs substantially from many others made of the hanging scene at the time, which imagined that the three were hanged simultaneously, side-by-side, or that Bhagat Singh had worn his hat until the end. In departing from this, *Hanging*

फांसी   HANGING

Raj Guru.   Bhagat Singh.   Sukhdev.

Figure 36: Roop Kishore Kapoor, 'Phansi' (Hanging), Kanpur: Shyam Sunder Lal, c. 1931. (Author's Collection). The image was proscribed in August 1931.

reveals mundane but significant detail—for example, that Bhagat Singh was taller than his friends.[14]

Only Rajguru's face is closely modeled on his photographic portrait, indicating a confidence in sketching Bhagat Singh and Sukhdev, perhaps based on familiarity, that did not extend to Rajguru. Rajguru was originally from Maharashtra (hence his codename, M), although he spent his youth in Banaras. Members and affiliates outside the inner circle of the HSRA in UP knew little about him, for he was by nature quiet and reserved.[15] He was brought to Lahore to shoot Saunders, and shortly after escaped with Bhagat Singh and Durga Devi Vohra, travelling with them on a train as far as Lucknow, where he alighted and slipped away.[16] Rajguru later took part in an action in Delhi in March of 1929 (which was aborted at the last minute).[17] Of the Lahore Conspiracy Case convicted, he evaded arrest for the longest period of time, discovered 'in possession of a fully loaded revolver and copies of a revolutionary leaflet' in Pune, on 30 September 1930.[18]

Kapoor's ability to accurately depict Sukhdev and Bhagat Singh in profile is indicative, as is the representation showing that they were not hanged simultaneously, of a familiarity with particulars not widely known outside revolutionary circles. The details of the hangings were most certainly communicated through sympathetic wardens to jailed revolutionaries, then through their visitors and in furtive letters to broader networks outside the prison.[19] Bhagat Singh's younger brother, Kultar Singh, described how many of Bhagat Singh's writings during this time were smuggled out of prison with the help of congenial wardens.[20] An anonymous image of Bhagat Singh and B.K. Dutt envisages knowledge of a final farewell, arranged by prison staff prior to Dutt's transportation, in contravention of jail operating procedure.[21] The illuminated handshake hovering overhead is suggestive of some sort of a pact, itself indicative of how narratives spread outside the prison through family, friends, and the networks established among prison employees and through poster artists to a broader public (Figure 37).

It was to break information channels such as these that the revolutionaries were dispatched to distant jails in 1931, far removed from their former stamping grounds in north India, to destinations such as Madras and the Andamans.[22] An

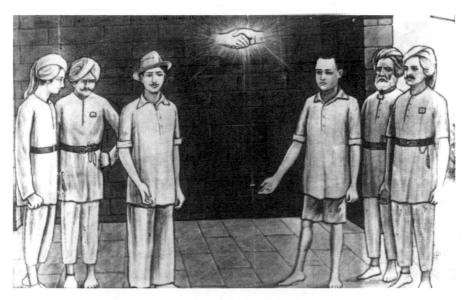

Figure 37: 'Separation of Mr B. K. Dutt from S. Bhagat Singh', Lahore: Hindi Bhavan, c. 1929–31. (Courtesy of NMML, Kulbir Singh Collection, Album 808, 36505)

image created to commemorate the decision of the Lahore Conspiracy Case indicates this severance, as the condemned trio is executed and those convicted to transportation are shipped off to isolation (Figure 18). In the middle of the scene, a coterie of Gandhi-*topi*-wearing satyagrahis—one of them is discernible by his distinctive turban and moustache as Madan Mohan Malaviya—stand behind bars and bid the revolutionaries, who are all carefully labelled by name, farewell. Unlike earlier images, which are named and copyrighted, this one is pointedly anonymous (other than an indication it is made in Lahore's Anarkali), as it reveals a certain complicity—in having access to the portraits of all the accused, and in being able to name them individually.

B.K. Dutt, who grew up and was educated in Kanpur, was frequently represented by Kapoor, and not only as Bhagat Singh's associate, as was common visual practice following the dual release of their photographs to the media. Figure 38 depicts B.K. Dutt alone, shackled and locked in the Andamans, minded by three guards, serving out his sentence of transportation for life. A tag around his neck specifies a prison identification number—2110404—and empty bowls beside him serve as a reminder of his epic hunger-strikes in 1929, 1930, and later on in the Andamans. Few outside revolutionary circles at the time would have been aware that he was imprisoned in the Andamans in yard no. 7, separate and alone.[23] It is the title, *The Caged Lion of India*, that imbues Dutt, about whom relatively little was publicly known, with a particular personality and heroism, a reminder of his years of struggle in jail. This image then, might be read as a sensitive reminder of the iconic revolutionary who survived, by someone personally acquainted with him. The styling of him as *Bharat ka Singh* seems to be a play on the name of his famous friend, Bhagat Singh.

Other images by Kapoor allude to his engagement in leftist politics in Kanpur. After Bhagat Singh's execution, following which communal rioting broke out in Kanpur after Congress workers attempted to enforce a *hartal* on Muslim shopkeepers, Ganesh Shankar Vidyarthi bravely threw himself into the heart of the conflict in an attempt to make peace.[24] He was stabbed and died on the spot. Roop Kishore Kapoor produced a powerful poster in Vidyarthi's honour, mourning a man who had been widely celebrated for his commitment to Hindu–Muslim unity (Figure 39). Many were shocked by Vidyarthi's death.[25] Kapoor communicates a contempt for the religious roots of the riot in his apocalyptic depiction of the communities at war, oblivious to Vidyarthi's efforts at bringing them together, indicated, again, by the visual trope of a handshake, past and forgotten.[26] He seems to have made multiple images of this nature, such as the even more emotive unsigned postcard, *Heart Rendering Effect of Hindu Muslim Riot at Cawnpore*, which features a strained Mother India, pierced by two arrows, cradling Vidyarthi in a pieta-like pose, surrounded by the two communities. Seeing the destruction they have wrought, those

भारत का सिंह पिंजड़े में

Figure 38: Roop Kishore Kapoor, 'Bharat ka Singh Pinjare main' (The Lion of India in a Cage), Kanpur: Shyam Sundar Lal, c. 1932. (Author's collection)

in the foreground are remorseful, but in the background, some are still bent on vengeance (Figure 40). While the vast majority of the images reproduced in this book were produced as posters for mounting on walls, *Heart Rendering Effect* is a handbill/postcard sized format, intended to be distributed, to be passed from person to person and to have the effect of arresting further violence. Just as those standing to the immediate left and right of Bharat Mata seem aghast at their role in slaying Vidyarthi, so too those receiving the handbill are compelled to reflect on the effects of communal violence.

Kapoor's penchant for representing revolutionaries suggests more than a distant admiration or an ideological concurrence. If we are to take images seriously as archival sources then the sheer volume of and detail in his depictions of HSRA members make it difficult to escape the conclusion that Kapoor was well-acquainted with his subjects. The extensive visual representations of the revolution-

Figure 39: Roop Kishore Kapoor, 'Ganesh Shankar Vidyarthi: Self Sacrifice in Mitigating the Riot of Cawnpore', Kanpur: Shyam Sunder Lal, c. 1931. (Author's collection)

aries in poster art during this period, not only by Kapoor but others, greatly assisted in communicating an anti-imperial, pro-revolutionary politics. The determination of artists like Kapoor in continuing to produce revolutionary art after it became explicitly illegal to do so is indicative of the desire to pursue ideology over and above the costs—both personal, as Kapoor was arrested for his work, and professional, as by mid-1931 martyr images could not be reproduced with copyright protection (meaningless as that may have been) that would identify the publisher or the artists.

There are some indications of how these images were circulated and displayed. Some (such as *Azad Mandir*) bear piercings in the upper corners, tell-tale signs of

Figure 40: 'Heart Rendering Effect of Hindu Muslim Riot at Cawnpore', Postcard, Kanpur: Bhargava Press, c. 1931. No artist listed, but it is in the style of Roop Kishore Kapoor. (Courtesy of Sandria Freitag)

having been pinned to a wall.[27] Banned images often bear the date of their proscription stamped on the image itself; otherwise it is often traceable in the pronouncements of Fortnightly Reports from the Home Department. Handwriting scrawled on *Sardar Bhagat Singh on the Scaffold* (Figure 31), for example, reveals that it was discovered in Delhi on 31 March, just days after the hangings on 23 March, indicating the degree to which the fateful event was anticipated by the artists and publishers, but also the extent of the Lahore-made image's mobility. Circulated in the final weeks of Bhagat Singh's life, the image was perhaps a provocative tool in the movement to save him from the gallows.

Finally, it has to be acknowledged that few of these images are visually pleasurable. Some pictures, when compared with rival posters produced for the mass market—the resplendent work of Ravi Varma, for example—are not particularly well crafted; their composition seems rather rudimentary, even in some of those made by the talented Roop Kishore Kapoor.[28] Painful to behold, they seem to go out of their way to emphasise the struggle and suffering in the anticolonial movement, and to incite the viewer to action. Consider *The End*, in which the artist has chosen to depict a bereft and dishevelled Mother India at the feet of her crucified son (Figure 41, compared with the styling of Bharat Mata in Figures 25, 35 and 40). This image, with its evocation of Christian symbolism, is arresting on a num-

THE END

Figure 41: Pandit Ram Saran Hind, 'The End', Ferozepur: Ram Saran Hind Picture Merchant, c. 1931. South Asia Microform Project, Reel 7, no. 8. This image seems to have been part of Gerald Barrier's personal collection.

ber of levels, almost certainly inspired by the inclusion of Jesus Christ in the *Chand ka Phansi Ank* as a martyr (Figure 42). Malcolm Darling was astounded to notice in Ludhiana, 'prominently displayed in a picture shop, a picture of Bhagat Singh crucified in a Homburg hat and at the foot of the cross a weeping figure of Mother India'.[29]

Martyr images defy the vernacular aesthetic of bazaar art, which generally privileges colour over monochrome, compelling the viewer to buy. Black and white posters were inexpensive to produce and affordable to purchase (*The End*, for example, cost just 2 *annas*). This is angry art; confronting, upsetting images calculated to dis-

 INRI

दे प्राण-दण्ड का गैमाशकारी दृश्य

भारतीय ध्वज

Figure 42: Crucifixion image from *Chand ka Phansi Ank*, 1926. South Asia Microform Project, Reel 15, No. 1.

turb and provoke the viewer. The disconcerting nature of such pictures, as Sumathi Ramaswamy has noted, is frequently contradicted by titles that affirm the gory executions as 'gifts' or 'wonderful presentations' to the nation,[30] suggesting an affinity with Sikh martyrology.

Visualising the Freedom Struggle

The inclusion of Motilal Nehru, Tilak and Lala Lajpat Rai in *The End* are a reminder that contemporary sources from the 1930s, as well as oral histories and

Figure 43: Nandlal, 'Dukhin Bharat ke Shahid' (Martyrs of Sad India), Lahore: Modern Half Tone Company, c. 1931. This particular image has been cropped, obscuring Rajguru's head in Bhagat Singh's left hand. (Courtesy of the Nehru Museum and Memorial Library, Kulbir Singh Collection, Album 808, 36517)

memoirs recorded later, reflect a perception that there was a convergence in the aims of the revolutionaries and the Congress. This was a sensibility which popular posters played a powerful a role in shaping. To return to *Desh Chintan* (Figure 33), it is notable that the image brings revolutionary and Congress methods—represented by the juxtaposition of the immolating moths and the spinning apparatus—together in the same frame. This cohabitation of violent and nonviolent means is reflective of more general sympathies in nationalist-minded circles, which saw no conflict in simultaneously supporting the Gandhian platform of nonviolence and honoring Bhagat Singh.[31] As the *Bhavishya* editorialised in August 1931, in the aftermath of Bhagat Singh's death:

If to-day the country worships Bhagat Singh, it is not for his mistakes, but for his unflinching patriotism, which if not greater, was not less [than] that of Gandhiji. To-day the life of

Bhagat Singh presents itself before the country as an emblem of genuine patriotism and sacrifice. To-day the memory of Bhagat Singh does not prompt anyone towards the path of violence; it evokes in the heart of men the pure spirit of asceticism. For this reason the worship of Bhagat Singh is the worship of the nation. To-day Bhagat Singh is before the country not in the form of the evils of violence, but as a pure embodiment of patriotism.[32]

This precise sentiment is echoed across many oral history interviews, in which the apparent contradiction is sometimes noted, but most often disregarded. Congressman Lala Jagat Narain reflected that Bhagat Singh's popularity might be attributed to a particularly Punjabi penchant for violence: 'it may be owing to our weakness, but as Punjabis, we praised our revolutionaries ... even though we honestly believed in Gandhism'.[33] Yet Narain's willingness to embrace colonial ascriptions of Punjabiness does not begin to explain the extent to which Bhagat Singh was revered after his death across much of India. As Durga Das, the eminent Delhi-based journalist who reported on the negotiations of the Gandhi–Irwin Pact, reflected when asked by B. R. Nanda in an oral history interview:

B. R. Nanda: Was there any inconsistency in the Indian opinion? On the one hand it accepted leadership of Gandhi, it accepted non-violence, on the other hand it had such passionate admiration for Bhagat Singh, because I lived through that experience myself.

Durga Das: There is no contradiction. The simple reason is this: There are two different emotions, one is the emotion of reverence for a holy man, a Messiah, a leader, a great man and a great Mahatma, that represented one compartment, the other was admiration for a hero, who had sacrificed himself for the country.

Nanda: May I say that showed some kind of split personality in the nation also where there are two separate compartments on such a crucial issue, violence and non-violence...

Durga Das: No, they were judging by only one yardstick, namely patriotism. They were not assessing violence or non-violence. They thought of Bhagat Singh as a man patriotically prepared to sacrifice himself for the cause of the nation. They took him as a hero, a martyr for the cause of the freedom for which Gandhi too was fighting.[34]

Such an interpretation, of there being one movement for independence regardless of formal differences about the means, comes across strongly in a range of materials from the 1930s. Manmathnath Gupta reflected that Shivprasad Gupta, the editor of *Aaj* and a Gandhian, was supportive of the revolutionaries, yet he did not see this as being incongruous: 'I think that most of the Gandhians were like this. There were very few who were sworn non-violence fanatics. Most Gandhiites wanted to be friendly to the revolutionaries; they had very great respect for the revolutionaries, but at the same time wanted to follow Gandhiji.'[35]

Chiranjilal Paliwal, a student leader in the early 1930s from the Delhi Student Union, considered himself a Gandhian and spent his college vacations at Sabarmati. Before he offered himself for arrest in October 1930 during civil disobedience, he came in contact with Chandrashekhar Azad at Hindu College, where HSRA mem-

141

ber Nand Kishore Nigam was employed as a lecturer.[36] Azad asked Paliwal to hold some weapons for safekeeping, and he agreed.[37] By the time Paliwal was released from jail in early 1931 following the amnesty of the Gandhi–Irwin Pact, Azad had been killed. In 1972, Paliwal surrendered the weapons to Prime Minister Indira Gandhi,[38] and in an interview two years later, defended his actions:

The question could arise that a man like me who was a follower of Mahatma Gandhi, was indulging in keeping such weapon[s] of violence and war. But these weapons were wielded by persons who were considered to be ardent patriots and they were prepared to sacrifice their lives for the sake of the country. We were also followers of Mahatma Gandhi, in a way were considered to be patriots but it was not for us to dissociate ourselves or to look upon them as something not belonging to the country or to us. Therefore, I kept only these weapons and carried out the wishes of these revolutionary friends to the last.[39]

Rana Jang Bahadur Singh, editor of the Lahore weekly, *Nation*, and a follower of Lala Lajpat Rai, confessed in an interview that he had sheltered the absconding Durga Devi Vohra and Sushila in his home for three weeks, before clarifying:

Now, from the episode to which I have referred, one can form some idea of the influence which this revolutionary movement exercised in the country. Even those like me and my wife who would never liked to have been involved actively in the revolutionary movement felt very strongly actuated to give help and shelter to those who had chosen the path of violence for liberating their country. It implies that in the country there was a large population which had active sympathy with the movement and there is no doubt about it that the revolutionary movement with all its weaknesses, as the use of terroristic techniques, succeeded in making a tremendous contribution to the success of the other forces of liberation.[40]

The revolutionaries themselves certainly saw their efforts as making a positive contribution to the broader nationalist movement. In her oral history testimony, Shanti Das, a Bengali revolutionary, reflected that the presence of violence on the political spectrum helped to throw the Civil Disobedience Movement into stark relief.[41] Bimal Prasad Jain, an HSRA member arrested for his role in the Delhi Conspiracy Case, maintained that the purpose of the revolutionary movement was to rouse the masses, and that this had strengthened Gandhi's capacity to organise them.[42]

Kapoor's picturing of the revolutionaries within the same frame as the Congress movement was therefore not unique. Conceptualising Bhagat Singh and his colleagues as part of the nationalist pantheon has become a staple visual referent in independent India, in pedagogical charts intended as teaching aids for school children, and in images which picture Bhagat Singh on the periphery of a nationalist galaxy orbiting around Gandhi (Figure 44; Bhagat Singh is nestled in the upper right hand corner, underneath the flag), indicating a commonsense acceptance of the role of revolutionaries in the freedom struggle. These images cut across other equally popular images of slightly later provenance, reflecting a nationalist taxonomy that isolates those who have fought violently (Figure 10). A genre of calendar

Figure 44: *Galaxy of Leaders*, Bombay: Bacchu Ragaviah & Jonnala Pentaliah, c. 1946. (Author's collection)

and poster art celebrating the votaries of violence alone, championed since the 1960s by the popular Meerut based artist H. R. Raja (Figure 45), appears as a cultural corrective to the dominance of Gandhian nonviolence at the highest levels of state discourse. In his fieldwork, Chris Pinney interviewed H. R. Raja, who has painted over 150 Bhagat Singh portraits, many in the same frame as his colleague Azad, and his contemporary Bose, frequently in the company of other 'lions' such as Shivaji and Maharana Pratap.[43] Raja had many imitators; some even revived the moth motif (Figure 46). Co-locating twentieth century advocates of violence with those from earlier eras serves to establish, legitimise and glorify a tradition of violent resistance.

The support for Bhagat Singh and his revolutionary colleagues at a grassroots level, as demonstrated in the cases of Kanpur, Delhi and Lahore, proved to be of

Figure 45: H. R. Raja, 'Bharat Mata ki Vir Santan' (Brave Sons of Mother India). Calendar image for Batra Glass House, 1980. (Author's collection)

fundamental importance in 1929, when debates within the Congress about means and ends peaked. Congress members who were close to the revolutionaries, both ideologically and personally, became important conduits in the Congress-revolutionary dynamic, not only in provincial Congress committees, but at an All-India level. Taken together, their roles plugged into some of the most important openings for leveraging political advantage and communicating the revolutionary message. Prominent journalists such as Ganesh Shankhar Vidyarthi and Chaman Lal's access to influential newspapers such as *Pratap* and the *Hindustan Times*, and the interventions of Feroze Chand, the editor of *Bande Mataram* in Punjab, ensured that the revolutionaries had a strong media presence, and the work of artists such as Roop Kishore Kapoor both created and fed into a market which desired images of Bhagat Singh and his comrades.

Figure 46: Untitled, Belgium Calendar Corporation, c. 1970s–80s. (Courtesy of Robin Jeffrey)

Equally significant in the unfurling political drama of the early 1930s were the All-India Congressmen who established tactical connections with the revolutionaries, among whom could be counted both senior and junior Nehrus. It is the connections of such high-profile leaders that compel a reconceptualisation of the way in which the conduct of the nationalist movement in the interwar period has been conceived in academic historiography. Scholars have long recognised that 'the Congress was not, as Gandhi wished it to be, a well-disciplined army unquestioningly obeying the orders of a central command',[44] and that on occasion, Gandhi's 'political program was ignored by the Indian National Congress'.[45] The extent of the division within the central command over the Congress program of nonviolence in the late 1920s warrants closer attention.

6

'GANDHI AND BALRAJ'

FROM DOMINION STATUS TO COMPLETE INDEPENDENCE

The historiography of the transition of the Congress demand from Dominion Status
to *purna swaraj*—which represented a dramatic escalation of the anticolonial movement following the post-Chauri-Chaura lull of the early 1920s—has logically been
focused on the machinations within the Congress movement in general and its so-
called 'High Command' in particular. The decision to agitate for complete independence was formalised at the Lahore Congress in December 1929, but had been a
matter of contention for some years. As Gerald Barrier wrote in 1974, 'Indian politics exploded in early 1930 as the Congress dramatically implemented its Lahore
resolve to confront the British' in the subsequent Civil Disobedience Movement;[1]
but even Barrier—who was sensitive to the popularity of Bhagat Singh and the revolutionaries as a result of his extensive work on Punjabi politics and banned literature—does not name the HSRA's role in the quite literal explosions that pressed
reluctant Congress elders towards the more radical demand of *purna swaraj*.

By contrast, the Kanpur artist Ramshankar Trivedi positioned Bhagat Singh and
B.K. Dutt prominently in a line up of Congress notables who lobby Gandhi for
action in *Shesh Shayi* (Figure 3). The latter's dominance of the Congress is suggested
by the depiction of him on the serpent-seat Naga Shesh—conventionally the preserve of Vishnu. Just as the *devas* in times of crisis come to Vishnu's abode to entreat
him to intervene in worldly affairs, Jawaharlal Nehru, Motilal Nehru, Madan
Mohan Malaviya, Vallabhbhai Patel, Subhas Chandra Bose, Bhagat Singh,
B.K. Dutt and Sarojini Naidu stand aside while Bharat Mata, in the role normally
ascribed to Lakshmi Devi, makes a persuasive case on their behalf, pointing to the
violence meted out by uniformed British officers wielding *lathis*. Just as political

147

expression inhabits religious art, as von Stietencron has shown, so political art deftly commandeers religious themes to communicate its message: now is the time for action.[2] The struggle for independence is lent a distinctly *puranic* flavour, inserted into a narrative and imbued with an epic but predictable outcome. Whether this particular rendering was intended to criticise or flatter the Mahatma is surely a matter of interpretation.

The likeness of Sarojini Naidu in *Shesh Shayi* is suggestive of a photograph taken of her on the Salt March, which dates the image no earlier than April 1930, and no later than February 1931, when Motilal Nehru had passed away and was therefore unlikely to have been included in the queue of nationalists who seem to have joined forces to press Gandhi towards an escalation of civil disobedience.[3] Based on received concepts of the centrality of nonviolence to the freedom struggle, the somewhat ecumenical line-up of revolutionaries and Congress leaders seems at best aspirational, but as I will show below, even the more notoriously conservative individuals in this queue were in various ways supportive of the revolutionaries in 1929–30. While in many of the political posters presented in these pages a number of leaders are represented in the same frame as the revolutionaries who were quite peripheral to their politics (such as Muhammad Ali, in Figure 30; and Dadabhai Naoroji, in Figure 25), the replication of Motilal Nehru in several of these (Figs. 3, 30, 41 and 43) calls for particular attention. Whereas Muhammad Ali and Dadabhai Naoroji inhabit a heaven for patriots, *Shesh Shayi* is not a posthumous image, I would suggest, but is representative of a particular present. Poster artists seem to have made clear demarcations between the worldly and heavenly realms that their subjects inhabited.

Jawaharlal Nehru and Subhas Chandra Bose, two figures frequently identified as leaders of an impatient and radical youth that pressured the 'old guard' of Congress towards *purna swaraj* in 1929, were both prone to making supportive statements about the revolutionaries. Under pressure from Gandhi to uphold the platform of nonviolence (and to evade the growing threat of imprisonment), Jawaharlal learned to be more guarded, and was frequently vague about the amorphous 'youth movement', which both supported and fuelled his confrontation with the moderate elders in Congress. Among Jawaharlal's many statements in 1929, 'the youth movement' emerges as a euphemism for a range of bodies 'to which I owe allegiance'.[4] These ranged from the All-India Youth Congress to the Naujawan Bharat Sabha, an organisation which Jawaharlal made many strenuous attempts to influence.[5] He had, on the news of the indiscriminate arrests of several NJBS members immediately after the Saunders assassination in Lahore, sent them a public note of support in a Patna newspaper, *The Searchlight*.[6] Freshly returned from a foray in Europe (where Scotland Yard concluded that his real purpose was 'to study Indian revolutionary movements on the Continent' and to engage with communism first hand, rather than to oversee his wife's convalescence), Jawaharlal was himself considered something of a revolutionary.[7] Frustrated with the limitations inherent in Dominion Status, Jawaharlal, Subhas Chandra Bose and Srinivas Iyengar had formed the Independence League of India in 1928,[8] tendering their resignations to the Congress on the basis that they did not share its limited goals.[9] Their resignations were rejected by the leadership on the basis that there was no occasion for such dramatic gestures, which would almost certainly have been followed by an exodus of their followers, diverting youthful energies away from the Congress.

Congress elders were faced with the task of containing an energetic and impatient body of youth, emerging from a range of nationalist educational outlets in the late 1920s, indignant at the excesses of colonialism. At the 1927 Madras Congress, Jawaharlal had moved a resolution for 'complete national independence' in Gandhi's absence, according to intelligence reports, at the instigation of 'the Bengal revolutionary group'.[10] A resolution expressing sympathy with those accused in the Kakori case also was passed at Madras.[11] Writing sternly to Jawaharlal, Gandhi objected to the precipitousness of the independence resolution ('Your plunging into the "republican army" was a hasty step'), adding, 'I do not mind these acts of yours as much as I mind your encouraging mischief-makers and hooligans.'[12] Jawaharlal was not in Europe any more.

Nor is it coincidental that much of the action of the period was driven by events in Punjab, India's 'garrison state', in which Congress organisation was demonstrably weak.[13] The strength of the youth movement, in the form of the NJBS as well as associated leftist groups, in concert with a sizeable population of groups alienated by recent policy—in particular the Nehru Report, criticised by both Muslims and Sikhs—forced the Congress to engage with the strategically important province in order to avert its further estrangement from mainstream anticolonialism.

Motilal Nehru and the Lahore Conspiracy Case

Motilal Nehru has long been characterised as a moderate politician. His metamorphosis to strident colonial critic was gradual, his relative conservatism apparent in his eponymous Report, written three years prior to his death. Among other things, the Nehru Report advocated Dominion Status—presumed to mean that India would be granted autonomy in all matters of governance, but remain within the British Commonwealth of Nations, on par with 'white' dominions. The government of India discerned his conservatism in letters intercepted in the name of intelligence-gathering, which expressed his concerns for the escalating radicalism of his son.[14] It was therefore with a sense of revelation that news of Motilal Nehru's support of the revolutionaries of the HSRA was first publicly acknowledged in the *Motilal Nehru Birth Centenary Souvenir Volume* in 1961. In this commemorative publication, endorsed by the Motilal Nehru Centenary Committee, a relative unknown, N. K. Bhartya, revealed that he was the middleman through whom Motilal Nehru donated money to and communicated with Chandrashekar Azad:

From amongst the few that still survive and who have had the good fortune of coming into contact with Motilalji, I have an exciting and revealing true story to relate. ... I was very lucky to have been entrusted with the duties of a liaison officer between Panditji and Shri Chandra Shekhar Azad, the then commander-in-chief of the Socialist Republican Army ... I had many occasions to meet revered Panditji at Allahabad in his home.[15]

This aspect of his personality has not been factored into political biographies, although readers of revolutionary memoirs have known for some time that Motilal Nehru quietly provided money to the revolutionaries of the HSRA, as disclosed by Jatindernath Sanyal in his 1983 edition of Bhagat Singh's biography.[16] J. N. Sahni, the former editor of the *Hindustan Times*, likewise reflected in his memoirs that:

Motilal Nehru was a grand large-hearted person. Unlike Gandhi, he had no inhibitions about revolutionaries. He considered them misguided, but treated them with affection. Once when these boys were being trailed from one rat-hole to another, spending their time in jungles and low-down slums, living sometimes on roasted gram and dried bread, he called me and gave me a thousand rupees to be passed on secretly to the revolutionaries for relief.[17]

Sahni passed the money on to a Congress worker in Delhi, Satyawati, who had contacts with the revolutionaries. He claimed that when he was called to visit her some time afterwards, Satyawati introduced him to Durga Devi Vohra. Vohra showed him two revolvers that had been smuggled from the North Western Frontier Provinces. Pointing to them, Satyawati remarked:

'Now you can tell Motilalji how the money has been utilised'. I protested that the money was intended to offer relief like food and clothes. She replied that what I saw before me was more vital to them than food and clothes. When I described the scene to the elder Nehru his eyes filled with moisture. In a hoarse voice full of emotion, he said: 'One thing is for sure. Even if we fail, these boys will see to it that India is free.'[18]

Such a reminiscence might be dismissed as too anecdotal, and far too over-wrought. Yet there are several corroborating references to Motilal Nehru's generous financial assistance to HSRA members, in particular to Chandrashekhar Azad. In an oral history interview, Rajendrapal Singh 'Warrior'—a peripheral member of the HSRA who later served as a member of the Delhi Pradesh Congress Committee—specified that Motilal had given Rs 500 to Azad, and that on another occasion, while attending a Congress Working Committee meeting in Allahabad, Jawaharlal had also given them Rs 1000, explicitly saying that he didn't approve of their methods.[19] One associate of the HSRA in Kanpur made a statement in the Lahore Conspiracy Case in October of 1929, testifying that Bejoy Kumar Sinha told him that the elder Nehru had donated to the HSRA, although this information does not seem to have been taken seriously by the investigators.[20]

The many public statements of both Nehrus regarding the revolutionaries that lie peppered through their published papers indicate that both closely followed and commented on the intrigues of the Lahore Conspiracy Case, although these are largely related to the revolutionaries' legal battles with the empire. Visits of both Motilal and Jawaharlal Nehru to the revolutionaries in 1929, in the courtroom and in prison respectively, were well-documented in nationalist newspapers of the day and disapprovingly noted in intelligence reports, as were their public appeals for funds to cover the revolutionaries' defence. This was not inconsistent with Motilal Nehru's other activities; he was equally concerned about the conduct of the Meerut Conspiracy Case, and made several public pleas for funds to cover their legal costs.[21] However post-colonial memoirs and oral histories, as the above examples indicate, suggest a more substantial level to Motilal's engagement with the revolutionaries of the HSRA.

Perhaps the elder Nehru was inexorably drawn into the intrigues of the Lahore Conspiracy Case; as an MLA and the leader of the Swarajya Party, he was in the chamber when Bhagat Singh and B.K. Dutt threw bombs and leaflets into the Legislative Assembly on 8 April 1929. The members of the HSRA who planned the attack—Shiv Verma, Jaidev Kapoor and Bhagat Singh—had been deeply troubled in the lead-up to the bombing, uneasy in the knowledge that many venerable nationalists would be present, and that there was a level of unpredictability to the operation. Jaidev Kapoor reported that Bhagat Singh considered warning Motilal Nehru prior to the attack, but they abandoned the idea on the basis that it may jeopardise the entire action. Instead, they drew up a small map, charting out where each Member sat in the Assembly, so that the bombs could be directed away from Indian Members.[22]

J.N. Sahni recalled that after the first bomb landed, while many in the chamber ran for the exits or cowered under their seats, the senior Nehru kept remarkably calm:

Pandit Motilal Nehru not only remained in his seat, but a little later advanced towards the official benches to see what had happened, and to render any help to the wounded if any. He was half way between his seat and that of the Home Member when the second bomb fell, which was followed by two revolver shots. But even after the second bomb Pandit Motilal Nehru did not waver or recede.[23]

Later that night, when it was established that none had been seriously harmed in the bombing, members of the Nationalist Party gathered at Madan Mohan Malaviya's home and 'cut jokes' at the expense of those in the Assembly who had panicked when the bomb went off.[24]

A number of nationalist leaders condemned the attack on the Assembly, as the government expected them to. Gandhi decried that 'the bomb throwers have discredited the cause of freedom in whose name they threw the bombs'.[25] Motilal chose a different path. Two days after, the Congress president delivered a speech in which he reflected on the significance of the attack:

It is wise statesmanship alone which can, by strengthening the forces of non-violence, meet the forces of violence. To say that 'This is a sad day for the future of India' or that 'Such an incident is a catastrophe to India' will do no good. ... The real India does not believe in the cult of the bomb, nor does she believe in the cult of the Statutory Commission. India believes in suffering, and if the Government does not weaken the hands of Mahatma Gandhi she will one day stagger the world by the magnitude of her suffering for freedom. Let the people and the Government see things in their true perspective. The choice lies between Gandhi and 'Balraj'.[26]

By inviting the British to make a choice between Gandhi or 'Balraj' (the signatory to the leaflets that Bhagat Singh and Dutt had rained on the Assembly after the bombs), Motilal sparked a controversy, prompting a stern intervention from the Viceroy.[27] In a speech addressed to the Assembly, Irwin animatedly criticised Motilal's failure to condemn the bombing outright.[28] The next day Jawaharlal entered the fray, defending his father's interpretation in an address in Allahabad, delivering a sharp retort:

While many of us may grieve over the incident, for reasons that the Viceroy may not appreciate, it is absurd to talk of unqualified condemnation of the young men who did it. ... Lord Irwin has told us of the naked conflict between two contradictory philosophies, that of physical violence and that of reason and argument. On which, may I ask, do Lord Irwin and his Government base their rule in India? Is the foreign Army of Occupation here to reason with us sweetly? Are the mercenary Indian armies the embodiment of persuasion, and the police and the shooting and the brutal assaults and vindictive legal processes? Were the *lathi* blows that fell on Lala Lajpat Rai an attempt to reason with him?[29]

Scotland Yard described this intervention as 'very objectionable'.[30] It would have objected even more, had it known that there was an important prequel to the attack on the Assembly.

In early March 1929, Bhagat Singh approached Kumari Lajjawati, a worker from the Punjabi Congress who was sympathetic to the Naujawan Bharat Sabha, complaining to her that 'your Congress leaders call us dacoits whenever we do anything'.[31] Bhagat Singh suggested that in doing so, the leaders were missing out on an opportunity to leverage the revolutionaries' actions against the government, to meet the ends of the Congress. Shortly after this exchange, Sukhdev visited Lajjawati to request that she liaise with the senior Congress leadership, specifically suggesting Motilal Nehru (with whom she was close, through the Zutshi–Sahgal family), inviting him to capitalise on the threat of violence posed by the revolutionaries when negotiating with the British.[32] This was confirmed by Lala Feroze Chand, the Lahore-based member of the Congress and editor of *Bande Mataram*, who enjoyed close working relationships with both Sukhdev and Bhagat Singh:

[Bhagat Singh] professed very advanced views, there is no doubt, and he criticised Congress programmes as much too mild; but he was willing to concede that both things were necessary. He was not like some other revolutionaries, altogether hostile to the sort of programmes that the Congress and other nonviolent leaders were placing before the country. He had this conveyed, I understand, to Pandit Motilal Nehru, and Pandit Moti Lal Nehru, in a speech that became famous at the time, had used this expression: 'The choice for the British is "Balraj" or Gandhi.' 'Balraj' was Bhagat Singh's coinage for 'force'. And this expression 'Balraj or Gandhi', this also I ascribe to Bhagat Singh, although Motilal Nehru made it current. He thought it would strengthen the hands of the Swarajists' work or Pandit Motilal's work, if 'Balraj' also asserted itself to some extent and if it could be made clear to the British that if they did not concede the demands put forward by Gandhi, Lajpat Rai, Motilal, then they would have to reckon with 'Balraj', because the nation had no other alternative. The British must either concede the demands or the nation must rise in violent rebellion against the British and fight for its freedom. Such was Bhagat Singh's thinking.[33]

Interestingly, in 1933, with the revolutionaries in north India largely suppressed, a report on *Terrorism in India* drew much the same conclusion, reasoning that managing 'the violence movement' depended on 'the extent to which coming constitutional changes satisfy reasonable political aspirations. If an impression is created that political progress cannot be obtained by constitutional methods or without resort to violence, conditions favourable to increased revolutionary activity ... will come into existence'.[34] But in 1929, as the reverberations of the Assembly Outrage rattled throughout the empire, such a concession was unthinkable.[35]

A year later, Motilal's 'Balraj or Gandhi' speech was still the topic of discussion in the Intelligence Bureau, ranked as the most significant of all 'public utterances by Congress leaders', that 'foster and stimulate the spirit of violence'.[36] The nationalist press had defended Motilal's statement, explaining that the Pandit was unequivocally in favour of nonviolence; that in making this speech, he merely sought to emphasise that 'the best way to relegate "Balraj" to the background is to bring Gandhiji into prominence and to strengthen his hands'.[37]

Motilal Nehru's involvement with the Assembly Bomb Case (prosecuted in Delhi, before Bhagat Singh and B.K. Dutt were moved to Lahore to face charges in the larger Lahore Conspiracy Case in June) did not end with this incident. He covertly made some significant legal interventions as well. From early newspaper reports covering the police investigation of the bombing, it is clear that the original defence proffered by Bhagat Singh and Dutt's lawyer, Asaf Ali, was that the attack was 'a mere school boy's joke'.[38] This was entirely counter to the HSRA plan, which was to flagrantly admit guilt and use the courtroom as a venue for expressing their ideology.[39] Chaman Lal said that Asaf Ali's first defence statement 'was torn to pieces by

Bhagat Singh, I remember that definitely.'[40] He then added: 'Pandit Motilal Nehru had helped to write the statement that Bhagat Singh actually made'.[41]

This has been attested to by J. N. Sahni, Chaman Lal's editor, who further elaborated that Bhagat Singh's father had come to Delhi to help organise his son's defence, and had brought the statement to him for advice: 'After incorporating the essence of their views, I rewrote the statement and confidentially took it to Motilal. He not only kept most of what the boys wanted intact, but made the language even more aggressive.'[42] Crucially, Motilal brought his legal nous to the document by reinserting a sentence from the leaflet signed by 'Balraj', stressing that their intent had *not* been to kill, but 'to make a loud noise' (a reference to the French anarchist, Auguste Valliant). This, Sahni believed, saved Bhagat Singh and Dutt from a death sentence for attempted murder in the Assembly Bomb Case.[43] Perhaps this anecdote explains the background to a letter Jawaharlal wrote to Gandhi, shortly after the stir created when the statement was read in court, in which Jawaharlal expressed his confidence that Asaf Ali had not been the author of the statement: 'I think you are mistaken in thinking that the statement was the work of their counsel. My information is that counsel had nothing, or practically nothing, to do with it. He might have touched up the punctuation. I think the statement was undoubtedly a genuine thing'.[44]

The Congress and the Hunger Strikers

A number of scholars agree that the hunger strikes of the jailed revolutionaries in 1929 popularised their cause,[45] bringing them closer to the Congress,[46] either as a matter of political expediency,[47] or due to a degree of ideological convergence.[48] Beginning on 15 June 1929, seventeen convicts and prisoners on trial in jails across Punjab and Delhi embarked on a coordinated hunger strike in protest at differential treatment meted out to Indian and European prisoners.[49] The hunger strikers demanded that political prisoners be treated differently to criminals, and be given a better standard of diet; no forced labour; the freedom to wear their own clothes; be confined together; to have access to books, a daily newspaper, and writing materials; and to be able to receive letters and visitors fortnightly, instead of monthly.[50] By 13 September, Jatindranath Das had died of starvation, and several others lay gravely ill.

It was by no means clear in mid-1929 that civil disobedience was immanent or inevitable. In July Gandhi had 'bluntly declared' that he saw no signs of the discipline required for him to lead a movement on his terms.[51] In Britain, the Conservative Party had recently lost the elections, and MacDonald's minority Labour government incrementally began to advance debates about India's status within the empire.[52] Irwin made conciliatory but calculated advances towards moderate nationalists, initiating discussions in London about a Round Table Conference, following through with the Irwin Declaration in October, the details of which an optimistic Viceroy had strategically leaked in India, before he was out-maneuvered by a Conservative-led 'political storm' at home.[53] It was not until 23 December 1929, just days before the Lahore Congress, at a meeting of Congress and liberal leaders in Delhi with the Viceroy, that it became apparent to the Congress moderates and the Liberals that Irwin's offer was thin.

Many elders within the Congress had nurtured hopes that the government would accept the demands of Dominion Status, precluding a major campaign of action.[54] They seem to have been decidedly nervous at the energies of younger activists who had begun to regard moderate politics with despair. A close reading of the politics within the Congress in 1929 suggests that it was the pressures from the youth movement following the hunger strikes that pushed Jawaharlal Nehru to the fore of political organisation. And while many have argued that Jawaharlal's leadership was dictated by Gandhi, D.A. Low argues that in December 1929, 'at this critical juncture at least, it was Gandhi who deferred to Nehru', withdrawing his resistance and making the demand for *purna swaraj* in December ineluctable.[55] Below, I wish to foreground some of the interactions that the revolutionaries had with Congress leaders during this period, with a view to knitting together the political landscape which has been so often bifurcated into discrete arenas of revolutionary and Congress activity.

The Naujawan Bharat Sabha propelled much of the agitation around the hunger-strikers by organising a series of rallies and *prabhat pheries* in June. These gained so much exposure that Congress activities in Punjab soon became oriented around the hunger-striking revolutionaries, aided in no small degree by NJBS–Congress connections. At a 'Bhagat Singh Day' in Amritsar on 30 June, 5000 people gathered in Jallianwala Bagh to listen to speeches, poems and songs celebrating the hunger strikers.[56] Several Punjabi Congress leaders with connections to the revolutionaries addressed the gathering, including Kitchlew and Faqir Chand, commending the hunger strikes, while exhorting the audience to follow the Congress.[57]

This was just one of many meetings, observed the CID, where 'the Congress and the Nau Jawan Bharat Sabha have combined forces to arouse public feeling against Government'.[58] It was interactions such as these that led the Intelligence Bureau to conclude that the NJBS was poised to 'convert the Congress policy of non-violent non-cooperation into a policy of violence'.[59] In Punjab, 'where the people are more apt to react to such appeals than in any other province', this was an issue of major concern to the government. However from his office in the Home Department in Simla, Emerson felt that the obvious course of action—declaring the NJBS as an unlawful organisation—ran the risk of throwing 'saner political elements' into the arms of 'the extreme left', creating an undesirable unity.[60]

Turning to the issue of the hunger strikers, Emerson observed that 'popular sympathy with them is increasing. The death of any of them is likely to be followed by a wave of sentiment, by which the real issues will be obscured. One effect of this will be a large accession of supporters to the Congress programme.'[61] Prison management was technically a provincial concern, however the Home Department stoutly refused to press Punjab to accommodate those accused or convicted of political violence within the Special Prisoner category, under which nonviolent political prisoners were detained. Again, in negotiating the politics of the demands made by the hunger-strikers, Emerson emphasised 'the desirability of conciliating moderate opinion and isolating extreme opinion'.[62]

Moderate opinion, however, seemed to have shifted. In June came the news that the reliably conservative Madan Mohan Malaviya, who had also been present at and had initially condemned the bombing of the Assembly, had provided support to the accused in the Lahore Conspiracy Case, pledging one thousand rupees from Seva Samiti funds.[63] Malaviya surprised many when he defended the revolutionaries' claims for political prisoner status, characteristically at great length, in the Legislative Assembly, reading out a letter Bhagat Singh wrote to the Inspector General of Prisons, and moving a vote in their favour which was carried by 55 to 47.[64] In July Jawaharlal Nehru published a statement by Bhagat Singh and B.K. Dutt in the *Congress Bulletin*, judging that there was 'very general appreciation of it among Congress circles', although he was chided by the Mahatma for doing so.[65] Undeterred, Jawaharlal drafted the August edition describing the attempts to force-feed the revolutionaries as 'extraordinarily brutal', and reporting that a protest by seven youths in Lahore supporting the hunger strikers had been attacked and 'beaten senseless' by three dozen police.[66]

Gandhi's displeasure at such coverage raises the issue of how the Congress as an institution responded to the rising popularity of the revolutionaries. While many eminent Congress leaders demonstrated their support for the hunger-striking revolutionaries, doing so was technically in breach of the Congress creed of nonviolence, the policy that had underpinned the nationalist movement since 1920. On 26 July 1929, the Congress Working Committee was formally forced to confront this apparent contradiction at a meeting in Allahabad, when N. M. Ghatwai and Hariharnath Shastri proposed resolutions sympathising with the hunger-strikers.[67] As Congress president and despite (or perhaps to obscure) his private actions, Motilal Nehru ruled out the resolution, reasoning that 'the Congress could not appreciate or recognise any act, however brave, which was done in a violent manner.'[68] Members in the audience objected, reminding him of a recent precedent: in 1924, the Bengal Provincial Congress under the presidency of C. R. Das had passed a resolution sympathising with Gopinath Saha.[69] However, in an effort to maintain appearances, to the CID and perhaps also to Gandhi,[70] Motilal stood firm in his refusal; marginalia jotted on the minutes of the meeting specifically note that the failed resolutions were 'repugnant to the Congress'.[71] Congressite and Kanpur-based trade unionist Hariharnath Shastri, who supported the motion, intimated to the press that Motilal disallowed the motion because 'he wished to avoid discussion on a controversial matter'.[72]

In an editorial in the *Pratap* shortly after, Ganesh Shankhar Vidyarthi complained:

The All India Congress Committee was not expected to support the bomb-and-pistol policy of Bhagat Singh and Dutt; but this much was expected of it: that it should consider and praise the grim struggle that is going on in the Lahore Central Prison and Borstal Jail between superhuman godliness and demoniac beastliness in order to win the rights of humanity for political prisoners and the heroism that our youths are exhibiting in the struggle. The country has done all that human efforts could do to solve this problem by constitutional methods, but to no effect. Even today these educated, cultured prisoners are kept like wicked, depraved and mean persons and are accorded that humiliating and hateful treatment which no civilised man would accord even to the most degraded person. We do not wish that the country would follow the path of murder, but we do wish that bravery should be recognised wherever it may show itself.[73]

The NJBS, which had postponed its own conference in order to attend the deliberations of the Congress in Allahabad, was equally displeased, and threatened to withdraw support from the Congress.[74] With the 1929 Congress in Lahore less than four months away, the risk of Punjabi youth withdrawing their support from the Congress began to loom large in Motilal's imagination. Back in Punjab, the NJBS convened a public meeting to censure Motilal's 'autocratic attitude', prompting the senior Nehru to clarify his position in the *Pioneer*, warning readers that 'we are living in critical times and the youth of the country are our only hope, but that hope rests entirely on their strict sense of discipline'.[75] Two days later, on 8 August, the younger Nehru—then heavily embroiled in negotiations about his candidature for the presidency of the upcoming Lahore Congress—paid a visit to Bhagat Singh, B.K. Dutt, and Jatindranath Das in their Lahore cells. In a press statement praising their 'magnificent suffering', Jawaharlal credited them with rousing a

new consciousness of political life [that] once more made us all yearn for the liberty of our country ... [before adding, rather pointedly] What a contrast this is, compared with the unfortunate wrangles among Congressmen and the fighting for securing positions in the Congress and reception committee![76]

The NJBS was not easily assuaged, again condemning Motilal at its annual provincial conference in Amritsar on 9 August. Jawaharlal Nehru was invited to speak on 10 August, attracting a crowd of 6,000—approximately double that of the other sessions—at which he took the opportunity to chide the youth of Punjab for their readiness to criticise the actions of their elders. ... His speech [surmised the intelligence department] was hardly calculated to pacify the feelings of the extremists present. He told his audience that it was most necessary for them to discipline themselves, and warned them against any attempt to destroy the structure of the Congress, which represented the work of the last forty-six years.[77]

The following day, the CID reported that he took to the dais with Saifuddin Kitchlew, together delivering a speech in which they 'hardly veiled their conviction that, before long, methods of violence would be adopted ... the Conference was undoubtedly a success, beyond the expectation of its organisers, and the position of the Sabha, vis-à-vis the Congress has been considerably strengthened'.[78] The conference concluded with a speech from the NJBS's president, Amir Alam Awan, who urged those present to support the coming Lahore Congress.[79]

In early August, a procession of Congressites prevailed upon the revolutionaries to conclude their strikes. After Kishan Singh failed to convince his son to eat, Gopi Chand Bhargava visited the prisoners in Lahore, pointing out to them that Gandhi had always concluded his hunger strikes 'before getting to the extreme stage of committing the sin of taking his own life with his deeds'.[80] This had no effect. Bhagat Singh indicated that he would no longer negotiate directly with the government, instead devolving it to 'a Congress worker' to arrive at a settlement, which he would observe as long as it was along the lines of what he had requested.[81]

At the beginning of September, Ganesh Shankar Vidyarthi visited the hunger strikers to make a series of assurances on behalf of the Punjab Jails Committee: in short, they would extend special treatment to political prisoners if they concluded their hunger strike.[82] On 2 September 1929, thirteen hunger strikers, including Bhagat Singh and B.K. Dutt, broke their fasts, although Jatindranath Das refused. He was so gravely ill that his condition could not be reversed. The fasting had taken its toll, and the brutal regimen of force-feeding with a nasal-gastric tube had resulted in milk being injected into Das' lungs, causing pneumonia. The revolutionaries demanded the unconditional release of the ailing Das on 6 September; the government refused, and so many of the revolutionaries resumed their hunger strikes.[83] It was on the pleas of Congress leaders that these prisoners finally broke their fast after Das had died, as Motilal Nehru later reminded Emerson, in abeyance to a 'resolution passed at the last meeting of the All India Congress Committee for which I was mainly responsible'.[84]

Jatindranath Das' death on 13 September created a sensation (Figure 47). The subsequent mourning brought together members of the Congress and the NJBS at an All-India level. His bier was carried through Lahore by members of the Punjab Provincial Congress, and handed formally to representatives of the Bengal Congress, which took charge of the arrangements to take his body back to Calcutta.[85] The Intelligence Bureau interpreted this as mere Congress opportunism, but remarked

Figure 47: The front page of *The Tribune*, reporting Jatindranath Das' death on 15 September 1929. (Courtesy of the Supreme Court of India Museum)

on the significance 'that, at a meeting held at Lahore on 13th September to mourn the death of Das, no less than 10,000 persons were present, while at a Congress meeting held on the 22nd, to stimulate the boycott of foreign cloth, the audience numbered less than 300.'[86] Yet another report concluded that in Bengal, the youth movement and student associations 'have been so mixed up with Congress activities in connection with the death of Jatindra Nath Das, that it is not possible in the majority of cases to separate youth from Congress'.[87] Of even more consternation was the fact that Das' death brought together extremists from the discrete provinces that from a British perspective were best kept apart, as had happened earlier when Punjabi members of the NJBS had travelled to Calcutta in early August 1929 to hold 'Political Sufferers Day' jointly with the Congress 'under the leadership of Subhas Chandra Bose'.[88] It seems no coincidence that a poster issued by Kanpur's Coronation Press to celebrate the Indian Independence League leaders, Jawahar and Subhas, framed them in a moth motif, innocuously linking their politics to the symbolism used at the time to evoke the revolutionaries (Figure 48).

Roop Kishore Kapoor commemorated the support of the Congress for the revolutionaries' hunger strikes in a poster of Jawaharlal, as Congress president-elect, presenting Jatindranath Das' head to Mother India in the presence of B.K. Dutt and Bhagat Singh (Figure 49). The image is undated, but was most likely issued in late 1929. The play on the title, *Swatantrata ki Bhent: Amar Shahid Yatindranath Das* (The Gift of Independence: The Immortal Martyr Jatindranath Das), frames Jatindranath's death as a contribution to the freedom struggle, but also as an overt boost to the pro-independence forces against those in the Congress who preferred Dominion Status.

In the Legislative Assembly, Motilal Nehru moved to adjourn the house to discuss the political situation facing the country following Jatindranath's death.[89] He casti-

Figure 48. 'Subhash Chandra Bose and Jawaharlal Nehru', Kanpur: Coronation Press, c. mid 1929. (Author's collection)

gated the government for its failure to intervene early enough to save one of 'these devoted, high-souled men'.[90] Malaviya also delivered a speech contending that while the government had a duty to punish the revolutionaries, 'the Courts and the Government have yet to remember that they are not ordinary criminals who are promoted by sordid personal motives. [These are] men of high ideals, and possessed of a high sense of national self-respect.'[91] The motion to adjourn was passed by 55 to 47, with members as ideologically diverse as G.D. Birla, Chaman Lal Diwan, Muhammad Ali Jinnah, Kartar Singh, Rafi Ahmad Kidwai, H. N. Kunzru, and B.S. Moonje voting in favour. This catalysed an hour-long meeting between Motilal Nehru and James Crerar on 18 September, followed by another with Emerson the

Figure 49: Roop Kishore Kapoor, 'Swatantrata Ki Bhent: Amar Shahid Yatindranath Das' (Independence Gift: Immortal Martyr Jatindranath Das), Kanpur: Shyam Sunder Lal Picture Merchant, c. 1929. (Author's collection)

following day, in which Motilal extracted another undertaking that the Punjab government would extend special treatment to the prisoners.[92]

The government was surprised to note that Gandhi had 'made no public reference' to Jatindranath Das' death;[93] indeed it was not until late October that Gandhi explained his reticence, 'observed entirely in the national interest'.[94] Gandhi made a clear moral distinction between hunger striking and fasting.[95] In late September, the AICC passed a resolution at Gandhi's instigation, 'that hunger-strikes should not be resorted to except in a grave emergency'.[96] The revolutionaries ignored this, and in early 1930, fifteen Lahore Conspiracy Case prisoners were again refusing to eat. Reluctant to create another martyr through force-feeding, the prison authorities began to debate the wisdom of using anaesthetics to subdue them in order to administer nasal-gastric feeding tubes. When this was overruled, they questioned whether they had a legal duty to keep the prisoners alive at all.[97]

Counting down the days to the Lahore Congress, the Home Department observed these machinations with a sense of foreboding, aware that the capability of Jawaharlal to push through *purna swaraj* was predicated on support from 'the young men. The latter are out of hand and could be satisfied by no conceivable concession'.[98] The danger, according to this analyst, was that one end of the Congress spectrum could become entrapped in attempts to accommodate the irreconcilable 'young men', who would then quickly manoeuvre to overwhelm the leadership. A letter written by Bhagat Singh and B.K. Dutt was conveyed to the Punjab Students' Conference held in Lahore on 19 October 1929, and was read out in the open session. It pressed the youth to leave aside 'pistols and bombs', and throw their weight behind the Congress at the Lahore session, 'taking inspiration from the martyr Yatindra Nath Das'.[99]

The hunger strikes brought the revolutionaries to the fore of nationalist agitation and the public imagination. This compelled the government to devise ways of expediting their trial. David Petrie wrote of the 'deplorable situation' facing the Lahore Conspiracy Case trial, reasoning that a special legal ordinance was necessary to convict the revolutionaries:

[T]he accused are allowed freely to receive in Court visits from outside political notabilities. In recent months, they have been visited by such people as Subhas Chandra Bose and Dr Satyapal, whose presence has invariably been the occasion of the raising of revolutionary shouts, or of other gestures of defiance. It will be noticed from 2 [i.e. a cutting from the *Hindustan Times*, 23 December 1929] that the latest visitor to the Court was Pandit Moti Lal Nehru, who took his seat in the dock with the accused, and held conversations with them. The report goes on to say that after half an hour's interview with Bhagat Singh and the other accused, Pandit Motilal and his companion, Mohan Lal Saxena, left the Court. The next sentence runs: 'Before taking leave, he shook hands with each of the accused, and saluted them with folded hands'. It is not quite clear whether this was done by Pandit Moti Lal or Mohan Lal Saxena; but there seems to be no doubt that it was done by at least one of them, and not improbably by both. The effect of such conduct on the minds of impressionable young men, in leading them to imitate the crimes for which Bhagat Singh and other accused are on trial, can be nothing but disastrous. Unless something can be speedily done to speed up and improve the conduct of the proceedings, the whole trial is bound to be productive of far more evil than good.[100]

Just as the government was plotting to minimise the revolutionaries' influence, Motilal was working to garner their support, hence the above-noted appearance in court. Despite suffering from a bout of malaria, Motilal Nehru travelled to Lahore to meet Provincial Congress and Naujawan Bharat Sabha leaders to shore up their support prior to the Lahore Session.[101] In a letter to Jawaharlal, Motilal's description of his visit to the revolutionaries in court was brief. 'They were a jolly lot and were evidently very well looked after ... Bhagat Singh expressed a desire to have an interview with me. As I have no time tomorrow and am leaving for Delhi by the night train I could not give him an appointment'.[102] This letter seems to have been drafted entirely for the benefit of the Intelligence Bureau, to underplay the substance of the meeting in court.

Jatindernath Sanyal, one of the accused in the Lahore Conspiracy Case, witnessed the hushed exchange in the courtroom, enigmatically writing in his 1931 biography of Bhagat Singh that 'the writer would have very much liked to publish the important conversation that ensued between Moti Lalji and Sardar Bhagat Singh, but expediency demands silence on this matter. He hopes that time may come when it would be possible to do it.'[103] In a revised edition of his book published decades after independence, Sanyal was finally able to add that Bhagat Singh 'asked Motilal to make full use of the Lahore case and assured him that the country would see more positive actions by the revolutionary party'.[104]

Jaidev Kapoor was also with Bhagat Singh in court that day, and he too reported the exchange in his oral history interview. According to Kapoor, Motilal confided to Bhagat Singh that while he recognised the role of the revolutionaries in leading youth opinion to support *purna swaraj*, in his view, complete independence was premature. Motilal expressed his concern that the youth were not sufficiently disciplined to advance the movement, but at the same time, he was well aware that the Congress could ill afford to lose their support at this critical juncture. In response, Bhagat Singh said that if the Congress declared *purna swaraj* at Lahore, the youth would fall behind them, as would others—this seems to have been an allusion to the growing strength of the left, both within and without the Congress.[105] Motilal seems to have been assuaged by the exchange, for he came away from the meeting and immediately wrote a letter to the *Leader*, making a public appeal for the Lahore Conspiracy Case Defence Fund, declaring that 'it is a mistake to think that those who subscribe to the defence fund in any way associate themselves with a crime of the nature of which the accused are charged with'.[106]

Two days later, members of the HSRA performed another daring action, bombing the Viceroy's train as it entered Delhi on 23 December 1929.

Motilal's lightning visit to Lahore indicates the apprehension that the 'Old Guard' experienced in the lead up to the Lahore Congress. British observers interpreted Gandhi's refusal to accept the presidency of the Congress as ominous evidence that the Mahatma had realised that 'the mask of nonviolent noncooperation is about to be dropped—or has already been dropped.'[107] The presence of the revolutionaries on the political spectrum certainly influenced the fixture of candidature for the Congress presidency on Jawaharlal. In a letter to Gandhi in July, Motilal had advised that

The revolt of the youth has become an accomplished fact and there is no province in India today where it is not widespread. It would be sheer flattery to say that you have today the same influence as you had over the youth of the country some years ago and most of them make no secret of the fact. All of this would indicate that the need of the hour is the lead of Gandhi & the voice of Jawahar. It must however be remembered that even Jawahar is not a persona grata with a good many of them, specially those of the school of violence but perhaps he will be tolerated to a greater degree than any of us.[108]

Jawaharlal's reluctant acceptance of the leadership has also been seen as an indication of his 'sincere desire to build bridges with the radical ranks within Congress',[109] and the foisting of it upon him by Gandhi has been interpreted as a ploy to curb 'Jawaharlal's revolutionary zeal' by the burden of office.[110]

The Anatomy of an Action: The Attack on the Viceroy's Train

In the days before the Lahore Congress, the HSRA hatched a plot to introduce additional pressure on the deadlock around constitutional reform, scheduled for discussion at a special meeting of the Viceroy with Gandhi, Motilal, Patel, Sapru and Jinnah on 23 December 1929.[111] The operation to bomb Irwin's train as it entered Delhi, in what was subsequently prosecuted as the Delhi Conspiracy Case, was planned and executed by Bhagwati Charan and Yashpal, with the involvement of several other HSRA workers.[112] The action failed to kill anyone: due to the dense winter fog, visibility was low, and the bomb was activated too early, exploding before the Viceroy's bogey had passed.

The meeting with Irwin later that afternoon was to negotiate the terms for what would be the first Round Table Conference, which the Viceroy had indicated would be convened in London to discuss proposals for reforms. Irwin's October statement had vouched that the government had come to accept that 'the natural issue of India's constitutional progress' was 'the attainment of Dominion Status'.[113] Senior nationalists—a loose coalition of Liberals and Congress elders—signed the Delhi Declaration in early November, laying out their conditions for the Round

Table, which they conservatively agreed would not be to decide a date for Dominion Status, but a 'scheme of Dominion Constitution for India'.[114] Subhas Chandra Bose refused to sign, and Jawaharlal had only done so under duress from Gandhi.[115] Jawaharlal immediately began to rue his signature on the manifesto, and two days later wrote to his father and Gandhi resigning from the secretaryship of the AICC, pressing Gandhi to take up the presidency.[116] It is clear from his correspondence with the Mahatma that he was deeply unhappy—'agitated' and 'dejected'—with settling for Dominion Status.[117] Gandhi seems to have consoled him and persuaded him not to resign, and arranged to discuss the matter further when they next met.

The pressure that Jawaharlal came under for signing the declaration was ominously noticed by the Intelligence Bureau:

the young intelligentsia of Lahore are deeply pessimistic of the Congress and are grievously disappointed at Jowahir Lal Nehru's capitulation to Mr Gandhi and the older leaders. They declare that Jowahir Lal has foolishly allowed himself to be ensnared in the trap prepared for him by the Mahatma, and that by his election as President of the Congress, he has lost his power to act independently.[118]

Within days it was evident to Gandhi that the signatories of the Delhi Declaration had 'put on the Viceroy's statement about Dominion Status a construction which may prove to be wholly unwarranted.'[119] Objections from diehards in Britain about putting an end date to the perpetual 'not yet' of empire had become irrepressible,[120] and Irwin had begun to retreat, refusing to promise that Dominion Status would be on the Round Table agenda.

No record of the meeting on 23 November, with what must have been a still-shaken Viceroy, concedes that the attempt to bomb his train overshadowed the proceedings. Yet it was a watershed moment, as Sapru reported the meeting:

Mr Gandhi arrived at Patel's house at about 4 p.m. broke his silence at 4.15.p.m. and quietly went into the motor car with Pundit Moti Lal Nehru and drove to the Viceregal Lodge. … When we went in Mr Gandhi first expressed his horror at the attempt to wreck the Viceregal train which had been made that very morning. After that throughout the conversation he was most truculent which took us all by surprise. Pundit Moti Lal Nehru was scarcely less stiff.[121]

Then, Sapru wrote, 'Mr Gandhi took Jinnah, Patel and me by storm and held out an ultimatum to the Viceroy'.[122]

This was indeed a surprising development. In the month leading up to the meeting, Gandhi had made it clear that he was disengaged from the negotiations, on 4 December writing to Motilal that his presence at the meeting with Irwin was 'wholly unnecessary'.[123] By 14 December, he seems to have agreed to attend, but maintained that he would follow Motilal's lead in the negotiations with the Viceroy.[124] On the day of the meeting however, Gandhi found his voice, and became 'the main spokesman'.[125] Gandhi and Motilal Nehru, Irwin wrote in a letter to his father, were 'intractable and unreasonable, and seemed to me quite clearly to have come with the intention of being obstructive. There was therefore nothing to be done with them'.[126] Low reads Gandhi's late change of heart—a capitulation to Jawaharlal, no less—as a master-stroke that precluded a split in the Congress,[127] which would have left him powerless to control the escalating radicalisation and tacit endorsement of political violence in nationalist circles.

It is hard to imagine that Gandhi's decision to throw himself back into political action was not impacted by the attack on the Viceroy's train. The day after the attempt on Irwin, Gandhi opened his presidential speech at the All-India Suppressed Classes Conference with the admonition that 'Freedom can never be attained by exploding bombs on an innocent man. I regard it as a most outrageous crime.'[128] For the assault on the Viceroy animated the political landscape, as the *Times of India* breathlessly reported on Christmas Day:

Lahore is seething with excitement on the eve of the Congress session. The attempt to bomb the Viceroy is the topic of the moment. Everything else has paled into insignificance. Congress circles are worried, not so much over the failure of the Gandhi–Nehru Conference with the Viceroy, as over the effect on public opinion in India and outside of the attempt made by revolutionary miscreants to murder Lord Irwin.[129]

The project to target the Viceroy had been devised early in 1929, and Phanindranath Ghosh, an HSRA member who became an approver, revealed in court that Azad had sanctioned it.[130] The HSRA had made at least two other attempts on the Viceroy, both aborted at various stages of execution. As the Lahore Congress loomed, the preparations to bomb the Viceregal Special became mired with disagreements within the party.[131] As Bimal Prasad Jain recalled:

Lord Irwin was to meet Congress leaders, Mahatma Gandhi and Motilal Nehru and others to give a final reply to their previous demand of 'substance of independence'. So the Central Committee of the Revolutionary Party was divided in its opinion, whether the train should be blown up before the meeting takes place, or not. Some people were of the opinion: let the Mahatma and his meeting with the Viceroy [take place first], others thought that it would be an insult to go down on your knees to the Viceroy to request him to grant independence. So nothing could be decided.[132]

It was into this deadlock that Ganesh Shankar Vidyarthi weighed in, after meeting Azad in Delhi the day prior to the planned action.[133] Whereas Vidyarthi had supported the revolutionaries ideologically, financially and legally in the past, he now urged caution, writing an editorial in early December requesting that the HSRA abandon violence and join the Congress.[134] Vidyarthi personally discouraged Azad from carrying out the action, and Azad deferred to him, calling it off action.[135] However, Yashpal and Bhagwati Charan had invested much time and effort into planning the action. They reasoned that the ultimatum given at the Calcutta Congress had been totally ignored, and that the bombing would serve 'to impress upon the Government the serious consequences of ignoring the people's demands'.[136] They quietly proceeded to carry out the action, armed with the additional justification that Bhagat Singh had approved of the attack from jail.[137] Azad was furious with this indiscipline, but Yashpal later defended his decision to carry out the action on the basis that the political timing was the overriding factor.[138]

The Viceroy, for his part, responded to the attack with a proverbial stiff upper lip, writing to his father the following day:

They all tell me that it was very fortunate that no harm was done, but I can't pretend that I personally was at any moment greatly disturbed by it. It went off about three coaches in front of me when I was sitting in my saloon reading Challoner. I heard the noise and said to myself 'That must be a bomb'; and fully expected to hear something further happen. I then smelt all the smoke which came down the train, and concluded that it was a bomb; but, as nothing happened, I went on reading Challoner until someone came along and told me it had been a bomb and I went to see the damage.[139]

Irwin supposed that the bomb was planned to commemorate the anniversary of the attack on a predecessor, Lord Hardinge, as he entered Delhi in 1912. This does not seem to have entered into any of the revolutionaries' calculations: they were entirely focused on upsetting his meeting with the nationalists. The revolutionaries were in this case focused on influencing future politics, not rehearsing the past. Irwin fancied that the attempt on his life would strengthen his own position in India, 'for what it is worth'.[140] He then proceeded to complain about his meeting with the nationalists, before giving his father an overview of his plans for Christmas. Other reports of the bombing were far less heroic. Malcolm Darling wrote to his wife of a 'vivid account' he heard from a Mrs West, who was in the train when the bomb exploded. The force of the bomb was such that it was as though 'some superhuman power' had thrown her the length of the bogey.[141] Arguably Irwin had no choice but to outwardly downplay the effect of the explosion,[142] but Darling observed that 'it looks as if HE [His Excellency] has had his balance upset by that attempt on his life'.[143]

The Lahore Congress

Gandhi's agenda at the Lahore Congress was, as Judith Brown has noted, unenviable. Among other objectives, most notably addressing rising communalism, the Mahatma 'needed to stem the rising tide of violence and provide another outlet for the feeling of which it was symptomatic'.[144] The attempt on the Viceroy a few days prior brought the issue of violence in the anticolonial struggle to the fore. Jawaharlal had on the first day of proceedings put the resolution expressing appreciation for the 'self-sacrifice of Jatindra Nath Das', which had been so controversial in the months before, to the vote, and it was carried, 'all standing'.[145] The following day, Gandhi introduced a motion to condemn the action and congratulate the Viceroy and Vicereine on their 'fortunate and narrow escape'.[146] Unlike Irwin, who by his own account had not bothered to put down his bible to see if anyone else was hurt in the explosion, Gandhi included in the resolution his relief that the Viceroy's Indian staff were not harmed.

In his speech, Gandhi reminded the Congress of his nonviolent rationale. He had taken upon himself the moral responsibility for 'any thing that any single person born in Hindustan might do'; and he believed that violence harmed the national cause, on the basis that 'every bomb outrage has cost India dear', by inspiring repressive state violence.[147] 'We are the protectors of the Viceroy', Gandhi declared. Emily Kinnaird, a proponent of women's education in Lahore who was closely watching the proceedings, quipped that it would have been more true had Gandhi said that he alone was the protector of the Viceroy.[148]

The resolution had been debated in the Subjects Committee days before, on 27 December, where it was opposed by a number of committee members as being 'practically a loyalty resolution', although it was carried by 48 votes.[149] In the open session, the resolution failed and had to be retaken, indicating 'the strength of feeling on the violence issue', particularly from representatives from the provinces of Bengal and Punjab.[150] Heated debate followed. It was formally opposed by Swami Govindanand, whose speech is recorded in the formal minutes, although the extent of the ensuing debate is not.[151] Baba Gurdit Singh ('of *Komagata Maru* fame') spoke strongly against it, arguing that firstly, he suspected that the bombing had been orchestrated by the CID to create sympathy for the Viceroy and to advance their chances for promotion; and secondly, if the perpetrators were Indian, it was their right to 'avoid a life of slavery', even if it meant marching to the gallows.[152] 'This resolution was passed it was true', observed a 'Brief note on the Alliance of Congress with Terrorism', 'but only by a majority of 148, no fewer than 794 votes being recorded against it.'[153] The significance of such a thin majority was not lost on the HSRA, which would later question whether it was a reflection of 'honest political convictions', or the machinations of the Mahatma.[154] Bimal Prasad Jain believed that the vote was not a 'true indication of Congress feelings, since many votes in favour of the resolution were given solely from a sense of loyalty to Mr Gandhi,' who had insisted on its passage.[155]

An indication of rank and file support for the revolutionaries was apparent when the police arrived at the Congress Camp, Lajpat Rai Nagar, to arrest several members of the NJBS in connection with the attack, only to be prevented entry. Congress workers—including Manmohini Zutshi, the first woman to be elected president of the Lahore Students' Union—formed a procession of honour to escort

168

the suspects, Kiren Das (the brother of the late Jatindranath), Ram Kishan and Dhanwantari to the entrance of the camp, where they were ceremonially handed over to the police.[156] Another indication of a pro-revolutionary ethos became apparent when an Indian CID constable deputed to the camp was confronted by a number of volunteers, his face blackened and his money taken, he was told, 'for Bhagat Singh's defence fund'.[157] Perhaps this story filtered back to the Mahatma, who later that evening, in his speech in support of the motion to congratulate the Viceroy, urged those assembled to consider 'CID Indians also to be our kith and kin'.[158]

The 1929 Lahore Congress was by all accounts an extraordinary event, culminating on the evening of 31 December when Jawaharlal Nehru raised the national flag, declared *purna swaraj* to be the new aim of the Congress, and 'along with other young men of Punjab, started doing *bhangra*'.[159] The Lahore gathering committed the Congress to civil disobedience, although what this would mean was open to debate within the Congress leadership, ranging from Motilal's conception of comprehensive non-cooperation to that of Bose, who envisaged setting up a parallel administration.[160] These were details to be negotiated later—at the close of 1929, it was the euphoria of a triumphant and energetic section of the Congress movement that prevailed. Emily Kinnard wrote to her friends in England of the excitement of the gathering:

as I sat in the great meeting of over 1000 voters and 12,000 people, with some dozen Americans and Britishers, all sitting Indian fashion, so simple on the ground, I could feel the pulse pulsating through the meeting and could recognize the patriotic sense.[161]

The Lahore Congress represented as much a triumph over moderate politics as over the British. In his presidential address, Nehru betrayed considerable ambivalence about nonviolence, arguing that 'violence is bad, but slavery is far worse'.[162] For the government, the speech confirmed suspicions that 'the violence movement' was on the rise, and would soon be formally incorporated into the Congress program.[163] An anonymous correspondent at Lahore confided that:

'Inkalab Zindabad' (Long Live Revolution) was the most popular cry here, thanks to the wisdom of the Government, who have imprisoned several students for shouting it in the streets. The 'volunteers' ape in every detail the militarism of the West—so far with an inefficiency that would earn the contempt of a militarist as surely as it is the despair of the pacifist. … How long the Mahatma can hold this at bay I don't know. People say that but for him there would be bomb-throwing and shooting all over the country, and he has been bitterly attacked for it.[164]

Analysis from the Home Department concluded that a 'powerful section of the youth movement' had 'terrorised' the All-India Congress leaders into submission at the Lahore Congress, leaving them no option but to abandon their aspirations for Dominion Status.[165] Subhas Chandra Bose saw it more pragmatically, noting that 'Mahatma Gandhi, by advocating independence, was able to win over some of the Left Wing elements'.[166] Posters issued in early 1930 by the Coronation Press in Kanpur to celebrate the inaugural Republic Day seemed to acknowledge that the achievement was a joint project. The artist incorporated Bhagat Singh into an All-India flag-hoisting ceremony, in which the effort was shared across India's regional leaders, exemplified by Congress notables Malaviya, Rajagopalachari, Bose, Sarojini Naidu, and Jawaharlal, with Gandhi steadying the flagpole at India's centre (Figure 50).

Figure 50: 'Rashtriya Jhanda' (National Flag). Postcard, Kanpur: Radhe Lal Agrewal Picture Merchant/Coronation Press, c. 1930. (Author's collection)

The relationship between Congress and the revolutionaries in the wake of the Lahore Congress was summed up in a CID report:

Gandhi and the Nehrus have advanced towards the revolutionaries to an extent which must be causing acute discomfort to the elder Nehru at least. They courted their support partly through fear of their vociferous opposition and physical hostility, but mainly because they regard the extension of Congress influence to the rural and industrial masses as essential, and hope to find an avenue of approach through the communistic organisations, to which the various groups of revolutionaries belong. In this action the Congress leaders have given away everything—their position as a powerful political party and their protection under the law—and have got in return an anarchist rabble as audience, but not as a following. The revolutionaries are elated at the advertisement they have obtained, but will not obey even Jowahir Lal Nehru, unless he hands himself over to them body and soul. They will take up vigorously any activities which Gandhi may initiate which are capable of being conducted in revolutionary channels, but they will brook no control.[167]

Manifesto Polemics: The Cult of the Bomb and the Philosophy of the Bomb

It was not Motilal's 'acute discomfort' that came to the fore in January 1930, but the Mahatma's. During the Lahore Congress, the revolutionaries had circulated a manifesto written by Bhagwati Charan Vohra with input from Yashpal, which aimed to clarify the motives of the HSRA.[168] The manifesto maintained that organised armed rebellion would make colonial governance impossible, and that this was necessary to expeditiously liberate India from foreign domination. The Manifesto offered a critique of Gandhi, even as it conceded that the revolutionaries would be ungrateful if they did not recognise his talent for awakening the masses. That said, the manifesto described the Mahatma as 'an impossible visionary', claiming that his insistence on nonviolence was unprecedented in the global history of struggle. They defined their use of violence as counter-terrorism; a just response to government violence. The manifesto concluded with exhortations to the youth to 'shake off the paralysing effects of long lethargy' and to 'sow the seeds of disgust and hatred against British imperialism ... water the seeds with your warm blood'![169] An intelligence summary concluded that the pamphlet was 'a more reasoned production than the average leaflet of its type, [which] instead of confining itself to dire threats against the Government, endeavoured to show that violence, when its object was the emancipation of India, was not a bad thing'.[170]

Responding to this provocation, Gandhi drafted 'The Cult of the Bomb', a detailed critique of revolutionary praxis, delineating his moral, practical and political arguments supporting nonviolence.[171] He denied that revolutionary actions favourably influenced negotiations with the government, and ventured to speculate 'what would have happened if the Viceroy had been seriously injured or killed. There certainly would have been no meeting of the 23rd ultimo and therefore no certainty as to the course to be adopted by the Congress. That surely would have been, to say the least, an undesirable result.'[172]

Needless to say, the revolutionaries were exasperated by Gandhi's intervention. Chaman Lal Azad later revealed that the HSRA had hoped that Gandhi would respond differently, recognising them as fellow critics of the Raj:

Gandhiji condemned this bold revolutionary action and in a speech at Lahore declared that those who throw bombs are cowards! This created great indignation among the revolutionaries. When the Irish leader Parnell was asked to condemn the revolutionaries he had replied that he was not going to act for the police. The revolutionaries of India also wanted Gandhi to follow Parnell's example ... [but] the revolutionary movement progressed by leaps and bounds and it become a challenge to the congress. Gandhiji had sensed this change and in another famous speech had declared it is necessary to condemn violence to re-establish the supremacy of the Congress in India's politics.[173]

In interpreting the HSRA's formal response to Gandhi's article, it is important to note the difficulty in defining the revolutionary ideology of the HSRA; not only did it morph and develop substantially from the Association's inception, but it varied from individual to individual within the party. The riposte, 'The Philosophy of the Bomb', was written by Bhagwati Charan in consultation with Azad,[174] who by a number of accounts, was Gandhi's most strident critic in the HSRA.[175] First distributed on Independence Day (26 January 1930) in the form of a printed four-page leaflet, it 'appeared in considerable numbers in Punjab and the United Provinces',[176] and by the time the government discovered it in Bombay in October, it had become 'notorious'.[177]

Compared to the Manifesto circulated weeks earlier, it was a much more defensive document, declaring at the outset that 'the Indian National Congress, in conjunction with Gandhi, has launched a crusade against the revolutionaries'. While the authors assured Gandhi of their appreciation of the Congress movement, they were openly dismissive of the project of constitutional reform, asserting that their goal was nothing less than complete independence and revolution. They triumphantly quoted Sarla Devi Chaudhurani, a member of the emerging left in Congress, who had privately conceded the difficulty that Gandhi had in passing his motion congratulating the Viceroy. Irwin, they insisted, was no friend of India, for he had 'succeeded in shattering the unity between different political parties in the country that had resulted from the boycott of the Simon Commission'.[178] Rhetorically, the document asked: 'why press for the acceptance of truth by non-violence alone? Why not add physical force also to it?'[179] It is this double-track strategy that the revolutionaries envisioned as a more effective weapon against imperialism, even though Gandhi himself was resolutely opposed to nonviolence being harnessed in this fashion.

Gajanand Potdar, an HSRA member who worked closely with Azad, elaborated on this rationale in an oral history interview:

there were leaders like Motilal Nehru, like Dr Kitchlew, and some other extremist leaders. They were all very sympathetic towards us. They were sure that if extremist movements, like the revolutionary movement, grew, the bargaining power of parties like the Congress, that is the constitutional and legal parties, would grow. They will have more bargaining power. That is why they wanted us to develop our movement. But they wanted that we should not be rash and we just should not start an orgy of violence, just for nothing. We must select our plans and execute them very carefully.[180]

The appearance of the 'Cult of the Bomb' and its rejoinder—embedded as they were with irreconcilable critique—served to assure the government that the Congress and the HSRA were discrete and antagonistic movements, despite their close encounters leading up to the 1929 Congress. Evidence of collusion between the two remained elusive. In 1933, the government of India sent out a request for all provinces to report on the connections between terrorism and the Congress. With the exception of Bengal, no province was able to demonstrate such a link, other than the observation that the unrest of the Civil Disobedience Movement seemed to create a general atmosphere of 'disgust and hatred of the British', in which acts of violence were more likely to be interpreted by the public as retribution than as an 'outrage' of moral and political ethics.[181] 'The connection between terrorism and Congress activities', concluded one official, 'though obscure, is probably more of sympathy between two organisations fighting a common enemy than one of active collaboration'.[182] Such an impression gave Congress members who were linked to the HSRA the pleasure of deniability.

Civil Disobedience, the NJBS and the Bhagat Singh Defence Committee

With the onset of civil disobedience in April, Durga Das Khanna recalled, the HSRA purposefully stayed its hand, 'because we did not want any blame to be cast on our party in case Gandhiji's Salt Satyagraha failed'.[183] This decision seemed to follow the precedent set by Bengal revolutionaries during the Non-Cooperation Movement.[184] Gandhi announced in the press that he had received a communication from 'an alleged terrorist', giving him 'three years to attain the freedom of India by non-violent methods'.[185] Although the Mahatma was uncertain of which revolutionary party his correspondent 'Colonel Bedy' represented, he welcomed its promise.[186] 'The terrorists', wrote an analyst in the Intelligence Bureau, 'have professed an indulgent readiness to stand aside until nonviolence had met its (to them) inevitable failure'.[187]

Many Naujawan Bharat Sabha members and some members of the HSRA took part in the Salt Satyagraha; Comrade Ram Chandra, Rajendrapal Singh 'Warrior' and the incorrigible Chaman Lal all served time in prison as satyagrahis.[188] In the Punjab, the NJBS and some members of the Kirti Kisan Party advocated for non-payment of taxes to become a plank of civil disobedience.[189] The NJBS had, since

1928, been distributing Urdu translations of communist tracts to Punjab peasants in an attempt to revive the non-payment of land revenue or water rates.[190] Workers from the NJBS in Gurdaspur and Amritsar enforced a *hartal* when they heard of Jawaharlal's arrest in April 1930.[191] As revolutionary groups observed the escalation of police violence against *satyagrahis*, 'knowing full well that Congressmen were incapable of retaliation', they began to plot to 'match the terror of the police'.[192] The Asthi Chakkar Party in Punjab, formed by Inderpal, a former HSRA member, began a campaign to target the police with bombs.[193]

The HSRA Central Committee was far from inactive during this time. Peripheral party members began to pursue approvers, punishing them for giving evidence against their colleagues.[194] Punjab-based workers were engaged in fund-raising and planning an action to free Bhagat Singh and B.K. Dutt from jail. The bombs made for this action were so unstable that they exploded prematurely on 28 May, killing Bhagwati Charan Vohra; and again on 2 June, combusting in the HSRA hideout in Bahawalpur road, which had to be hastily abandoned.[195] In Delhi, Azad ordered a 'money action', holding up Gadodia Stores in July, on the basis of which they established an ammunitions factory under the front of 'Himalayan Toiletries' on Jhandewala Road.[196] Kailashpati, one of the HSRA's Delhi workers, was arrested on 28 October and agreed to become an approver, leading to a sweep of arrests that effectively wound up the HSRA's Delhi operations. Azad and Nigam left their refuge in Hindu College, returning briefly to Kanpur before setting up a base in Allahabad.[197]

The beginning of 1930 was initially a time of rapid expansion for the NJBS, with the organisation expanding to produce four newspapers—*Naujawan, Naujawan Sarhad, Naujawan Sarfarosh* and in Urdu, *Piam-i-Jang*. After several provocations in print and in public, the NJBS was progressively declared illegal across north India, its newspapers subjected to a Press Ordinance in key provinces; on 3 May, in the NWFP; in Punjab, on 23 June; and in the United Provinces on 30 June.[198] The ban on the NJBS coincided with a general sweep of arrests of Congress leaders, including Gandhi himself, who was arrested on 5 May. When Motilal applied for permission to visit Gandhi in Yeravda, the Viceroy determined that his intention was to inflame matters. The Viceroy discerned that Motilal was working to 'increase Congress militancy and attack Government's weak spots',[199] and so he too was arrested in Allahabad on 30 June, although he was released on 8 September 1930, due to his declining health. Durga Das Khanna claims that after his release, Motilal called Azad to his home in Allahabad to discuss revolutionary strategy, exhorting him to escalate the HSRA's campaigns.[200]

The formal ban on the NJBS seemed to change little, with an intelligence report observing that it simply recommended operations under a slightly different name.[201] In Punjab, the NJBS operated in camouflage as the Bhagat Singh Defence

Committee, which orchestrated an appeal for signatures for clemency following the announcement of the death sentences on 9 October 1930.[202] The government censor intercepted a communiqué from Motilal Nehru, which instructed that *hartal* be observed in protest against the convictions, and condemned the government for failing to ensure that the trio could adequately defend themselves, although he added the rider that during the *hartal* 'the creed of nonviolence should be especially enjoined'.[203] 'Eight Days Interlude', a Congress publication issued to chronicle Jawaharlal's brief release from jail to visit his father, contained a speech in which Jawaharlal reflected on both Mahatma Gandhi's nonviolence and Bhagat Singh's bravery.[204]

Bejoy Kumar Sinha recalled that Motilal sent messages to the revolutionaries from his sick bed, recommending that they appeal against their sentences.[205] Kumari Lajjawati, by this time working as a secretary of the Bhagat Singh Defence Committee, confirmed this. In her oral history interview, she recalled that Motilal had dispatched his son-in-law, Ranjit Pandit, to Lahore to bring her to Agra, where he gave her his legal opinion on the special ordinance that allowed for the revolutionaries to be tried in absentia.[206] He asked Lajjawati to bring him a copy of the ordinance and the judgement, and having read through them, he recommended that they take the case to the Privy Council.[207] Motilal had been thinking along these lines for some time. He had written to Purushottamdas Thakurdas in May, raising 'what I consider to be a very important matter', asking him to challenge the special ordinance to try the Lahore Conspiracy Case prisoners before the highest judiciary:

I have carefully studied this ordinance and am definitely of opinion that it is *ultra vires* of the Governor-General to pass it under Sec. 72 of the Government of India Act. ... the guilt or innocence of the accused is wholly immaterial. The only point is whether the Governor-General has any power to withdraw the case from a court which is seized of it and provide a special procedure for trial by a special tribunal.[208]

Bhagat Singh did not expect a reprieve, but agreed to the case being taken to the Privy Council in London, reasoning that it would popularise their case internationally and undermine the British reputation for impartiality and rule of law.[209] Additionally, Sanyal argues that there was a tactical advantage in prolonging the challenge: 'Bhagat Singh and others had an apprehension that the Congress might come to a dishonourable settlement with the Government; so he wished that the Government should hang him and his comrades at such a time when the hangings would strengthen the hands of the extremists and the younger party, and would reveal the weakness of the Congress.'[210] The Bhagat Singh Defence Committee advertised widely for donations to support the costs of the appeal, and received approximately two thousand rupees.[211] On 6 February 1931, Motilal died, apparently confident that the three condemned prisoners would not be hanged.[212] Five days later, on 11 February, leave to apply to the Privy Council was rejected.

Hearing of Motilal's death, Lord Irwin ventured to speculate how this loss would play out in the Congress, musing that 'on the whole, it will not be unhelpful, for he was so devoted to his extreme son that he was always concerned to support and shield him to the utmost extent possible. The result was that over Jawaharlal's extremer programme and policy there was thrown a cloak of moderation which tended to mislead many'.[213] In retrospect, the reverse seems to be true: after decades at the forefront of constitutional anti-imperial politics, in his final days, Motilal's revolutionary sympathies went undetected because the attention of the CID was focused warily on his son.

The Death of Chandrashekhar Azad

In his autobiography, Jawaharlal Nehru recalled

a curious incident about that time, which gave me an insight into the mind of the terrorist group in India. This took place soon after my discharge from prison, either a little before father's death or a few days after. A stranger came to see me at our house, and I was told that he was Chandrashekhar Azad. I had never seen him before, but I had heard of him ten years earlier, when he had non-cooperated from school and gone to prison during the NCO movement ... I was surprised, therefore, to see him. He had been induced to visit me because of the general expectation (owing to our release) that some negotiation between the Government and the Congress was likely. He wanted to know if, in case of a settlement, his group of people would have any peace ... they were convinced now that purely terrorist methods were futile and did no good. He was not, however, prepared to believe that India would gain her freedom wholly by peaceful methods.[214]

This particular reminiscence, curiously omitted in the American edition of Jawaharlal's autobiography, indicates that Jawaharlal might have inherited his father's clandestine relationship with Azad.[215] Yashpal, however, who was in Allahabad at the time, recalls that Azad was unhappy with the meeting, in which Nehru not only expressed his reservations about the utility of terrorism, but expressed his dislike of the HSRA's autocratic organisation. Subsequently, Yashpal also met with Jawaharlal, who refused to fund any 'terroristic activities', but agreed to pay for Yashpal and Azad to go to Russia for training.[216] Azad expressed some concerns that 'Indian revolutionaries should work for India's freedom only and not become Russian agents'.[217] This was not to be, for a week later Azad was gunned down by two police officers in Allahabad's Alfred Park, scarcely a stone's throw from the Nehru residence, Anand Bhavan, on 27 February 1931. Azad returned fire and the gun battle lasted half an hour,[218] but he died, according to Yashpal, with 500 rupees from Jawaharlal still in his pocket.[219]

Chandrashekhar Azad's death provided the occasion for the CID to note 'another striking example of the relations between the Congress and the terrorists', after the leaders of the Provincial Congress Committee in Allahabad 'took an active interest in the cremation of Azad's body'.[220] Purushottamdas Tandon, the president of the UP Congress Committee, collected Azad's ashes and organised a procession through Allahabad, culminating in a public meeting in Purushottamdas Park, where Kamala Nehru and Mrs Sachindranath Sanyal, 'the wife of a notorious terrorist convict', addressed a meeting organised by the Allahabad Students' Association. 'The immediate result of this public adulation', according to an intelligence report, 'was that later the same night a secret meeting was held, attended by some 40 students, all of whom took an oath, while rubbing the ashes of Azad on their heads, to avenge his death by killing the officer responsible for it.'[221] In closing, the report urged that these details remain strictly confidential, as their airing would undoubtedly expose their undercover informant.

A few days later, Chaman Lal organised a meeting in Delhi to mourn Chandrashekhar Azad's death, 'ostensibly under the auspices of the Naujawan Bharat Sabha but Shankar Lal Basal, president of the Delhi Congress Committee, took the chair'.[222] The meeting passed a motion 'congratulating Azad on his brave martyrdom' with the caveat that the meeting differed 'with his creed and line of action, [but] it appreciates his great patriotism, sincere bravery and selfless sacrifice'. A memorial fund was formed, with donors urged to send money to 'Pt. Jawarhar Lal Nehru, the President of the All-India National Congress, who would spend it as he thought proper'.[223] Chaman Lal circulated a photograph of Azad's body in Alfred Park,[224] and delivered a speech which was transcribed by a CID officer:

Many people say that why the Congressmen congratulated men like the late Azad. He added that the day before yesterday the Superintendent of Police CID asked him not to hold this meeting, because by holding such meetings he helped the men of violence creed. He remarked that they were the followers of the policy of non-violence but it was their duty to congratulate the martyrs like Azad. The speaker said that what ever the trouble comes, he will face it.[225]

By 1931, a discourse had been negotiated and established in the Congress of acknowledging revolutionary bravery while formally, and sometimes procedurally (as in Chaman Lal's case) invoking the policy of nonviolence. Ironically, the precedent for this contradictory policy came from Gandhi himself, in his addendum to the Saha resolution in 1924.[226] Renegotiating and ultimately retracting this discourse would be Gandhi's difficult task in 1931, in the aftermath of Bhagat Singh's death.

The insertion of the revolutionaries of the HSRA into the politics of the Civil Disobedience Movement invites a fresh consideration of the Congress–Revolutionary nexus, and of Motilal Nehru, for it complicates the conclusion of his contemporaries,[227] historians and biographers that 'for Motilal ... the only authentic expression of militant nationalism in India was the Gandhian weapon of satyagraha'.[228] Presumptions that it was Motilal who consistently dampened Jawaharlal's militancy in the late 1920s need to be reconsidered, as it would appear that as his health began to falter, the father exceeded the son by advancing towards more strident means and methods to help deliver what had been almost a lifelong struggle. And yet Motilal was mourned by the British-owned newspaper, the *Pioneer*, which lamented that had he survived his illness, he would 'at the present critical juncture have exercised a moderating influence in the counsels of his political colleagues',[229] as Gandhi proceeded to negotiate a truce with Lord Irwin. Revolutionary memoirs maintain that Chandrashekhar Azad joined Motilal's funeral procession, from Anand Bhavan to the Triveni, incognito.[230] Motilal's death was commemorated by Roop Kishore Kapoor, who created a powerfully poignant homage to the veteran Congressman with revolutionary sympathies (Figure 51).

Figure 51: Roop Kishore Kapoor, 'Mata ki Vilaap: Anant Shaiyya', (Mother's Lamentation: The Eternal Rest), Kanpur: Shyam Sunder Lal, c. 1931. (Author's collection)

The interactions between the HSRA and members of the Congress High Command were politically significant, and were mediated by individuals whose sympathies overlapped with both Congress and NJBS ideologies. These collaborations operated around and despite Gandhi. When provoked, the revolutionaries could be harshly critical of the Congress's formal adherence to nonviolence and the Mahatma, as the polemical 'Philosophy of the Bomb' shows. Means aside, the HSRA had a more comprehensive social revolution as their ultimate goal, yet the overall aim of expelling the British converged with those of the Congress. As such, they justified shaping Congress programs, and saw their own actions as injecting impetus to the government's general intransigence. They did not conceive of themselves as operating entirely independently of the larger Congress movement, and they actively encouraged the convergence of patriotic interests, believing that their own interventions made strategic contributions to the broader anticolonial struggle. The repercussions of this tactic would become clear in March of 1931.

PART III

THE AFTERMATH

GANDHISM AND THE CHALLENGE
OF REVOLUTIONARY VIOLENCE

7

THE KARACHI CONGRESS, 1931

In 1931, India's ides of March were charged with a combination of expectation and tension, a complex and contradictory convergence of emotions following the excitement and the strain of civil disobedience. As a result of the Gandhi–Irwin Pact, concluded on 5 March, the movement was withdrawn, government ordinances pertaining to the movement expired, and all nonviolent prisoners were freed. In a letter to the Secretary of State for India, Irwin surmised that 'the country is generally tired of strife' and welcomed 'the restoration of normal conditions'.[1] But conditions were far from normal. In Punjab alone, the release of 12,000 prisoners in mid-March had 'inevitably resulted in a considerable increase in excitement', in which celebrations of their release merged with protests over the impending executions.[2]

It is usually at this moment that Bhagat Singh enters the annals of mainstream historiography, as historians almost invariably note in passing the pressure that the impending executions placed on the negotiation of the pact, and subsequently on Gandhi at the Karachi Congress. A sizeable body of literature has grown up around what has become a polarised debate about why Gandhi was unable to save Bhagat Singh, Sukhdev and Rajguru from their fate.[3] Many of these debates attempt to establish the degree of vehemence with which Gandhi requested that the executions be halted, or question why he did not make it one of the terms of his pact with the Viceroy.[4] This debate has raged in India ever since 1931, even though it was a series of British judgments that sent the trio to the gallows.

A great many imperatives were brought to bear on Irwin and the India Office in the lead up to the Gandhi–Irwin Pact and the second Round Table Conference.[5] The presumption that Gandhi was in a commanding position with the British was imagined in a poster produced by the Shyam Sunder Lal Press in Kanpur, in which the King eagerly reaches out to pump the hand of a relaxed, if not jubilant,

Mahatma in London (Figure 52). This was not borne out by the Gandhi–Irwin negotiations (regarded as a squandered opportunity by Jawaharlal, among others), or indeed by the ultimate failure of the pact.[6] The conclusion that he was responsible for the executions fails to consider the extraordinary pressure exerted on British decision-makers to implement the maximum punishment. As a communist contemporary from the M. N. Roy camp—otherwise a harsh critic of Gandhi—reflected, the 'Mahatma could not save Bhagat Singh and others, even if he wanted to. He cannot get from the reluctant hand of imperialism any more than it is prepared to grant voluntarily without injuring its position.'[7] The face of empire had much to lose at home and in India by showing clemency, which given the political pressures of the time, it was not prepared to risk. The executions need to be woven into a broader, empire-wide fabric, which unfurls with the politics of expatriate Britons in India and their ability to play to Conservatives in London who were frankly aghast at the idea of constitutional reforms.

Panic in the Punjab

The Gandhi–Irwin Pact was negotiated in Delhi behind closed doors. Prior to its conclusion on 4 March 1931, there was considerable speculation about its terms;

Figure 52: 'Mahatmaji meeting the King-Emperor in Buckingham Palace', Kanpur: Shyam Sunder Lal, c. 1931. (Courtesy of Claudia Hyles)

according to R. E. Hawkins, an interested observer in Bombay, 'the great public has been fed exclusively on rumour'.[8] The prevalence of one rumour in particular seems to have animated nationalist circles in mid-February. News that the Viceroy had confidentially given Gandhi an in principle agreement to commute the death sentences began to spread, and many eminent Congress leaders, including Motilal Nehru and Subhas Chandra Bose, seemed utterly confident that the Viceroy would honour this commitment.[9]

However in a public statement on 20 February, Gandhi's secretary Mahadev Desai categorically denied any such concession had been made, claiming that the source of the rumour—Dr Satyapal, in 1931 serving as a member of the Congress Working Committee—had either been misquoted or was misinformed.[10] Several oral history testimonies disclosed that Satyapal had given a speech in Punjab, in which he assured his audience that Gandhi had broached the topic with Irwin in early February.[11]

It is unclear whether this story was based on a misinterpretation, at some point of communication, about the fate of 'political prisoners' who had been arrested during the Civil Disobedience Movement, whose freedom Gandhi did negotiate in the Pact. The term 'political prisoners' had been much used since 1929, and was often used—particularly by the revolutionaries and their supporters—to describe revolutionaries in jail.[12] The principal claim during the hunger strikes was that the revolutionaries ought to be treated as political prisoners, not criminals, and this was eventually tacitly although uneasily accepted by the government. It was more common, however, for the government to make a distinction between political prisoners and 'prisoners guilty of crimes of violence' or similar discursive formulations, as euphemisms; when under pressure, they wrote of 'murderers' or 'terrorists'.[13]

There were die-hards in the Civil Service who felt that even negotiating for the freedom of nonviolent political prisoners was folly, as we will see below. Given the infamous fuss Winston Churchill had created in England upon hearing that Irwin had condescended to negotiate with a certain 'seditious saint … striding half-naked up the steps of the Vice-regal Palace',[14] it is understandable that the Viceroy might have been anxious to avoid the perception that he was, via the Mahatma, negotiating on the behalf of 'terrorists', which he had vowed in July 1930 never to do.[15] On 13 March 1931, Irwin had written to the King acknowledging the impropriety of a Viceroy meeting 'the principal leader of a subversive movement', but pointed out that this was mitigated by the exigencies of public opinion in India and in the US.[16] By the end of the year, the King himself would receive Gandhi, although perhaps not in the warm fashion imagined by the artist in Figure 52.

Oral history accounts maintain that the news that the three condemned men were to be awarded clemency leaked out and soon reached the ears of Punjab's civil service. Wincing under the weight of a series of attacks on public servants, and especially the police, 'the entire civil service in the Punjab, including the Governor' are said to have panicked, cabling the Secretary of State in the India Office with the threat to resign en masse if the sentences were commuted.[17] Rumours of this ultimatum quickly disseminated in the Punjabi public sphere: they were noted in Lahore's weekly, *The People*, reproduced in the *Tribune*;[18] and reflected in reportage in Patna's *Searchlight*.[19] But they find no mention in Anglo-Indian newspapers such as Lahore's *Civil and Military Gazette* or Bombay's *Times of India*, or for that matter the *Times* of London, despite their obviously sensational news value. There is no mention in the Halifax collection of any threatened resignation from the Punjab, nor in the private papers of Punjab-based officials.[20] No cable is held in the correspondence of Wedgewood Benn, the Secretary of State, although Benn did write to Irwin in April about a 'mere rumour [in January 1931] of an amnesty for political prisoners [which] had caused a good deal of increased activity against the law by those who were anxious to take the opportunity of indulging in a short term of martyrdom. This kind of thing is certainly very embarrassing and tends, I fear, to distract from the value of any act of amnesty'.[21]

It is this confusion—about whether the amnesty of the Pact would extend to those accused of violence—that seems to have given rise to a general expectation that the executions would be stayed. Penderel Moon was surprised at the extent of this belief, writing to his father from Lyallpur that '[m]any people were strangely of the opinion that the Viceroy would commute the sentences, and I was fortunate enough to win a bet that they would be hanged.'[22]

Traces of the resignation story are still circulated in India today, sometimes with minor reassignments of the characters threatening to resign. A relatively recent version has it that 'the police officers in Punjab and also British members of the Indian Civil Service had in a letter to the Viceroy and the Government threatened resignation unless Bhagat Singh and his compatriots were hanged'.[23] The tale of the threatened resignation suggests fissures in imperial governance, revealing a gulf between 'men on the ground' in Punjab, Delhi and in London, at a time when elements in the Conservative Party clustered around Churchill were resolutely opposed to the Pact about to be negotiated with Gandhi by one of its own, Lord Irwin.[24] It seems unlikely that an ultimatum could have been delivered without so much as a paper trail, a ripple of controversy, or a frisson of triumph from the British community of Punjab when the hangings did take place. Yet there are a few grains of truth in the rumour, inasmuch as there was speculation and substantial division within the British Indian body politic, perhaps best illustrated by the divide between the Governor of Punjab and the Viceroy.

Apart from a colonial grand tour in 1904, in which he sailed to Australia via Bombay and overland to Calcutta, pausing in Delhi to stay with the Curzons, Irwin had very little experience in India prior to his appointment as Viceroy. He was known to be out of step with Conservative interests in London, who rued that he had become worn down by 'those Indian politicians who come to talk to him + are no doubt most persuasive + damnably clever'.[25] The Governor of Punjab, Sir Geoffrey de Montmorency, the other important figure in this scenario, was an experienced India hand. He had joined the Indian Civil Service (ICS) in 1899, arriving in India one year later, where he served in Punjab before being transferred to Delhi.[26] His most distinguished role was as private secretary to Viceroy Reading (1922–26); prior to that he had organised the controversial Indian tour of the Prince of Wales in 1921. After Reading's departure, he served under Irwin for a few months until his appointment to the Governorship was confirmed.[27] De Montmorency was a diligent bachelor with a reputation in the ICS for an 'incapacity for personal relationships'.[28] Unsurprisingly, de Montmorency's correspondence with Irwin from late 1930, when he was shot at by Hari Kishen, reveals a Governor under considerable strain. He had struggled with a substantial rise in political violence in his province; he oversaw the administration that pursued the complicated Lahore Conspiracy Case trial, engaging the hunger striking revolutionaries in a long and dramatic stand-off, before urging for a special ordinance to try them in absentia and sentence three of them to death. For precisely these reasons, de Montmorency became a target of the HSRA.

By January 1931, both the Viceroy and the Governor had survived revolutionary actions, but each seems to have responded differently to their brush with death. Without question, de Montmorency's encounter was much more dramatic than Irwin's experience; the former's escape was both very narrow and very recent, and no doubt foremost in his mind as the executions edged nearer.[29] De Montmorency described his near-miss in a letter to Irwin, written the day after the incident, on 23 December 1930:

I seem to have had a very lucky escape. As I was just moving out of the door of the University Convocation Hall, after the end of the Convocation, six shots were fired from behind me by someone nearly at point blank range. So far as I can recollect, the first and second shot hit me: in both cases, the assassin was behind his bird, as the first shot passed through the upper part of my left arm, which happened, apparently at the moment, to be behind my body, and the second grazed my ribs along the back on the left side. I think I had just turned the corner beyond the door, when the other four shots went off. I am sorry to say they did damage, one of them wounding and subsequently killing a poor sub-inspector. … I had a rather painful afternoon yesterday and a somewhat restless night but I am feeling much better today and have no temperature and the wounds seem to be going on all right. I shall take it quietly for a day or two.[30]

In his New Year's message to the Viceroy a few days later, de Montomorency wrote '1930, the more I look back on it, has been a bad one, and the worst part of it to me at any rate has been the coincidence of the economic worries with the political ones'.[31] For a man who had come under fire the week before, this seems like an understatement.

De Montmorency's correspondence reveals that he was on several occasions at odds with the Viceroy.[32] De Montmorency believed that Irwin was a little too gentle and far too liberal in his handling of the nationalists. He was disparaging of 'Grandpa Gandhi', and in early 1931 was generally 'pessimistic' at the idea of releasing nonviolent political prisoners and told Irwin so.[33] He predicted that the Congress would not hold to any terms they agreed to in the Pact, maintaining that the release of Congress workers would undermine the morale of the Indian police who had arrested them, leading to a situation in which they would, rather sensibly, question any future orders to arrest their satyagrahi-compatriots.[34]

De Montmorency vociferously defended his administration and saw the police as its backbone, strongly recommending senior members of the Punjab police for King's Birthday Honours for their service in controlling the 'unprecedented' wave of revolutionary activity in the province.[35] Given this, he was frankly aghast at the Viceroy's suggestion in early 1931 that the provinces voluntarily submit to budget cuts as a prudent response to the depression.[36] Yet at no stage in the available correspondence does the issue of whether to carry out the executions arise. A meeting of officials from the Home Department and the Punjab administration was convened on 17 February in New Delhi to discuss issues of procedure and the timing of the executions.[37] When it was all over, on 30 March, Irwin wrote to the Secretary of State praising de Montmorency for his 'adroit handling' of the executions.[38]

While the story of the telegrammed ultimatum remains unsubstantiated, what can be established is that the *notion* that Gandhi had covertly supported Bhagat Singh, Rajguru and Sukhdev by advocating for their clemency obtained contemporary currency.[39] It is graphically illustrated in *The Lone*, in which the Mahatma opens his chest to reveal the hanged trio peering out from within (Figure 53). The scene is dignified by the memory of the same three, framed in stars, accompanied by a portrait of Bhagwati Charan (top right of the picture). The image evokes a story widely celebrated in Hindu visual culture. Hanuman's devotion to Sita, Ram and Lakshman was once questioned by impetuous courtiers who dismissed him as 'just another monkey'. In response to this insult, the divine Hanuman tore open his heart to reveal Sita, Ram and Lakshman inside.[40] The adaptation of this chest-opening device, suggesting a self-disclosure, indicates a secret knowledge of Gandhi's sympathies; that he did indeed apply himself to the task of saving the trio. Unable to publicly reveal that he did so, he opens his heart to B. K. Dutt, and as the title would suggest, B. K. Dutt alone.[41]

The posthumous presence of Bhagwati Charan Vohra is another distinctive aspect of this image. Like Azad, Vohra died a wanted man. His portrait was never publicly circulated while he was alive, nor was it released to the media immediately after his accidental death. Printed by a Lahore-based publisher whose dominant trade was religious pictures, this image is based on a portrait most likely sourced from revolutionary contacts; perhaps this interpretation of events was communicated to the artist at the same time.[42]

Murderous Outrages in the Punjab

By March 1931, the cumulative effect of 'outrages' piled upon the British community in Punjab became focused on Bhagat Singh, its most notorious representative. The escalation of violence in British India led to outbursts of threatened

Figure 53: 'The Lone', Lahore: Krishna Picture House, c. 1931. (Courtesy of NMML, Kulbir Singh Collection, Album 808, 36509)

vigilantism, and in both Bengal and Punjab, branches of the European Association called town hall meetings to complain about what they saw as a soft government unwilling to exert its authority to the full extent. Such concerns were no doubt aggravated by dramatic changes in the imperial zeitgeist in the early the 1930s.[43] Cherished ideologies of the Raj were being slowly but surely dismantled, apparent in the rejection of the paternalism of the Simon Commission and its replacement with Round Table Conferences, even if one of the most valuable outcomes of this was 'the education of British opinion'.[44] More alarmingly for Britons in India, long-established patterns of colonial violence had begun to be reversed. Since 1929, violent attacks on Europeans in India had escalated dramatically. The arrests of key members of the HSRA and the subsequent airing of their objectives through the court had only inspired more 'outrages' on British interests and persons (Table 1).

Table 1: Tabular Statement of the number of Crimes of a Terrorist Nature committed in India during the years 1929 and 1930.[45]

Year	Bengal	Bihar & Orissa	Bombay & Sind	Burma	Central Provinces	Delhi	NWFP	Punjab	United Provinces	Total
1929	8	1	2	Nil	Nil	2	Nil	3	3	19
1930	34	2	7	3	1	4	2	17	4	74
Grand Total										93

While colonial data indicated that Bengal was the most 'unruly' province, consistently exceeding the number of 'crimes of a terrorist nature' committed elsewhere, there was a dramatic increase in the Punjab. Three violent incidents in 1929 escalated to seventeen in 1930, at a time when Irwin wrote that 'the violence party are holding their hand to a considerable extent while they await results of civil disobedience'.[46] This argument no doubt was intended to put pressure on debates among Conservatives in Britain who were resisting a renegotiation of India's relationship with the Empire.

The government of India could not seem to check the growth of violence, with various indications that anticolonial violence was morphing in its modality, making it harder to predict and detect. Violence was no longer the preserve of organised parties, noted the government of the United Provinces, but was 'committed by persons who … by improving on the insane methods of Mr Gandhi, thought they could do something to free the country by exploding bombs at odd places, by cutting telegraph wires and such like stupid methods.'[47] This rise in political violence injected an overdose of anxiety into British residents in India, greatly undermining 'the pleasure of ruling', as Bhagat Singh himself noted.[48] Such pleasures had already been dramatically scaled back during the Civil Disobedience Movement, which (in concert with the depression) substantially interrupted the profitability and the predictability of British India.[49] By early 1931, the Anglophone public sphere in India resonated with shrill arguments that repeatedly alleged that the Civil Disobedience Movement was responsible for the rise in violence.[50]

The level of panic in the European population of Punjab escalated considerably after the murder of an Englishwoman in the Lahore Cantonment on 13 January 1931. Sajjan Singh's initial plan was to kill Captain Curtis, who according to one account he held responsible for his dismissal from the army. Arriving at the Curtis home in the Lahore cantonment, Singh learned that his target was out of station. In the statement he gave in court, he saw Mrs Curtis and 'it struck me Europeans had killed many of my brethren, and that I should not return empty-handed.'[51] He 'murderously assaulted first Mrs Curtis, and then her two children',[52] reasoning that in Jallianwala Bagh women and children had also been killed.[53] Mrs Curtis' two daughters were hospitalised after the attack and survived, but she did not, succumbing to her injuries later that evening. This attack on the vulnerable underbelly of the Raj—an innocent mother and her daughters—sparked indignant outbursts of fear and outrage from the British community in India and beyond. Particularly graphic accounts of the murder were published in the dominions, incorporating fictional twists in which the assailant was construed to have killed his mistress.[54] Such reportage was deliberately redolent of mutiny narratives, which emphasised the sudden and undue transition from servitude to treachery. Nor was this the first time that the British community in Punjab 'took fright', anticipating a resurgence of 1857.[55] In Punjab, the murder raised memories of the attack on Marcia Sherwood which in 1919 provoked one of the most notorious instances of colonial humiliation, the 'crawling order'. Government policy was blamed for the violence; 'Result of Labour's Laxity', proclaimed one tabloid.[56] Despairing that Bhagat Singh and his colleagues had still not been hanged, one anonymous correspondent wrote that 'If conviction and execution (preferably in public) were to follow close on the heels of a murderous outrage such as occurred in Lahore Cantonments last week, the Government will have provided the strongest possible deterrent to potential evil-doers'.[57]

In mid-January 1931, the Punjab Legislative Council convened to discuss 'anarchical crimes' at length. Responding to a suggestion mooted by Mahomed Din Mahomed, Sir Henry Craik (the Finance Member, representing the Civil Service in the debate), said:

One speaker in this debate commented that this outbreak of revolutionary crime coincided with the start of the civil disobedience movement and he is perfectly right. Nobody who has studied the civil disobedience movement closely can come to any conclusion other than that the persons promoting the movement are in sympathy with, and have incited the commission, of violent crime. The movement calls itself non-violent, or did call itself non-violent.

We do not hear very much about non-violence now and I think it is almost time that people running the movement should drop this futile mask of non-violence.[58]

Craik went on to quote extensively from Jawaharlal Nehru's speeches in support of the Lahore Conspiracy Case hunger strikers, and similar public statements by Sen Gupta, Satyapal and Kitchlew, castigating the Congress for its links with the Naujawan Bharat Sabha.[59] However he maintained that there was no need to seek further powers from the center in order to deal with the situation.[60]

The British expatriate community in Lahore felt differently. Robert Owen, a businessman and Member of the Legislative Council, convened a meeting of Europeans and Anglo-Indians at which he 'accused the Punjab Government of complete ineptitude and said that the entire responsibility for the increase in terrorist crimes in the Province could be laid at its door'.[61] The meeting at the Lahore Gymkhana was ostensibly to condole Mr Curtis, and was so densely attended that many could not gain entry. An anonymous correspondent to the British newspaper of Lahore, the *Civil and Military Gazette*, proposed the formation of a 'League of Loyal Citizens', intended to pressure the government into ensuring that justice be 'meted out to the loyal people as well as to the Congress Wallahs'.[62] Such activism was encouraged by sensationalism that the *Gazette* had indulged in following the attack on de Montmorency ('Terrorist Outrages: The Forces of Lawlessness have been set Loose'), and more anonymous letters published by the editor, which vented moral outrage at the rising violence that Lahore's 'law-abiding citizens' were forced to endure.[63] 'I hope we get through this phase', wrote a worried de Montmorency to Irwin, 'but in my past experience there is always a danger of a Tommy with a glass or two inside him taking reprisals off some Indian that falls into his hands'.[64]

It did not help that during the trial, Sajjan Singh had declared himself to be a member of the Congress,[65] feeding the perception in the European community in Lahore that the nonviolent platform of the Congress masked a covert program of anarchy.[66] David Petrie argued that

it is clear that he is typical of many others who have imbibed the teachings of the Congress, and it would be hypocrisy to deny that the agitation which seeks protection behind the threadbare cloak of non-violence is responsible for their production. The seeds shown by the recognised leaders of the Congress movement, by their veiled hints in favour of violence, are now bearing fruit. It was inevitable that raw uneducated country youths, whose natural instincts led them to violence, once caught in the maw of the Congress, would not be able to appreciate the subtlety of non-violence.[67]

Representatives of the Sikh community went to press with a statement that the attack was entirely contrary to the principles of Sikhism and repugnant to its followers;[68] and Indian representatives in the Punjab Legislative Council went to great lengths to explain that the violence movement was a separate current to Gandhi's.[69]

Sajjan Singh was swiftly tried, and sentenced to death on February 7. In court he gave a long account of the history of British oppression since the mutiny, before summarising that

he had come to warn the British Government that a revolution had started in the villages and only a match was required to kindle the conflagration. In the end he said he admitted having murdered Mrs Curtis and would again do similar acts if allowed to live. He did not want to give a defence, and urged that he be hanged without delay.[70]

Sajjan Singh's lawyers appealed against his death sentence on the basis that he was insane, but this was rejected by the Lahore High Court[71] and he was hanged on 9 April 1931. It is clear that he had acted alone and was not connected to any revolutionary movement,[72] but he had adapted some of the tactics of the Lahore Conspiracy Case prisoners by refusing to give much of a defence, in his discourse of revolution, and in actively embracing execution. These similarities allowed a panicked population to make unwarranted conceptual leaps, wildly extrapolating on the direction of things to come. A long letter signed by 'Justice' asked 'Will the last act of "non-violence" in the name of Congress arouse our apparently spineless Government to the fact that a state of disorder exists in the country? ... As a citizen and taxpayer of this country, I ask with thousands of others "are our wives and little children to be left open to such outrages on the part of an unlawful body?"'[73]

In the wake of the death of Mrs Curtis, following close on the heels of numerous other attempted or failed attacks amounting to 'seventeen outrages in ten weeks',[74] It mattered little to the stressed population of Lahore that from jail Bhagat Singh had surmised that violent tactics should be of strictly limited and careful application, writing, in a manifesto aimed at the youth movement:

Terrorism is a confession that the revolutionary mentality has not penetrated down into the masses. It is thus a confession of our failure. In the initial stages it had its use, it shook the torpor out of the body politic, enkindled the image of the young intelligentsia, fired their spirit of self-sacrifice and demonstrated before the world and before our enemies the truth and strength of the movement. But by itself it is not enough. ... The pleasure of ruling may be bombed out or pistolled down, but the practical gain from exploitation will make him [the imperialist] stick to his post.[75]

Bhagat Singh's musings in jail urged restraint on the revolutionary movement. They were smuggled out of prison and circulated in underground circles. However by 1931, violent attacks were no longer the preserve of revolutionary organisations, as demonstrated by Sajjan Singh's case. Such individual acts were not constrained by the codes of discipline intended to regulate actions coordinated by the HSRA; but in the eyes of the European community in India the two were conflated. The Punjab government was staffed with citizens alarmed by what they saw as a state of anarchy in the province that could in their eyes only be restored by the state summarily executing those convicted of murder.

The Gandhi–Irwin Pact and the Road to Karachi

When his agreement with the Viceroy was finally announced on 4 March, Gandhi directly addressed the revolutionaries:

There is ... a small but active organisation in India which would secure India's liberty through violent action. I appeal to that organisation, as I have done before, to desist from its activities, if not yet out of conviction, then out of expedience ... I want them to be patient, and give the Congress, or if they will, me, a chance to work out the plan of truth and non-violence ... Let them preserve their precious lives for the service of the Motherland to which all will be presently called and let them give to the Congress an opportunity of securing the release of all the other political prisoners and maybe even rescuing from the gallows those who are condemned to them as being guilty of murder. But I want to raise no false hopes. I can only state publicly what is my own and the Congress aspiration.[76]

Following Gandhi's declaration in February that the release of political prisoners accused of violence would not be a condition of the impending pact, Chaman Lal swung into action. He produced and began to circulate a one-page polemic on red paper, 'Where is Peace?'. One breathlessly long sentence adequately communicates Chaman Lal's indignation at what he saw as Gandhi's abandonment of those accused of violence, whose sacrifice, in his view, had energised the anti-colonial struggle:

And those who could not believe in the Policy of the Mahatma and the path shown by him, *who went through the penance of liberation by shedding fresh blood from their heart*, who left their homes called to the play of fire by the exuberance of rising Youth, who could never lower their heads before with the meanness of supplicants before the oppressive rules, who had not the effrontery or hypocrisy of making a show of war with the determination of a compromise, who yearned for liberation through the path leading to the scaffold with the vow of death, *who thrusted sharp dagger into the heart of the oppressor with the accumulated wrath caused by minds receiv*ed, who tried to pay the oppressors in their own coin, *who created terror in the heart of the enemy with the terrible roar of fierce fire arms*, who cleared the path to the next world of a few Englishman as a reply to the persecution of the English, who showed valour by snatching away from the persecutor the means of his persecution, who removed the blot of cowardice of the Bengalis, *who showed the living path as though the English could be injured by armed rebellion*, and whom the English are determined to crush either by hook or by crook and by staging false trials with a view to efface even their very memory from the heart of the country, for them this is not peace.[77]

On 7 March, following a meeting in Delhi at which Gandhi addressed an estimated crowd of 50,000, Chaman Lal's sister-in-law Satyawati delivered a copy of 'Where is Peace' to the Mahatma.[78] According to a fortnightly report, Gandhi was compelled to explain to the audience that while 'he was unable to obtain the release of violent political prisoners at present, he was averse to any form of corporal punishment and hoped to be able to obtain their release when the reins of power were in the hands of the Congress.'[79] Gandhi knew that Chaman Lal was the author of 'Where is Peace', and yet he continued to work with his critic, apparently unperturbed.[80] By provocatively signing the manifesto 'Young India', Lal suggested that Gandhi was no longer representative of the youth that he invoked weekly in his newspaper of the same name.[81] 'I have claimed to be a young man of 62', retorted the Mahatma, 'But even if I were to be labeled as a dilapidated old fogey, I have a right to appeal to your good sense.'[82]

With the annual Congress meeting to ratify the Gandhi–Irwin Pact scheduled to open on 29 March, Irwin was aware that this was a critical time for Gandhi and the Congress as a whole. The Pact had been criticised by 'the extremist section of the Congress and particularly by the youth element', and Irwin confided to Benn that 'many believe that a split in the near future is almost inevitable'.[83] It is also clear that the Viceroy knew that the executions of the Lahore Conspiracy Case prisoners would 'gravely prejudice' an already sensitive political situation.[84] The Punjab government proceeded to make arrangements for the executions, debating with the Home Department whether to carry them out before or after the Karachi meeting.[85] The government of India favoured afterwards, but realised that this might create unreasonably false hope for a reprieve, or leave an opening for commutation of the sentences to be a condition of the acceptance of the pact by the Congress. After much discussion, the Home Department accepted the Punjab government's decision to execute the prisoners 'no later than March 23, and earlier if practicable'.[86]

Speculation was rife among nationalist circles in Lahore that if the executions were carried out prior to the Congress session, the meeting would be cancelled altogether. Many concluded that the government would not risk such a calamity, which would imperil the Gandhi–Irwin Pact. Vallabhbhai Patel's presidential address could not be finalised until the prisoners' fates were known, although a report carried in the *Tribune* claimed that a draft had been made assuming commutation.[87] As late as 25 March, the *Tribune*'s editor dedicated three columns to a plea to 'Commute those Sentences', reasoning that the government's only capacity to disarm revolutionaries lay in doing so, and threatening that no peace or truce would be gained by execution.[88] Typeset too late to retract, the editorial was published in the same edition that announced the executions on its front page.

The Evening Executions

The Punjab government had presumed that news of the evening executions would not spread until the following morning, 'but an inkling of this had already leaked out from some pressmen and youths who had collected in the house of Santanam, a Congress leader, just opposite the jail' shortly after the event.[89] The political response to the executions was immediate. Branches of the Naujawan Bharat Sabha had been energetically working to avert the executions, taking 'full advantage of the many processions and meetings, which have taken place in honour of the released prisoners, to proclaim its sympathy with proclaimed murderers'.[90] Hearing the executions had been carried out, the NJBS branch in Jhang sent urgent telegrams to the Congress Secretary in Karachi insisting that the Pact be immediately revoked and that civil disobedience recommence.[91]

In the days after the executions, the fate of the pact seemed grim. As a fortnightly report dryly noted, 'Gandhi's failure to secure their reprieve confirmed the view of many that his victory at Delhi had not been so complete as his followers had been at some pains to make out it was.'[92] Jawaharlal Nehru's public comment—that the corpse of Bhagat Singh would stand between the Congress and the British—quickly reverberated in British circles, introducing an element of dread for those who had welcomed the Gandhi–Irwin agreement.[93] Even Lahore's *Civil and Military Gazette* published the circumspect views of their Delhi correspondent, that 'sane and sober elements of the European community', felt that the executions were impolitic and inopportune.[94] Horace Alexander—the Quaker who had visited India to study the plight of political prisoners the year before—wrote of his conviction that the executions had been expedited by 'sworn enemies' of Mahatma Gandhi, Lord Irwin and the Delhi Agreement.[95]

News of the executions came as Congressites were en route to Karachi. Chiranjilal Paliwal was present when the Viceroy's secretary delivered the news to Gandhi, boarding a train at Delhi Railway Station:

Gandhiji kept quiet. Nehru read it and fell as if into a trance. Then he regained his composure, and said: well, let us see, lest we forget, lest we forget … He repeated these two-three words. And then Gandhiji was dumbfounded.[96]

Chaman Lal was on the same train to Karachi. When people came to greet Gandhi at the railway stations en route, Chaman Lal intercepted them, crossly instructing them not to shout 'Mahatma Gandhi ki jai', because he had failed to save the three convicted prisoners in Lahore. He later marveled at the Mahatma's response to this provocation in his oral history testimony: 'Gandhiji simply smiled and would say: "All right, now that you have had your lecture, give me your shoulder so that I can go outside and address the audience." Never once—from Delhi to Karachi—Gandhiji felt angry at my rude behaviour.'[97]

On 21 March, in anticipation of the executions, Mahatma Gandhi had taken the precaution of wiring Karachi Congress organisers with a request to abandon the traditional procession to welcome the president, Vallabhbhai Patel.[98] To forestall a similar reception for himself, Gandhi made arrangements to alight from the train at Malir, one station before Karachi. Arriving on 24 March, he was received by protesting NJBS volunteers; neither Chaman Lal nor Comrade Ram Chandra knew how they had learned of Gandhi's plan to alight there, although it would seem to be indicative of a level of communication between Congress and NJBS workers in Sindh.[99] They presented him with a garland of black cloth flowers, 'representing, I imagine, the ashes of the three patriots'.[100] Malaviya was furious, turning on Chaman Lal and scolding him for the NJBS's disrespect of elders.[101] But Gandhi graciously accepted the garland, and addressed the crowd, disconcerting the protesters, as one of the NJBS workers, Jeet Mal Lunia wrote:

Look at the magic of the magician! A big meeting takes place. He talks to the youth about Bhagat Singh's hanging and his own personal feelings. He praises their wisdom in their offering him black flowers also. Instead of expressing displeasure, he showers his love on them. He forgets his insult and instead feels sorrow for their pain, the wounds inflicted on their hearts and tells them that they could lop off his head if they wanted to, but they could not kill Gandhism.[102]

The remarks of Jaidev Gupta, Bhagat Singh's childhood friend, also in Karachi for the Congress, concurred: 'The atmosphere was of mixed nature. There were two camps, one was anti and the other was pro [Gandhi]. But Mahatma Gandhi was such an orator ... who by his reasoning, sweet voice, calm and quiet manner, would convince the public that what could be done was done.'[103]

At a press conference on his arrival in Karachi, in the presence of several foreign correspondents, Chaman Lal challenged Gandhi openly, asking why he had not secured the release of all political prisoners and a reprieve for the condemned revolutionaries. Gandhi's response exposed both Chaman Lal's complicated subjectivity and the Mahatma's quick wit:

Gandhiji evaded the question with a very interesting joke. He said: 'I have known four Chaman Lals, one whom I met in his village in 1920, one who worked under me in the Congress for so many years, one who is secretary of the Nau Jawan Bharat Sabha and one who is representative of the *Hindustan Times*. Which Chaman Lal is asking this question?' Everybody burst into laughter and the question was avoided.[104]

It was only later, in private, that Gandhi confided to Chaman Lal that he had done all he could to avert the executions, but that pressure from the Punjab had compelled Irwin to proceed.[105] Chaman Lal concluded his oral history interview with the view that 'it is important that historians and people in India know that it was not Gandhiji who failed.'[106]

Other journalists at the press conference pressed Gandhi on the issue of the executions, and he conceded that the timing of the hangings was 'a first class blunder' jeopardising the truce, and declared that he would go into retirement if the pact was not ratified.[107] He concluded by predicting that the revolutionaries would realise the error of their ways, declaring that 'whatever may be true of other countries, in this country, with its teeming famishing millions, the cult of violence can have no meaning'.[108] The CID was closely watching Bose and Jawaharlal to gauge their responses, knowing that if there were to be a challenge to Gandhi from within the Congress, it would come from them.

The Naujawan Bharat Sabha in Karachi

In Karachi, the news of the executions was met with a silent procession of 8,000—that it was a silent procession indicates that it was organised by the Congress in accordance with Gandhi's instructions—followed by a public meeting attended by 15,000.[109] However, in Punjab, the Naujawan Bharat Sabha dominated the protests over the executions, its 'undisguised or thinly veiled repudiation of Gandhi and the Congress … frightening most politicians who possess any sense of responsibility'.[110]

The NJBS had organised its annual conference to coincide with the Karachi Congress, commencing on 27 March. On the morning of the conference, 400 NJBS members took 'what they declared to be a charred remnant of Bhagat Singh in procession' through Karachi 'without any untoward incident', although there was trepidation in the report that they intended to 'force entry to the Congress Pandal'. The police, the Commissioner assured the Home Department, 'are taking necessary precautions'.[111] A band of seven NJBS workers, 'all but one Punjabis', stormed the Congress camp, and 'Jawaharlal had to save Gandhi from physical attack'.[112] Later that evening, Gandhi granted members of the NJBS an interview, in which 'they explained that it was never their intention to do any physical harm to him … and that individual terrorism was not their creed'.[113] They pressed upon Gandhi the idea of the formation of a socialist republic in India, and expressed their dissatisfaction with the pact.

The NJBS's 1931 conference was presided over by Subhas Chandra Bose, who was 'confidentially reported to have accused Gandhi at an AIWC [All-India Working Committee] meeting of blundering in making peace'.[114] The accuracy of this report is implied in *Indian Struggle*, where Bose used precisely the same language—that by suspending civil disobedience, the party leaders were 'committing a blunder'.[115] The same tone was carried into his 'militant' presidential speech at the NJBS conference,[116] which castigated the 'vagueness and mental reservation in the mind of the leaders' of the Congress,[117] before embarking on an extensive and eloquent critique of the pact as 'exceedingly unsatisfactory and highly disappointing', delineating no less than seven weaknesses.[118]

However instead of leading a breakaway faction from the Congress, as many analysts had anticipated, Bose argued for restraint. He later reflected that if 'the Government was so anxious to create a split, there was something to be said in favour of avoiding it'.[119] He announced that the left wing of the Congress would support the Pact, even though they disapproved of it, and he urged those present to refrain from confrontational politics. Hearing of this, the Home Department concluded that Bose had been 'completely won over' by the Mahatma.[120] However the *Bombay Chronicle's* interpretation favoured the notion that there was a pragmatic view about the importance of unity in March of 1931: 'The youths realised that the execution of Bhagat Singh and his companions was carried out on the eve of the Karachi Congress with a view to create a split in the ranks of Congressmen. Therefore they had in the interests of the country decided to stand solidly behind Mahatma Gandhi and send him to London as the accredited representative of the country.'[121]

While the Congress avoided the predicted split at Karachi, the NJBS did not. Its annual meeting was attended by political notables, including Madan Mohan Malaviya and two of his sons, Kamala Nehru, and Kamaladevi Chattopadhya. The conduct of the meeting revealed a deeply divided movement.[122] The presence of Congress members made it difficult to pass resolutions. Comrade Ram Chandra moved a resolution denouncing the Gandhi–Irwin agreement, but this was countered by 'most of the prominent Congressmen present'.[123] At the same time, large numbers of members of the Kirti Kisan group, who had been working with the NJBS for some time, began to assert their increasingly communist politics. Malaviya had been invited by one section of the NJBS to speak, but he was shouted down by the Kirti Kisan faction so boisterously that he had to be escorted safely from the dais.[124] Bose too recalls that this faction of the NJBS 'openly declared that they were against terrorism and that they believed in mass action on Socialist lines'; this would appear to have been the faction that went to confront Gandhi.[125]

The Congress Proceedings

Zaidi was not exaggerating when he referred to the proceedings of the 45th annual session of the Indian National Congress as being held 'under circumstances which were memorable and unique'.[126] Additional pressures were brought to bear on the gathering when the news of the rioting in Kanpur filtered though. The violence had started 'as an anti-English demonstration' after the news of the executions spread on 24 March,[127] but quickly turned into a communal affray when Muslim shopkeepers refused to close their shops as instructed by a resolution of the Kanpur Congress.[128]

Overzealous Congress workers had attempted to forcibly close the stores, inflaming existing tensions and sparking a riot in which 'probably between four and five hundred' were killed.[129] Several members of the AICC were sent abusive letters from Kanpur Muslims who blamed the Congress for the violence,[130] and a subsequent government enquiry into the outbreak concurred. There was also an element of personal loss for many Congressites with the arrival of the news of Ganesh Shankar Vidyarthi's death, in which, as an editorial in the *Tribune* reflected, 'the

United Provinces have lost a great patriot, the Mussalmans have lost a great friend'.[131] When the news of Vidyarthi's death was delivered to the AICC, a pall fell over the session, as Jawaharlal would recall: 'A telegram came and it broke our hearts—there was sudden darkness before our eyes'.[132] Paliwal went so far as to say that it was not until Vidyarthi's death that the Congress began to take communalism seriously.[133] This sounds like a significant claim, but the Kanpur riots were momentous and inspired 'the first attempt by the Congress Party to comprehensively state their position on Hindu–Muslim relations',[134] in the form of the weighty Kanpur Riot Commission Report.

The violence in Kanpur emphasised not only the gravity of communalism, but the depth of feeling that Bhagat Singh's execution had stirred in Congress circles. The first day of the Congress meeting began with a motion by Jawaharlal to adjourn the Committee for fifteen minutes 'as a mark of respect for Bhagat Singh and others executed at Lahore'. This was seconded by Maulana Zafar Ali, who added that 'Bhagat Singh was an institution who, next to Gandhiji, had drawn the whole of India towards himself'.[135] In the open session, Bhagat Singh was the second item of business, following a condolence motion for Motilal Nehru. Jawaharlal rose to put a resolution (which had been drafted by Gandhi) to the vote:

The Congress, while disassociating itself from and disapproving of political violence in any shape or form, places on record its admiration of the bravery and sacrifice of the late Sardar Bhagat Singh and his comrades Sriyuts Sukhdev and Rajguru and mourns with the bereaved families the loss of these lives. This Congress is of the opinion that Government have lost the golden opportunity of promoting goodwill between the two nations, admittedly held to be essential at this juncture, and of winning over to the method of peace the party which, being driven to despair, resorts to political violence.[136]

Having dutifully read out the statement, Jawaharlal departed from the script, stating that 'it would have been more appropriate if the resolution was moved by Gandhiji who had drafted it, or Mr Vallabhbhai Patel who was at the helm of Congress affairs today'. He then went on to praise Bhagat Singh, remembering him as 'a clean fighter who faced his enemy in the open field. He was a young boy full of burning zeal for the country.[137]

Nehru's speech was applauded, and the motion was seconded by Malaviya, who said that 'the fact that young men took to violence showed that all was not well in the country and something had made them desperate.'[138] While acknowledging that the government had 'a large share' in making young men into revolutionaries, Malaviya spoke the language of caution, requesting the audience to desist from violence 'because we love you young men and we know too well the dangers of the cult and we do not wish to sacrifice any more Bhagat Singhs.' Malaviya emphasised that bravery and courage were equally required in nonviolent action, before introducing Bhagat Singh's father and Rajguru's mother to the audience. Kishan Singh spoke for over half an hour, appealling to the youth for patience and wisdom, and relating episodes from his son's life, which was received with 'thunderous cheering' and cries of 'Bhagat Singh zindabad!'[139]

When the Bhagat Singh resolution was put to the vote, V. L. Shastri, a delegate from Andhra Pradesh, stood to move an amendment to delete the clause 'disapproval of political violence'. Shastri carefully explained that he was 'a humble apostle of Mahatma Gandhi', who had 'lived the life of non-violence for 365 days of the year ... facing all the attacks of violence that the Government was capable of'.[140] Yet Shastri felt moved to put on the record that the disapproval clause 'did not do justice to the sacrifice' of the hanged trio, and he deplored what he saw as 'half-hearted, stinting, grudging compliments to the great men who had been executed'.[141] Shastri's objection to the 'disapproval' clause drew attention to the complicated manner in which the Congress had formally negotiated instances of political violence since the Saha resolution was passed and amended in 1924.

The Congress leadership had expected this challenge, and had made contingency plans. Kamaladevi Chattopadhyaya had initially agreed to second Shastri's amendment, but had since been prevailed upon not to proceed, although a seconder was found in Tarachand Lalwani.[142] Anonymous others 'who had given notice of their intention to move and second two amendments' to the Bhagat Singh resolution withdrew them.[143] Shastri had addressed the audience in English, and requested that his translator be allowed to speak so that the Hindi speakers in the audience might follow him. This was denied, and Shastri began to argue with Patel, who firmly told him 'to sit down and obey the chair; his amendment went to a vote and lost'.[144] According to the *Tribune*'s correspondent, when Shastri objected, 'the loud speakers fouled and Mr Shastri protested that they had been put out of order'.[145] Further discussion was firmly closed.

An assessment by the CID, cabled to the Secretary of State by the Viceroy, was impressed that Gandhi had been able to brook so much opposition. 'Extremists probably realised from outset that they are not at present in position to detach themselves from main body of Congress which follows Gandhi who has probably persuaded them to keep quiet until they see what he can do at the Round Table Conference.'[146] The left, however, was beginning to consolidate its position. The CID heard rumours that M. N. Roy had been at Karachi, which his biographer confirms.[147] Intelligence reports noted that the circulation of revolutionary literature, 'much, but not all, of it Communist', at the Karachi Congress was 'stupendous'.[148] The publishers of *The Masses*, 'the organ of the committee for organising the revolutionary working class party of India', was dismissive of the Karachi Congress, describing it as 'a congregation of blind devotees come on pilgrimage to the shrine of a saint'; 'a political *Kumbh Mela*, where the occasional cry of "Inqilab Zindabad" could be uttered only on sufferance'.[149] It was after the Karachi Congress that the left within the Congress began to move towards organised socialism, which later fed into the formation of the Punjab and Congress Socialist Parties in 1933 and 1934.[150] Many former HSRA members would follow.[151]

The Karachi Compromise

In balancing the politics of the pact against the executions, Gandhi 'was caught between incompatible demands'.[152] Intelligence analysts later concluded that the combined pressures from the NJBS, radical elements of the press and those sympathetic to their politics had intimidated the Congress into passing the Bhagat Singh resolution.[153] As Bose conceded, Gandhi was in an extraordinarily difficult position, forced to choose between his own commitment to nonviolence and conceding the popularity of the revolutionaries: at Karachi Gandhi 'had to make his conscience somewhat elastic'.[154] As a result the Bhagat Singh Resolution he drafted was fraught with tension, rejected by supporters of the hanged men, and criticised by the government and in the British press for its 'half-hearted condemnation of political violence'.[155] Gandhi would later regret the resolution, 'not because it was wrong in principle, but for the misinterpretation it has lent itself to.'[156]

Yet an assessment of the annual session by the Home Department concluded that the conference represented a win for Gandhi, for he managed to avoid the widely-predicted split by drawing the radicalised youth back to the Congress. The cost of this manouvre was high, as one report concluded: 'Mr Gandhi managed to secure their silence at the price of sympathetic resolutions on the subject of terrorism in general and Bhagat Singh and his confederates in particular'.[157] This was coupled with the Fundamental Rights resolution, aimed at satisfying leftist circles within the Congress, who might have led a breakaway faction.[158] Judith Brown felt that it would do an injustice to the friendship of the Mahatma and Jawaharlal to conclude that the Fundamental Rights resolution was a 'blunt quid pro quo for Jawaharlal's public support' at Karachi, although this is precisely how government reports accounted for Jawaharlal's assent to the Gandhi–Irwin Pact in March 1931.[159]

Within a week, Gandhi felt the repercussions of the Karachi compromise. On 8 April, the Mahatma travelled to Amritsar with other Congress leaders to attend a meeting of the Central Sikh League, in an attempt to address the general alienation of Sikhs from the Congress movement.[160] The strain of recent events must have overwhelmed him, for he fell ill and was unable to attend the meeting on 9 April, attended by 20–30,000 people. Bhagwan Das, who had witnessed much in his time as a long-serving member of the CID in Punjab, described the four-hour meeting as 'too bad for words'.[161] He went on to describe the 'poisonous atmosphere' of the meeting, redolent with speeches 'full of vituperation and abuse of the worst type and open defiance of authority or inflammatory to violence'.

Satyapal's speech in particular was 'very objectionable and full of praises of Bhagat Singh etc., and badly critical of Government'.[162] Sarojini Naidu and Subhas Chandra Bose were reported to have eulogised Bhagat Singh, and a resolution in his honour was passed.

The following day, on 10 April, in the absence of senior Congress leaders an amendment was proposed to add the name of Sajjan Singh, the murderer of Mrs Curtis (executed the day before), to a motion appreciating the sacrifice of Bhagat Singh, Rajguru and Sukhdev. 'Votes for the amendment were more than those against it', a CID agent noted, and Master Tara Singh attempted to overrule it, but lost.[163] The vote was widely recorded in reportage implying that Congress members present the previous day had enthusiastically congratulated Mrs Curtis' murderer.[164] This conflation in the public sphere of the murders of two Britons—Saunders and Mrs Curtis—forced Gandhi to intervene.

In a statement in *Young India*, published the following week, he reasserted his arguments in favour of nonviolence, and opined that

The extolling of murderers is being overdone. ... The praising of Sajjansingh as a hero raises a doubt in my mind about the wisdom of my having been the author of the Congress resolution about Bhagatsingh. My motive was plain enough. The deed was condemned. The spirit of bravery and sacrifice was praised. The hope behind that was that we would hereby be able to distinguish between the deed and the motive, and thereby learn to detest deeds such as political murders, no matter how high the motive might be. But the effect of the Congress resolution has been perhaps quite the contrary. It seems to have given a passport for extolling murder itself.[165]

A month later, Gandhi was called to a series of meetings with Emerson in Delhi. Emerson claimed that ongoing eulogies to Bhagat Singh by Congress members constituted a new and subtle form of exhortation to violence, constituting a breach in the terms of the Delhi Pact.[166] Gandhi was shown pages of evidence collected by the government that the Pact was being abrogated daily by rank-and-file Congress workers speaking in support of Bhagat Singh.[167] In response to this and other infractions of the terms of the agreement, Rajgopalachari issued a ten-point circular with clear behavioural guidelines to all party workers, which concluded with the following admonition:

We should not make any approving references to acts of violence. Congratulation of bravery and self-sacrifice on the part of persons committing acts of violence are unnecessary and misleading, except when made by persons absolutely pledged to non-violence in thought and deed as Gandhiji.[168]

Emerson 'seems to have been well pleased' with Rajagopalachari's circular, writing to Gandhi in May of his satisfaction.[169] However exhortations such as these were only going to constrain those followers of the Congress who were readily restrained by the niceties of resolutions and the threat of jail. Many were not, such as the Karachi-based publisher of a poster discovered in June 1931, in which 'John Bull is confronted by Gandhi holding the banner of freedom, while a masked revolutionary holds a pistol to his head. The publisher was sent to jail during the civil disobedience movement and appears to be anxious to return there'.[170] The poster and its publisher were indicative of a crossover between revolutionary and Congress methodology, evidence of a strategy of the simultaneous exertion of violence and nonviolence as part of the anticolonial struggle, in which the threat of the former would compel the British towards the latter. In the coming months, both the government and Gandhi turned their attention to the elimination of violence from nationalist sympathies.

8

CONTROLLING POLITICAL VIOLENCE

THE GOVERNMENT, THE CONGRESS AND THE HSRA

At the beginning of 1931, the government of Punjab concluded that violence was incited and nurtured by three sources: 'Congress leaders, the press, and demonstrations glorifying the perpetrators of such crimes',[1] and it proceeded to exert pressure on each of these in an effort to restore security. Notably absent from any of these factors was any sense of governmental responsibility, which was often central to the statements of those accused of violence.[2] In government circles, the role played by economic factors in pressing the youth to extremes was debated, but generally ruled out of contention, on the basis that youth unemployment was an All-India phenomenon, yet anticolonial violence seemed to be confined largely to north India and Bengal.[3] Even more constructive critics read political violence as an unrestrained, unprovoked and immature outburst, surmising that 'it is not hunger, but emotion and sentiment that lead at least to 90 per cent of the terrorists to paths of violence.'[4] While the government would later congratulate itself on its effective management of the revolutionary challenge in north India, many groups including the HSRA began to re-think the role of violence in political action in the 1930s. The ebbing of the revolutionary wave of political violence therefore had as much to do with ideological factors within the remnants of the HSRA as with governmental repression.

In the immediate aftermath of Bhagat Singh's death, it became evident to the government that the maximum use of the punitive apparatus of the state actually encouraged assassinations. The widespread acceptance of Bhagat Singh, Rajguru and Sukhdev as martyrs proved to be a powerful inducement to more violence, not less. The Home Department began to grapple with 'a comparatively new phenomenon', for 'terrorists can now be found who are prepared to commit outrages in circumstances which must almost inevitably result in their death or capture'.[5] In Bengal, Shanti Ghosh and Suniti Choudhury, who shot and killed a British Magistrate on 14 December 1931, were frustrated to be sentenced to transportation—their aim had been to 'become the first women martyrs'.[6] Whereas previously 'terrorists had been content to target European officials', the spin placed on the murder of Mrs Curtis allowed the British to deduce that revolutionaries had come to regard 'any important non-official European as fair game'.[7] These new variables injected urgent imperatives into the task of countering anticolonial violence, and the government set its sights on redefining the definition of incitement to violence in the press.

Eulogy as Incitement: The 1931 Press Ordinance

Not long after the onset of civil disobedience, the government promulgated a Press Ordinance in April 1930 allowing for a loose interpretation of what constituted 'seditious material'.[8] This was subsequently lifted on 5 March 1931 as one of the terms of the Gandhi–Irwin Pact.[9] As a result, there was technically little restraint on the press in the weeks prior and months following the executions, a situation which the nationalist media, which had been heavily monitored during civil disobedience, took full advantage of. In the months after their deaths, Bhagat Singh, Rajguru and Sukhdev were more popular than ever. Bhagat Singh in particular was the subject of speeches, the object of *pujas*, and the name in whose honour people observed fasts and *hartals*, the star character in plays, poems and songs.[10] The 'epidemic' of eulogy literature, according to one analyst, 'is very serious, for it gets youth thinking on terrorist lines and this widens the field for terrorist recruitment to huge dimensions. It also incites persons unconnected with terrorist organisations to commit crimes on their own'.[11]

The response of the press to the executions was particularly strong in Punjab, placing the administration in the difficult position of balancing the spirit of the pact with the need to manage the public response to the executions, in which eulogies became construed as incitement. Irwin, whose attention was more focused on his immanent departure, gave de Montmorency permission to prosecute any who could be found inciting violence: 'I see no reason at all, under the terms of my agreement with Gandhi, why we should find ourselves debarred from dealing with incitement to violence and the like'.[12] In reality, this was legally questionable, although several arrests were indeed made under Section 302 of the Penal Code (which related to actual murder) for speeches, before a separate ordinance was introduced to cover such prosecutions.[13]

In the meantime, Geoffrey de Montmorency was left to deal with a difficult province. With Lord Willingdon, recently bereaved by the sudden death of his son, still settling into the rhythms of Viceregal office, de Montmorency gave a frustrated speech in Simla in late April, complaining that 'the patience of the Punjab Government has been abused by disregard of the Delhi Agreement by the rank and file of the Congress'.[14] The speech was repeated in the House of Lords, where Lord Reading quoted his former secretary as opining that British 'toleration has only in the end bred licence'.[15] De Montmorency's anxiety was thus introduced into the political debates in London leading up to the Second Round Table Conference. Die-hard sections of the Conservative Party, led by Winston Churchill and supported by Lord Rothermere and the Indian Empire Society, a body of 'old India hands' formed by former Punjab Governor Michael O'Dwyer, cohered to avert the devolution of power to Indian hands.[16]

At the end of April 1931, the government of Punjab sent a file of eulogy literature—comprising twenty articles and seven images, including *The End*, which rendered Bhagat Singh as a crucified Jesus (Figure 41)—to the Home Department, in an effort to demonstrate 'how seriously the tone of the press had deteriorated' since the repeal of the Press Ordinance.[17] An even fatter file was despatched to the India Office.[18] Another report pointedly noted that many speeches and gestures of support were traceable to 'public bodies', most notably members of the Punjabi Congress.[19] Feeling especially vulnerable after carrying out the death sentences, the Punjab government urged that the Home Department institute a fresh Press Ordinance. From the relative safety of New Delhi, Emerson rejected the request, reasoning that the situation was exceptional and that the excitement was bound to recede.[20]

It did not. From April to December 1931, a string of officials, high and low, were shot, five fatally, the majority of attacks occurring in Bengal.[21] While Bengal was traditionally considered a separate analytical entity when it came to political violence, in 1931 the targets were so high-profile and the perpetrators so brazen that the Home Department aggregated them to supplement their data. Collectively, these figures suggested the serious escalation of a problem that substantially undermined the confidence of members of the European community in India. Australian-born R. G. Casey, who would serve as the penultimate Governor of Bengal in British India, lightly quipped in a memoir that several of his predecessors had been 'shot at on quite a number of occasions', to the extent that in the Indian Civil Service an appointment to the position of Governor of Bengal was considered 'the greatest curse of all'.[22]

The string of attacks began on 7 April 1931 when the District Magistrate of Midnapore, James Peddie, was shot and killed; on 27 July R. R. Garlick, the judge who had tried the Bengali revolutionary Dinesh Gupta, was gunned down in his own courtroom days after receiving a death threat—his assassin evaded the wrath of colonial justice by committing suicide on the spot. Attempting to milk the controversy around Sajjan Singh, the *Pioneer* complained that 'the Congress camp' had been 'strangely quiet' after Garlick's murder, implying its tacit approval of the crime.[23] Finally, the assassination in December 1931 of Mr Stevens, a District Magistrate in the division of Chittagong, introduced a new angle of anxiety when it was revealed that the perpetrators were girls (the aforementioned Shanti Ghosh and Suniti Choudhury). The discovery of congratulatory leaflets issued by the HSRA in honour of Shanti and Suniti in both English and Bengali implied a level of cross-provincial complicity and cooperation which served to justify the Home Department's recent tendency to consider the escalation of political violence as an All-India phenomenon.[24]

The majority of attacks on Europeans in 1931 were not carried out by the HSRA, but by individuals who seemed to be inspired by them, such as the two employees of the Great Indian Peninsula Railway, who decided to avenge Bhagat Singh's death by slaying a subaltern.[25] Similarly, on 26 July 1931, police arrested two youths in Amritsar who had formed a revolutionary party 'for the purpose of murdering high officials'.[26] Subsequent investigations of the pair exposed the conspiracy's 'genesis in a Congress volunteer corps', and it was found that the youths had 'styled their organisation the Republican Socialist Party and were imbued with Bhagat Singh's revolutionary ideals'.[27] The role of the press in encouraging such attacks was underscored in a report which demonstrated that a number of those convicted or accused in the Lahore Conspiracy Case had 'imbibed revolutionary ideas from the reading of newspapers', including the publication of apparently innocuous facts, which proved to be of pedagogical value in planning subsequent attacks.[28]

This was most evident in the case of V.B. Gogate, who on 22 July 1931 shot at Sir Ernest Hotson, the Acting Governor of Bombay, at Pune University. Gogate's oral history testimony shows that he had closely studied the reportage of the Lahore Conspiracy Case, and had been struck by the mistake made by Jaigopal, who had mistaken Saunders for Scott in Lahore:

I had read the stories of revolutionaries and I found that some revolutionaries made a mistake between the Europeans. They could not identify them correctly because, for us Indians, all Europeans are practically alike. I thought to myself that I should not commit such a mistake, and therefore, I had kept a photograph of Sir Ernest Hotson in my pocket.[29]

The university convocation ceremony emerged as a preferred site of action, with attempted hits on Governors—who could be relied upon to grace such an event—featuring at three convocations in a twelve month period. In addition to Gogate's attack, was that on de Montmorency by Hari Kishen, on 23 December 1930; the latter was hanged on 9 June 1931. In January 1932, the Governor of Bengal, Sir Stanley Jackson, was fired upon at Calcutta University by Bina Das, but he too survived.[30] Of these, only Hari Kishen had links to the HSRA (and they were sufficiently indirect to enable him to convince prosecutors that he acted alone);

Gogate was strongly inspired by the HSRA; and Bina Das was linked to an underground Bengali organisation.[31]

The university's inadvertent role in hosting such actions was additionally reflective of the support among students for revolutionary actions.[32] Envisioning the rousing support of his fellow students as he was being arrested was one of the reasons that Hotson's would-be nemesis planned their encounter on campus, in the Wadia Library at Fergusson College. His colleagues did not disappoint him, responding thunderously to his shouts of 'Bande Mataram' and 'Inqilab Zindabad' as he was led away by police, and later on, a group of students broke into the library and stamped the books 'Gogate Library' in his honour.[33] James Peddie was fatally shot while inspecting a school exhibition.

The government suspected that the role of teachers in schools was pivotal in sowing the seeds of virulent disaffection, noting in Calcutta what seemed to be a pernicious policy of 'staffing their schools with ex-detenus and the like'.[34] Willingdon briefly countenanced this view, implementing a scheme 'to enlist support of mass opinion among students by working on the self-interest of the majority'.[35] He proposed that all students enrolled in government education institutions that hosted an 'outrage' would be instantly rendered ineligible for government employment, reasoning that this would inject into the student body an impetus to retard assassinations during the plotting stage. This met with no support from the would-be targets, the Governors, who argued that such a policy would lead to resentment and merely fuel anti-imperial sentiments on campus.[36]

Policing and prosecuting became increasingly challenged by the fact that as the revolutionaries became celebrated figures, vital colonial collaborators—CID agents, Indian police constables, informers, and approvers—were subjected to threats, intimidation and retribution. In some instances, such pressure was exerted by revolutionary organisations as a matter of policy. Investigations of violent attacks were increasingly obfuscated by the refusal of witnesses to testify against revolutionaries, some out of active sympathy, and some responding to intimidation.[37] One of the approvers in the Lahore Conspiracy Case, former HSRA member Phanindranath Ghosh, survived one attempt on his life in 1930,[38] before he was fatally stabbed by Baikunth Sukul on 9 November 1932. Given state protection after providing evidence in several cases related to HSRA actions, Phanindranath was attacked in Mina Bazaar in Betia while the constable deputed to protect him was distracted, apparently answering the 'call of nature'.[39] Ghosh died just over a week later.

Crackdown

British attempts to prevent political violence were undermined by their own narrow analysis. A general inability to move beyond the righteous conviction that violence in the hands of non-state actors was unprovoked and illegitimate foreshadowed most attempts to come to terms with underlying grievances. British intelligence simply did not agree with any justifications of political violence, such as that given at a meeting at Albert Hall in Calcutta: 'just as in the Great War killing of Germans was no offence, so, in the war with the British, Indians could not be morally wrong in killing their enemies'.[40] Frequent comparisons between colonial and anticolonial violence were made in the public sphere. A condolence speech for Chandrashekhar Azad explained to the audience that 'Azad had committed the same offence which had been committed by the warriors of these English men ['mutiny heroes'] whose statues had been placed outside Kashmerigate in Nickelson Garden'.[41]

Pressure from Britain and from Britons in the subcontinent urged the government of India to forcefully implement justice, and plans of action invariably revolved around repression. The lessons from the government of Bengal's perpetual struggle with political violence were extrapolated to north India. In the early 1930s, seven battalions had been deployed to Bengal 'for the sole purpose of assisting in the campaign against terrorism'.[42] The militarisation of the public sphere—in the form of flag marches, military displays, an increase in platoon posts, and the 'active use of troops in guarding, patrolling and general surveillance of suspects' was proposed in order to create a certain 'moral effect'. Such overwhelming displays of force were to be balanced with propaganda and the education of public opinion.[43]

Whether the use of aggressive flag displays was productive is debatable. The journalist and filmmaker K. A. Abbas recalled that as a schoolboy in the early 1920s, he and his fellow students had been forced to line up and watch a detachment of the British Army—'the cavalry, the artillery, the big guns, the rifles, the bayonets shining on these rifles'—marching to Lahore, that was so lengthy that it took two hours to pass. What frightened the boys the most 'was the red and what seemed to us the angry faces of the British soldiers mounted on these horses':

And it was only later on, years later, that I understood the significance of what I had seen that morning. We were made to stand there to see the might of the British Army, so that this terror could fill our hearts and that we should be over-awed by the mighty forces at the disposal of British imperialism. Later on, I learnt that another little boy, who stood on the same road, not in Panipat but in Amritsar, happened to be a young man who, when he grew up, was called Bhagat Singh ... the name of Bhagat Singh became synonymous with the youthful revolutionaries. And it was the same experience for Bhagat Singh, of standing and watching this British Army that turned him into a revolutionary. His whole psychology was changed by this one event.[44]

The accuracy of this particular recollection of Bhagat Singh is less important in this context (it is clear that the influences that pressed Bhagat Singh extended well beyond this single incident) than is the point that such displays of force might not invariably inspire awe and submission, but invoke humiliation and rebelliousness.

The government of India also introduced a fistful of legislative measures, including the Indian Press Emergency Powers Ordinance, the Special Powers Ordinance and amendments to provincial criminal law that enabled the detention of suspects without evidence.[45] The compilation of a list of 3,000 'irreconcilables' in the Punjab, in concert with these newly enhanced powers made it possible for pre-emptive arrests to be made, allowing Willingdon to visit Lahore in 1933 unmolested, amid rumours of an assassination plot.[46] Other measures sought to make it possible to prevent the formation of secret societies, such as an amendment to the Punjab Criminal Law Act in 1932, which operated on the rather endearing assumption that such organisations aspired to remain within legal parameters.[47]

In 1933, the Indian Press Ordinance was credited with bringing an era of 'laudation of murderers in the press' to a definitive close, thereby reducing the incidence of revolutionary violence.[48] There were still incidences of conspiracies, some still disconcertingly close to Congress circles, such as the premature explosion of a bomb in a Gandhi Ashram in the United Provinces in December 1933, which took off the hands of the conspirator clasping it.[49] Individuals kept on perpetuating the memory of revolutionaries, such as one Shiv Shankar Prasad Bhartiya in Allahabad, who produced leaflets in honour of Azad and Bhagat Singh on their death anniversaries as late as 1936, but evaded capture.[50]

The government of Punjab, in an effort to assuage the tide of panic that had engulfed its administration and inspired expressions of vigilantism, resorted to the artful application of statistics, drafting in 1934 a mind-bogglingly obfuscating table that aimed 'to give an impression of the comparative efficiency of the terrorists and the Police preventative measures during the past six years' (Table 2). Just as Bengal's statistics were incorporated or excised in analyses of anticolonial violence according to administrative or political expediency, so too figures could be presented to demonstrate the efficacy of governmental repression.

An accompanying explanation clarified that Column B was not intended to demonstrate 'the results of investigations of cases mentioned in Column A'; rather, readers of the table were invited to observe that 'the terrorists definitely had the upper hand in 1930 and that the position was reversed in the following three years'.[51] The table reads as a scoreboard; yet from such data it is impossible to compare the gravity of each case, or the comprehensiveness of police initiatives. And yet this was the data relayed to London, intended to calm a debate driven by members of the Conservative Party about the calamity of self-determination in India, made all the more shrill by instances of political violence.[52]

Other figures on political violence collected by the government during this period are equally difficult to work with. The definition of 'outrage' was so elastic as to include several modes of violent criminality. While the discovery of bomb factories and the premature or planned explosion of incendiary devices almost certainly point to conspiracies, the number of dacoities and robberies committed in this period simply cannot be attributed to revolutionary parties or individuals, who by no means had a monopoly on this sector of activity. Yet the data in Table 3, compiled in response to a question from the formidable Duchess of Atholl in the House of Commons to the Secretary of State, makes no distinction between instances of murder, failed assassination attempts or occurrences of dacoity, making it difficult to discern trends in revolutionary activity.

Table 2: Outrages in Punjab, 1928–33.

'Column A: All instances where initiative lay with the terrorists, whether successful outrages or incidents such as the premature explosion of bombs, of the existence of which the Police were unaware.

Column B: Occasions in which the initiative lay with the Police, such as the frustration of crimes by the timely capture of arms or explosives.'[53]

	A	B
1928	2	–
1929	2	1
1930	25	7
1931	5	12
1932	2	3
1933	–	2

Table 3: Number of Terrorist crimes and offences, actual and attempted, in the provinces of British India other than Bengal for 1933.[54]

Province	First six months of 1933	Second six months of 1933
United Provinces	7	1
Bihar and Orissa	1	3
Punjab	1	–
Delhi	Nil	–
Bombay	3	5
Madras	5	1
Central Provinces	Nil	Nil
Assam	3	2
NWFP	Nil	Nil

* Official figures not yet received [as of March 21, 1934].

This particular dataset seemed to be designed to suggest a phenomenon under control and on the decline. An experienced India hand might have questioned such a conclusion, given the glaring absence of figures for political violence in Punjab and Delhi, two of the most active regions outside Bengal. Indeed, the above statistics do not align with figures held in the India Office, which sketch the details of no less than '43 incidents indicating revolutionary conspiracy' in Punjab in 1933, which included the recovery of bombs, pistols and cartridges from student premises in Lahore and Amritsar, the throwing of a crude bomb at a police post in Lahore, and the stabbing to death of an informer on 9 December.[55] Added to this was the complication that not every attack was indicative of conspiracy; in 1933 alone, two 'outrages' in the Punjab turned out to be 'engineered by an informer in the hopes of financial gain', and a similar case was discovered in Delhi.[56]

Pressuring the Congress

The government may have appreciated Gandhi's readiness to make appeals and issue circulars enjoining the policy of nonviolence on the Congress, but it was evident in April 1931 that the acceptance of such appeals was far from unanimous. While Congress leaders after Karachi were more likely to toe the nonviolent line, discipline in the Congress rank and file remained less reliable. Following Gogate's attempt on the life of Sir Ernest Hotson on 22 July and the murder of Judge Garlick in Alipur on 27 July 1931, Gandhi wrote an article in *Young India* in which he 'congratulated His Excellency Sir E. Hotson on his providential escape' and made his strongest statement yet, of which there could be no ambiguous interpretation:

Bhagat Singh worship has done ... incalculable harm to the country. Bhagat Singh's character, about which I had heard so much from reliable sources, ... carried me away and identified me with the cautious and balanced resolution passed at Karachi. I regret to observe that the caution has been thrown to the winds. The deed itself is being worshiped as if it was worthy of emulation. The result is goondaism and degradation.[57]

At its very next meeting, on 6–8 August 1931 in Bombay, the AICC passed the Public Violence Resolution. This resolution deplored the attacks on Hotson and Garlick, warning 'those who secretly or openly approve of or encourage such murders that they retard the progress of the country'.[58] Speaking in favour of the motion, Jawaharlal Nehru addressed the AICC. Indicating a rethink on the role of violence since the Karachi Congress, he declared that 'We can have either nonviolence or violence but certainly we cannot play with both ... If we really believe in nonviolence we must follow it irrespective of what the government do. If we do not believe in it, we must have the courage to say so openly.'[59]

Further, the AICC appealed for 'special propaganda against all acts of public violence, even where provocation is given', and made a special plea to the nationalist press to support the campaign.[60] According to the Home Department, the resolution had a 'salutary effect on the accredited leaders of the Congress of the Punjab', who had been openly patronising 'such questionable objects as the Bhagat Singh Memorial Fund', and who withdrew in response to the resolution—with the notable exception of Satyapal.[61] It was also at this meeting that the Bhagat Singh Cremation Committee was declared closed, and there was no further discussion of a Bhagat Singh Memorial backed by the Congress.[62]

When the Public Violence Resolution was placed before a meeting of the Kanpur Congress later that month, the meeting erupted in 'pandemonium'. A young man 'leapt to the stage and gave a speech denouncing the Congress policy of non-violence and advocated progressing individual terrorism to mass terrorism', refusing to withdraw unless his proposal was put to the vote, which 'less than one hundred out of four hundred' voted for.[63] The Director of Intelligence concluded that 'generally speaking, Congress leaders have realised their moral responsibility for recent terrorist outrages and are prepared to make amends, [however] the younger Hindu element, of which the Congress rank and file is largely composed, is intransigent'.[64]

Such incidents spurred the All-India Congress leadership to draw a tighter rein on its subsidiary organisations, such as the Hindustani Seva Dal, a volunteer organisation for Congress workers under the age of eighteen, formed in order to channel youth energies towards the Congress.[65] According to Jawaharlal, during the Civil Disobedience Movement there was a substantial body of volunteers who worked within but also beyond the Congress, who 'had little discipline and there was no uniformity in their training and their organisation'.[66] Given the hurried recruitment of a large quota of workers prior to the 1929 Congress, this is hardly surprising, but it was perhaps a veiled reference to the Naujawan Bharat Sabha. The AICC implemented a series of measures to coordinate the activities of the Seva Dal, and to prevent auxiliary organisations 'not recognized by the Working Committee' from working in the name of the Congress. Additionally, new formalities were introduced to regulate institutional membership, with enrolment, training and form-filling seen as necessary to establish belonging and affiliation. This included a vow to accept 'the Congress creed', and hereafter officers were required to hold certificates of membership.[67] A pledge was established, in which the first clause was to solemnly affirm to 'strive for the attainment of Purna Swaraj by peaceful and legitimate means'.[68]

Responding to the accusations of the *Pioneer* that the Congress was complicit in political assassinations, Jawaharlal wrote that:

It is clear enough that if anyone has to regret terrorist outrage in India, it is the Congressman. It is impossible for this peaceful struggle to be carried on simultaneously with a contrary method. Therefore, it becomes essential for us even from the lower ground of expediency, to counteract with all the strength that we have, any attempts at violence. Apart from this, terrorist outrages on individuals are bad from every point of view. They are confessions of despair and only when an individual or a country is full of despair are they indulged in.

They demoralise and let loose the spirit of violent revenge. Thus they may be condemned on human grounds as well as on political grounds.[69]

Jawaharlal now named and rejected the dual strategy of exerting pressure on the government using both violence and nonviolence as 'fencing'.[70] He attended the Punjab Political Conference on 26 September 1931, urging the youth to consolidate its energies into Congress activity,[71] and within weeks visited Bengal on a similar mission. In a speech in Calcutta on 17 November 1931, he appealed to the youth of Bengal to

adhere strenuously and absolutely to the path of non-violence ... I say and I say it definitely, and I challenge anyone to contradict me, that individual terrorism today in this country or in any other has always been resorted to just to wake up and rouse the people and to remind them that there are some who do not tolerate alien rule; but it has never succeeded in freeing a country.[72]

This speech was delivered on 17 November 1931 to commemorate the anniversary of Lala Lajpat Rai's death, which had inspired the HSRA's first action. Within three years, key Congress leaders were no longer prepared to publicly endorse political violence.

The Congress's conformity to a unilaterally nonviolent stance reduced an important element of support for revolutionary action from the field of politics. While the revolutionaries had always maintained a high level of independence from the Congress, it had nonetheless relied upon Congress workers for financial backing for revolutionary activities and for legal defence. Together with the untimely deaths of key intermediaries and members of the Congress High Command (such as Ganesh Shankar Vidyarthi and Motilal Nehru), by mid-1931 the revolutionaries lost an important source of moral support. Chaman Lal withdrew from the political fray after civil disobedience, managing to secure a passport. He began to travel the world, leaving in his wake a 95-page file in Scotland Yard, which warned that he was 'a mischievous person who is apt to cause trouble wherever he goes.'[73]

The deaths of iconic revolutionary leaders—especially Bhagat Singh and Chandrashekhar Azad—hit the HSRA hard, and while their appeal was substantially enhanced by their status as martyrs, this came at an enormous cost. Not only were key members such as Durga Devi Vohra personally destabilised by the executions (recall that Manmohini Zutshi supposed that she lost heart after their deaths, compelling her to surrender to the police), but the loss of their organisational skills removed a vital element of focus and restraint that had informed HSRA actions. These factors, combined with the multifaceted repression of absconding revolutionaries that slowly culminated in the arrests of much of the HSRA, substantially limited the scope for organised revolutionary activity in north India after 1932.

The Demise of the HSRA, 1930–34

While relentless government crackdown and withdrawal of overt support from the Congress movement exerted considerable strain on the HSRA's internal mechanisms, ideological shifts within the remnants of the party were equally important in the association's reassessment of its tactics. By late 1930 the organisation had been substantially depleted, with the majority of its Provincial and Central executive in jail. As the party's inner circle was reconstituted, it was simultaneously destabilised by a number of factors. These included consistent shadowing by the CID, with several near-miss encounters;[74] the frustrating failure to progress important actions such as freeing Bhagat Singh from jail in mid-1930 (partly due to his own reluctance to be rescued),[75] and the statements of approvers—former revolutionaries—in court cases, which had a demoralising effect on the organisation. Ajoy Ghosh remarked that the HSRA never recovered from Azad's death, particularly because party members felt Azad's presence had been betrayed by one of their own; 'there was no knowing who would be the next traitor … none was exempt from suspicion'.[76] For a time the HSRA's energies were directed towards targeting approvers and evading the police rather than organising actions, as handsome rewards offered for information leading to arrests of members bore fruit.[77]

Given this, from 1930 provincial units of the HSRA began organising actions without the approval of the Central Committee. In Bombay, the Lamington Road Outrage was perpetrated autonomously, bypassing the usual operational formalities; this was dictated by the urgency felt by Durga Devi Vohra and her accomplices to respond to Bhagat Singh's death sentence. The attack on the Viceregal train was a more grave example of party authority being subverted, with Azad specifically withdrawing his approval for the plan, largely in deference to the wishes of his long-term friend, Ganesh Shankar Vidyarthi.[78] Both of these actions might be seen as attempts by party members whose revolutionary reputations had been individually questioned—Durga Devi, Bhagwati Charan and Yashpal—to demonstrate their commitment. Other members, such as Inderpal, formed breakaway organisations or masterminded independent actions, unsanctioned by Azad or the Central Committee.

From their jail cells, HSRA leaders issued pleas for order to be restored to revolutionary activity, writing letters and manifestoes which were intended to be published in the press or disseminated in underground circles.[79] In a letter written in October 1930, addressed to 'bhaiya', Sukhdev denounced these independent operations, pointing out that they were divorced from the HSRA's primary aim when planning actions, which was to arouse public support.[80] Shortly before his execution Bhagat Singh wrote a lengthy manifesto, urging the youth to refrain from assassinations and acts of political violence, for these were 'reserved for a chosen few' to attract publicity for the movement; 'terrorist outrage', he warned, was a limited means to the larger goal of capturing political power 'by the masses for the masses'.[81] This document was extensively distributed, and was later attributed to the decline in political violence, as well as for diverting youthful energies towards communist thinking.[82]

These forces ultimately combined to force a crisis in the organisation, as a result of which—according to Yashpal—Azad decided to disband the HSRA's Executive in September 1930.[83] This did not dissuade the Punjab-based operatives, Durga Das Khanna, Virendra and Chaman Lal, who proceeded to plan the attack on de Montmorency on 23 December. Indeed, the decision to proceed was symptomatic of the problems besetting the HSRA.[84] Jawaharlal Nehru's account in his autobiography of his discussion with Azad in February 1931 after Motilal's death seems to indicate that the revolutionaries were indeed rethinking their tactics.

However within days, Azad himself was no more, his death eliminating, in the words of the Director of the Intelligence Bureau, 'the moving spirit of terrorism in Upper India' from the political scene.[85] There were several attempts to hunt down and murder Virbhadra Tiwari, the HSRA member thought responsible for alerting the police to Azad's whereabouts,[86] although there was disagreement within the party as to whether he was in fact responsible for this.[87] Yashpal claims that he was appointed Commander in Chief of the organisation after Azad's death;[88] however his own arrest in January 1932 in Allahabad put an end to that. By 1932, the overwhelming majority of the HSRA's key party members had been either jailed, executed, killed, or placed under preventative detention.[89]

In 1932, the intelligence department surmised that despite these measures, the 'central council still seems to exist', directed by persons who 'are in some form of custody but who manage surreptitiously to communicate their wishes to the residue of their followers who are still at large'.[90] Shiv Verma, Bejoy Kumar Sinha and Jaidev Kapoor had been imprisoned in distant provinces, before eventually being transferred to the Andamans. Hereafter the agenda of the HSRA was picked up by figures sufficiently peripheral to have evaded detection and therefore arrest, as a British report noted: 'the movement degenerated into small local conspiracies and numerous, but isolated, cases of bomb-throwing'.[91] Actions seemed to be devised on a smaller scale so that in the event of detection, 'the party would not be completely crippled'.[92]

Manifestoes were still being produced in the HSRA's name in 1933, one timed to commemorate Azad's death, and another to commemorate anniversaries of the deaths of Bhagat Singh, Sukhdev and Rajguru a month later.[93] Hans Raj Sikka, who had been imprisoned in Borstal Jail at the same time as Bhagat Singh and had corresponded with him by passing messages through sympathetic sweepers, pasted red posters around Lahore on 23 March 1933.[94] A third leaflet circulated in May celebrated the 1857 uprising, with copies posted to members of government, including the Viceroy and the Home Member.[95] The tone of these was pronounced to be 'definitely Communistic', and intelligence networks reported that a meeting of the HSRA in Delhi in July 1933 had agreed to dissolve the organisation 'for the time being' and that 'study circles' should be organised.[96] A number of unaffiliated individuals performed actions which symbolically referenced the HSRA, fashioning derivative organisations, and performing acts of commemoration. In 1934, a cracker bomb exploded near the home of the police inspector in Bihar and Orissa on the third anniversary of Bhagat Singh's death.[97] These were low-order, small-scale actions, compared to the ambitious plans to target the Viceroy just a few years earlier.

Prison as Pedagogy

The revolutionaries of the HSRA had been largely action-focused, with much of their energies oriented towards procurement of funds and arms, and the manufacture of bombs.[98] By contrast, their prison time proved to be instructive, providing them with the time to read and discuss ideology, to the extent that Bejoy Kumar Sinha described jail as 'university for politicals'.[99] The extent to which Bhagat Singh was able to use his incarceration to study leftist literature is evident in his Prison Diary, filled with his cursive notes on the writings of Marx, Engels, and a range of Western political philosophers, but also the literature of Dostoyevsky and Ibsen, to name a few.[100] Other HSRA members agreed that jail was a formative experience, specifically naming the years 1930 to 1935, which was periodically shared with so many satyagrahis.[101] For Sinha, serious and systematic study of leftist and revolutionary literature was profoundly enlightening:

We were realising our mistakes, but not without much pain and suffering. Sometimes when we had finished discussions, some one of us would march away from the rest to a remote corner and think for himself. Was it all for nothing that so many of our comrades fought and perished on the scaffold? The next moment he would reply, 'No, martyrdom never goes in vain. They had defied British imperialism and broken its spell of terror. They had awakened their countrymen and inspired in their hearts a self confidence and a spirit of unbending resistance. They had left for us a noble tradition of iron will, supreme self-sacrifice and dogged persistence.' … From our analysis of the past we had found that it was the absence of revolutionary theory that had been our greatest drawback.[102]

Initially the life convicts of the Lahore Conspiracy Case—Kamalnath Tiwari, Bejoy Kumar Sinha, Mahaveer Singh, Gaya Prasad, Jaidev Kapoor and Shiv Verma—were sent to Madras, dispersed across different jails.[103] Jail policy reasoned that difficult prisoners were likely to improve when removed from their local environment; their supporters argued that isolating prisoners from those who could speak their language was an additional form of persecution.[104] As dangerous revolutionaries, many of them were initially kept in separate cells, as opposed to barracks, although jailers had the capacity to waive this, and many did, allowing them to mix with satyagrahis.[105]

In Vellore Jail, Jaidev Kapoor had the opportunity to associate with Madras Congress leaders such as Rajagopalachari, Satyamurti, N. G. Ranga, Sambamurti, T. Prakasam and Gopalareddy, and they formed a regular discussion group to talk about north Indian politics and the revolutionary movement.[106] When it became evident that Kapoor and Verma were integrating with the other prisoners, and even learning Tamil, they were transferred again.[107] Kapoor resorted to elaborate ruses in order to meet with other nationalists, in one case feigning illness to be transferred to a medical unit where he met with medically trained prisoners, such as Dr Pattabhi Sitaramayya and, on other occasions, E. M. S. Namboodripad.[108] Similarly, in Punjab, Congress leaders such as Bhim Sen Sachar (later a Chief Minister) found himself jailed with 'terrorist friends, Sardar Gulab Singh, Kundan Lal, Roop Chand and others of the Lahore Conspiracy Case'.[109] Sachar described his jail time in the 1940s with great affection:

Lot of reading was done, discussions were held, but all in a very good spirit. I remember those days with a nostalgia. The friendships made during those days were really abiding friendships. They stick to you.[110]

These prison friendships certainly counted; in 1946, Sachar would have the pleasure of releasing the Lahore Conspiracy Case convicts from their life sentences, after decades of agitating and hunger striking.[111] There were also political outcomes that emerged as a result of long periods of incarceration together: both Shilabhadra Yaji and Bejoy Kumar Sinha noted that the Congress Socialist Party was heavily consolidated on the basis of jail networks formed during the Civil Disobedience Movement,[112] and intelligence authorities were alerted to reports that J.P. Narayan had canvassed the support of incarcerated revolutionaries.[113]

In June 1933, Kapoor, Verma and Sinha were sent to the Andamans.[114] They were delivered to Port Blair, arriving shortly after three prisoners, Mahavir Singh, Mohit Mitra and Mohan Kishore, had died as a result of hunger strike, creating a state of excitement.[115] Initially, the Lahore Conspiracy Case prisoners had welcomed going to the Andamans, reasoning that they would meet with their comrades there. However the conditions on the island were intolerable; cholera and malaria were rampant, and the food was inedible, with the dal infested by worms and the chapatis gritty with dirt.[116] After another hunger strike, conditions improved and they were provided with the ability to cook and eat their own food together with meat and fish twice a week, access to a local newspaper, the right to meet with family annually, and to correspond once per month, although letters continued to be censored.[117]

Kapoor explained that in the Andamans many of the revolutionaries established formal links with the Calcutta Communist Party through Adbul Halim, who provided them with books by Lenin, Marx and R. P. Dutt, smuggled in through a sympathetic contractor. Prison officers did not intervene—'they also longed for a peaceful living', remarked Kapoor—believing that as long as the prisoners were engaged in study, they were less inclined to indiscipline.[118] The prisoners formed a communist study cell which produced two monthly magazines—handwritten affairs containing articles, pictures, cartoons and poems by prisoners—which were circulated secretly throughout the prison. The CID was aware of and uncomfortable about this development, but reasoned that the spread of communist ideology represented a distant menace, which, all things considered, was preferable to the immediate threat of terrorism.[119] By 1940, when Ajoy Ghosh was arrested and joined his former HSRA colleagues in Lucknow District Jail, he noted that they were 'now mature convinced communists'.[120]

The bulk of the memoirs, oral histories and visual artefacts that I have drawn on to demonstrate the intersection between revolutionary and Congress activity in 1929–1930 are so heavily focused on the lives and adventures of personalities, especially the charismatic Bhagat Singh and the more enigmatic Chandrashekhar Azad, that evidence of revolutionary energies being channeled into Congress activity in the aftermath of their deaths becomes elusive. From the perspective of Manmathnath Gupta, after the loss of these two figureheads, the revolutionary movement 'became divorced from its moorings and was more artificial and people came into it because of the romantic glamour attached to it, not out of any deep idealism.'[121] N.K. Nigam, a Delhi-based organiser from Hindu College who had been close to Azad, and was arrested in late 1930, concurred.[122] He was released from jail in 1934 and, unable to find any recognisable revolutionary organisation or employment, eventually fell into Congress work.[123] It was around this time that in Kanpur, Roop Kishore Kapoor painted *Desh Chintan*, an image communicating his own despair, heavily coded to sail beneath the radar of the censors, but perhaps also the Congress leadership.

CONCLUSION

THE DYNAMICS OF ANTICOLONIAL VIOLENCE

This book aims to position the role of violence in the freedom struggle, with special reference to the revolutionary interlude in north India, by paying attention to a fusion of textual, oral, visual and other 'unarchived' histories. This reconstituted archive brings into focus a formative time in India, when nationalistic institutions were porous, and anti-British sentiment was sufficiently capacious to absorb a broadly anti-imperial ethos that formed in response to the violence of the Raj. This study reveals that in many circles in interwar India, the necessity of returning that violence was absorbed into the larger nationalist picture. But this changed. Subsequently, narratives about revolutionaries have inhabited the margins of history, at best relegated to the edges of 'official' Congress nationalism, while they are simultaneously celebrated in popular culture. Bringing the two into alignment throws up the challenging prospect that nonviolence is, at least in some contexts, much more compelling when attended by its disruptive opposite.

Yet historians have come to see violence and nonviolence as rival forms of political action, remaining conspicuously reticent when violence intruded into later campaigns, such as the Quit India movement.[1] But it is far more productive to see 'all of these movements as parts of a single formation of anti-colonial nationalism, linked to each other by complex discursive and organisational connections'.[2] As alumni of the Non-Cooperation Movement, the revolutionaries of the HSRA for the most part enjoyed collegial relationships with many leading Congressites at the provincial level, which facilitated and shaped the politics and organisation in both the HSRA and the Indian National Congress. Revolutionaries from north India and Bengal made substantial contributions as volunteers in the annual Congress sessions in Kanpur, Calcutta and Lahore. Their influence can be read in resolutions—the urgency of which expedited declarations for complete independence in 1927 and 1929—as well as in the ambivalence on the utility of nonviolence that was so discernible at the Lahore session.

A REVOLUTIONARY HISTORY OF INTERWAR INDIA

In the introduction to his memoirs, written in 1939 after his release from jail, Bejoy Kumar Sinha explained:

Revolutionaries do not want to be awe-inspiring figures. They wish to be recognised as common soldiers in our common struggle for social and political emancipation. It becomes all the more imperative when the released prisoners have in their hundreds to take their stand, shoulder to shoulder with their struggling people. I would feel satisfied if this book goes even a little way forward to facilitate this task. In all these pages my main object has been to bring my imprisoned comrades nearer to their fighting countrymen.[3]

Sinha's message, more than half a century later, is more important than ever. Even those who had explicitly supported the HSRA were reticent about their activities in the first few decades after independence. The incorrigible Bhikshu Chaman Lal went on to write several books, none of which owned up to his revolutionary entanglements; not even *Martyrs of India*, published by the Kapoor Publishing Press in Kanpur to commemorate the centenary of the 1857 rebellion.[4]

Compelled by the burdens of statesmanship after 1947, Nehru also had difficulty reconciling his earlier connections with the revolutionaries. In 1949, he declined an invitation to lay the foundation stone for a memorial in honour of Khudiram Bose being erected in Muzaffarpur, on the basis that 'the principle of non-violence was involved'.[5] Hearing of this, Durga Das Khanna wrote a letter to the Prime Minister, reminding him of his extensive linkages with the revolutionaries and of their sacrifice.[6] Khanna received only a dull form letter in reply. But he ran into Nehru at a function some time later, where Nehru privately upbraided Khanna, explaining that it was impolitic for a prime minister, 'even if he was in the thick of the revolutionary movement' in his youth, to publicly own it.[7]

But the revolutionaries *did* capture the imagination of the masses. While Gandhi was undoubtedly an astute journalist, communicating his politics through his body as well as through newspapers, he was 'dismissive of the potential of the new media of film, recordings and radio in carrying messages of the nation and its rebirth to ordinary people.'[8] By contrast, a younger generation, disaffected with colonialism and impatient for political change, embraced these new media enthusiastically. This was a powerful blend. Bhagat Singh delighted in the cinema hall, enthralled with films concerned with social justice, but he also revelled in the pleasurable escapism of comedy and gangster films.[9] Perhaps it was there that he honed his sense of thriller nationalism, already keened on the stories of those who had sacrificed their lives before him. Bhagat Singh was unquestionably an aesthete with a deep appreciation of the affective,[10] and he brought these qualities to the revolutionaries' communications strategy, crafting an image and positioning a narrative in the public sphere that attained an iconicity that was, as the younger Nehru marvelled in his autobiography, 'something amazing'.[11]

Artists sympathetic with or connected to the revolutionaries replicated their portraits, illustrating the revolutionary struggle with graphic and dramatic idioms.

The resulting body of martyrology, in concert with dramas, poems, songs and slogans, fed into an underground culture of defiance, intersecting with the ethos of civil disobedience. Interpretations of these formats did not always align with revolutionary ideas, themselves so dynamic and accretive that they defy easy categorisation.[12] The religious imaginaire that anchored illustrations of martyrdom, which repeatedly featured gods or Bharat Mata (for Kanpur images alone, see Figures 3, 26, 33, 34, 35, 40, 49), suggested that revolutionary politics aligned with a Hindu framework. This was despite the absorption of the Arabic concept of *shaheed* into discourses of nationalist martyrdom—emotive images arguably linger longer than words. This faultline perhaps begins to explain the alienation of Muslims from the Congress-organised protests and *hartals* in Kanpur following Bhagat Singh's death in 1931. And yet in Figure 40, Roop Kishore Kapoor centered his critique of communalism around a larger-than-life Mother India, mutely accusing her contrite sons, when indeed they might turn the gaze of incrimination back at her divine form.[13] The revolutionaries' ubiquity in material culture of the period provides not only evidence of their popularity, but is also one of the richest sources for unpacking the ways that their politics resonated and were interpreted by 'the masses' that they sought to mobilise. Viewed alongside a critical reading of archival sources, oral history interviews, memoirs, rumours and hearsay, a picture of revolutionary politics and praxis begins to emerge which challenges existing nationalist narratives.

Revolutionising the Congress

By focusing on the revolutionaries as isolated actors, many scholars have concluded that, as an organisation, the HSRA failed on several counts. Bipan Chandra's assessment was that the revolutionaries failed in their own objectives of popularising socialism in India, but that

They succeeded in arousing the country and in winning the love and respect of their countrymen, but for the cause of nationalism. This was no mean success. But the fruits of their success were gathered by the traditional Congress leadership which they had denounced as bourgeois and middle class and which they had hoped to replace, but which was actually and actively heading the anti-imperialist struggle.[14]

While it is important to note again that the revolutionaries' ultimate objectives were not the same as those of the Congress, freedom from British rule was a common goal. However, the preceding chapters demonstrate that in 1929 the HSRA *invited* senior members of the Congress to leverage their violent acts against the state in their negotiations. This collaboration, as short-lived as it was, has largely gone unnoticed and unremarked, clouded by the dominance of nonviolence in nationalist historiography.

For the most part, revolutionary interactions with the Congress leadership were indirect. They were nurtured by intermediaries—political workers who were active in a range of fringe movements and satellite organisations which orbited around the greater Congress movement. Some of these workers were extraordinarily fluid, reflective of a political ethos that was broadly anticolonial, and an environment in which the discipline of the Congress and the acceptance of nonviolence was far from total. Institutional affiliations would become less agile and more exclusive from the early 1930s. Interestingly, it was also around this time that wry presswallahs came up with the term 'High Command' to describe the Congress Working Committee,[15] a term which quickly lost its irony and has endured in the language of Indian politics, where it gestures to a leadership at odds with its base.

More importantly, the revolutionary challenge reinvigorated Congress strategy. In early 1928, the Congress movement seemed to be at an impasse, with Gandhi withdrawing from high politics to engage in constructive work in his ashram. According to Chaman Lal, Gandhi had confided in him in 1928 that he had not the energy for another campaign,[16] and he seems to have been somewhat removed from the constitutional framework being constructed by Motilal Nehru. The campaigns conducted by the revolutionaries excited a youth alienated by the Old Guard's chaffering and bargaining over Dominion Status. This exuberance forced nationalist leaders away from staidly moderate means, escalating nationalist demands and reinvigorating debates within the Congress about the utility of nonviolence.

The political conflict between the Nehrus, father and son, over whether *purna swaraj* was premature has been remarked upon by several biographers, as it was by intelligence officers who intercepted Motilal's correspondence, revealing his dismay at Jawaharlal's growing radicalism.[17] With this in mind, British analysts struggled to make sense of Motilal Nehru's very public visit to Bhagat Singh and the prisoners of the Lahore Conspiracy Case in the courtroom, just prior to the momentous Lahore Congress in 1929, which was to mark the expiry of the ultimatum to the government to accept Dominion Status or face civil disobedience.

While Motilal's courtroom visit was exceptional, necessitated by his anxieties about the possibility of a split at Lahore, it is clear that the revolutionary challenge engaged him keenly. As his health began to fail, the serving Congress president covertly provided financial, legal and a degree of moral support to the revolutionaries, while Jawaharlal worked with them and their base in the Naujawan Bharat Sabha in an attempt to draw them into the orbit of the Congress. The Nehrus cannot have failed to notice that their correspondence was being intercepted, and were careful to censor themselves, even to the extent of feeding their readers with misinformation. Writing to his son shortly after the Assembly attack, Motilal mused: 'What a coincidence. People will think that we settled our press statements together on the phone before one was issued from Allahabad and the other from Delhi. Even some of the words are the same. The idea of course was bound to be the same.'[18]

CONCLUSION

The Civil Disobedience Movement and its most prominent campaign, the Salt March, were directed at the British, but they were partially devised as a response to revolutionary actions, particularly the attempt to kill the Viceroy in December 1929. The Mahatma conceded on a number of occasions that civil disobedience was an attempt to stem 'the tide of onrushing violence',[19] and Subhas Chandra Bose indicated the same in an interview to Horace Alexander.[20] The Gandhian activist B. R. Durandhar even claimed that the Salt March was

the most brilliant strategy which enabled Gandhiji to fight both the repression of the government and the terrorists of Bengal and the Punjab, who were getting very impatient and might have got out of hand. … The full significance of the Dandi March will be realised when we take into consideration that after the march there was no terrorism. Dandi March buried the bombs.'[21]

This outcome was not as immediate as Durandhar remembered it—the daring Chittagong Armory Raid by Bengali revolutionaries led by Surya Sen in mid-April of 1930 being just one indicator to the contrary.[22] However, his testimony adds weight to a view that nonviolent mobilisation out-manoeuvred the revolutionaries by engaging the energies of the masses.

There is much to suggest that, Gandhi and his closest followers aside, support for anticolonial activities was not so neatly compartmentalised into rival camps, 'violent' and 'nonviolent'. Many remembered the exhilaration of the time when each spilled into and reinforced the other—together presenting the British with a formidable challenge. The different strategies of violence and nonviolence, rather spectacularly illustrated by occasional polemics between Gandhi and the revolutionaries, served to assure the government that the two movements were oppositional, despite some evidence of collusion, especially at the provincial level. At the same time, these debates were a reminder that even though the revolutionaries were amenable to their actions feeding into Congress objectives, they were not going to dance to the Congress tune.

The HSRA did not entirely abhor nonviolence, but they saw a dialogical relationship between it and violence, in which the latter was regrettably indispensable, but to be used sparingly. By the same token, while Gandhi strove to eliminate violence altogether, many of his followers were more pragmatic, seeing nonviolence as a tactic rather than a moral imperative. As Jaidev Gupta recalled of Bhagat Singh:

His philosophy on violence was subtly mixed with non-violence. He shed minimum blood at a time and in such a way that it was appreciated by all the freedom-loving people. He conducted the whole struggle in such a manner that the British were placed always in the wrong. He forced the hands of the alien rulers to hang him at a time when the whole propaganda of his movement was at its full height in his favour in the whole world and thus created unprecedented clamour and efforts for throwing away the British by force.[23]

This history has been obscured by accounts that suggest that Gandhi's opposition to revolutionary violence was embraced by the Indian National Congress as a whole. Additionally, the Mahatma's more concerted campaign against political violence following the Karachi session has been revised to predate 1931. But until that point, Gandhi was somewhat constrained, perhaps realising that the Congress would not survive the fallout if he chose to suspend another campaign, as he had suspended non-cooperation following Chauri Chaura.[24] Additionally, the popularity of the revolutionaries made it difficult for him to denounce them. Gandhi's studied silence on the death of Jatindranath Das—an event which by all other accounts created great excitement in the country—is perhaps one of the clearest indicators of the Mahatma's dilemma. The groundswell of nationalist support from the youth and the left made the reluctant Jawaharlal's candidature as president vital, and *purna swaraj* and civil disobedience inevitable.

It can be said therefore that the revolutionary challenge re-energised the Congress, shaking it from the stagnation of the mid-1920s, leading to a mass recruitment drive launched prior to the Lahore session. This was replaced later by a fresh emphasis, in the wake of the executions in 1931, on nonviolence and discipline.[25] The revolutionary interlude in north India concluded when Gandhi strove to re-emphasise nonviolence as the basis of the Congress creed as a prelude to the Second Roundtable Conference in London. The Mahatma would have strenuously disagreed, but it is difficult to avoid the conclusion that the political violence orchestrated by the HSRA threw nonviolence into sharp relief, making Gandhi a viable and desirable option for the British.

The Experience of Political Violence

Bhagat Singh is said to have once described the task of his party as 'the disorganising of the British rulers'.[26] What did the broader anticolonial movement look like from the perspective of its most immediate target, the European communities settled in India? To be sure, there was a good degree of stiff-upper-lippery on the part of the administration—'We are in India to keep our tempers', Irwin reportedly declared to his military secretary, not long after his appointment as Viceroy.[27] In Punjab—until the early twentieth century, one of the more sought-after and hospitable postings for ambitious members of the Indian Civil Service—the European community saw the rise in political violence in the interwar period as a corollary to Gandhian nonviolence.[28] They pressured their government accordingly, and the government, too, could not help noticing that Congress campaigns created an atmosphere of flagrant disregard for its authority, in which the revolutionaries' defiance was celebrated. Motilal Nehru's rhetorical challenge, 'Balraj or Gandhi?', served as a not-so-gentle reminder that the latter, with his perplexing politics of nonviolence, was eminently favourable to the revolvers and bombs of Balraj. Political assassinations directed at Britons in high posts during this period injected urgency into the stately talkfest about the process of constitutional reform then going on in London. This played into the hands of the Congress.

Some historians have concluded that the revolutionaries of the HSRA failed because its key leadership died, and that the colonial state triumphed because within a few years, they had quashed the revolutionary movement.[29] This is a narrow conceptualisation. Setting aside the ongoing social and political potency of revolutionary martyrdom (which continues to be celebrated and appropriated in contemporary India), the decline of the revolutionary movement in north India had as much to do with ideological developments in revolutionary circles as outright repression. As Dennis Dalton has pointed out, across the empire colonial authorities 'evidenced no qualms of guilt in their ruthless execution of terrorists'.[30] But Bhagat Singh and the other young activists of the HSRA who had their portraits taken to commemorate their actions never expected anything less.

It is hard to imagine that the escalation of political violence in 1931–2 did not prompt some career reassessment in the minds of civil servants, or shake the colonial mindset. Recall that Scott, the intended target of the Lahore assassination who had ordered the *lathi* charge on the anti-Simon protestors, did not tarry in the town long after his young colleague was killed. Bengali revolutionaries dispatched James Peddie not long after he recommended 'a few more shootings' of protesting villagers in June 1930.[31] It was at this time that British recruitment for the Indian Civil Service became sluggish, a rather surprising trend given the lack of employment at home during the depression.[32] While other forces were certainly in play,[33] a potentially short and violent career in His Majesty's Indian Empire was not a tempting proposition, as former Governor of Bengal R. G. Casey quipped in his memoirs.[34] Belief in the imperial idea began to wane as the level of coercion required to maintain the Raj in the face of such attacks escalated.[35]

The HSRA's acts of violence were small in number, but powerful and memorable. They were amplified by their extensive coverage in the press and material culture. They were replicated by the actions of independent activists who sought martyrdom, and by supporters who performed acts of retribution directed at approvers, law enforcement authorities and other government targets. Certainly, their actions were not endorsed by all, and there were several approvers and a great number of witnesses who shuffled forth to give evidence against them in the Lahore Conspiracy Case.[36] However, later court cases such as the Lamington Road and Delhi Conspiracy Cases collapsed due to lack of evidence; in the former, only one approver could be coaxed to testify. This gives us a sense of how quickly the idea of revolutionary violence as a project worthy of support caught on, even if by simply refusing to give evidence in court.

In the Lahore Conspiracy Case, the government was determined to hang the accused as terrorists, crafting an ordinance that would allow them to do so expeditiously. It could also be argued that the anti-terrorist project accentuated the righteousness of the British in India, lending it, in the words of Reinhold Niebuhr, 'a moral potency which it does not deserve'.[37] Yet acts of violence directed at the administration—predominantly at British targets—served to provide a depth to the political spectrum which made nonviolent action, with its unpredictable and chaotic ramifications, look desirable. This raises the rather unsatisfactory proposition that there is only a finite amount of political energy to be sequestered, which, if not adequately channelled into moderate outlets and other forms of allowable protest, bursts forth in paroxysms of terrorism. This in itself is a supposition worth pressing further, especially given its currency in debates around the tail end of the War on Terror. It is evident that in its more reflective moments, this was precisely what the British government of India believed. 'It is not altogether new in the history of terrorism in Upper India', wrote an intelligence report in 1936,

that the thoughts of young men turn towards terrorism at a time when other self-styled patriots are, more or less, quiescent. At the present time, with no civil disobedience and with Congressmen mainly engaged in making wordy speeches, it is, perhaps, not surprising that the younger generation should be getting impatient.[38]

By 1931, to the horror of much of the Conservative Party, the acknowledged leader of a subversive movement was striding up the stairs of the Viceregal palace in Delhi to negotiate a truce. While many had reason to be disappointed with the outcome of these negotiations,[39] the Karachi Congress that ratified the Gandhi–Irwin Pact weeks later proved to be pivotal not only for the reasons described in Chapter Seven, but also because it was there that the emerging forces of the left—aggrieved by the pact, the executions, and the violence in Kanpur—were able to leverage these to push through the Fundamental Rights Resolution.

The idea of a Fundamental Rights Resolution came from M. N. Roy, whose draft was proffered to the AICC at the Karachi Congress.[40] *The Masses* reported that Roy's supporters 'submitted to the Congress a resolution containing the programme of relentless struggle for the capture of the political power of the masses', which was rejected, but 'the pressure was felt nonetheless.'[41] Nehru crossly rejected the widespread rumour that Roy 'drew up this resolution, or the greater part of it, and thrust it down upon me at Karachi';[42] and a comparison of the final resolution and Roy's draft does reveal significant differences. The editors of *CWMG* claim that the resolution was 'presumably drafted by Gandhi',[43] and while Gandhi's influence is visible—his own eleven points from 1930 are reflected among the twenty—other accounts suggest that it was a collaborative effort. According to Kamaladevi Chattopadhyay, the document was put together by a number of leftist Congress members, and passed to Nehru, on the understanding that he would edit and present the document to Gandhi.[44]

The Fundamental Rights Resolution provided for the first time a concrete vision of the basic civil and economic rights citizens could expect in an independent India. As Chattopadhyay later reflected, 'We felt it was very necessary that when we were calling upon the people to wage this big struggle for freedom, they should be guaranteed the substance of it'.[45] Many of the aspirations in the document remain elusive today, but the Resolution was 'remarkable' at the time, and remains 'one of the most important documents of the Indian National Congress', laying the ground for the human rights claims against the state from marginalised groups and communities, and the framework for what would become the Indian Constitution of 1950.[46] Nehru resented the interpretation that Gandhi agreed to pass the edited resolution as a way of mollifying his unhappiness with the Pact,[47] but this was widely taken to be the case, as the Viceroy explained to the Secretary of State:

[Gandhi] placated them to some extent by resolution advocating release of all political prisoners violent or otherwise and his so-called description of Swaraj was also intended to appeal to Socialists and specially Jawahar Lal Nehru.[48]

The revolutionaries were not engaged in the drafting of the resolution, but their politics and fate helped to create the conditions for its acceptance by the Congress in the face of some determined opposition.[49] The resolution not only injected a socialist tinge to Congress objectives, but 'served to provide a powerful stimulus to the growth of the socialist movement in the country'.[50] This was an outcome that was consistent with the HSRA's own objectives.

Revolutionary Reflections

Several surviving revolutionaries concluded in their memoirs and testimonies that the HSRA's actions and subsequent martyrdoms reinvigorated a culture of sacrifice into Indian politics, even as they acknowledged that Gandhi too worked to achieve this in life and in his eventual death.[51] Several revolutionaries became politically active after the Jallianwalla Bagh massacre, and continued to be actuated by the injustice and high-handedness perpetrated by the British that they saw around them.[52] Many in interwar India were animated by the humiliations of colonialism, and incensed by its violent excesses. Consider, for instance, an encounter recorded in *Congress Bulletin* in 1930, between a twelve year old boy and a British Superintendent of Police in Bombay. Not intimidated by the Superintendent's uniform, the boy shouted the banned slogan, '*Inquilab Zindabad!*' Enraged, the 'Police Superintendent caught him and gave him a slap on his face and the boy fell down', but the boy leapt to his feet and repeated the slogan. The process was repeated no less than four times, before the Superintendent 'had to yield and went off'.[53]

Many surviving revolutionaries believed that their violent actions avenged the national honour, and in the process made the government more circumspect in its deployment of violence. Durga Das Khanna related that Saunders was killed because

it had become necessary to avenge a national insult. Lalaji was a leader of world fame... I may recall the statement of Shrimati Basanti Devi... If he could be manhandled that way, then Gandhiji, Jawaharlal, Motilal and other leaders could also be handled in the same way.[54]

Likewise, Shiv Verma reflected that after the assassination in Lahore, 'we felt a confidence, and we felt: No, India is not impotent as they think of us to be.'[55] Verma then referred his interviewer to Jawaharlal Nehru's comment in his autobiography that Saunders' death 'seemed to vindicate, for a moment, the honour of Lala Lajpat Rai, and through him of the nation'.[56] Seen in this light, the revolutionaries took up the role of protecting Congressmen who had pledged not to defend themselves. They vowed to answer colonial violence with revolutionary violence.

Saunders' assassination was an act performed with relative detachment and with discernible regret, as a necessary restoration of order. Frantz Fanon would later reflect that in this modality, 'violence is a cleansing force. It frees the native from his inferiority complex and from his despair and inaction; it makes him fearless and restores his self-respect.'[57] Fanon would later reprimand nationalists in Algeria for appropriating revolutionary violence for their own ends,[58] but in India the nationalist left (as well as the Indian internationalist communists)[59] in 1929 was still in a formative phase, and was aligned or connected, however uneasily, with the Congress. The Fundamental Rights Resolution notwithstanding, the Karachi Congress sowed some of the seeds for its detachment, with the formation of Congress Socialist parties in Bihar, Delhi, Uttar Pradesh, Bombay and Punjab by 1934, aimed at pressing the Congress to the left.[60]

The progressive arrests of HSRA members in 1929 and the subsequent conduct of the Lahore Conspiracy Case threw the British legal framework into disrepute, further undermining confidence in the Raj. As Jaidev Gupta recalled:

the rulers were placed in a tight corner. The Indians were abused openly in the court by an English judge. This was the point which straightaway went into the minds of the masses. Their boycotting the court and their cause gained them respect of great magnitude. ... [T]he hollowness of the so-called British justice, which they were proclaiming to the whole world that they were governing us for our benefit and giving justice to the Indians was proved nonetheless.[61]

Partha Chatterjee has drawn attention to the 'significant shift' taking place in colonial courtrooms from the 1920s and 1930s, as Indian lawyers began to come into their own. This, Chatterjee argues, represented in microcosm 'the secret story of the transfer of power in late colonial India, carried out not so much in street demonstrations, prisons, and conference tables but within the interstices of the governmental apparatus itself'.[62] The nationalist lawyering that was brought to bear on the Lahore Conspiracy Case, evident in legalistic speeches from leaders such as Jinnah and Malaviya, but also the legal interventions of Motilal Nehru to the Privy Council, substantially complicated what was a high-level, high-stakes case. The early 1930s, when Bhagat Singh, Rajguru and Sukhdev were hanged, represented the final hurrah of die-hard imperialism, that would be worn down by the Government of India Act (1935), before being extinguished by the Second World War.

Bimal Prasad Jain's reflections are also instructive:

After my release from jail, I was interested in working with the Congress, because the independence movement had gone down to the masses and that was the only purpose of the terrorist movement—to rouse the masses for a mass movement. Gandhiji played a very important role in making it a mass movement. Our role as a terrorist movement was equally important because when Gandhiji could not do anything—not a single man was behind him and people were so much upset—our supreme sacrifices created two things among masses. One, fearlessness towards the English rule, and for confidence in themselves. And two, a spirit of sacrifice to achieve independence.[63]

Finally, Bhagat Singh explained that political assassination was intended to gain public support, to 'create a mentality and an atmosphere which shall be very necessary to the final struggle. That is all.'[64] But the final struggle that he imagined never came. Writing from jail, Bhagat Singh warned the youth against 'the vicious circle of aimless outrages and individual self-immolation', which now seemed to be of limited use:

terrorism can at most force the Imperialist power to come to terms with [the Congress] party. … Terrorism thus hope[s] to wring out what Gandhism bids fair to attain—a compromise and an installment of reforms—a replacement of a white rule at Delhi by a brown rule.[65]

In one of his final reckonings, Bhagat Singh concluded that, on balance, political violence profited organised nationalism more than it did revolutionary purposes, although in this he made exceptions for both Nehrus.[66] And yet the last phrase in the above quote is redolent of Gandhi's own demurral in *Hind Swaraj*, that to aspire for mere 'English rule without the Englishman' would not do.[67] For the HSRA operated at the fringes of the nationalist movement, studying, critiquing and at times converging with Congress agendas; this was where they had located their opportunities for popularising their socialist politics. There was, in short, an intersection between the mainstream Congress and the revolutionaries, which allowed the latter to shape nationalist choices and strategies to an extent historians of the Congress movement have never fully appreciated.

Thus Bhagat Singh became famous *both* because he was willing to use violence, and despite it. J. P. Narayan reflected that his death

was one of the most tragic incidents in our national history, which made an indelible mark particularly on the minds of the youth of India and that one incident had alienated the youth of India much more from the British than any other single incident I can think of had done before.[68]

The impact of the revolutionaries was endorsed by others as well. The Congress leader Lala Jagat Narain assured an interviewer, 'I can tell you that ninety per cent of the public were in sympathy with the revolutionaries'.[69] Durga Das Khanna proudly recalled the day, some time in the 1950s, when he happened to meet the president of India, Dr Radhakrishnan. They discussed the convocation ceremony in Lahore in late 1930, when Hari Kishen misfired at Geoffrey de Montmorency. Radhakrishnan leaned towards Khanna, telling him that the assassination attempt 'stepped up the prestige of the country and even brought the Gandhi–Irwin Pact nearer.'[70]

Modalities of Violence

If the revolutionary contribution to the mainstream nationalist movement was so fundamental, why did it lose the support of important Congress leaders who continued to shape the nationalist movement—in particular, of Jawaharlal Nehru? The answer to this, I believe, lies in Jawaharlal's judgement of the complex inter-relationship between various modalities of violence in the aftermath of the Kanpur riots.

It was the violence caused by economic disparity that turned many early moderate nationalists to organise against the government,[71] calling attention to, as Dadabhai Naoroji had so neatly put it, the link between 'Poverty and UnBritish Rule in India'. Similarly, heinous acts of state violence employed against nationalist protest, particularly the massacre in Jallianwala Bagh in April 1919, have long been acknowledged as pivotal in providing an impetus for nationalist mobilisation and militancy. More recently, in the wake of a body of scholarship concerned with epistemological violence, studies of colonialism have shifted back to examine the everyday violence exacted upon the Indian body under colonialism.[72] Elizabeth Kolsky has recently emphasised that 'white violence' perpetrated by Britons on Indian subjects was 'a constant and constituent element of British dominance in India';[73] and Taylor C. Sherman has demonstrated the degree to which the state relied upon physical force to exact colonial compliance.[74]

By contrast, as Shahid Amin argues in his book on Chauri Chaura, nationalist violence has been seen as an uncomfortable aberration that disrupts the nonviolent narrative.[75] For the most part, communal violence between Hindus and Muslims is considered under an entirely separate rubric,[76] with the lauded success of nonviolence in delivering the nation to independence remaining difficult to reconcile with the extraordinary scale of partition violence. Slavoj Žižek has recently concluded that:

The lesson of the intricate relationship between subjective and systemic violence is that violence is not a direct property of some acts, but is distributed between acts and their contexts, between activity and inactivity.[77]

Violence, once initiated, becomes self-perpetuating and spills across the discursive categories that aim to conscribe it. In this mélange, there is a troubling crevice between action and intention, interpretation and outcome.

Following this conceptualisation of the inter-relatedness of different modalities of violence, it becomes difficult to partition colonial and anticolonial violence from communal violence. This was certainly what Jawaharlal Nehru came to believe in the aftermath of the Kanpur riots, counted as the worst 'since Banaras 1809 in terms of the causalities that occurred'.[78] From other writings we know he was deeply troubled by communal violence,[79] and he was especially haunted by the death of Vidyarthi: 'All the time I see his face before me'.[80] He concluded his speech at the Karachi Congress by explaining:

My regard for Bhagat Singh is no less than that of any of you. I shall not conceal anything from you. I declare openly that only by the method of Mahatma Gandhi will we gain freedom and if we leave the path of nonviolence we shall not be free for years to come. This is my opinion. I honestly believe that we cannot gain independence by violence. I am fully confident that those who think violent means would solve the problem are wrong. The way of violence is a dangerous way for our country. It will ruin the country and set brother against brother and, God forbid, they may start killing each other.[81]

The influence of Gandhi's analysis of violence in this formulation is unmistakeable. Many biographers have attempted to account for Jawaharlal's capitulation to Gandhi after his father's death, suggesting that Gandhi became his surrogate father-figure.[82] The months following his father's death were certainly difficult ones for Nehru, with the Viceroy describing his mood as 'impossible' and 'very mercurial'.[83] His dissonance seemed to have peaked at the Karachi Congress, where 'his sadness impressed Gandhi and induced him to have a heart-to-heart talk with him.'[84] The outcome of this *tête à tête* was Nehru's support for the pact, secured against the Bhagat Singh and Fundamental Rights Resolutions. This was not the first time Jawaharlal had unhappily reconciled himself to Gandhi, nor would it be the last. In this particular instance, his earlier pragmatic attitude to nonviolence seems to have given way to a more ideological commitment. This was prompted not only by the death of Motilal, nor by the manoeuvring of the Mahatma; but by his meditations on the overwhelming scale of communal violence that killed Ganesh Shankar Vidyarthi.

EPILOGUE

CONGRESS AND THE REVOLUTIONARIES, 1937–1946

The Government of India Act of 1935, negotiated and drafted following the second phase of civil disobedience, introduced a level of provincial autonomy. In 1937, elections were called to establish Indian-led governments in the provinces; the Congress would emerge as the strongest political party, winning in all provinces save Bengal and Punjab. The Congress Election Manifesto, drafted in 1936, declared that the release of political prisoners would be the priority of any Congress Ministry. After the elections, when Congress-led provinces proceeded to free their political prisoners, the Viceroy and respective Governors blocked the release orders. This forced a political crisis, with the Congress accusing the Governors of unacceptable interference; in Bihar and the United Provinces the newly-appointed Chief Ministers resigned.[1] Political prisoners embarked upon a fresh round of hunger strikes, and Gandhi began to plead with them to abandon them.[2] The Bengali revolutionary Shanti Das recalled that it was through the Mahatma's intervention that she was released early from her prison sentence, heralding 'a new chapter in my life'.[3]

Some of the Lahore Conspiracy Case convicts were less amenable to negotiation, despite their ideological transformation in prison. Jaidev Kapoor, Narain Rai and Niranjan Sen formed a committee through which they communicated, via the Commissioner, with Gandhi.[4] Gandhi was, at the time, negotiating with political prisoners in several provinces to vow to renounce violent activities after their release. Jaidev Kapoor refused to give any such undertaking, maintaining that 'violence or non-violence would depend upon the ruler's behaviour'.[5] Gandhi also negotiated with the government to return revolutionary prisoners to jails in the provinces that had convicted them.

While the Lahore Conspiracy Case prisoners declined to be freed under these terms, Bejoy Kumar Sinha, Shiv Verma, Gaya Prasad, Kamalnath Tiwari and Jaidev

Kapoor left the Andamans and were returned to Punjab, from where they commenced an appeal to be sent to the United Provinces, to be close to their families.[6] The Punjab government, formed by the Unionist Party under Sikander Hyat Khan, was not amenable to this, anticipating that if they were returned to the United Provinces, the Congress would indulge the revolutionaries with an amnesty. Following the direct intervention of Jawaharlal Nehru, the UP-based revolutionaries were eventually transferred to Naini Jail, with the proviso that because they had been convicted in Punjab, any acquittal must be secured from that province alone.

At Naini, they met with Nehru, Ranjit Pandit and K. N. Katju, who secured them reasonable facilities for reading, writing and receiving visitors, and eventually the government agreed to their request to be transferred to Lucknow.[7] Jawaharlal appealed to Kapoor to assist in negotiations with the Kakori prisoners, who had been freed earlier by the Congress government, but who had made several violent speeches, 'causing embarrassment to the United Provinces Ministry'.[8] Nehru reasoned that the Kakori convicts would defer to Kapoor, because he 'was one of them'. Nehru organised for Kapoor to be released temporarily from prison, travelling to the United Provinces Provincial Congress meeting in Ayodhya to meet with Pandit Parmanand and Raj Kumar Sinha, where he urged them to recalibrate their activities. Six of the released Kakori prisoners, including Manmathnath Gupta, were unable to tolerate the quiescence expected of them, and actively courted re-arrest within months of their release by breaching their parole conditions, entering Delhi to attend an Ex-Political Prisoners Conference organised by Durga Devi Vohra, in her capacity as president of the Delhi Congress Committee.[9] Jawaharlal Nehru threw a tea party in their honour, 'but very shrewdly converted it into a meeting' in which he would be seen to be instructing them.[10]

In 1938, following Subhas Chandra Bose's election as Congress president, Jaidev Kapoor wrote to Chandrabhanu Gupta requesting that Bose visit them in jail on his next visit to Lucknow.[11] As Jail Minister, Rafi Ahmad Kidwai facilitated the visit, and one fine November day Bose arrived, bringing with him Sachindranath Sanyal. The Lahore Conspiracy Case prisoners requested that Bose negotiate an amnesty with the government in Punjab, in return promising not to enter the province.[12] Bose was unable to progress the issue before the outbreak of the Second World War the following year.

A breakthrough of sorts came in March 1941, when Jawaharlal was transferred with Ranjit Pandit to Lucknow Jail, while serving a sentence of rigorous imprisonment for breaching the Defence of India Rules. This gave both Nehru and the remaining UP revolutionaries the opportunity to spend time together. While Nehru was kept in a separate barracks at night, during the day he freely mixed with other prisoners.[13] Nehru noted in his prison diary that 'we were glad to be with them both for our sakes and theirs. This gives us an opportunity to get to know them and already we have found them to be jolly and attractive, despite their long confinement'.[14] The revolutionaries equally enjoyed Nehru. Kapoor recalled Jawaharlal's personal touch and concern for the welfare of those around him, and they engaged in long conversations about politics, comparing socialist and capitalist economic theories. Kapoor's hobby in jail was gardening, and he taught Nehru how to graft and bud roses, which Nehru remarked upon in his diary.[15] Shiv Verma recalled that Nehru took charge of the cooking, making tasty omelets which gave the revolutionaries welcome respite from B Class Prisoner fare.[16] Both Kapoor and Verma were deeply impressed by Nehru's personality, and after spending some days with him without witnessing his famous temper, approached him, saying:

'Panditji, we are very disappointed in you. ... We had heard a lot about you that you perform a very good drama and it is about a month since you have come here but there has been no throwing of pillows or thalis.' Immediately he caught the hint... 'I have to travel for the whole night, and when I reach the station in the early morning hours, an open car awaits for me. Pandit Nehru is there, slogan shouting and demonstrations start. Nobody is worried that human needs are there. I want to ease myself, relax myself, but there is slogan shouting. So, I lose my temper!'[17]

In his prison diary, Nehru commented on the same discussion, marveling, 'They had been told that I had a frightful temper and was unsocial and difficult to get along with. What a reputation to have!'[18]

It was not until after the 1946 elections, when the Congress and the Muslim League formed a joint ministry in Punjab, that the possibility of the Lahore Conspiracy Case prisoners being freed was raised. Kapoor believed that Nehru was a prime mover behind this.[19] The remaining political prisoners of the Lahore Conspiracy Case were released in April 1946.[20] In the UP, there was some delay in releasing the revolutionaries due to a disagreement over terms between the Governor and the Congress Ministers which came to a head when an MLA, Anant Prasad Dube, demanded the resignation of the Ministry.[21]

A number of released revolutionaries, though not all, turned to the Congress Socialist Party or the Communist Party of India after their release.[22] Some, like B.K. Dutt, retreated from political life altogether. Shiv Verma, on the other hand, concluded his oral history interview with constructive advice to future activists:

Never think you can befool the police by saying wrong things. Once you open your mouth, it is very difficult to save yourself. I have emphasised more on my mistakes because if somebody reads this record, he may get a lesson out of it.[23]

Such was the commitment of a veteran radical, pledged to the cause of revolution to the end.

APPENDIX

THE MARTYR'S CONFERENCE IN PARADISE

Surgpuri 12ᵗʰ April 1931.

To-day a conference of all the India's martyrs was held in Paradise. Hundreds of holy souls who had shed their blood for Indian liberty were adorning the conference in their respective seats. The names of Khudi Ram Bose, Mr Ram Parshad Bismil, Mr Ishfaqullah, Mr Hari Bhai Balmukand, martyr Khushi Ram etc are worthy of note among those who occupied higher places. The Martyrs of Jallianwallah Bagh looked smart in bloody uniforms. The enthusiasm of the Sholapur martyrs was also worthy of note. A high place was vacant for martyr Jatindra Nath Das, Chairman of the Reception Committee, Sardar Bhagat Singh President of the Conference, and his comrades Messers Rajguru and Sukhdev. The arrival of those young men who had to arrive from the Mother country after attaining martyrdom was being anxiously awaited. About this time conches were blown, the gods began to shower flowers and Sardar Bhagat Singh, Mr Rajguru and Shriyut Sukhdev came to the conference amidst such shouts as these:—'Mukammal azadi zindabad' (Long live complete independence), 'Shahidon ki jai' (victory to the martyrs), 'Bartania ka khuni insaf murdabad' (May England's bloody justice be dead). A look at the signs of the hangman's rope round their neck showed as if they were wearing necklaces of shining jewels, their faces indicated glory and their eyes contained a glimmer of sanctity. They were accompanied by martyr Jatindra Nath Das. The martyrs of the Jallianwala Bagh after raising their red arms high presented arms to Bhagat Singh and his comrades. Sardar Bhagat Singh and his comrades embraced each and every votary of the Mother country and then took their seats. A newly married young man, who was the husband of Shrimati Rattan Devi and who was killed by Dyer's bullet in the Jallainwalla Bagh, performed the Arti ceremony. After that Sardar Bhagat Singh rose from his seat and greeting the martyrs said 'A country where bridegrooms are so brutally murdered, cannot remain a slave for much longer'. Poems entitled 'Shahidon ka Tahara' and Ram Parshad Bismil's well known poem 'Ham abhi se kiya batain kiya hamare dil mein hai' were recited. Thereafter Jatindranath Das read his address as Chairman of the Reception Committee in the course of which he said:

'The bloody Baisakhi of Amritsar will ever remain memorable in the history of India's liberty. The English rulers have proved it to God and to the whole world that the English nation has not procured only one Dyer. General massacres and executions continue; and by shedding the blood of our countrymen from time to time we are being told that seventy thousand Dyers are working in India. Time has come when the blood of the martyrs will certainly bear fruit and hundreds of Khudi Rams, thousands of Bismils and lakhs of Bhagat Singhs will come out into the field in order to have their heads struck off for the same of liberty. It is a matter for pride to me that I am welcoming my three comrades'.

At this moment Jesus Christ arrived. Sardar Bhagat Singh said: 'India's martyrs greet the martyr of Jerusalem.' Voices were raised by the Jallianwala Bagh martyrs: 'Accept our salutation O peaceful shepherd of bloodthirsty sheep'. The Sholapur men said: 'Turn your wolves into sheep again'. In short the welcin [sic] resounded with shouts like the above. Jesus met every one cordially and after kissing the Cross he said: 'An innocent man's blood never goes in vain'. 'Dyer is to-day being burnt in hell fire. He is crying to me for intercession but can I intercede on the behalf of executioners, murderers, and assassins? I swear by this sacred Cross that there is absolutely no nearness between me and these white people whose hearts have become black with the blood of oppressed people. They will get their desserts and no heavenly power can save them from the wrath of my Holy Father. Rest assured, God will never forgive your murderers.'

After having made the above remarks Jesus patted Sardar Bhagat Singh and gave benedictions to all the martyrs.

In the course of his presidential address, Sardar Bhagat Singh is reported to have said: 'I have merely done my duty. I want to sacrifice myself for the sake of my country's freedom by taking several births. Before putting the hangman's rope around my neck I kissed it. Our dust is flying not only on the banks of the Sutlej but in all corners of India, so that it might enter the eyes of those rulers who have become blind through their setting store by their power and authority and they might become absolutely incapable of seeing the truth. It is in this way that a tyrannical Government can come to an end. The fleet of Sin sinks when it has been fully loaded. The day is not far off when the blind rulers of India will once again cause the blood of the innocents to run in streams. At that time death will be standing over their heads but they will not be able to see it. Those who bathe in the blood of martyrs are cowards. No resolution should therefore be passed respecting them. You are lions. You gave up your lives like lions. It is an insult to us to censure cowards. Their own high priest, their own Prophet, their own Apostle has refused to intercede for them. There could be no greater humiliation than this.'

The idea of passing a resolution of censure was therefore given up.

In the course of his speech Martyr Khudi Ram Bose, representing the martyrs of Bengal, said: 'I wish I could again take birth in the Mother Country and sacrifice my life to cut asunder the chains of Bharat Mata. The war of Mahabharat is again in progress in India. A peaceful man like Mahatma Gandhi cannot quarrel with anyone. He is simply working as the tool of this Just God. The disc of Lord Krishna is working and British rule is coming to an end in India every moment. Lord Krishna is drinking the blood of the witch of slavery and munching her bones'.

Punjab delegate-martyr Khushi Ram who boldly faced death through Police Bullets in Hira Mandi, Lahore (in 1919) said: 'By her stratagems England is digging her own grave. She gave us a chance to become martyrs for which we are grateful to her. The English have to cross the stream of the blood of us—innocent people—which is flowing between the Heaven and the Earth. This stream is so dreadful that they will not be able to cross it even if they give crores of cows in charity. The white-skinned people should remember that the blood of a single martyr possesses the power of causing a flood in this dreadful stream and the blood which they regard to-day as so cheap its cheapness will cost them very dear.'

Speaking on the behalf of the martyrs of the Delhi Conspiracy Case Bhai Balmukand said: 'we want to die for the country and if we again get this element of dust we will again sacrifice ourselves like moths at the lamp of freedom.'

Bhai Balmukand's wife said: 'The authorities must understand that the husband of an Indian woman can throw their contemptible government to the ground in an instant.'

In the course of his speech Babu Ram Pershad speaking on behalf of the UP and Kakori Martyrs read the verse:

'Fairs will be annually held at the cremation places of the martyrs.
This will be the name and vestige of those who become extinct for the country'.

After reciting the above verse, he said:

'The numbers of martyrs is increasingly largely in India. I have no personal quarrel with the English but my blood begins to boil in my veins when I see on the Union Jack the stains of the blood of my countrymen, that is why I refuse to bow before this bloody flag. The greater the increase in the number of martyrs the greater becomes the number of (blood) stains on this Flag. Those who honestly believe that British rule is based on justice are under a delusion. Time is coming when the nations of the world will jeer on seeing their blood-stained flag'.

In his inaugural address the President said: 'I do not know to what extent the martyr's colony in Paradise will grow. My heart says that until spouts of our blood go forth from the sacred soil of India liberty cannot be attained. I think that in two or four days at least four young men will join us after putting on the crown of martyrdom. O God! Send us to the world again so that we might be able to shorten the oppressed Mother Country's period of slavery by our fresh sacrifices'.

After these proceedings all the souls left for their respective abodes, the Conference came to an end but the redness of the atmosphere is still there.[85]

NOTES

A NOTE ON SPELLING

1. Arne Naess, 'Nonviolence', in *The Selected Works of Arne Naess*, Vol. 1, Dordrecht: Springer, 2005, p. 41.

INTRODUCTION: VIOLENCE AND ANTICOLONIALISM IN INDIA

1. *Hind Swaraj* was in part an interlocution with those who supported the assassination of Wylie Curzon in London by Madanlal Dhingra. Anthony Parel (ed.), *Hind Swaraj and Other Writings*, Cambridge: Cambridge University Press, 1997, pp. 77–78.
2. C. F. Andrews, 'Introduction', to H. G. Alexander, *The Indian Ferment: A Traveller's Tale*, London: Williams and Norgate, 1929, p. 1.
3. Cf. Gyanendra Pandey, 'Un-archived Histories: the "Mad" and the "Trifling"', *Economic and Political Weekly*, XLVII, no. 1, 2012, pp. 37–41.
4. For the purposes of this book, references to 'revolutionaries' will refer to the members of the Hindustan Socialist Republican Army/Association (HSRA), although they by no means had a monopoly on the use of the term, nor did they claim one. For a more nuanced consideration of what constitutes 'revolutionary' in South Asian histories, see Kama Maclean and J. Daniel Elam, 'Who is a Revolutionary?', *Postcolonial Studies*, Special Issue: Reading Revolutionaries—Texts, Acts, and Afterlives of Political Action in Late Colonial South Asia, 16(2), 2013, pp. 113–123.
5. Mrinalini Sinha, *Specters of Mother India: the Global Restructuring of an Empire*, Durham: Duke University Press, 2006, pp. 23–4.
6. It is for this reason that I generally favour the term 'Congressite' over 'Congressman', which not only evades gender assumptions, but is a reminder of the relative porousness of the Congress at the time, while circumventing anachronistic slippage between the Congress as a movement and as a later election-contesting party.
7. Faisal Devji, *The Impossible Indian: Gandhi and the Temptation of Violence*, London: C. Hurst & Co., 2012, p. 2.
8. Christopher Pinney, *'Photos of the Gods': The Printed Image and Political Struggle in India*, London: Reaktion Books, 2004, p. 118.

243

9. Shahid Amin, *Event, Metaphor, Memory: Chauri Chaura, 1922–1992*, Berkeley: University of California Press, 1995, p. 3.

10. Sumit Sarkar, *Modern India, 1885–1947*, Delhi: Macmillan, 1983, p. 251; Bipan Chandra, *Nationalism and Colonialism in Modern India*, Delhi: Orient Longman, 1979, p. 225.

11. See, for example, Subhas Chandra Bose's reflections in *The Indian Struggle: 1920–1942*, New York: Asia Publishing House, 1964, Chapters 9 and 10.

12. Neeti Nair has recently argued that Bhagat Singh's popularity was *not* a result of his violence, but due to a recognition that he was engaged in the dialectic of Satyagraha in his well-publicised hunger strikes in jail. Neeti Nair, 'Bhagat Singh as "Satyagrahi": The Limits to Non-Violence in Late Colonial India', *Modern Asian Studies*, 43(3), 2009, p. 678.

13. This is discussed in some detail in Chapter Six, however the welcoming address of Saifuddin Kitchlew and the presidential address of Jawaharlal Nehru at the Lahore Congress in 1929 were indicative of Congress discourses conceding the possibility of anticolonial violence. National Archives of India (henceforth NAI), Home Political (henceforth HP), 65/1930.

14. Judith Brown, *Gandhi and Civil Disobedience: The Mahatma in Politics, 1928–34*, Cambridge: Cambridge University Press, 1977, p. 16. Nanda also reflects that in 1924, Gandhi was 'bitterly disillusioned' when he realised that 'some of his senior colleagues should have mental reservations about non-violence even in its political applications'. B.R. Nanda, *The Nehrus*, Chicago: University of Chicago Press, 1974, p. 240.

15. Perry Anderson, 'Gandhi Centre Stage', *The London Review of Books*, 34(13), 2012, at http://www.lrb.co.uk/v34/n13/perry-anderson/gandhi-centre-stage (last accessed 10 September 2012).

16. Amit Kumar Gupta, 'Defying Death: Nationalist Revolutionism in India, 1897–1938', *Social Scientist*, 25(9/10), 1997, p. 4; for a reading of Savarkar within a revolutionary framework, see Vinayak Chaturvedi, 'A Revolutionary's Biography: the Case of V. D. Savarkar', *Postcolonial Studies*, 16 (2), 2013, pp. 124–139.

17. Gupta, 'Defying Death', p. 17.

18. More on this in Chapter Seven, but we might briefly reflect that Gandhi too courted martyrdom by undertaking several fasts to the death, cognisant of the political pressures on the government that his death would bring. See Kevin Grant, 'The Transcolonial World of Hunger Strikes and Political Fasts', in Durba Ghosh and Dane Kennedy (eds), *Decentering Empire: Britain, India and the Transcolonial World*, Delhi: Orient Longman, 2006, pp. 243–269.

19. Parel (ed.), *Hind Swaraj*, p. 78.

20. Interview with the *Times of India*, 5 June 1924.

21. See Gandhi's letter to Darcy Lindsay, 8 May 1931, *CWMG*, Vol. XLVI, p. 120.

22. Taylor C. Sherman, *State Violence and Punishment in India*, London/New York: Routledge, 2010; Elizabeth Kolsky, *Colonial Justice in British India*, Cambridge: Cambridge University Press, 2010.

23. Maclean and Elam, 'Who is a Revolutionary?', *passim*.

24. Maia Ramnath, *Haj to Utopia: How the Ghadar Movement Chartered Global Radicalism and Attempted to Overthrow the British Empire*, Berkeley: University of California Press, 2011, p. 8.

25. On this point, see Benjamin Zachariah, 'Internationalisms in the Interwar Years: The Traveling of Ideas', in Ali Raza, Franziska Roy and Benjamin Zachariah (eds), *The Internationalist Moment: South Asia, Worlds, and World Views, 1917–1939*, New Delhi: Sage, 2015, pp. 1–21.

26. Bipan Chandra, 'Bhagat Singh and Atheism', in *Ideology and Politics in Modern India*, New Delhi: Har-Anand Publications, 1994, p. 261.

27. Kris Manjapra, *M. N. Roy: Marxism and Colonial Cosmopolitanism*, London: Routledge, 2010, p. 71.

28. Bipan Chandra argues that the left in India was bifurcated by two trends: 'they either cut themselves off from the nationalist stream or became its "tail"'. 'Marxism in India', in *Ideology and Politics*, p. 201. See also Sanjay Seth, *Marxist Ideology and Nationalist Politics: The Case of Colonial India*, New Delhi: Sage, 1995; Stephen Sherlock, 'Berlin, Moscow and Bombay: The Marxism that India Inherited', *South Asia*, 21(1), 1998, pp. 63–76.

29. Shiv Verma, *Samsmritiyan: Krantikari Shahidon ke Samsmarnatmak Rekhichitra*, Lucknow: Rahul Foundation, 2006, p. 41. The NJBS had invited prominent communists to its Punjab Provincial Conference in 1929, such as P. C. Joshi, but they did not attend. Extract from weekly report of the Director, Intelligence Bureau (henceforth DIB Report), 28 February 1929. IOR, L/PJ/12/375, p. 16.

30. Mridula Mukherjee, *Peasants in India's Non-Violent Revolution: Practice and Theory*, New Delhi: Sage, 2004, p. 62.

31. Bhagat Singh's personal reading program, in which Marx, Engels, and Lenin featured prominently, can be discerned from his Prison Diary, a facsimile of which is held in NMML and has been published as K.C. Yadav and Babar Singh (eds), *Bhagat Singh, Ideas on Freedom, Liberty and Revolution: Jail Notes of a Revolutionary*, Delhi: Hope India Publications, 2007.

32. Bhagat Singh, 'Letter to Sukhdev', in Shiv Verma (ed.), *Bhagat Singh: on the Path of Liberation*, Chennai: Bharathi Puthakalaya, 2007 p. 131.

33. See, for example, 'To the Young Political Workers', in IOR, L/PJ/12/391, pp. 61–74.

34. On the nexus between the coterminous Lahore and Meerut Conspiracy Cases, see Franziska Roy and Benjamin Zachariah, 'Meerut and a Hanging: "Young India", Popular Socialism, and the Dynamics of Imperialism', *Comparative Studies of South Asia, Africa and the Middle East*, 33 (3), 2013, pp. 360–77.

35. Indications of this particular usage are evident in Balshastri Hardas, *Armed Struggle for Freedom: Ninety Years of Indian Independence, from 1857 to Subhash*, translated by S. S. Apte, Poona: KAL Prakashan, 1958; and also in contemporary popular posters which memorialise militant leaders from different epochs (See Figures 10 and 46).

36. Sugata Bose and Ayesha Jalal, *Modern South Asia: History, Culture and Political Economy*, Delhi: Oxford University Press, 1997, p. 150; Jim Masselos, *Indian Nationalism: A*

History, New Delhi: New Dawn Press, 2005, p. 175; Ravinder Kumar, *The Making of a Nation: Essays on Indian History and Politics*, Delhi: Manohar, 1989, p. 46–7.

37. See David M. Laushey, *Bengal Terrorism and the Marxist Left: Aspects of Regional Nationalism in India, 1905–1942*, Calcutta: Firma K. Mukhopadhyay, 1975; Durba Ghosh, 'Terrorism in Bengal: Political Violence in the Interwar Years', in Ghosh and Kennedy (eds), *Decentering Empire*; Peter Heehs, *The Bomb in Bengal: The Rise of Revolutionary Terrorism in India, 1900–1910*, Oxford: Oxford University Press, 1993; Roma Banerjee, *Subhas Chandra Bose and the Bengal Revolutionaries*, New Delhi: Reference Press, 2006; Hiren Gohain's recent *The Contribution of the Revolutionists in India's Freedom Struggle*, translated by Amrit Jyoti Mahanta, New Delhi: National Book Trust, 2010, includes north Indian and Punjabi developments, but its timeframe from the early 1900s skews the weight of the book towards Bengal.

38. 'Terrorism in India outside Bengal, Assam and Burma', 1933, IOR, L/PJ/12/398, p. 58.

39. Partha Chatterjee, 'Bombs and Nationalism in Bengal', paper presented at 'Subaltern Citizens and their Histories', 13–14 October 2006, Emory University. www.icis.emory.edu/subalterndocs/Chatterjee.pdf (last accessed 6 August 2014), p. 27.

40. Brown, *Gandhi and Civil Disobedience*, p. 36.

41. D. A. Low, 'The Purna Swaraj decision 1929', in *Britain and Indian Nationalism: The Imprint of Ambiguity, 1929–1942*, Cambridge: Cambridge University Press, 1997, p. 68.

42. Gandhi to Irwin, May 4, 1930, *CWMG*, Vol. XLIII, p. 389; Interview with *Young India*, March 11, 1930, *CWMG*, Vol. XLIII, p. 42.

43. Irfan Habib, 'The Congress and the Revolutionaries', in Kapil Kumar (ed.), *Congress and Classes: Nationalism, Workers and Peasants*, New Delhi: Manohar, 1988; Peter Heehs, 'Revolutionary Terrorism in British Bengal', in Elleke Boehmer and Stephen Morten (eds), *Terror and the Postcolonial*, London: Blackwell, 2010, pp. 153–176.

44. *Fortnightly Reports* are the important exception to this, although they tend to be somewhat curt summaries, rather than the lengthy documents which bounced between departments and provinces, accumulating anecdotes and analysis, however flawed, as they travelled.

45. http://www.nationalarchives.gov.uk/A2A/records.aspx?cat=059-lpj12&cid=-1&Gsm=2008–06–18%20-%20–1#-1 (last accessed 18 September 2012).

46. David Arnold has discerned a similar trend in post-colonial studies of labour history, in which 'a lingering Gandhian tradition' has resulted in industrial violence being 'regarded as too morally reprehensible and politically deviant to warrant serious analysis.' David Arnold, 'Industrial Violence in Colonial India', *Comparative Studies in History and Society*, 22(2), 1980, p. 235. Scholarship has been remarkably reticent on the violence of the Raj, a trend which is beginning to turn. See Jonathon Saha, 'Everyday Violence in British India', *History Compass*, 9(11), 2011, pp. 844–853; Anupama Rao, 'Problems of Violence, States of Terror: Torture in Colonial India', *Interventions: International Journal of Postcolonial Studies*, 3(2), 2010; Kolsky, *Colonial Justice in British India*. In a more confessional vein, see Bart Moore-Gilbert, *The Setting Sun: A Memoir of Empire and Family Secrets*, New York: Verso, 2014.

47. For example, M. K. Gandhi, 'The Curse of Assassination', *Young India*, 27 December

1928, *CWMG*, Vol. XXXVII, pp. 274–6; 'The Bomb and the Knife', 18 April 1929, *CWMG*, Vol. XL, p. 260.

48. Ravinder Kumar, 'The Place of Oral Sources in Historical Research', in *The Making of a Nation*, p. 245.
49. http://www.s-asian.cam.ac.uk/audio.html (last accessed 5 September 2012).
50. Compare Bhikshu Chaman Lal, Nehru Memorial Museum and Library (henceforth NMML), Oral History Transcript (henceforth OHT), with B. C. Lal, Centre of South Asian Studies, University of Cambridge (henceforth CSAS), Oral History Collection (henceforth OHC). The recent debates around the Belfast Oral History Project are a cogent reminder of the sensitivity of political context. Beth McMurtrie, 'Secrets from Belfast', *Chronicle of Higher Education*, 26 January 2014.
51. Arjun Appadurai, whose father had thrown his lot in with Subhas Chandra Bose's Indian National Army, wrote feelingly of his estrangement from the nonviolent mainstream: 'When my father returned to India in 1945, he and his comrades were unwelcome heroes, poor cousins in the story of the nationalist struggle … [T]o the end of their lives, my father and his comrades remained pariah patriots, rogue nationalists'. 'Patriotism and Its Futures', *Public Culture*, 3(5), Spring 1993, p. 415.
52. To qualify for 'Freedom Fighter' status, one's name had to be registered in the *Political Who's Who*, a list of dissidents complied by provincial governments in 1936. While this document did indeed contain many revolutionaries, those who died before, or joined the freedom struggle after 1936, were summarily excluded. Personal communication, Durba Ghosh, 7 August 2012. M. D. Thapar, Sukhdev's younger brother, was most resentful of this, writing to Kuldip Nayar that 'other political sufferers like Dr Kichloo's son, got a monthly packet of Rs. 5,000 and a flat free of cost. Against Dr Kichloo's son, compare our clan's sacrifice'. Kuldip Nayar, *Without Fear: The Life and Trial of Bhagat Singh*, New Delhi: HarperCollins, 2007, p. xiii.
53. Manmohini Sahgal (Zutshi), NMML, OHT, no. 65, 4 June 1970. p. 62. Durga Devi Vohra is one such example, see Chapter Three.
54. Manmathnath Gupta, *They Lived Dangerously: Reminiscences of a Revolutionary*, Delhi: People's Publishing House, 1969; Yashpal, *Singhavalokan*, Allahabad: Lokbharati Prakashan, 2007 (initially published in Lucknow by Viplav Karyalay, the author's own press, in three volumes, 1958–64); Verma, *Samsmritiyan*.
55. Manmathnath Gupta, NMML, OHT, p. 54. See also the introduction of M. Gupta's book, *They Lived Dangerously*.
56. Vinay Lal, *The History of History*, Delhi: Oxford University Press, 2003, p. 88. This is not to say that a substantial body of work on revolutionary history does not exist—there is an enormous body of Bhagat Singh biographies published in India alone, many of which challenge popular hagiographies. However, such scholarship rarely engages with mainstream nationalist narratives, with the result that revolutionary history tends to be seen as an outlier, a speciality niche of activity which inhabits the margins of scholarly understandings of anticolonialism in India. Sarvapelli Gopal's official biography of Nehru, for example, is exasperatingly silent on the issues that were so central to Jawaharlal's presidency of the Lahore Congress (that I discuss in Chapter Six). There

are some important exceptions to this, such as Sumit Sarkar's *Modern India*, and the work of Bipan Chandra.

57. Here I have in mind A. G. Noorani, *The Trial of Bhagat Singh: The Politics of Justice*, Delhi: Oxford University Press, [1996] 2008; Nayar, *Without Fear*; and Manini Chatterjee, *Do and Die: The Chittagong Uprising, 1930–1934*, New Delhi: Penguin, 2010 [1999].

58. Durba Ghosh, 'National Narratives and the Politics of Miscegenation', in Antoinette Burton (ed.), *Archive Stories: Facts, Fictions, and the Writing of History*, Durham: Duke University Press, 2005, p. 41.

59. See, for example, entries on HSRA members in P. N. Chopra (ed.), *Who's Who of Indian Martyrs*, New Delhi: Government of India, 1969.

60. Tellingly, there has been much less coverage of Gandhi in Hindi film. Rachel Dwyer, 'The Case of the Missing Mahatma: Gandhi and the Hindi Cinema', *Public Culture*, 23(2), 2011, pp. 349–376.

61. *Amar Shahid Bhagat Singh*, Chandigarh: Suchna, Prachar and Paryatan Vibhag, Punjab, 1968; *Fiftieth Anniversary of Martyrdom of Bhagat Singh, Rajguru and Sukhdev*, Chandigarh: Punjab Government Publication, 1981.

62. Jitendra Nath Sanyal, *Sardar Bhagat Singh* (revised edition), Nagpur: Vishva Bharati Prakashan, 1983, p. 102.

63. S. L. Manchanda, personal communication, 9 November 2010.

64. M. Gupta, NMML, OHT, pp. 47–8.

65. Ranajit Guha, 'The Prose of Counter-Insurgency', *Subaltern Studies II: Writings on South Asian History and Society*, New Delhi: Oxford University Press, 2007 [1983], pp. 1–42.

66. Motilal to Gandhi, 18 February 1930, *SWMN*, Vol. 7, p. 181.

67. Mahua Sarkar, 'Between Craft and Method: Meaning and Inter-subjectivity in Oral History Analysis', *Journal of Historical Sociology*, 25 (4), 2012, p. 10.

68. See David Petrie's notes on Verma's arrest in NAI, HP, 192/1929, KW I.

69. Verma, 'Preface', *Bhagat Singh: on the Path of Liberation*, p. 13.

70. See, for example, the HSRA Manifesto and 'The Philosophy of the Bomb' (both in Verma (ed.), *Bhagat Singh: on the Path of Liberation*); and 'To the Young Political Workers' and 'Our Opportunity', both written by Bhagat Singh in early 1931, both held in IOR, L/PJ/12/391, pp. 47–74.

71. On the legality of the Lahore Conspiracy Case trial, see Noorani, *The Trial of Bhagat Singh*; Sherman, *State Violence and Punishment*, Ch. 6.

72. Sohan Singh 'Josh', 'My Meetings with Bhagat Singh', in *My Meetings with Bhagat Singh and on Other Early Revolutionaries*, New Delhi: Communist Party Publication, 1976, p. 19.

73. Hardas, *Armed Struggle for Freedom*, pp. 317–8.

74. Gandhi, 'The Bomb and the Knife', *CWMG*, Vol. XL, pp. 259–60.

75. Verma, NMML, OHT, p. 95.

76. Thus Prakash Tandon, who in 1927 was enrolled in Lahore Government College and on the path to entry into the Indian Civil Service, pronounced that 'Punjabis, with one exception, made poor terrorists'. *Punjabi Century, 1857–1957*, Berkeley: University of

California Press, 1961, p. 195. See also Chatterjee, 'Bombs and Nationalism in Bengal', pp. 9–10.

77. Kapoor, NMML, OHT, p. 113; Verma, NMML, OHT, p. 95.

78. Report by Petrie, June 10 1929. NAI, HP, 192/1929, K.W. II, p. 90.

79. Report by Petrie, June 10 1929. NAI, HP, 192/1929, K.W. II, p. 90.

80. Yashpal, *Singhavalokan*, pp. 227–8.

81. Khanna, NMML, OHT, p. 38.

82. K. Murty Ashok Vohra, *Radhakrishnan, His Life and Ideas*, New York: SUNY, 1990, p. 48.

83. 'It is rare', de Montmorency is said to have quipped, 'for a man to receive at once an honour from the king and the homage of a revolutionary'. Sarvepalli Gopal, *Radhakrishnan: A Biography*, London: Unwin Hyman, 1989, p. 136.

84. Notice issued by the Hindustan Socialist Republican Army and a Statement issued on the behalf of J. N. Sanyal and five others to the Commissioner, the Special Tribunal, Lahore Conspiracy Case, December 1928–1930. NMML, Private Papers, Acc. 822.

85. 'Beware, Ye Bureaucracy', in Verma (ed.), *Bhagat Singh: on the Path of Liberation*, pp. 72–3.

86. Potdar, NMML, OHT, p. 4. Such reasoning pre-empts Frantz Fanon's dictum that colonialism 'is naked violence and only gives in when confronted with greater violence'. Frantz Fanon, *The Wretched of the Earth*, translated by Richard Philcox, New York: Grove Press, 2004 [1963], p. 23.

87. Potdar, NMML, OHT, p. 4.

88. J. Gupta, NMML, OHT, pp. 81–2.

89. For example, Partha Mitter, *Art and Nationalism in India, 1850–1922*, Cambridge: Cambridge University Press, 1994; Marcus Banks, 'Views of Jain History', in David J. Parkin, Wendy James and Paul Dresch (eds), *Anthropologists in a Wider World: Essays on Field Research*, New York: Berghan, 2000; Raminder Kaur, 'Martial Imagery in Western India: the Changing Face of Ganapati', *South Asia*, 25(1), 2002, pp. 69–96.

90. As evidenced by a range of manuals: Marcus Banks, *Visual Methods in Social Research*, London: Sage, 2001; Gillian Rose, *Visual Methodologies: an Introduction to the Interpretation of Visual Materials*, London: Sage, 2001; and more recently, Marcus Banks and Jay Ruby (eds), *Made to be Seen: Historical Perspectives on Visual Anthropology*, Chicago: University of Chicago Press, 2011.

91. Pinney, *'Photos of the Gods'*, p. 117.

92. Pinney, *'Photos of the Gods'*, p. 117.

93. Pinney, *'Photos of the Gods'*, p. 117.

94. Sumathi Ramaswamy, *The Goddess and the Nation: Mapping Mother India*, Durham and London: Duke University Press, 2010, p. 296.

95. Partha Chatterjee, 'Critique of Popular Culture', *Public Culture*, 20(2), 2008, p. 331.

96. In my article on 'The Portrait's Journey', I was more hesitant in this, resisting claims of the autonomy of the image, instead arguing for an 'awareness of visuality' in historical inquiry. 'The Portrait's Journey: The Image, Social Communication and Martyr-Making in Colonial India', *Journal of Asian Studies*, 70(3), 2011, pp. 1052–3.

97. That this strategy is effective is indicated by its carriage into the mediated spectacles of violence scripted by twenty-first century insurgents, enhanced with digital technologies and social networking facilities. See Neville Bolt, *The Violent Image: Insurgent Propaganda and the New Revolutionaries*, London: Hurst & Co., 2012.

98. Yashpal, *Singhavalokan*, pp. 239–240.

98. Pinney notes that in the central Indian village of Bhatisuda, god posters are known as *bhagawan ke photo* (god-photos). Pinney, '*Photos of the Gods*', pp. 18 and 226.

100. Kajri Jain, *Gods in the Bazaar: The Economies of Indian Calendar Art*, Durham: Duke University Press, 2007, pp. 7–8.

101. See Fig. 5.1 in Kama Maclean, *Pilgrimage and Power: The Kumbh Mela in Allahabad, 1765–1954*, New York: Oxford University Press, 2008, p. 148.

102. Christopher Pinney, *The Coming of Photography in India*, New Delhi: Oxford University Press, 2008.

103. Pinney, '*Photos of the Gods*', p. 31.

104. Ramaswamy, *Goddess and the Nation*, p. 224.

105. For example, *Desh Chintan*, Fig. 33, is discussed in detail in Chapter Five, and I have offered alternative readings of it in 'Imagining the Nationalist Movement: Revolutionary Metaphors in Imagery of the Freedom Struggle', *Journal of Material Culture*, 19 (1), 2014.

106. Stuart Hall, 'Encoding/decoding' in S. Hall, D. Hobson, A. Lowe, and P. Willis (eds), *Culture, Media, Language*, London: Hutchinson, 1980, p. 134.

107. Judith Brown, *Gandhi's Rise to Power, Indian Politics 1915–1922*, Cambridge: Cambridge University Press, 1972; Brown, *Gandhi and Civil Disobedience*.

108. On the personal and political differences between Motilal Nehru and Madan Mohan Malaviya, see my 'Hybrid nationalist or Hindu nationalist? The life of Madan Mohan Malaviya' in Kate Brittlebank (ed.), *Tall Tales and True: India, Historiography and British Imperial Imaginings*, Melbourne: Monash Asia Institute, 2008.

109. Sandria Freitag, 'More than Meets the (Hindu) Eye: The Public Arena as a Space for Alternative Visions', in Richard H. Davis (ed.), *Picturing the Nation: Iconographies of Modern India*, Delhi: Orient Longman, 2007, p. 94.

110. Chandra, 'The Revolutionary Terrorists in Northern India', in *Nationalism and Colonialism in Modern India*, pp. 223–51; S. K. Mittal and Irfan Habib, 'The Congress and the Revolutionaries in the 1920s', *Social Scientist*, 10(6), June 1982, pp. 20–37; Bipan Chandra, 'Bhagat Singh and his Comrades', in Ravi Dayal (ed.), *We Fought Together for Freedom*, Delhi: Oxford University Press, 1995, pp. 137–151; Irfan Habib, 'Civil Disobedience, 1930–31', *Social Scientist*, 25(9/10), 1997, pp. 43–66; Irfan Habib, *To Make the Deaf Hear: Ideology and Programme of Bhagat Singh and His Comrades*, New Delhi: Three Essays Collective, 2007.

111. Note by O'Cleary, February 21 1928. IOR, L/PJ/12/292, p. 14.

112. B. R. Nanda, 'Nehru and the British', *Modern Asian Studies*, 30(2), 1996, p. 471.

113. See, for example, his appeal to the revolutionaries in 'The Cult of the Bomb', in which he argued that anticolonial violence spurred military spending and repression. 2 January 1930, *CWMG*, Vol. XLVIII, p. 185; Brown, *Gandhi and Civil Disobedience*, pp. 88–93.

114. Judith Stiehm, 'Nonviolence is Two', *Sociological Inquiry*, 38, Winter, 1968, p. 26.

115. Victor Lidz, 'A Note on "Nonviolence is Two"', *Sociological Inquiry*, 38, Winter, 1968, pp. 31–6.

116. Pandey, 'Un-archived Histories', p. 37.

117. Indeed, as this book was in press, the beginnings of a body of such scholarship began to emerge. For example, Durba Ghosh, 'Revolutionary Women and Nationalist Heroes in Bengal, 1930 to the 1980s', *Gender & History*, 25 (2), 2013, pp. 335–75; Nikhil Govind, *Between Love and Freedom: the Revolutionary in the Hindi Novel*, New Delhi: Routledge, 2014; Harald Fischer-Tiné, *Shyamji Krishnavarma: Sanskrit, Sociology and Anti-Imperialism*, London: Routledge, 2014; Ali Raza, Franziska Roy and Benjamin Zachariah (eds), *The Internationalist Moment: South Asia, Worlds and World Views, 1917–39*, New Delhi: Sage, 2015.

1. OF HISTORY AND LEGEND: REVOLUTIONARY ACTIONS IN NORTH INDIA, 1928–31

1. Bipan Chandra, 'Bhagat Singh and his Comrades', in Dayal (ed.), *We Fought Together for Freedom*, p. 137; Bipan Chandra, Mridula Mukherjee, K. N. Panikkar and Sucheta Mahajan, *Independence, 1857–1947*, Delhi: Penguin, 1988, p. 247.

2. Michael Silvestri, '"The Sinn Fein of India": Irish Nationalism and the Policing of Revolutionary Terrorism in Bengal', *The Journal of British Studies*, 39(4), 2000, p. 456.

3. Chandra et al., *India's Struggle for Independence*, p. 247.

4. See IOR, L/PJ/12/397, pp. 79–144.

5. DIB Report, 24 September 1931. IOR, L/PJ/12/390, p. 80; Laushey, *Bengal Terrorism and the Marxist Left*, p. 34.

6. 'Constitution of the HRA', in Verma (ed.), *Bhagat Singh: on the Path of Liberation*, p. 196.

7. H. W. Hale, *Political Trouble in India, 1917–1937*, Allahabad: Chugh Publications, 1974, p. 56.

8. Verma, 'Ideological Development of the Revolutionary Movement', in *Bhagat Singh: on the Path of Liberation*, p. 39.

9. The letterhead that the organisation used in Delhi in April 1929 was 'Hindustan Socialist Republican Army' (Fig. 1). However by November 1929, when the party circulated its manifesto at the Lahore Congress the letterhead had changed to 'Hindustan Socialist Republican Association'. Different HSRA members seem to have been responsible for producing the two letterheads in Punjab and Uttar Pradesh/Delhi; it may also be the case that the later use of 'Association' was reflective of a transition away from militancy in the organisation.

10. Verma, 'Ideological Development of the Revolutionary Movement', p. 39.

11. Corinne Friend (ed.), *Yashpal Looks Back: Selections from an Autobiography*, Delhi: Vikas, 1981, p. 26.

12. Ghosh, 'Terrorism in Bengal', p. 276; Verma, *Samsmritiyan*, p. 24.

13. Statement of Manmohan Bannerji, 24 July 1929, in Malwinderjit Singh Waraich and

Harish Jain (eds), *The Hanging of Bhagat Singh, Vol. III: Confessions, Statements and Other Documents*, Chandigarh: Unistar, 2007, p. 271.

14. N.K. Nigam, NMML, OHT, p. 17. It is worth noting here that the structure of the HSRA closely modeled that of the Indian National Congress, with both central and provincial committees.

15. Friend (ed.), *Yashpal Looks Back*, p. 70. It is equally telling that even though Azad doubted the fidelity of Virabhadra Tiwari, suspecting him of having CID links, he did not immediately dispense with him, as only Tiwari knew all of the UP members, and was in possession of valuable weapons. Nigam, OHT, pp. 19–20. In the aftermath of Azad's death, many in the party felt that Tiwari had alerted police in Allahabad to Azad's whereabouts and there were several attempts to eliminate him. DIB Report, 3 December 1931. IOR, L/PJ/12/390, p. 116.

16. Ironically, it is approver testimonies that provide valuable clues to party structure and operation, even though many of them are partial. See Aparna Vaidik, 'History of a Renegade Revolutionary: Revolutionism and Betrayal in Colonial India', *Postcolonial Studies*, 16(2), 2013, pp. 216–229.

17. 'Names of Accused', 2 May 1929, in Wariach and Jain (eds), *The Hanging of Bhagat Singh, Vol. III*, p. 29.

18. Yashpal, NMML, OHT, p. 10.

19. Lal, 'Introduction', *The Jail Notebook*, p. 12.

20. R. T. Peel, 'Unrest: A Note on Revolutionary Movements in Bengal, the United Provinces and the Punjab', IOR, L/PJ/12/404.

21. CID file no. 9249/1926. Facsimile reproduced in Malwinder jit Singh Wariach, *Bhagat Singh: The Eternal Rebel*, Government of India, Publications Division, 2007, p. 58.

22. Bhagat Singh, 'Why I am an Atheist', in Verma (ed.), *Bhagat Singh: On the Path to Liberation*, p. 120.

23. Chand, CSAS, OHC, no. 205, p. 44.

24. Kapoor, NMML, OHT, p. 80.

25. Channan Singh's death was not intended; according to Jai Gopal's statement, the assailants 'had to shoot him merely with a view to save themselves'. Wariach and Jain (eds), *The Hanging of Bhagat Singh, Vol. III*, p. 77.

26. 'Notice issued by the Hindustan Socialist Republican Army', December 1928, NMML, Acc. no. 822.

27. Kapoor, NMML, OHT, p. 112.

28. Note the censorious tone of the editorial, 'Bombs in the Assembly', published in the pro-Congress Lahori newspaper, *Tribune*, 10 April 1929, p. 8. By late July, when they were fasting in protest at jail conditions, the same newspaper was reporting the observance of Bhagat Singh and Dutt Day in Lahore, under the auspices of the Congress Committee. *Tribune*, 21 July 1929, p. 2.

29. *Hindustan Times*, 11 April 1929, p. 1.

30. Excluding edited collections of Bhagat Singh's writings, a sampling of such scholarship would include J. S. Grewal, (ed.), *Bhagat Singh and his Legend*, Patiala: World Punjabi Centre, 2008; Habib, *To Make the Deaf Hear*; L. P. Mathur, *Bhagat Singh: the Prince of*

Martyrs, Jaipur: Aavishkar Publications, 2001; plus the work of two journalists, Nayar, *Without Fear*; Noorani, *The Trial of Bhagat Singh*.

31. Kamlesh Mohan, *Militant Nationalism in the Punjab, 1919–1935*, Delhi: Manohar, 1985; Taylor Sherman, 'The Hunger Strikes of the Lahore Conspiracy Case Prisoners', in *State Violence and Punishment in India*; Shalini Sharma, *Radical Politics in Colonial Punjab: Governance and Sedition*, London: Routledge, 2009; Nair, 'Bhagat Singh as "Satyagrahi"'; Chris Moffat, 'Experiments in Political Truth', *Postcolonial Studies*, 16(2), 2013, pp. 185–201.

32. Simeran Gell, 'L'Inde aux deux visages: Dalip Singh et le Mahatma Gandhi', *Terrain*, 31 September 1998, p. 22 (thanks to Rachel Routley for translating this fascinating article); Christopher Pinney, 'The Body and the Bomb', in Davis (ed.), *Picturing the Nation*, p. 63.

33. Ishwar Dayal Gaur, *Martyr as a Bridegroom: A Folk Representation of Bhagat Singh*, Delhi: Anthem, 2008, p. 6.

34. Himadri Banerjee, 'Bhagat Singh in Bengali Writings', at http://bhagatsinghstudy. blogspot.com/2008/01/bhagat-singh-in-bengali-writings.html (last accessed 3 April 2010).

35. See Prem Singh, 'Bhagat Singh in Hindi Literature'; Ashok Chousalkar, 'Bhagat Singh in Marathi Literature', and Raj Kumar Hans, 'Bhagat Singh in Gujarati Literature', in Grewal (ed.), *Bhagat Singh and his Legend*. For more regional language materials, see Gurdev Singh Sidhu (ed.), *The Hanging of Bhagat Singh, Vol. IV: The Banned Literature*, Chandigarh: Unistar, 2007.

36. Pinney, '*Photos of the Gods*', p. 126; see also Pritam Singh, 'Why the Story of Bhagat Singh Remains on the Margins?' www.sacw.net/article22.html (last accessed 11 November 2009).

37. Pinney, '*Photos of the Gods*', p. 117.

38. Christopher Pinney, 'Visual history tells us about repressed histories', *Tehelka*, 5(37), September 2008, p. 20.

39. J. Gupta, NMML, OHT, p. 88.

40. DIB Report, 24 June 1926. IOR, L/PJ/12/375, p. 1.

41. Daniel Elam notes the inspiration of Giuseppe Mazzini's Young Italy in the NJBS. 'The "Arch Priestess of Anarchy" Visits Lahore: Violence, Love, and the Worldliness of Revolutionary Texts', *Postcolonial Studies*, 16(2), 2013, p. 152.

42. DIB Report, 20 December 1928. IOR, L/P&J/12/60, p. 3.

43. Bhagat Singh, 'Why I am an Atheist', in Verma (ed.), *Bhagat Singh: on the Path of Liberation*, p. 120.

44. M. Gupta, NMML, OHT, p. 61.

45. Letter by M. D. Thapar to Shanta Kumar, 18 April 1978. Sukhdev Papers, NMML, Acc. no. 190, LLXVI (116).

46. 'Crown Complainant Vs Sukh Dev and others', in Wariach and Sidhu (eds), *The Hanging of Bhagat Singh, Vol. I: Complete Judgement*, Chandigarh: Unistar, 2005, p. 82.

47. Avinash Kumar, 'Nationalism as Bestseller: The Case of *Chand*'s "Phansi Ank"', in Abhijit

Gupta and Swapan Chakravorty (eds), *Moveable Type: Book History in India*, Delhi: Permanent Black, 2008, p. 176.

48. Petrie had served as one of the investigators in the bomb attack on Lord Hardinge in Delhi in 1912. Jason Tomes, 'Sir David Petrie', *Oxford Dictionary of Biography*, online edition, 2008.

49. Letter from Petrie, 25 May 1929. NAI, HP, 192/1929, KW I. The appellation 'Balraj' had been adapted from the HRA; Sachindranath Sanyal had signed the HRA manifesto with the name in 1924. For further discussion on the meaning of 'Balraj', see Chapter Six.

50. Verma (ed.), *Bhagat Singh: on the Path of Liberation*, p. 78, fn; see also Nigam, NMML, OHT, p. 29.

51. Max Harcourt, 'Revolutionary Networks in North Indian Politics, 1907–1935', unpublished D. Phil. thesis, University of Sussex, 1974, p. 264.

52. See the descriptions in *The United Provinces Political Who's Who 1936*, Second Edition, Allahabad: Superintendent of Printing and Stationary, 1936.

53. CID file no 9249/1926, facsimile reproduced in Wariach, *Bhagat Singh*, p. 58.

54. Kapoor, NMML, OHT, p. 61; Statement of Jai Gopal, in Wariach and Jain (eds), *The Hanging of Bhagat Singh, Vol. III*, p. 61.

55. Verma, NMML, OHT, p. 87.

56. Jitendra Nath Sanyal, *Sardar Bhagat Singh (A Short Life-sketch)*, Allahabad: J.N. Sanyal, 1931, NAI, Proscribed Literature section, Acc. 969, p. 42.

57. Vohra, NMML, OHT, p. 15.

58. Sohan Singh 'Josh', *My Meetings with Bhagat Singh*, p. 25.

59. Chhabil Das, NMML, OHT, pp. 34–5.

60. According to Jaidev Gupta, the first Congress Session Bhagat Singh attended was in Ahmedabad, in 1921. J. Gupta, NMML, OHT, p. 28.

61. This is elaborated in Part II.

62. DIB Report, 12 January 1928. IOR, L/P&J/12/59, p. 17. See also the report by Fryer, 19 April 1929. NAI, HP, 192/1929, K.W. II, p. 14.

63. Laushey, *Bengal Terrorism and the Marxist Left*, p. 59.

64. Sanyal, *Sardar Bhagat Singh*, 1931, p. 44; Kapoor, NMML, OHT, p. 93.

65. Statement of Lalit Kumar Mukherji, Confession Exhibit PBV/1/28.6.29, in Wariach and Jain (eds), *The Hanging of Bhagat Singh, Vol. III*, p. 247.

66. Potdar, CSAS, OHC, p. 5.

67. DIB Report, 8 April 1929. IOR, L/PJ/12/389, p. 3.

68. Friend (ed.), *Yashpal Looks Back*, p. 47.

69. Kapoor, NMML, OHT, pp. 103–5.

70. This was in fact a point of much debate within the HSRA, as Azad initially favoured an escape—not a surrender—after the attack on the Assembly; other members differed in opinion as to who they could afford to lose to the action. For details see Kapoor, NMML, OHT, pp. 101–119.

71. DIB Report, 18 April 1929. IOR, L/PJ/12/389, p. 2.

72. Note by David Petrie, 25 May 1929. NAI, HP 192/1929, KW I.

73. Kapoor, NMML, OHT, pp. 125–6.
74. The original document, with deletions marked, is held in NAI, Private Papers, Acc. No. 246.
75. 'Bhagat Singh and Dutt's Sensational Statement', *Hindustan Times*, 8 June 1929, pp. 1, 5.
76. DIB Report, 3 October 1929. IOR, L/PJ/12/389, p. 25.
77. 'Statement Before the Lahore High Court Bench', in Verma (ed.), *Bhagat Singh: on the Path of Liberation*, p. 147–8.
78. For a discussion of *Inquilab Zindabad*, see Moffat, 'Experiments in Political Truth'.
79. Delhi Bomb Case, Statement in Court. NAI, Private Papers, Acc. No. 246, p. 6.
80. Kris Manjapra, 'Communist Internationalism and Transcolonial Recognition', in Sugata Bose and Kris Manjapra (eds), *Cosmopolitan Thought Zones: South Asia and the Global Circulation of Ideas*, London: Palgrave Macmillan, 2010, pp. 159–177.
81. J. Gupta, NMML, OHT, p. 69.
82. 'USA and Canada', 9 March 1931. IOR, L/PJ/12/434, p. 20.
83. The Communist Party of Great Britain, Lahore Conspiracy Case, March 5 1931. IOR, L/PJ/12/377, pp. 23–5.
84. 'Labour Government Executes 3 India Rebels Frame-up Revolutionists for British Imperialism', in Verma (ed.), *Bhagat Singh: on the Path of Liberation*, pp. 181–2.
85. 'Message of the Martyrs! A Call to Arms!', poster issued by the Hindustan Gadar Party, NAI, HP, 29/7/1931.
86. Sidhu (ed.), *The Hanging of Bhagat Singh, Vol. IV*, p. 196.
87. Telegram from Home Department to Commissioner of Sind, 25 March 1931. NAI, HP 4/21/31.
88. Two sources, each quoting different newspapers, provide a graphic description of the torture that some of the prisoners suffered. See C.S. Venu, *Sirdar Bhagat Singh*, Madras, c. 1931, p. 22; the Communist Party of Great Britain, 'Lahore Conspiracy Case', 5 March 1931. IOR, L/PJ/12/377, p. 24.
89. See Butler's undated letter to Crombie, in IOR, L/PJ/12/314, p. 40.
90. Horace Alexander, *Political Prisoners In India: A Statement Issued by Direction of the Society of Friends*, January 1937, p. 18. IOR, L/PJ/12/314. The majority of the inner circle of the HSRA was well educated, and had met while studying in nationalist schools or colleges. N.K. Nigam had an MA, and was a class 'topper' who taught history at Hindu College, in Delhi. Nigam, NMML, OHT, p. 11.
91. N.G. Barrier, *Banned: Controversial Literature and Political Control in British India, 1907–1947*, Columbia: University of Missouri Press, 1974, pp. 206–9 lists 29 entries on Bhagat Singh; G. Shaw and M. Lloyd (eds), *Publications Proscribed by the Government of India: A Catalogue of the Collections in the India Office Library and Records and the Department of Oriental Manuscripts and Printed Books, British Library Reference Division*, London: British Library, 1985, p. 192, has over seventy relevant entries on Bhagat Singh alone.
92. Sidhu (ed.), *The Hanging of Bhagat Singh, Vol. IV*.
93. Sidhu (ed.), *The Hanging of Bhagat Singh, Vol. IV*, p. 8.

94. Report on the Political Situation in Bengal for the second half of April 1931. NAI, F/18/3/1931.
95. Chaman Lal, 'Bibliography on Bhagat Singh', in Grewal (ed.), *Bhagat Singh and his Legend*, pp. 255–69.
96. *Tribune*, 7 March 1931, p. 7.
97. *Tribune*, 6 March 1931, p. 5.
98. It appears from correspondence between the Home Department and Punjab government that a date for the executions was not fixed until 17 March. Telegram, 17 March 1931. NAI, HP, 4/21/31, p. 18.
99. *Tribune*, 4 March 1931, p. 7.
100. *Tribune*, 5 March 1931, p. 7.
101. See NAI, Home Judicial, 152/I/31 and K.W.
102. Bose, *Indian Struggle*, p. 204.
103. See the mortuary images of Ramprasad Bismil and Roshan Singh in *Chand ka Phansi Ank*, South Asia Microform Project, Reel 15, pp. 316, 321; Roshan Singh's is reproduced in 'Azad Mandir', Fig. 34.
104. Nair, 'Bhagat Singh as "Satyagrahi"', p. 659.
105. Kapoor, NMML, OHT, p. 184; Report on the political situation in Bengal for the fortnight ending the first half of September 1929. IOR, L/PJ/12/686.
106. Telegram from Home Secretary, Punjab, to Home Department, New Delhi, 18 March 1931. NAI, HP 4/21/31.
107. Section 872 of the *Manual for the Superintendence and Management of Jails in the Punjab* dictated that executions from November–March be carried out at 8 am. Lahore: Civil and Military Gazette Press, 1916, p. 273.
108. Bhagat Singh had been partly raised by his childless aunt, Harnam Kaur, and so the question of who constituted 'immediate family' even within the context of the Indian extended family unit, was not a straightforward one. J. Gupta, NMML, OHT, p. 14.
109. *Tribune*, 25 March 1931, pp. 1, 5.
110. Report on the political situation in the Punjab for the fortnight ending the 31st of March 1931. NAI, F/18/3/1931.
111. 'The Official Cremation', *Tribune*, 27 March 1931, p. 9.
112. *The Indian Annual Register: an Annual Digest of Public Affairs of India*, Vol. 1, January–June 1931, Calcutta: Annual Register Office, 1931, p. 215.
113. Report on the political situation in the Punjab for the fortnight ending the 31st of March 1931. NAI, F/18/3/1931.
114. Emerson to Gandhi, March 20 1931. NAI, HP, 4/21/31, p. 66.
115. 'Irritation is undoubtedly there. It would be better to allow it to find vent through meetings etc.' Gandhi to Emerson, 20 March 1931. NAI, HP, 4/21/31, p. 65.
116. *Tribune*, 24 March 1931, p. 3.
117. Letter from Emerson, 18 February 1931. NAI, HP, 4/21/31, p. 43.
118. Cawnpore Riots Enquiry Committee Report, in *The Indian Annual Register*, Vol. 1, p. 96.

119. Report of the Commission of Inquiry into the Communal Outbreak at Cawnpore, Cmd. 3891, June 1931, p. 4.
120. *The Indian Annual Register*, Vol. 1, p. 30.
121. J. Gupta, NMML, OHT, p. 62.
122. Letter from G.F.S. Collins to Emerson, 1 April 1931. *Fortnightly Reports for the Second Half of March 1931*, NAI, F/18/3/1931.
123. *Tribune*, 4 April 1931, p. 1.
124. Resolutions adopted by CWC, Karachi, 1–2 April 1931, in A. M. Zaidi (ed.), *Congress Presidential Addresses*, Vol. 10, 1930–35, Delhi: Indian Institute of Applied Political Research, 1988, pp. 184–5.
125. Letter from Satyapal to Janam Das (Gen. Secretary), 13 September 1931. NMML, AICC Papers, 43/1931.
126. Telegram from Commissioner of Sind, to Home Department, 28 March 1931. NAI, HP, 136/1931.
127. Friend (ed.), *Yashpal Looks Back*, p. 218.
128. Bose, *Indian Struggle*, pp. 204–5.
129. Report on the political situation in the Punjab for the fortnight ending the 31st of March 1931. NAI, F/18/3/1931.
130. Report of the Commission of Inquiry into the Communal Outbreak at Cawnpore, Cmd. 3891, June 1931.
131. Report on Bengal for second half of March 1931. NAI, F/18/3/1931.
132. Speech by Jawaharlal Nehru, originally in Hindi, delivered at the Karachi Congress, 1931, in Zaidi (ed.), *Congress Presidential Addresses*, Vol. 10, p. 77.
133. Reproduced from *Piyam* in the *Zamindar* (Lahore) on 3 April 1931. NAI, HP, 13/XI/1931 & KW.
134. 'The Martyr, Sardar Bhagat Singh', in NAI, HP, 13/XI/1931, & KW.
135. This particularly graphic metaphor was drawn from one of Bhagat Singh's articles, written about the six Babbar Akalis who were executed on the day of Holi in 1926, which in turn invokes Ram Prasad Bismil's celebrated poem, 'Sarfaroshi ki Tamanna'. Ek Punjabi Yuvak, 'Blood Sprinkled on the Day of Holi', *Pratap*, 15 March 1926, reproduced in Verma (ed.), *Bhagat Singh: on the Path of Liberation*, p. 67.
136. Jatindranath Sanyal, the author of *Sardar Bhagat Singh*, was also trialed in the Lahore Conspiracy Case. He was acquitted, only to be jailed for two years, convicted of sedition for writing and publishing his book in 1931.
137. Chandravati Devi, 'Shahid Sardar Bhagat Singh', NAI, HP, 4/22/1931, p. 32.
138. See 'Watan de Lal', in Sidhu (ed.), *The Hanging of Bhagat Singh, Vol. IV*, pp. 47–8.
139. Thus it was recently published in a collection of short stories, Rustom Rai (ed.), *Pratibandhit Hindi Sahitya*, Part 1, Delhi: Radhakrishnan Prakashan, 1999, p. 185. Two other eulogies, 'Bhagat Singh Kirtanamrutam' and 'Quami Shahid', both in Sidhu (ed.), *The Hanging of Bhagat Singh, Vol. IV*, p. 131, 119 respectively, also profess that he was innocent of Saunders' murder.
140. 'Petition of Sardar Kishan Singh', Shaheed-e-Azam Bhagat Singh Museum, Khatkarkalan, courtesy of the Supreme Court of India Museum, p. 5.

141. See 'Letter to Father', in Verma (ed.), *Bhagat Singh: on the Path of Liberation*, p. 170; *Tribune*, 4 October 1930, p. 1.
142. Vidyavati to Irwin, 19 February 1931. NAI, Home Judicial, 152/I/31 & KW.
143. Telegram from Commissioner of Sind, Karachi to Home Department, 26 March 1931. NAI, HP, 136/1931.
144. NAI, HP, 139/1931.
145. 'For Public Information! Sukh Dev's Posthumous Letter', *Tribune*, 28 March 1931, p. 7.
146. This had also been alleged by Kishan Singh. 'Petition of Sardar Kishan Singh', pp. 3–4; Venu, *Sirdar Bhagat Singh*, p. 65.
147. Sidhu (ed.), *The Hanging of Bhagat Singh, Vol. IV*, p. 34.
148. 'Khoon ke Ansu', in Sidhu (ed.), *The Hanging of Bhagat Singh, Vol. IV*, p. 75.
149. Nayar, *Without Fear*, p. xii. By this, the government of Pakistan was alluding to the Khalistan movement of the 1980s; research for Nayar's book on Bhagat Singh was conducted in the 1990s.
150. Ali Hasan Cemendtaur, 'On disowning Bhagat Singh and Other Vagaries', http://www.chowk.com/articles/12840 (last accessed 11 November 2009).
151. Kuldip Nayar, 'People want to bury the hatchet but Pakistan government stands in the way', *Tribune*, 30 March 2007.
152. Anita Joshua, 'It's now Bhagat Singh Chowk in Lahore', *The Hindu*, 1 October 2012; 'Shadman Chowk won't be renamed after Bhagat Singh', *Pakistan Today*, 13 December 2012.
153. Louis E. Fenech, 'Contested Nationalisms, Negotiated Terrains: The Way Sikhs Remember Udham Singh 'Shahid' (1899–1940), *Modern Asian Studies*, 36(4), 2002, pp. 833.
154. Letter from Mathura Das Thapar, to S. Giani Zail Singh, dated 10 November 1976. NMML, Sukhdev Papers, 190, LLXVI, Serial 9.
155. Letter from Kultar Singh to Y.B. Chavan (Minister for External Affairs), 20 October 1976. NMML, Sukhdev Papers, Acc. No. 190, LLXVI.
156. In 2007 a selection of materials was published in volume 3 of the series *The Hanging of Bhagat Singh*.
157. Mubarak Ali, 'Remembering Bhagat Singh', *Dawn Magazine*, 7 October 2007.
158. Harcourt, 'Revolutionary Networks', p. 312.
159. See the speech reproduced in Noorani, *Trial of Bhagat Singh*, pp. 270–282.
160. Kumar, 'Nationalism as Bestseller', p. 178.
161. For a discussion of the recent Bhagat Singh film phenomenon, see Philip Lutgendorf's review of 'The Legend of Bhagat Singh', http://www.uiowa.edu/~incinema/LegendBhagat.html (last viewed July 22, 2010).
162. The film's 'distortion of facts about Bhagat Singh and other national figures' was raised by P. Sundarayya (CPI M) in the Rajya Sabha. 'Film on Bhagat Singh', *The Hindu*, 11 September 1954 (reproduced in *The Hindu*, 11 September 2004).
163. Pinney, *'Photos of the Gods'*, p. 177.
164. *23rd March 1931: Shaheed*, directed by Guddu Dhanoa, 2002, Captain DVD.

165. Lutgendorf, Review, 'Legend of Bhagat Singh'.

166. Jagmohan Singh, 'Distorting Bhagat Singh's Legacy', *Alpjan*, April–June 2002, pp. 65–6. Jagmohan Singh is the son of Bibi Amar Kaur, the eldest of Bhagat Singh's sisters.

167. Aarti Wani, 'Uses of History: *Rang De Basanti* and *Lage Raho Munnabhai*', *Monthly Review Magazine*, 12 February 2007.

168. Neelam Srivatsava, 'Bollywood as National(ist) Cinema: Violence, Patriotism and the National-Popular in Rang de Basanti', *Third Text*, 23(6), 2009, pp. 703–16.

169. Karline McLain, *India's Immortal Comic Books: Gods, Kings and other Heroes*, Bloomington: Indiana University Press, 2009, p. 172.

170. Ramchandra Guha, 'The Challenge of Contemporary History', *Economic and Political Weekly*, 28 June 2008, p. 198.

171. Pritam Singh, 'Review Article', *Journal of Punjab Studies*, 14(2), 2007, p. 298.

172. *The Hanging of Bhagat Singh*, a ten-volume project still in progress, under the general editorship of Malwinderjit Singh Waraich.

173. For example: K.C. Yadav and Babar Singh (eds), *Bhagat Singh, Ideas on Freedom, Liberty and Revolution: Jail Notes of a Revolutionary*, Gurgaon: Hope India Publications, 2007; Verma (ed.), *Bhagat Singh: on the Path of Liberation*; and Lal (ed.), *The Jail Notebook*. All three anthologies include the prison notebooks, with the first offering a facsimile of each diary page so that the reader is able to see Bhagat Singh's own handwriting, where necessary translated into English; the latter two have additional writings and useful introductions.

174. See *Rajya Sabha Debates*, 3 May 2007, p. 331; 'JNU to set up Bhagat Singh chair', *Hindustan Times*, 16 September 2007, p. 6.

175. *Inquilab*, directed by Gauhar Raza, 2007. 'New film tells "real" Bhagat Singh story', *Hindustan Times*, 14 July 2008, p. 3.

176. 'Documentary on DD today', *Hindustan Times*, 27 September 2007, p. 17.

177. Chandravati Devi, 'Sardar Bhagat Singh', in NAI, HP, 4/36 Part 1, 1931, p. 28.

2. THAT HAT: INFAMY, STRATEGY AND SOCIAL COMMUNICATION

1. 'Karachi Congress Proceedings, Resolution on Bhagat Singh passed', *Tribune*, 1 April 1931, p. 3.

2. For example, 'Bhagat Singh and Others: S. Sardul Singh's Statement', *Tribune*, 12 March 1931, p. 7; 'Commute Death Sentences: Will Bhagat Singh be saved?', *Tribune*, 24 March 1931, p. 1.

3. The Lahore Conspiracy Case Charge Sheet, 10 July 1929, India Office Records, African and Asian Studies, British Library (henceforth IOR), L/PJ/12/377.

4. Ramaswamy, *Goddess and the Nation*; Pinney, *'Photos of the Gods'*, p. 117.

5. Pritam Singh, 'Why the Story of Bhagat Singh Remains on the Margins?' www.sacw.net/article22.html (last accessed 11 November 2009). Chaman Lal, 'Introduction', *The Jail Notebook*, p. 11.

6. C. A. Bayly, *Empire and Information: Intelligence Gathering and Social Communication in India, 1780–1870*, Cambridge: Cambridge University Press, 1996, p. 2.

7. Sandria Freitag, 'More than Meets the (Hindu) Eye: The Public Arena as a Space for Alternative Visions', in Davis (ed.), *Picturing the Nation*, p. 94.

8. Roland Barthes, *Camera Lucida: Reflections on Photography*, London: Vintage, 1993, p. 26.

9. Kapoor, NMML, OHT, p. 61.

10. The phenomenon of 'iconic processing', i.e. relying on attributes to identify famous faces, has been described by Claus-Christian Carbon, 'Famous faces as icons: The illusion of being an expert in the recognition of famous faces', *Perception*, Vol. 37, 2008, pp. 801–806.

11. Fenech, 'Contested Nationalisms', p. 850. Such images were encouraged by the discovery of a photograph of Bhagat Singh taken during his first arrest. Milkha Singh Nijhar, 'Bhagat Singh ki chori-chhipe khinche gaya chitra (Bhagat Singh's Secret Photograph)', in M. M. Juneja (ed.), *Bhagat Singh par Chuninda Lekh*, Hisar: Modern Publishers, 2007, pp. 205–51.

12. For example, Jaidev Kapoor refers to Bhagat Singh as 'Sardarji' in his oral history interview, *passim*; as does the caption for fig. 17; Venu, *Sirdar Bhagat Singh*. See also Bhagat Singh, 'Why I am an Atheist', in Verma (ed.), *Bhagat Singh: on the Path of Liberation*; Bejoy Kumar Sinha, *Memoirs of a Revolutionary: Andamans, the Indian Bastille*, Delhi: Mittal Publications, 1987 [1939], p. 27.

13. Gell, 'L'Inde aux deux visages', pp. 129–144.

14. Pinney, '*Photos of the Gods*', pp. 127–8.

15. In the next chapter, I argue that this was only half of his disguise; it was equally pertinent that he posed as a married man.

16. Neeti Nair (quoting Pinney, '*Photos of the Gods*'), 'Bhagat Singh as "Satyagrahi"', p. 677.

17. This, however, does not negate the idea that Bhagat Singh was popular because he was violent; it simply establishes that many were oblivious to Bhagat Singh's thinking on the role of violence in anticolonial struggle.

18. Nair, 'Bhagat Singh as "Satyagrahi"', p. 676.

19. Nair, 'Bhagat Singh as "Satyagrahi"', p. 677.

20. Sharma, *Radical Politics in Colonial Punjab*, p. 46.

21. See the testimonies of Jaidev Kapoor, Jaidev Gupta, Chhabil Das, et al.

22. Kapoor, NMML, OHT, p. 311; J. Gupta, NMML, OHT, p. 77.

23. Jawaharlal Nehru, *Toward Freedom: An Autobiography*, Boston: Beacon Press, 1958 [1936], p. 134.

24. DIB Report, 25 April 1929. No. 16. IOR, L/PJ/12/292.

25. Jawaharlal Nehru, 'Eight Days Interlude', October 1930, South Asia Microform Project, Indian Prescribed Tracts, Reel 3, p. 6.

26. See, on this point, Gaur, *Martyr as a Bridegroom*.

27. Jawaharlal Nehru, 'On the Lahore Executions', Speech at the Congress Session, Karachi, 29 March 1931. *Selected Works of Jawaharlal Nehru* (henceforth *SWJN*), Vol. 4, Delhi: Orient Longman, p. 505.

28. 'Bhagat Singh and others: S. Sardul Singh's Statement', *Tribune*, 12 March 1931, p. 7.

29. Kapoor, NMML, OHT, p. 116.

30. Kapoor, NMML, OHT, p. 116. This would seem to mirror the social practice of formally photographing the elderly, that they may be properly memorialised in death. Christopher Pinney, *Camera Indica: the Social Life of Indian Photographs*, London: Reaktion Books, 1997, p. 147.

31. Kapoor, NMML, OHT, p. 117.

32. 'Note on the Assembly Bomb Case' by A. Fryer, Superintendent of Police, CID, Delhi, dated 19 April 1929. NAI, HP 192/1929; 'Accused in Assembly Bomb Outrage refuse to give any information', *Tribune*, 24 April 1929, p. 3.

33. Verma, NMML, OHT, p. 99.

34. Kapoor, NMML, OHT, p. 118. The original photographs were cabinet cards, approximately 16 x 10 cm, and the negatives were glass.

35. Kapoor, NMML, OHT, p. 128.

36. 'Government and Delhi Outrage', *Tribune*, 12 April 1929. p. 8.

37. 'The Bomb Outrage', *Hindustan Times*, 12 April 1929, p. 10.

38. Friend (ed.), *Yashpal Looks Back*, pp. 63–4. Yashpal estimated that he had received the negatives in Lahore on 4 or 5 April, but the date is most likely later, as indicated by both Kapoor and Verma's accounts that they collected the negatives after the attack on the Assembly on 8 April.

39. Unfinished letter written by Sukhdev to his brother, in Sukhdev Papers, 190, LLXVI (116), NMML.

40. J. Gupta, NMML, OHT, pp. 29, 39, & 89.

41. Verma NMML, OHT, p. 23; see also Kumar, 'Nationalism as Bestseller', p. 178.

42. Verma, NMML, OHT, p. 25.

43. J. Gupta, NMML, OHT, p. 88.

44. Recovery from the House of Prem Dutt, in Wariach and Jain (eds), *The Hanging of Bhagat Singh, Vol. III*, p. 39. NJBS meetings featured lantern slide presentations of the Kakori martyrs. NJBS, DIB Report, 21 May 1929. IOR, L/PJ/12/375, p. 25.

45. Bhagat Singh, Prison Notebooks, NMML, Acc. No. 716, pp. 22, 30.

46. Bhagat Singh, 'Letter to the Second Lahore Conspiracy Case Convicts', 22 March 1931, in Verma (ed.), *Bhagat Singh*, p. 135.

47. In Bhagat Singh's home state of Punjab, literacy ranged between 8–15% of the population. Baljit Kaur, 'Pattern of Literacy in the Punjab, 1931', in *Punjab History Conference Proceedings*, 25th Session, 5–7 May 1992. Patiala: Department of Punjab Historical Studies, 1992. p. 189.

48. Sumathi Ramaswamy links representational conventions which picture Baba Deep Singh, who valiantly fought a battle with his decapitated head aloft in one hand, to those of Bhagat Singh, where he is shown offering his head to Mother India. Sumathi Ramaswamy, 'Maps, Mother/Goddesses, and Martyrdom in Modern India', *Journal of Asian Studies*, 67(3), August 2008, p. 840–2.

49. Kapoor, NMML, OHT, p. 118.

50. Jain, CSAS, OHC, p. 3.

51. Kapoor, NMML, OHT, p. 128.

52. Letter from Graham to Haig, 23 April 1929. NAI, HP 391/1930.

53. *Tribune*, 4 May 1929.

54. Prosecution Witness 193, *Lahore Conspiracy Case*, Vol. 2, p. 149. NAI, Private Papers.

55. Prosecution Witness 193, *Lahore Conspiracy Case*, Vol. 2, p. 148. NAI, Private Papers; Kapoor, NMML, OHT, p. 132.

56. Chand, CSAS, OHC, p. 42.

57. Chand, CSAS, OHC, p. 75.

58. 'Bombs and Pistols Create Chaos in Assembly', *Hindustan Times*, 10 April 1929, p. 1.

59. 'Assembly Bomb Outrage', *Hindustan Times*, 17 April 1929, p. 1.

60. '"Bomb Factory" discovered by Police in Lahore', *Hindustan Times*, 17 April 1929, p. 1. It was a routine police tactic to tell suspects that their colleagues had made full confessions and agreed to become prosecution witnesses, in return for freedom. Jaidev Kapoor was also (falsely) told by inquisitors that Bhagat Singh had turned 'approver' in an effort to get him to confess. Kapoor, NMML, OHT, p. 151.

61. '"Saunders Murderer is Present", Curious placards at Sikhs' Meeting', *Hindustan Times*, 17 April 1929, p. 11.

62. 'Hysteria in London', *Hindustan Times*, 17 April 1929, p. 10.

63. Kapoor, NMML, OHT, p. 131.

64. 'The Assembly Outrage', *Hindustan Times*, 11 April 1929, p. 10.

65. 'Sir Michael O'Dwyer's Hysterics', *Hindustan Times*, 12 April 1929, p. 1.

66. Memo by Fryer, 21 April 1929. NAI, HP 192/1929.

67. 'Another "Red" Army Letter to Hindustan Times editor', *Hindustan Times*, 18 April 1929, p. 1.

68. 'An Indian Episode', Jack Morton Papers, BL, Eur Mss D1003/1, p. 41.

69. 'Police Unearth Plot: Mr Scott Leaves', *Hindustan Times*, 28 April 1929, p. 1.

70. 'Red Posters in Cawnpore', *Hindustan Times*, 24 April 1929, p. 1.

71. Motilal Nehru to Jawaharlal, 4 May 1929. In *Selected Works of Motilal Nehru* (henceforth *SWMN*), Vol. 7, New Delhi: Vikas, 1986, p. 44.

72. *Pioneer*, June 1 1929, quoted in letter to editor; *Pioneer*, 2 June 1929; *SWMN*, Vol. 7, p. 56.

73. Haig to Thompson, 25 April 1929. NAI, HP, 192/1929.

74. Thompson to Haig, 26 April 1929. NAI, HP, 192/1929.

75. Thompson to Haig, 26 April 1929. NAI, HP, 192/1929.

76. Kapoor, NMML, OHT, p. 128.

77. 'The Hindustan Socialist Republican Army', *Hindustan Times*, 10 April 1929, pp. 1–2.

78. Report by Jeffreys, 4 May 1929; Note by Fryer, 11 May 1929; NAI, HP 192/1929.

79. 'Police Enquiry into Assembly Outrage', *Hindustan Times*, 22 April 1929, p. 1.

80. Jain, CSAS, OHC, p. 3.

81. 'Confiscation of the pass supplied to the Hindustan Times', NAI, HP 235/1931. This Chaman Lal is not to be confused with Diwan Chaman Lal, MLA, whom we encountered a few pages earlier.

82. Bhikshu Chaman Lal, CSAS, OHC, p. 18.

83. Bhikshu Chaman Lal, NMML, OHT, p. 16.

84. J. N. Sahni, *Truth about the Indian Press*, Delhi: Allied Publishers, 1974, p. 75.

85. Bhikshu Chaman Lal, CSAS, OHC, p. 17.

86. Sahni, *Truth about the Indian Press*, p. 75.

87. Letter from Thompson to Haig, 26 April 1929. NAI, HP, 192/1929.

88. Bejoy Kumar Sinha worked as a journalist for major British-owned Indian newspapers, such as the *Statesman* and *Pioneer*. Hans Raj Vohra later gave evidence against the revolutionaries, but at the time of the Assembly bombing worked with Feroze Chand at the office of *Bande Mataram*; Statement of Hans Raj Vohra, in Wariach and Jain (eds), *The Hanging of Bhagat Singh, Vol. III*, p. 116; Sinha, *Memoirs of a Revolutionary*, p. 2. For further details on Vohra, see Vaidik, 'History of a Renegade Revolutionary'.

89. Friend (ed.), *Yashpal Looks Back*, p. 75.

90. Kapoor, NMML, OHT, p. 137

91. NAI, Private Papers, Proceedings of the Lahore Conspiracy Case, Vol. 2, p. 40.

92. DIB Report, 23 May 1929. IOR, L/PJ/12/389; Telegram from Viceroy to Secretary of State for India, 6 May 1929. NAI, HP, File 192/1929. The first Lahore Conspiracy Case was trialled in 1915.

93. DIB Report, 23 May 1929. IOR, L/PJ/12/389.

94. DIB Report, 23 May 1929. IOR, L/PJ/12/389.

95. Wariach and Jain (eds), *The Hanging of Bhagat Singh, Vol. III*, p. 113.

96. Copy of Judgment on Trial of Messers B.K. Dutt and Bhagat Singh, NAI, Private Papers, Acc. no 246, p. 11.

97. Letter to Emerson, undated. NAI, HP 21/57 1929.

98. 'Md. Ali Jinnah, Speech in the Legislative Assembly', 12 September 1929, quoted in Noorani, *The Trial of Bhagat Singh*, p. 271.

99. 'Naujawan Bharat Sabha', Intelligence Report, undated [c. July 1929]. NAI, HP 130/1930, p. 47.

100. Nehru, 'On the Lahore Executions', p. 505.

101. 'The Naujawan Bharat Sabha of Peshawar, 1929–1930'. IOR, L/PJ/12/375, p. 69.

102. Nehru, *Toward Freedom*, p. 144.

103. 'Note regarding the celebration of "Bhagat Singh Day" at Amritsar', NAI, HP 130/1930, p. 11.

104. Letter from Roy to Collins, dated 11 October 1930. NAI, HP, 498/1930, p. 4.

105. *Liberty*, 24 March 1931, quoted in NAI, HP, 4/36, Part 1, 1931.

106. Letter to Emerson, 6 July 1929. IOR, L/PJ/12/691.

107. Letter to Emerson, 6 August 1929. IOR, L/PJ/12/691.

108. Letter to Emerson, 6 September 1929. IOR, L/PJ/12/691.

109. One was celebrated in the Punjab on 30 June 1929. DIB Report, 4 July 1929. IOR, L/PJ/12/377; and another in October, 'Bhagat Singh Day Observance', *Tribune*, 12 October 1930, p. 2.

110. Celebrated on 23 March 1931, reported in *Liberty* (Calcutta), 24 March 1931. NAI, HP, 4/36, Part 1, 1931.

111. DIB Report, 11 December 1930. IOR, L/PJ/12/390.

112. *Council of State Debates*, 11 March 1931, p. 21. This will be explored in Chapter Seven.

113. DIB Report, 9 October 1930. IOR, L/PJ/12/389. The attack was most likely the work of Asthi Chakkar, an organisation which broke away from the Lahore-based HSRA. Friend (ed.), *Yashpal Looks Back*, p. 177.

114. Gogate, CSAS, OHC, p. 2.

115. Nawalkar, CSAS, OHC, p. 2.

116. A method of reproducing a photograph in the absence of its negative, whereby a fresh photograph was taken of an existing photograph. Testimony of Prosecution Witness 94, Balraj, Photographer, Anarkali, Lahore, in NAI, *Proceedings of the Lahore Conspiracy Case*, Vol. 2, p. 40.

117. Pinney, '*Photos of the Gods*', p. 128.

118. See, for example, G. Shaw and M. Lloyd (eds), *Publications Proscribed by the Government of India*.

119. Verma, NMML, OHT, p. 165.

120. Shahid Amin, 'Gandhi as Mahatma: Gorakhpur District, Eastern UP, 1921–2', in Ranajit Guha (ed.), *Subaltern Studies III*, Delhi, Oxford University Press, 1984, p. 2.

121. A clear statement of HSRA ideology lies captured in IOR, L/PJ/12/391, pp. 47–60. The manifesto, named 'Our Opportunity', was seized by intelligence officers in 1932 and was attributed to Bhagat Singh. DIB Report, 2 February 1932. IOR, L/PJ/12/391, p. 45. This document has been verified by JNU scholar Chaman Lal as Bhagat Singh's.

122. Sarkar, *Modern India*, p. 288.

123. See, for example, Sidhu (ed.), *The Hanging of Bhagat Singh, Vol. IV*; Gaur, *Martyr as a Bridegroom*, *passim*.

124. Sinha, *Memoirs of a Revolutionary*, pp. 21–2.

125. See, for example, the anxiety in the discussions contained in 'Regarding demonstrations in connection with the execution of Bhagat Singh, Sukh Dev and Rajguru', NAI, HP 4/21/31.

126. DIB Report, 19 September 1929. IOR, L/PJ/12/389, p. 19.

127. Ramaswamy, 'Maps, Mother/Goddesses, and Martyrdom', p. 849.

128. See, for example, the pictorial advertisement for Lal-Imli Pure Wool in the *Hindustan Times*, 27 April 1929.

129. Kapoor, NMML, OHT, p. 114.

130. Bharti, NMML, OHT, p. 32.

131. Durga Das, NMML, OHT, p. 33; Kapoor, NMML, OHT, p. 116.

132. 'Bombs and Pistols Create Chaos in Assembly', *Hindustan Times*, 10 April 1929, p. 1. The author was most likely Chaman Lal, who years later admitted that he wrote the lead articles on the case. Bhikshu Chaman Lal, CSAS, OHC, p. 18.

133. Kapoor, NMML, OHT, p. 116; Manmathnath Gupta, *Bhagat Singh and His Times*, Delhi: Lipi Prakashan, 1977, p. 114.

134. J. Gupta, NMML, OHT, p. 58.

135. Ramaswamy, *Goddess and the Nation*, p. 297.

136. DIB Report, 5 September 1929. IOR, L/PJ/12/375, p. 33.

137. North-Western Frontier Province Fortnightly Report for the second half of March 1931; Gauhar Raza, personal communication, 15 February 2009; Dastur, CSAS, OHC, p. 4.

3. THE REVOLUTIONARY UNKNOWN: THE SECRET LIFE OF DURGA DEVI VOHRA

1. Pinney, '*Photos of the Gods*', p. 127; Gell, 'L'Inde aux deux visages'.
2. Bharti, NMML, OHT, p. 50.
3. Viceroy to Secretary of State for India, 18 December 1928. IOR, L/PJ/12/377, p. 2.
4. Leela Kasturi and Vina Mazumdar, 'Women and Indian Nationalism', in *Women and Indian Nationalism*. New Delhi, Vikas, 1994, p. 2; Suruchi Thapar-Bjorkert, *Women in the Indian Nationalist Movement: Unseen Faces and Unheard Voices, 1930–1942*. Delhi: Sage, 2006, p. 47.
5. This case is more convincingly argued with reference to the revolutionary movement in Bengal, where Bengali men, and occasionally women, challenged colonial concepts of Bengali effeteness by taking up arms. Purnima Bose, 'Engendering the Armed Struggle: Women, Writing and the Bengali "Terrorist" Movement', in T. Foster, C. Seigel and E. E. Barry (eds), *Bodies of Writing, Bodies in Performance*, New York: New York University Press, 1996', p. 159. This argument does not align well with the HSRA, a large number of whose members were Punjabi, and as such were more likely to have imbibed the inverse colonial discourse—that Punjabis constituted a 'military race'. Colonial discourses aside, it is demonstrable that witnessing the violence of colonialism was a humiliating experience, and answering colonial violence, such as the attack on Lala Lajpat Rai, with counter-violence was seen by the HSRA as 'avenging the national honour'. Khanna, NMML, OHT, p. 70.
6. Vohra, NMML, OHT.
7. S. L. Manchanda, personal communication, 9 November 2010. Durga Devi's testimony transcript runs to 36 pages; whereas Sridevi Musaddi's interview, which I draw on below, fills 140 pages.
8. See, for example, 'Bhagat Singh ki Smritiyan', in *Homage to Martyrs*, Delhi: Freedom Fighters Association, 1981, pp. 15–21. In 1976 she was interviewed by Koushalya Devi Dublish, in which she very briefly mentioned the Lamington Road case. Kaushalya Devi Dublish, *Revolutionaries and their Activities in Northern India*, Delhi: B. R. Publishing Corporation, 1982, Appendix XIII, pp. 209–11.
9. Geraldine Forbes, 'Goddesses or Rebels? The Women Revolutionaries of Bengal', in *Indian Women and the Freedom Movement: A Historian's Perspective*, Mumbai: Research Center for Women's Studies, 1997, pp. 112–134; Sandip Bandyopadhyay, 'Women in Bengal Revolutionary Movement (1902–35)', *Manushi*, July–August 1991, pp. 30–35.
10. J. Gupta, NMML, OHT, p. 29.
11. J. Gupta, NMML, OHT, p. 14.
12. M. Gupta, NMML, OHT, p. 66.
13. C. Das, NMML OHT, p. 26.

14. Verma, NMML, OHT, p. 42.

15. Prasad, NMML, OHT, p. 54; M. Gupta, NMML, OHT, p. 64.

16. Verma, NMML, OHT, p. 166.

17. Suruchi Thapar-Bjorkert interviewed Mishra's wife, Sushila Devi Mishra, in the 1980s, and while Sushila Devi mentioned her husband's arrest, Thapar-Bjorkert noted that she would not discuss the incident in which she challenged her husband's integrity, possibly because she considered it 'inappropriate for a woman of traditional values to criticise her husband', although that was precisely what she had done in 1929, that too supported by her mother-in-law. Suruchi Thapar-Bjorkert, 'Nationalist Memories: Interviewing Indian Middle Class Women', *Oral History*, 27 (2), 1999, p. 42.

18. J. A. Alter, 'Celibacy, Sexuality, and the Transformation of Gender into Nationalism in North India'. *Journal of Asian Studies*, 53(1), 1994, pp. 45–66; Carey A. Watt, *Serving the Nation: Cultures of Service, Association, and Citizenship*. New Delhi: Oxford University Press, 2005; Friend (ed.), *Yashpal Looks Back*, p. 6.

19. Kapoor, NMML, OHT, p. 97; R. Singh 'Warrior', NMML, OHT, p. 45.

20. Khanna, NMML, OHT, p. 84. See Yashpal's account of this incident, in 'Yashpal ko Prandand ka Nirnay', *Singhavalokan*, pp. 342–62.

21. Friend (ed.), *Yashpal Looks Back*, p. 178.

22. Khanna, NMML, OHT, p. 84. See also 'Warrior', NMML, OHT, p. 44; Yashpal, *Singhavalokan*, p. 330; Friend (ed.), *Yashpal Looks Back*, p. 161; and Harcourt, 'Revolutionary Networks, p. 345.

23. Musaddi, NMML, OHT, p. 58.

24. M. Gupta, CSAS, OHC, p. 24. This additional danger was that women might face sexual abuse in prison or during questioning. The humiliation of women in custody in the 1920s was well known, and had been the subject of a report by the journalist and Congress leader Ganesh Shankar Vidyarthi. M. L. Bhargava, *Ganesh Shankar Vidyarthi*, Delhi: Publications Division, Government of India, 1988, p. 100; See also Geraldine Forbes, *Women in Modern India*, Cambridge: Cambridge University Press, 1996, p. 152.

25. DIB notification, 2 February 1932, IOR, L/PJ/12/391, p. 45.

26. 'Our Opportunity', IOR L/PJ/12/391, p. 49.

27. 'Our Opportunity', IOR L/PJ/12/391, p. 59. On the biological construction of women's passivity, see Cynthia Enloe, *Manoeuvres: The International Politics of Militarising Women's Lives*, Berkeley: University of California Press, 2000; Neloufer de Mel, *Militarising Sri Lanka: Popular Culture, Memory and Narrative in the Armed Conflict*, New Delhi: Sage, 2007.

28. *The United Provinces Political Who's Who*, entry no. 101.

29. Interview with Durga Devi Vohra, 3 March 1986, in I. Mallikarjuna Sharma (ed.), *In Retrospect: Sagas of Heroism*, Vol. 1, Hyderabad: Ravi Sasi Enterprises, 1999, p. 8.

30. Vohra, NMML, OHT, p. 2.

31. Bhagwati Charan Vohra, NMML Private Papers, Acc. No. 720.

32. Durga Devi Vohra had known Bhagat Singh since 1921. Vohra, NMML, OHT, p. 32.

33. 'Provincial Nau Jawan Bharat Sabha', in NAI, HP, 130 & K. W., 1930, unpaginated.

34. Friend (ed.), *Yashpal Looks Back*, p. 36.

35. Vohra, NMML, OHT, p. 4.

36. Vohra and several other revolutionary memoirs disclose that Jaichand Vidyalankar, a mentor to party members in Lahore, suspected that Bhagwati Charan was a CID informer. These aspersions were conveyed to Azad, who at one stage refused to accept the funds that they donated to the party. Azad ultimately was reassured of Bhagwati Charan and Durga Devi's commitment, but she remained resentful of the allegations even when she was interviewed in the 1970s. See Vohra, NMML, OHT, p. 7; Gupta, *Bhagat Singh and his Times*, p. 125.

37. Jain, CSAS, OHC, pp. 7–8; Verma, *Samsmritiyan*, p. 160.

38. Vohra, NMML, OHT, p. 11.

39. Lajjawati, NMML, OHT, pp. 136–7.

40. The *United Provinces Political Who's Who* noted that there were records of several revolutionaries' photographs and handwriting on record, but they lacked Durga Devi's, according to her entry, no. 101.

41. Vohra, NMML, OHT, p. 10.

42. Vohra, NMML, OHT, p. 12.

43. Vohra, NMML, OHT, p. 12. Lajjawati, NMML, OHT, p. 99. Yashpal, *Simhavalokan*, p. 114–6.

44. Kapoor, NMML, OHT, p. 91.

45. Vohra, NMML, OHT, p. 13

46. C. Das, NMML, OHT, pp. 34–5.

47. Verma, NMML, OHT, p. 88.

48. Vohra, NMML, OHT, p. 15.

49. Vohra, NMML, OHT, p. 17.

50. Vohra, NMML, OHT, p. 18.

51. Vohra, NMML, OHT, p. 18.

52. 'Lahore Bomb Factory Discovered', *Hindustan Times*, 28 April 1929, p. 1.

53. 'Attachment of Lahore Congressman's House', *Times of India*, 15 May 1929.

54. Comrade Ram Chandra, *Naujawan Bharat Sabha and Hindustan Socialist Republican Association/Army*, New Delhi: published by the author, 1986, pp. 116–7.

55. Sahni, *Truth About the Indian Press*, p. 78.

56. Jain, CSAS, OHC, p. 5.

57. Vohra, NMML, OHT, p. 20.

58. Friend (ed.), *Yashpal Looks Back*, pp. 143–5.

59. DIB Report, 11 September 1930. IOR, L/PJ/12/389, p. 65. The details of Bhagwati Charan's death were aired in February 1931 in an approved statement submitted by Inderpal for the Delhi Conspiracy Case prosecution. 'Terrorist Killed by a Bomb', *Civil and Military Gazette*, 11 February 1931, p. 5.

60. In an undated interview with K. C. Yadav, Vohra ended her story with her husband's death. K. C. Yadav and Babar Singh (eds), *Bhagat Singh: Making of a Revolutionary: Contemporaries' Portrayals*, Delhi: Hope India Publications, 2006, pp. 162–70.

61. Lajjawati, NMML, OHT, p. 137. See also Chandra, *Naujawan Bharat Sabha*, 1986, p. 123; Friend (ed.), *Yashpal Looks Back*, p. 145.

62. Vohra, NMML, OHT, pp. 20–1.

63. Chandra, *Naujawan Bharat Sabha*, p. 124

64. Singh, CSAS, OHC, p. 30.

65. Musaddi, NMML, OHT, pp. 51, 60.

66. Nigam, CSAS, OHC, p. 8.

67. 'Bhagat Singh and Dutt's Hunger Strike', *Tribune*, 16 July 1929, p. 9; 'Jatin's Death: Hartal in Lahore', *Tribune*, 15 September 1929, p. 2.

68. 'Note on Terrorism', 1932, IOR, L/PJ/12/404, p. 106.

69. 'Twelve men arrested in Police Raids', *Times of India*, 11 October 1930.

70. 'Twelve men arrested in Police Raids', *Times of India*, 11 October 1930.

71. 'Shots fired at Lahore Police Officer', *Times of India*, 14 October 1930.

72. 'Bombay Police Hunt for Absconding Gujarati Couple, *Times of India*, 15 October 1930.

73. Vohra, NMML, OHT, p. 24.

74. DIB Report, 11 December 1930. IOR, L/PJ/12/390, p. 4.

75. In her interview, Durga Devi recalled that Prithvi Singh and Bapat were in the car with her. However the prosecutors in the court case alleged that Bapat, S. N. Rao, and Durga Devi were in the car at the time of the shooting. The discrepancy could be a result of aliases, or the prosecutors could have been wrong—all of the accused entered a not guilty plea.

76. 'The Lamington Road Case', *Times of India*, 6 May 1931, p. 1.

77. Jain, CSAS, OHC, p. 9.

78. Sinha, *Memoirs of a Revolutionary*, p. 26.

79. Vohra, NMML, OHT, p. 22.

80. 'Bombay Outrage', *Times of India*, 14 October 1930; 'Bombay Shooting Outrage', *Times of India*, 20 October 1930.

81. Vohra, NMML, OHT, p. 26.

82. Vohra, NMML, OHT, p. 26.

83. 'The Lamington Road Outrage', *Times of India*, 2 February 1931, p. 11.

84. 'Wanted Woman in Lamington Road Conspiracy Case: is She the Durga Devi of Lahore Case?', *Times of India*, 30 January 1931, p. 10. 'All accused acquitted in Lamington Road Case', *Times of India*, 5 May 1931, p. 9.

85. 'Police hunt for absconding Gujarati Couple', *Times of India*, 15 October 1930.

86. Lajjawati, NMML, OHT, pp. 116–8.

87. Ghosh, 'Terrorism in Bengal', p. 287.

88. Vohra, NMML, OHT, p. 33.

89. Friend (ed.), *Yashpal Looks Back*, p. 58.

90. In an exception that proves the rule, Yashpal did on one occasion don an elaborate disguise as a suited, London-returned lawyer to visit Sukhdev, in an attempt to make contact with the HSRA branch in UP. Crucially, to seal the performance he brought a girl by the name of Shakuntala with him, who posed as Sukhdev's sister. On cue, she burst into an elaborate performance of wailing at the sight of a perplexed Sukhdev, in order

to convince the jailers of her (and ultimately Yashpal's) legitimacy. Friend (ed.), *Yashpal Looks Back*, p. 70.

91. Ghosh, 'Terrorism in Bengal', p. 288.

92. He is styled as such in 'Attachment of Lahore Congressman's House', *Times of India*, 15 May 1929.

93. This would have been between 17 February, when Gandhi arrived in Delhi, and 4 March, when the talks were concluded. C. B. Dalal, *Gandhi: 1915–1948, A Detailed Chronology*, New Delhi: Gandhi Peace Foundation, 1971, pp. 86–7. Vohra, in Dublish (ed.), *Revolutionary Activities in Northern India*, p. 210.

94. Nehru, *Toward Freedom*, p. 144.

95. Vohra, NMML, OHT, p. 27; Lajjawati, NMML, OHT, p. 136.

96. B. R. Grover, *Civil Disobedience Movement in the Punjab, 1930–1934*, New Delhi: B. R. Corporation, 1987, pp. 31, 65, 68.

97. *India in 1930–31*, New Delhi: Anmol Publications, 1985 [1931], p. 73.

98. NAI, F/18/3/1931, *NWFP Fortnightly report for the second half of March 1931*.

99. *Tribune*, 29 March 1931, p. 5; and 28 March 1931, p. 1.

100. Gaur, *Martyr as a Bridegroom*; Panchal, CSAS, OHC, p. 2.

101. Interview with Shiva Dua, 4 March 1986. *In Retrospect*, in Sharma (ed.), p. 53.

102. 'Collection of violent speeches made in the Punjab', NAI, HP, 33/9/1931, p. 146–7.

103. 'The Naujawan Bharat Sabha', NAI, HP 130/1930, p. 49.

104. Panchal, CSAS, OHC, p. 2.

105. Panchal, CSAS, OHC, p. 3.

106. Chandra, *Naujawan Bharat Sabha*, p. 187.

107. Geraldine Forbes (ed.), Manmohini Zutshi Sahgal, *An Indian Freedom Fighter Recalls Her Life*, London: M.E. Sharpe, 1994, p. 95.

108. *The United Provinces Political Who's Who*. IOR, L/PJ/12/672, p. 101.

109. *The United Provinces Political Who's Who*, p. 101.

110. Vohra, NMML, OHT, p. 26.

111. Vohra, NMML, OHT, p. 29; M. Gupta, CSAS, OHC, p. 19.

112. *Times of India*, 30 July 1938, p. 5.

113. '"Durga Bhabhi" Dead', *Tribune*, 16 October 1999.

114. Chaman Lal, *The Vanishing Empire*, Tokyo: Kyodo Printing Co., 1937, pp. 203–4.

115. K. Kutralam Pillai, 'Sentamil Manjari, Part 1', in Sidhu (ed.), *The Hanging of Bhagat Singh, Vol. IV*, p. 151.

116. Chand, CSAS, OHC, p. 44.

117. DIB Report, 17 December 1931. IOR, L/PJ/12/391, p. 4.

118. Bose, 'Engendering the Armed Struggle', p. 159.

119. *India in 1930–31*, p. 73.

120. Tanika Sarkar, 'Politics and Women in Bengal: The Conditions and Meaning of Participation', *Indian Economic and Social History Review*, 21(1), 1984, p. 99.

121. Friend (ed.), *Yashpal Looks Back*, p. 146.

122. Musaddi, NMML, OHT, p. 60.

123. She specifically named books written by Vishnu Prabhakar, Rajendra Kishwar and

Sukhdevraj's *Jab Jyoti Jagi*. Vohra, in Sharma (ed.), *In Retrospect*, p. 12. Shiv Verma also denied these allegations, and was critical of Sukhdevraj's book. Interview with Shiv Verma, 10 October 1988, *In Retrospect*, pp. 73, 77.

124. Vohra, NMML, OHT, p. 13.

125. Vohra, NMML, OHT, p. 24.

126. 'Our Opportunity', L/PJ/12/391, p. 57.

127. On this general point, see Thapar-Bjorkert, *Women in the Indian Nationalist Movement*, p. 74.

128. Khanna, NMML, OHT, p. 32.

129. A note on Terrorism in India, 19 August 1933, L/PJ/12/397, p. 100. See also NAI, HP, 130/1930 for references to women activists.

130. Paliwal, NMML, OHT, p. 76.

131. *The United Provinces Political Who's Who*, p. 311.

132. Thapar-Bjorkert, 'Nationalist Memories', p. 43.

133. Kasturi and Mazumdar, 'Women and Indian Nationalism', p. 17.

134. Thapar-Bjorkert, 'Nationalist Memories', p. 42.

135. K. K. Khullar, 'Durga *Bhabhi*: A Forgotten Revolutionary', *Tribune*, 14 November 1999.

136. Shiv Verma, Manmathnath Gupta, Yashpal, Bejoy Kumar Sinha and Sukhdevraj each published memoirs; the first three were the authors of more than one volume. Durga Devi contributed an interview to a volume on Bhagat Singh, but in it did not reflect on her own broader contribution to the party. See Yadav and Singh (eds), *Bhagat Singh: the Making of a Revolutionary*.

4. INTERMEDIARIES, THE REVOLUTIONARIES AND THE CONGRESS

1. *Vir Bharat* (Lahore), 13 April 1931. NAI, HP, 13/XI & KW/1931, pp. 49–57.

2. *Tribune*, 28 March 1931, p. 7.

3. *Vir Bharat*, 14 April 1931, in NAI, HP, 13/XI & KW/1931. Sections that are under-lined are done so in pencil on the file.

4. Mukherjee, *Peasants in India's Non-Violent Revolution*, p. 105. On the agile nature of nationalist inspiration, see Chaturvedi, 'A Revolutionary's Biography', pp. 135–9; and Zachariah, 'Internationalisms in the Interwar Years', pp. 14–5.

5. *Vir Bharat* was considered Hindu paper, with a circulation of around 2,500 between 1930–1932. Grover, *Civil Disobedience Movement in the Punjab*, p. 310.

6. Gyanesh Kudaisya, *Region, Nation, "Heartland": Uttar Pradesh in India's Body Politic*, Delhi: Sage, 2006.

7. One of the first in this genre was represented by S.A. Dange's 1921 pamphlet, *Gandhi vs. Lenin*. Debates or ideological clashes to follow include Gandhi versus Bose, Gandhi versus Aurobindo, and Gandhi versus Ambedkar. See also Harold Coward (ed.), *Indian Critiques of Gandhi*, Albany: SUNY Press, 2003.

8. M. Gupta, NMML, OHT, p. 54; *They Lived Dangerously*, Introduction.

9. M. Singh, NMML, OHT, p. 135.

10. 'Our Opportunity', IOR, L/PJ/12/391, p. 54.
11. Mittal and Habib, 'The Congress and the Revolutionaries in the 1920s', pp. 20–37; Habib, 'Congress and the Revolutionaries'; Sharma, *Radical Politics in Colonial Punjab*.
12. Khanna, NMML, OHT, p. 90.
13. Prasad, NMML, OHT, p. 55; Verma, NMML, OHT, p. 64.
14. Friend (ed.), *Yashpal Looks Back*, p. 73.
15. Sarkar, *Modern India*, p. 251; Mohan, *Militant Nationalism in the Punjab*, p. 197.
16. DIB Report, 2 January 1930. IOR, L/PJ/12/389, p. 29. This amounted to only three Congresses, as there was no annual meeting in 1930.
17. Narain, NMML, OHT, p. 32.
18. M. Singh, NMML, OHT, p. 134.
19. Kishan, CSAS, OHC, p. 2.
20. DIB Report, 3 May 1928. IOR, L/PJ/12/375, p. 3.
21. Mittal and Habib, 'The Congress and the Revolutionaries', pp. 20–37.
22. Interview with Comrade Ram Chandra, in Sharma (ed.), *In Retrospect*, p. 41. Chandra claimed to have a role in the formation of the NJBS, although this did not come to the attention of the CID. See IOR, L/PJ/12/375; NAI HP, 130 & KW, 1930.
23. DIB Report, 3 May 1928. IOR, L/PJ/12/375, p. 4.
24. EMDC to Hirtzel, 28 December 1928, IOR, L/PJ/12/404, p. 1; a full list of arrested persons is in G42/1929, AICC Papers, NMML.
25. Narain, NMML, OHT, p. 34–43.
26. Report on the political situation in Punjab for the fortnight ending the 28 February 1931. NAI, HP 18/1/31.
27. This was contradicted by a CID officer, who clarified that based on his close observations, Bhagat Singh was the primary force behind the NJBS's inception. 'The Nau Jawan Bharat Sabha', NAI, HP 130/1930, p. 36; IOR, L/PJ/12/375, p. 21.
28. For a list compiled using CID files, see Rama Hari Shankar, *Gandhi's Encounter with the Indian Revolutionaries*, New Delhi: Siddharth Publications, 1996, Table II, 'List of prominent revolutionaries who participated in the Non-Cooperation Movement', pp. 84–6.
29. Chand, CSAS, OHC, p. 42.
30. See M. Singh, NMML, OHT, p. 134; and Narain, NMML, OHT, p. 31.
31. Bhikshu Chaman Lal, CSAS, OHC, p. 16.
32. 'The Nau Jawan Bharat Sabha', NAI, HP 130/1930, pp. 36, 99.
33. DIB Report, 21 May 1929. IOR, L/PJ/12/375, p. 22; Singh, CSAS, OHC, p. 17.
34. 'Josh', 'My Meetings with Bhagat Singh', p. 13.
35. Beazely to GOI, 21 May 1929. NAI, HP, 130/1930, p. 99; 'Josh', 'My Meetings with Bhagat Singh', pp. 12–13.
36. 'Josh', 'My meetings with Bhagat Singh', pp. 15, 29.
37. DIB Report, 10 May 1928. IOR, L/PJ/12/375, p. 11.
38. DIB Report, 29 May 1929. IOR, L/PJ/12/375, p. 26.
39. G. Heeger, 'The Growth of the Congress Movement in Punjab, 1920–1940', *Journal*

of Asian Studies, 32(1), 1972, p. 41. Tai Yong Tan suggests that the weakness of the Congress in Punjab might be partly related to the heavy presence of military families and their dependence on pensions. Tai Yong Tan, *The Garrison State: The Military, Government and Society in Colonial Punjab*, Delhi: Sage, 2005, p. 181. This however fails to explain the strength of organised movements such as Ghadar; anticolonial strains within the Akali Movement; or for that matter the 'Punjab Disturbances' of 1919, let alone the HSRA and satellite parties. For a more nuanced exploration of the subjectivities of colonial soldiers, see Gajendra Singh, *The Testimonies of Indian Soldiers and the Two World Wars: Between Self and Sepoy*, London: Bloomsbury, 2014.

40. Shalini Sharma, 'Developing a Communist Identity: The Case of the Naujawan Bharat Sabha', *Journal of Punjab Studies*, 14(2), 2007; Grover, *Civil Disobedience Movement in the Punjab*, pp. 11–12.

41. S. K. Mittal and Irfan Habib, 'Towards Independence and Socialist Republic: Naujawan Bharat Sabha', *Social Scientist*, 8(2), 1979, p. 20.

42. Sharma, 'Developing a Communist Identity', p. 177.

43. NAI, HP, 130, 1930, p. 101; IOR, L/PJ/12/375, p. 4.

44. Chandra, *Naujawan Bharat Sabha*, p. 68; Khan, NMML, OHT, p. 32; Friend (ed.), *Yashpal Looks Back*, pp. 31–2.

45. Chandra, *Naujawan Bharat Sabha*, p. 39.

46. The longer incarcerations of its leaders, such as Ram Chandra, Abdul Majid Khan and Kedar Nath Sehgal (the latter two accused in the Meerut Conspiracy Case) removed skilled and committed organisers from the field. Chandra, *Naujawan Bharat Sabha*, p. 75; Beazely to GOI, 21 May 1929. NAI, HP, 130/1930, p. 104. See also Ali Raza, 'Separating the Wheat from the Chaff: Meerut and the Creation of "Official" Communism in India', *Comparative Studies of South Asia, Africa and the Middle East*, 33 (3), 2013, pp. 316–333.

47. 'Revolutionary movements in Bengal, the United Provinces and the Punjab', L/PJ/12/404, p. 82.

48. Khan, NMML, OHT, p. 33.

49. 'Notes on Terrorism', 1933, IOR, L/PJ/12/397, p. 150. This mix of agendas was evident at the NJBS's tumultuous meeting in Karachi in 1931, described in Chapter Seven.

50. Satyabrata Ray Chowdhuri, *Leftism in India, 1917–1947*, Palgrave Macmillan, 2007, p. 145.

51. Vinay Bhal, 'The Attitude of the Indian National Congress towards the Working Class Struggle in India, 1918–1947', in Kumar (ed.), *Congress and Classes*, p. 22.

52. Mushirul Hasan, 'Communalism in the Provinces: A Case Study of Bengal and Punjab, 1922–1926', *Economic and Political Weekly*, 15, 33, 1980, p. 1404.

53. Report on the political situation in Punjab for the fortnight ending the 31st August 1929. IOR, L/PJ/12/694; Khan, NMML, OHT, p. 39; Sachar, NMML, OHT, p. 103.

54. Report on the political situation in Punjab for the fortnight ending the 31st August 1929. IOR, L/PJ/12/694. See undated letter from Jawaharlal to Satyapal, AICC Papers, G-99/1929, p. 23; Gandhi, 'Appeal for Punjabi unity', *Young India*, 7 November 1929, *CWMG*, Vol. XLII, p. 111.

55. DIB Report, 3 May 1928. IOR, L/PJ/12/375, p. 3. Chandra, *Naujawan Bharat Sabha*, p. 26.

56. Khan, NMML, OHT, p. 33.

57. DIB Report, 15 August 1929. IOR, L/PJ/12/375, p. 34.

58. Emerson to GOI, 25 February 1930. NAI, HP 130/1930, p. 121.

59. Gyanendra Pandey, *The Ascendency of the Congress in Uttar Pradesh, 1920–1940*, London: Anthem Press, 2002 [Second Edition], p. 78.

60. Chandra, *Naujawan Bharat Sabha*, pp. 46–7.

61. 'The Naujawan Bharat Sabha', 1929. NAI, HP, 130/1930, p. 37.

62. DIB Report, 28 February 1929. IOR, L/PJ/12/375, p. 16.

63. Beazley to GOI, 21 May 1929. NAI, HP 130/1930, p. 99.

64. Kitchlew had also donated funds to Bhagat Singh, and had been startled to see him in Delhi, hair cut and clean shaven, at the Legislative Assembly. Kapoor, NMML, OHT, p. 107.

65. Bhargava too had a connection to the revolutionaries; in 1928 Yashpal worked for Bhargava as his secretary, although Yashpal left his service in early 1929, their relationship strained by Bhargava's realisation of his links with the Saunders assassination. Friend (ed.), *Yashpal Looks Back*, p. 23, 42. Later in 1929, however, Bhargava made politically expedient interventions on the behalf of hunger-striking revolutionaries.

66. *Tribune*, 13 March 1929, quoted in Grover, *Civil Disobedience Movement in the Punjab*, p. 18.

67. Grover, *Civil Disobedience Movement in the Punjab*, p. 18. With 27,490 enlisted by September 1929, the quota was not fully realised, partly as a result of the schism in the Congress leadership in Punjab. Grover, *Civil Disobedience Movement in the Punjab*, p. 20.

68. Verma, NMML, OHT, p. 95.

69. Nigam, CSAS, OHC, p. 7; Hale, *Political Trouble in India*, p. 67; Statement of Political Crimes and other Manifestations of the Revolutionary Movement, September 1929 to December 1930, L/PJ/12/396, p. 18.

70. 'Notes on Terrorism', 1933, IOR, L/PJ/12/397, p. 46. Nigam, CSAS, OHC, p. 6.

71. Nigam, CSAS, OHC, p. 6.

72. Nigam, CSAS, OHC, p. 6.

73. Progress report for week ending 28 February 1931. NAI, HP, 4/13/30, p. 179.

74. 'History Sheet', 1928, IOR, L/PJ/12/168, p. 5.

75. Bhikshu Chaman Lal, NMML, OHT, p. 22.

76. Subhash Chander Arora, *Turmoil in Punjabi Politics*, Delhi: Mittal Publications, 1990, p. 20.

77. For this he earned special mention in Bhagat Singh and B.K. Dutt's statement: 'We are neither perpetrators of dastardly outrages, and therefore a disgrace to the country, as the pseudo-socialist Dewan Chaman Lal is reported to describe us'. Statement of Bhagat Singh and B.K. Dutt in the Sessions Court. NAI, Private Papers, Acc. No. 246, p. 2.

78. Question in Legislative Assembly, 17 August 1929. NAI, HP, 21/57 1929.

79. IOR, L/PJ/12/375. Born Chaman Lal Kapoor, 'Azad' (freedom) was a name he adopted,

perhaps following the example of Chandrashekhar Azad. Bhagwat Ram Talwar, 'Martrydom of Hari Kishan', *Homage to Martyrs*, p. 46.

80. Khanna, NMML, OHT, p. 32.
81. Khanna, NMML, OHT, p. 32.
82. 'Attack on Punjab Governor', *Civil and Military Gazette*, 31 December 1930, p. 5.
83. Hale, *Political Trouble in India*, p. 70.
84. Khanna, NMML, OHT, pp. 47–50.
85. Letter from M. G. Hallett, 30 March 1933. NAI, HP 44/46, 1933, p. 24.
86. Khanna, NMML, OHT, p. 30; Bhikshu Chaman Lal, NMML, OHT, pp. 13–4.
87. Bhikshu Chaman Lal, CSAS, OHC, p. 2.
88. Bhikshu Chaman Lal, NMML, OHT, p. 8.
89. Bhikshu Chaman Lal, CSAS, OHC, p. 4.
90. Bhikshu Chaman Lal, CSAS, OHC, p. 6.
91. Bhikshu Chaman Lal, CSAS, OHC, p. 6
92. Sahni, *Truth about the Indian Press*, p. 51.
93. Bhikshu Chaman Lal, NMML, OHT, p. 12.
94. 'Assembly Attaché Case Incident', *Times of India*, 13 March 1928, p. 10.
95. 'Assembly Attaché Case Incident', *Times of India*, 13 March 1928, p. 10.
96. Bhikshu Chaman Lal, CSAS, OHC, p. 12–14.
97. Bhikshu Chaman Lal, CSAS, OHC, p. 16.
98. Letter from Thompson to Haig, 26 April 1929. NAI, HP, 192/1929.
99. Note by Fryer, 11 May 1929. NAI, HP 192/29 & KW, p. 54.
100. Bhikshu Chaman Lal, CSAS, OHC, p. 19.
101. Bhikshu Chaman Lal, CSAS, OHC, p. 15.
102. Khanna, CSAS, OHC, pp. 8–9; Sahni, CSAS, OHC, pp. 15–20.
103. Bhikshu Chaman Lal, CSAS, OHC, p. 26.
104. Bhikshu Chaman Lal CSAS, OHC, p. 29.
105. See Bolt, *The Violent Image*, Introduction, on the creation of media events through political violence.
106. David A. Thomas, 'Lucknow and Kanpur, 1880–1920: Stagnation and Development under the Raj', *South Asia*, 5(2), 1982, p. 75.
107. G. K. Leiten, 'When Communism Came to India', *South Asia*, 5(1), 1975, p. 91.
108. Hardas, *Armed Struggle for Freedom*, p. 310.
109. 'Notes on Terrorism', 1933. IOR, L/PJ/12/397, p. 46; *The United Provinces Political Who's Who*, pp. 113, 147, 324, 330.
110. G. Pandey, *The Ascendancy of the Congress in Uttar Pradesh, 1920–1940*, London: Anthem Press, 2002, p. 109.
111. 'Notes on Terrorism', 1933. IOR, L/PJ/12/397, pp. 49–51.
112. 'Notes on Terrorism', 1933. IOR, L/PJ/12/397, pp. 109–10.
113. 'Notes on Terrorism', 1933. IOR, L/PJ/12/397, pp. 110.
114. NAI, Home Judicial, 152/I/31 & K.W.
115. *Report of the Commission of Inquiry into the Communal Outbreak at Cawnpore*, Cmd. 3891, June 1931, p. 4.

116. S. D. Tripathi, 'Politics of a Multi-Union Plant: The Swadeshi Experience', *Indian Journal of Industrial Relations*, 3(4), 1968, pp. 441–458; S.M. Pandey, 'Ideological Conflict in the Kanpur Trade Union Movement, 1934–45', *Indian Journal of Industrial Relations*, 3(3), 1968, pp. 243–68.

117. Francesca Orsini, *The Hindi Public Sphere, 1920–1940: Language and Literature in the Age of Nationalism*, Oxford: Oxford University Press, 2002, p. 65.

118. Orsini, *Hindi Public Sphere*, p. 65.

119. Gyanendra Pandey, 'Mobilisation in a Mass Movement: Congress "Propaganda" in the United Provinces (India), 1930–1934', *Modern Asian Studies*, 9(2), 1975, Table 1; p. 209.

120. Kapoor, OHT, p. 107; Verma, OHT, p. 32; Bhargava, *Ganesh Shankar Vidyarthi*, p. 87.

121. Orsini, *Hindi Public Sphere*, p. 451.

122. Lal, 'Introduction', *The Jail Notebook*, p. 14.

123. Verma, NMML, OHT, p. 23.

124. Bhargava, *Ganesh Shankar Vidyarthi*, p. 44.

125. Kapoor, NMML, OHT, p. 307. It was from this book that the revolutionaries learned of the efficacy of the political hunger-strike. Silvestri, '"The Sinn Fein of India"', p. 469.

126. Silvestri, '"The Sinn Fein of India"', p. 469.

127. Verma, NMML, OHT, p. 17–23; Kumar, 'Nationalism as Bestseller', p. 172; Bhargava, *Ganesh Shankar Vidyarthi*, p. 15.

128. Verma, NMML, OHT, p. 20.

129. Kapoor, NMML, OHT, p. 229; 'Warrior', NMML, OHT, p. 45.

130. Verma, NMML, OHT, p, 16.

131. Prasad, NMML, OHT, p. 81.

132. Bhargava, *Ganesh Shankar Vidyarthi*, p. 31.

133. Cf. Richard Gordon, 'The Hindu Mahasabha and the Indian National Congress, 1915 to 1926', *Modern Asian Studies*, 9(2), 1975, pp. 145–203.

134. Indeed there are closer studies of Gandhi's interactions with revolutionaries than of the larger Congress movement. See Shankar, *Gandhi's Encounter with the Indian Revolutionaries*.

135. Quoted in Nanda, *The Nehrus*, p. 243.

136. Kumar, 'From Swaraj to Purna Swaraj', in *Making of a Nation*, p. 47.

5. THE REVOLUTIONARY PICTURE: IMAGES AND THE DYNAMICS OF ANTI-COLONIALISM

1. Pinney, '*Photos of the Gods*', p. 135.

2. Pinney, '*Photos of the Gods*', p. 136.

3. Ramaswamy, *The Goddess and the Nation*, p. 218.

4. Proceedings of the Lahore Conspiracy Case, NAI, Private Papers, Vol. 2, p. 40.

5. Comrade Ram Chandra, *Ideology and Battle Cries of Indian Revolutionaries*, New Delhi: Published by the Author, 1989, pp. 212–3.

6. Thanks to Amit Ranjan for his poetic translation of the Awadhi.

7. I have extended this rather rudimentary analysis elsewhere, offering a range of other interpretations of this picture. See my 'Imagining the Nationalist Movement'.

8. Chris Pinney, personal communication, 9 June 2011.

9. Pinney, *Photos of the Gods*, p. 128.

10. Pinney, 'Iatrogenic Religion and Politics', in Raminder Kaur and William Mazzarella (eds), *Censorship in South Asia: Cultural Regulation from Sedition to Seduction*, Bloomington: Indiana University Press, 2009, p. 52.

11. Report by Superintendent of Police, 14 April 1931. NAI, HP, 159/1931.

12. DIB Report, 23 May 1929. IOR, L/PJ/12/389; Graham to Haig, 23 April 1929. NAI, HP, File 391/1930.

13. Bhargava, *Ganesh Shankar Vidyarthi*, p. 31.

14. Vohra, NMML, OHT, p. 18; Yashpal, NMML, OHT, p. 17. According to Sanyal, Bhagat Singh was 5' 11". *Sardar Bhagat Singh*, 1983, p. 80.

15. Vohra, NMML, OHT, pp. 11–12. L. F. Chand reflected that Rajguru made a great impression upon him, 'and this impression was made by his silence. He seldom ever uttered a word'. Chand, CSAS, OHC, p. 62.

16. Vohra, NMML, OHT, p. 12.

17. Shiv Verma claimed that this action was on the Viceroy, however Jaidev Kapoor provides the greater detail, explaining that they were targeting Sir John Simon, travelling in a convoy en route to a party in Talkatora Gardens on 25 March. This is consistent with Simon's social program in Delhi at the time, although it is likely that the Viceroy attended the same event. Kapoor, NMML, OHT, p. 111–2. Verma, NMML, OHT, p. 95. 'Social and Personal', *Times of India*, 25 March 1929, p. 12.

18. Statement of political crimes, 1933. IOR, L/PJ/12/396, p. 17. This explains why Rajguru is not represented in posters representing the 1929 hunger strikes.

19. Gulab Singh, who was also accused in the Lahore Conspiracy Case, notes that in Lahore Central Jail after the hangings 'every jail employee who met us' told them details about the hangings. Gulab Singh, *Under the Shadow of the Gallows*, Delhi: Rup Chand, 1963, p. 132.

20. K. Singh, NMML, OHT, pp. 66–7.

21. Surviving revolutionaries describe being taken to say farewell to Bhagat Singh before they were transferred from Lahore Central Jail in December 1930. Verma, NMML, OHT, p. 168; Kapoor, NMML, OHT, p. 237.

22. Kapoor, NMML, OHT, p. 285.

23. Sinha, *Memoirs of a Revolutionary*, p. 39.

24. *Report of the Commission of Inquiry into the Communal Outbreak at Cawnpore*, June 1931, CMD 3891, p. 25.

25. Sahai, NMML, OHT, pp. 22–25; 'Warrior', NMML, OHT, p. 45; Verma, NMML, OHT, p. 23; Jain, CSAS, OHC, p. 5. See also Chapter Seven.

26. An indication of the tone of Vidyarthi's writings about communalism can be found in Gyanendra Pandey, *Construction of Communalism in North India*, New Delhi: Oxford University Press, 2006, pp. 238–9.

27. That said, none of the Kapoor images in my own collection bear the signs of having

been displayed—they are mostly clean and reasonably intact, and bear no pockmarks that suggest they have ever been hung. Perhaps this has something to do with the route they travelled to the Delhi dealers that I purchased them from. I suspect these posters were remaindered, or perhaps hidden In the 1930s, and only relatively recently rescued from a godown, as I have frequently seen multiple versions of them for sale over time and have recognised similar prints in the collections of other enthusiasts.

28. Compare, for example, his masterly images (Figures 17, 33, 39 and 49) with his more rudimentary (Figures 36 and 38).

29. Darling to Irene, 20 April 1931. CSAS, Darling Papers, 1:10, envelope 2, p. 182.

30. Ramaswamy, *Goddess and the Nation*, p. 219.

31. There is a large genre of leaflets and booklets in proscribed tracts collections in a range of languages which include poems and songs in praise of Congress leaders, including Gandhi and Nehru, alongside Bhagat Singh. IOR, PP Hin B55, pp. 16; and *Sardar Bhagat Singh Povada*, a Marathi pamphlet of 1931 presents two ballads, one to Bhagat Singh and the other to Motilal Nehru. IOR, MAR D 5/2.

32. Quoted in 'Note on the Press', 8 August 1931. NAI, HP 4/22/1931.

33. Narain, NMML, OHT, p. 66.

34. D. Das, NMML, OHT, p. 49. Curiously, Nanda never elaborated on this puzzle in his own scholarship.

35. M. Gupta, NMML, OHT, p. 43.

36. Nigam, CSAS, OHC, p. 1.

37. Paliwal, NMML, OHT, p. 99.

38. Arvind Kala, 'Embodiments of Saga of Courage', *Indian Express*, 19 August 1972.

39. Paliwal, CSAS, OHC, p. 11.

40. Singh, CSAS, OHC, p. 30.

41. S. Das, NMML, OHT, p. 17.

42. Jain, CSAS, OHC, p. 18.

43. Pinney, '*Photos of the Gods*', pp. 175–7.

44. B. R. Tomlinson, *The Indian National Congress and the Raj, 1929–1942: The Penultimate Phase*, Cambridge: Cambridge University Press, 1976, p. 4.

45. Brown, *Gandhi and Civil Disobedience*, p. xiii.

6. 'GANDHI AND BALRAJ': FROM DOMINION STATUS TO COMPLETE INDE-PENDENCE

1. Barrier, *Banned*, p. 109.

2. Herman von Steitencron, 'Political Aspects of Indian Religious Art', in *Hindu Myth, Hindu History: Religion, Art, and Politics*, Delhi: Permanent Black, 2005, p. 13.

3. I am grateful to Philip Lutgendorf for his analysis of this picture as respondent to my paper at the AAS and ASAA conferences.

4. Jawaharlal to Gandhi, 4 November 1929. *SWJN*, Vol. 4, p. 166. On this point, see Franziska Roy, 'International Utopia and National Discipline: Youth and Volunteer Movements in Interwar South Asia', in Raza, et al (eds), *The Internationalist Moment*, pp. 150–87.

5. Both British and Congress definitions of the contemporary youth movement make this clear. See 'Youth Movement in India, 1929–1936', IOR, L/PJ/12/60; AICC papers, 'Youth Movement in India', G39/1929; G-39/1930.

6. 'Pt. Jawaharlal's Sympathy: No Terrorism can Damp Youngmen's Ardour', *The Searchlight*, 11 January 1929, p. 7.

7. DIB Report, 5 August 1926 and 5 April 1928. IOR, L/PJ/12/292, pp. 2–14.

8. J. Coatman, *India in 1928–29: A Statement Prepared for Presentation to Parliament*, New Delhi: Anmol Pubs, 1985 [1929], p. 48.

9. 'Resignation of Pt. Nehru and Bose', *Forty-Second Session of the INC*, Madras, 1927; A. M. Zaidi and Shaheda Zaidi (eds), *The Encyclopaedia of the Indian National Congress* (henceforth *EINC*), Vol. 9, New Delhi: Chand & Co., 1980, p. 519.

10. R. Ray, 'Brief Note on the Alliance of Congress with Terrorism in Bengal', IOR, L/PJ/12/391, pp. 89–90. The same report claims that Bengali revolutionaries also had a role in the formation of the Independence League in 1928, intending 'to capture the Bengal Provincial Congress Committee'. p. 90.

11. *EINC*, Vol. 9, pp. 306–8.

12. Gandhi to Jawaharlal, 4 January 1928. *CWMG*, Vol. XXXV, p. 433.

13. Tan, *Garrison State*, pp. 171–2.

14. DIB Report, 26 April 1928. IOR, L/PJ/12/292.

15. N.K. Bhartya, 'A Friend of Revolutionaries', L. R. Nair (ed.), *Motilal Nehru: Birth Centenary Souvenir*, New Delhi: Motilal Nehru Centenary Committee, 1961, p. 133.

16. Sanyal, *Sardar Bhagat Singh*, revised edition, Nagpur: Vishva Bharati Prakashan, 1983, p. 66.

17. Sahni, *Truth About the Indian Press*, p. 78.

18. Sahni, *Truth About the Indian Press*, p. 78. Sahni indicates that this exchange took place prior to Vohra being widowed (on 28 May 1930).

19. 'Warrior', NMML, OHT, p. 37; this is corroborated by several other revolutionaries, including Surendranath Pandey. See his testimony in Sharma (ed.), *In Retrospect*, p. 134.

20. Confession Statement of Santosh Kumar Mukherjee, 19 October 1929, in Wariach and Jain (eds), *The Hanging of Bhagat Singh, Vol. III*, p. 296.

21. See *SWMN*, Vol. 7, p. 469.

22. Kapoor, NMML, OHT, pp. 125–6.

23. J. N. Sahni, 'Two Incidents', in Nair (ed.), *Motilal Nehru*, p. 141. Motilal's response was also noted by Sanyal, *Sardar Bhagat Singh*, 1931, p. 48; and Kapoor, NMML, OHT, p. 127.

24. Rai, NMML, OHT, p. 23.

25. Statement in *Young India*, 18 April 1929, in *CWMG*, Vol. XL, p. 26.

26. 'Pandit Motilal's Statement', *Times of India*, 10 April 1929, p. 9.

27. Reginald Craddock, *The Dilemma in India*, London: Constable & Co., 1929, p. 323. The impact of the controversy was muted somewhat in the Indian-owned press, coming as it did amid Baisakhi celebrations, when many newspapers were closed.

28. 'Viceroy's Statement to the Central Legislature', *Hindustan Times*, 14 April 1929, p. 1.

29. 'Assembly Outrage', *Hindustan Times*, 18 April 1929, p. 3.

30. DIB Report, 25 April 1929. IOR, L/PJ/12/292, p. 31.

31. Lajjawati, NMML, OHT, p. 93. This is a reference to the Congress response to the Saunders assassination. An oral history interview with her sister, Kumari Shiva Dua, offers a sketch of Lajjawati's biography. Sharma (ed.), *In Retrospect*, pp. 52–4.

32. Lajjawati, NMML, OHT, p. 94. Sukhdev seems to allude to this in a letter he wrote in October 1930 which was intercepted by prison guards, in which he wrote that 'we desired that they [Congress leaders] should write in round about way that it was a political murder and was the result of Government's policy and that it was responsible for such an action'. NAI, HP, 135/1931, p. 35.

33. Chand, CSAS, OHC, pp. 43–4. It may even be the case that Motilal was given an inkling of the attack from Chaman Lal, which would explain his calm response to it, when other nationalists reacted in panic. See Rai, NMML, OHT, pp. 23–4.

34. Note by the government of the United Provinces, 1933. IOR, L/PJ/12/397, pp. 85–6.

35. 'Hysteria in London', *Hindustan Times*, 17 April 1929, p. 10.

36. 'The Growth in the Spirit of Violence', DIB Report, 11 December 1930. IOR, L/PJ/12/390.

37. 'Gandhi or Balraj', *Tribune*, 18 April 1929, p. 8. Similarly, G. D. Birla would write to Samuel Hoare in 1932, urging him to think of Gandhi as a friend; 'if his just demands were accepted, it would be better in the long run than the alternative of rejecting them, which would simply strengthen the socialists'. Cited in Benjamin Zachariah, *Developing India: An Intellectual and Social History*, New Delhi: Oxford University Press, 2005, p. 215.

38. NAI, HP 192/29 & KW, see also 'Bhagat Singh and Dutt Still Silent', *Pioneer*, 10 May 1929. Asaf Ali was perhaps influenced by Bhagat Singh's father Kishan Singh, who came to Delhi to try to exonerate his son.

39. Kapoor, NMML, OHT, pp. 103–5.

40. Bhikshu Chaman Lal, CSAS, OHC, p 10.

41. Bhikshu Chaman Lal, CSAS, OHC, p. 18. V. N. Datta has recently claimed that it was Jawaharlal Nehru who wrote the statement. *Gandhi and Bhagat Singh*, New Delhi: Rupa, 2008, p. 74. Datta does not explain why he thinks this is the case, but it might be informed by edits on the original statement, held in the NAI. The statement clearly shows deletions throughout the document which are accompanied by initials, which seem to read 'JN'. While these initials do admittedly resemble Jawaharlal's characteristic signature, a note at the end of the statement makes it clear that they are the penmanship of the Sessions Judge, J. Middleton (JM), who marked up sections of the statement to be expunged on 9 June 1929. NAI, Private Papers, Acc. No. 246; Acc. No. 306, Vol. 1.

42. Sahni, *Truth about the Indian Press*, pp. 78–9.

43. Sahni, *Truth about the Indian Press*, p. 79. As a result, they were charged under section 3 of the Explosive Substances Act, 1908. The argument that the revolutionaries were not actuated by malice complicated the prosecution's case. NAI, Assembly Bomb Case Papers, Acc. 306, Vol. 6, p. 6.

44. Jawaharlal to Gandhi, 13 July 1929. *SWJN*, Vol. 4, p. 157.

45. Ujjwal Kumar Singh, *Political Prisoners in India*, Delhi: Oxford University Press, 1998, Chapter 4.

46. 'There can be little doubt', writes Gyan Pandey, 'that the nationalist fervour generated [by Jatindranath Das' death] did much to strengthen the hands of the younger Nehru and the Congress "Left" … and helped them carry the party into a more militant stance'. Pandey, *Ascendancy of the Congress*, p. 78. See also Sharma, *Radical Politics in Colonial Punjab*, p. 36.

47. 'The case was prosecuted at a time when the Indian National Congress was preparing for another nationwide anti-British campaign, the civil disobedience movement, and many Congressmen (some with reluctance, some with alacrity) were drawn to support the hunger strikers'. Taylor C. Sherman, 'State Practice, Nationalist Politics and the Hunger Strikes of the Lahore Conspiracy Case Prisoners', *Cultural and Social History*, 5(4), 2008, p. 498.

48. 'With regard to the strategic use of non-violence and the relationship between means and ends, Bhagat Singh was ideologically closer to the Mahatma than the latter cared to acknowledge'. Nair, 'Bhagat Singh as "Satyagrahi"', p. 676.

49. The hunger strikers were convicted in a range of conspiracy cases, and included Ghadarites, Kakori convicts, and the Lahore Conspiracy Case accused, who were still under trial. See *Tribune*, 12 September 1929, for a list of hunger strikers.

50. 'Bhagat Singh and Dutt send letter to Home Member', *Tribune*, 13 July 1929.

51. Sarkar, *Modern India*, p. 282.

52. While these failed in the short term, Bridge and Brasted contend that these were substantial advances that the Conservative Party would never have countenanced. Carl Bridge and Howard Brasted, 'The British Labour Party "Nabobs" and Indian Reform, 1924–31', *Journal of Imperial and Commonwealth History*, 17(3), 1989, p. 397.

53. Andrew Roberts, *'The Holy Fox': The Life of Lord Halifax*, London: Weidenfeld and Nicolson, 2001, p. 29.

54. Low, *Britain and Indian Nationalism*, pp. 60–6; Andrew Muldoon, *Empire, Politics and the Creation of the 1935 India Act*, Farnham: Ashgate, 2009, p. 55.

55. Low, *Britain and Indian Nationalism*, pp. 68–9.

56. 'Note regarding the celebration of "Bhagat Singh Day" at Amritsar'. NAI, HP, 130/1930, p. 11.

57. 'Note regarding the celebration of "Bhagat Singh Day" at Amritsar', NAI, HP, 130/1930, p. 13.

58. DIB Report, 26 September 1929. IOR, L/PJ/12/389, p. 21; Emerson, 'A Note on the Political situation in Punjab', 7 July 1929. NAI, HP, 130/1930, p. 16.

59. DIB Report, 15 August 1929. IOR, L/PJ/12/375, p. 34.

60. Emerson, 'A Note on the Political situation in Punjab', 7 July 1929. NAI, HP 130/1930, p. 18.

61. Memo from Emerson, 6 August 1929, in NAI, HP, 242/1929.

62. Memo from Emerson, 6 August 1929, in NAI, HP, 242/1929.

63. Report on the political situation in Punjab for the fortnight ending the 15 June 1929. IOR, L/PJ/12/694.

64. *Legislative Assembly Debates*, Vol IV, no. 9, 14 September 1929. NAI, HP, File 137/1930.

65. Jawaharlal to Gandhi, 13 July 1929, in *SWJN*, Vol. 4, p. 157.

66. *Congress Bulletin*, no. 12, 1 August 1929. AICC Papers, G-97/1929, pp. 13–5.

67. AICC Papers, G-11/1930, p. 6; *Leader*, 29 July 1929, quoted in Chandra, *Naujawan Bharat Sabha*, p. 88.

68. Report on the Political Situation in the United Provinces for the second half of July 1929. IOR, L/PJ/12/695.

69. Chandra, *Naujawan Bharat Sabha*, p. 88; Gupta, 'Defying Death', p. 17.

70. Ghosh, 'Terrorism in Bengal', p. 281.

71. AICC Papers, G-11/1930, p. 6. The *Fortnightly report for the United Provinces for the first half of August 1929* quoted the resolution at length, indignantly but incorrectly claiming that Motilal had supported the resolution.

72. 'AICC & Hunger-Strike', *Tribune*, 16 August 1929, p. 1; Nair, 'Bhagat Singh as "Satyagrahi"', p. 661.

73. Editorial, *Pratap*, 7 August 1929, in 'Note on the Press in United Provinces of Agra and Oudh', for the week ending 10 August 1929, no 32 of 1929.

74. DIB Report, 25 July 1929. IOR, L/PJ/12/375, p. 29.

75. 'On Naujawan Bharat Sabha meeting', 6 August 1929. SWMN, Vol. 7, pp. 340–1.

76. 'On a Visit to Prisoners on Hunger Strike' and 'On Hunger Strikes', 9 August 1929. *SWJN*, Vol. 4, pp. 13–5.

77. DIB Report, 15 August 1929. IOR, L/PJ/12/375, p. 30.

78. DIB Report, 5 September 1929. IOR, L/PJ/12/375, pp. 33–4.

79. DIB Report, 15 August 1929. IOR, L/PJ/12/375, p. 30.

80. Note from de Montmorency, 7 August 1929. NAI, HP, 242/1929.

81. Note from de Montmorency, 7 August 1929. NAI, HP, 242/1929.

82. M. Gupta, CSAS, OHC, p. 15. However, as Gupta recalled, the 'government cheated Ganesh Shankar Vidyarthi', failing to follow through with the promised concessions.

83. 'Bhagat Singh and Dutt Segregated', *Tribune*, 13 September 1929, p. 9; 'Hunger Strikes in the Lahore Conspiracy Case'. NAI, HP 36/III/1930.

84. Motilal to Emerson, 17 October 1929, in *SWMN*, Vol. 7, p. 129; Report on the political situation in Punjab for the fortnight ending 15 October 1929, BL, IOR, L/PJ/12/694.

85. Report on the political situation in Bengal for the fortnight ending 15 September 1929. IOR, L/PJ/12/686.

86. DIB Report, 26 September 1929. IOR, L/PJ/12/389.

87. DIB Report, 25 September 1929, quoted in Fortnightly Report for Bengal, second half of September 1929. IOR, L/PJ/12/404, p. 40.

88. Telegram from Viceroy to Secretary of State for India, 30 August 1929. IOR, L/PJ/12/389, pp. 13–15.

89. Motilal to the president of the Legislative Assembly, 13 September 1929. NAI, HP, File 137/1930. See also 'Conference at Pt. Motilal's House', *Tribune*, 15 September 1929, p. 1. Figure 47.

90. Extract from *Legislative Assembly Debates*, Vol. IV, no 9. 14 September 1929. NAI, HP, File 137/1930.

91. Extract from *Legislative Assembly Debates*, Vol. IV, no 9. 14 September 1929. NAI, HP, File 137/1930.

92. 'Note of conversation with James Crerar', 18 September 1929, in *SWMN*, Vol. 7, pp. 297–300.

93. Fortnightly report for the United Provinces for the second half of September 1929.

94. 'My Silence', 17 October 1929. *CWMG*, XLII, pp. 6–7.

95. See Kevin Grant, 'The Transcolonial World of Hunger Strikes and Political Fasts, c. 1909–1935', in Ghosh and Kennedy (eds), *Decentring Empire*. See also Sherman, 'State Practice', p. 501.

96. Fortnightly report for the United Provinces for the second half of September 1929.

97. Letter from Inspector General of Prisons, Punjab, 18 February 1930. NAI, HP, 125/1929. For further details of these 'cat and mouse' tactics deployed in dealing with hunger strikers, see Singh, *Political Prisoners in India*, pp. 122–157.

98. Telegram R, to Private Secretary to the Viceroy, 24 November 1929. NAI, HP, 98/1930.

99. 'Message to Punjab Students Conference', in Verma (ed.), *Bhagat Singh: on the Path of Liberation*, p. 88.

100. Petrie, 24 December 1929. NAI, HP, File 172/1930.

101. Jawaharlal to Satyapal, 14 December 1929. NMML, AICC Papers, G-100/1929–30, p. 72.

102. Motilal to Jawaharlal, 20 December 1929. SWMN, Vol. 7, p. 340.

103. Sanyal, *Sardar Bhagat Singh*, 1931, p. 82.

104. Sanyal, *Sardar Bhagat Singh*, 1983, pp. 65–6.

105. Kapoor, NMML, OHT, p. 218.

106. 'Appeal for Lahore Conspiracy Case Defence Fund, December 20, 1929', *Leader*, 22 December 1929. *SWMN*, Vol. 7, pp. 342–3.

107. Fyfe to Inchacape, 4 September 1929. IOR, L/PO/6/65 (ii), p. 210.

108. Motilal to Gandhi, 13 July 1929, in *SWMN*, Vol. 7, p. 86.

109. Habib, 'Civil Disobedience, 1930–31', p. 52.

110. Benjamin Zachariah, *Nehru*, London/New York: Routledge, 2004, p. 65.

111. Chandra, *Naujawan Bharat Sabha*, p. 118.

112. Chandra, *Naujawan Bharat Sabha*, pp. 118–9.

113. D. A. Low, 'Sir Tej Bahadur Sapru and the First Round Table Conference', D. A. Low (ed.), *Soundings in Modern South Asian History*, Berkeley: University of California Press, 1968, p. 304.

114. 'All-Parties Leaders' Joint Statement', 2 November 1929. *CWMG*, Vol. XLII, pp. 80–1; also as 'The Delhi Manifesto', 1 November 1929. *SWJN*, Vol. 4, p. 165.

115. Gandhi to Jawaharlal, 4 November 1929, *CWMG*, Vol. XLII, p. 96.

116. Jawaharlal to Gandhi, 4 November 1929. *SWJN*, Vol. 4, p. 167.

117. Telegram from Gandhi to Jawaharlal, 6 November 1929; Letter from Gandhi to Jawaharlal, 8 November 1929. *CWMG*, Vol. XLII, p. 116.

118. DIB Report, 19 December 1929. IOR, L/PJ/12/60, p. 48.

119. 'Is it true?', 7 November 1929. *CWMG*, Vol. XLII, p. 112.

120. I refer here to Dipesh Chakrabarty's now-famous observation that under colonialism

'some people were less modern than others, and that the former needed a period of preparation and waiting before they could be recognised as full participants in political modernity.' *Provincialising Europe: Postcolonial Thought and Historical Difference*, Princeton: Princeton University Press, 2000, p. 9.

121. Sapru, to Graham Pole and Polak, 9 January 1930, Sapru Papers, quoted in Low, 'Sir Tej Bahadur Sapru', p. 306.

122. Sapru to Ali Imam, 5 January 1930, Sapru Papers. Quoted in Low, *Britain and Indian Nationalism*, p. 67.

123. Gandhi to Motilal, 4 December 1929. *CWMG*, Vol. XLII, p. 244.

124. Gandhi to Motilal, 4 December 1929. 'A Letter', unaddressed and undated but before 23 December 1929; *CWMG*, at http://www.gandhiserve.org/cwmg/VOL048.PDF, p. 128 (last accessed 6 December 2013).

125. Brown, *Gandhi and Civil Disobedience*, p. 73; Gandhi's dominance is clear in the notes of the meeting reproduced in Nanda, *The Nehrus*, pp. 322–3.

126. Irwin to Viscount Halifax, 24 December 1929. BL, Halifax Papers, Mss Eur C152/26.

127. Low, *Britain and Indian Nationalism*, p. 69.

128. 'Speech at All-India Suppressed Classes Conference', Lahore, 24 December 1929. *CWMG*, Vol. XLII, p. 313.

129. 'Eve of the Congress', *Times of India*, 25 December 1930, p. 13.

130. Report for week ending 11 January 1930. NAI, HP, 4/13/30, p. 29.

131. Friend (ed.), *Yashpal Looks Back*, p. 101.

132. Jain, CSAS, OHC, p. 6.

133. 'Warrior', NMML, OHT, p. 45; Chandra, *Naujawan Bharat Sabha*, p. 118.

134. Editorial, *Pratap*, 1 December 1929, quoted in Bhargava, *Ganesh Shankar Vidyarthi*, p. 46.

135. Jain, CSAS, OHC, p. 6; 'Warrior', NMML, OHT, p. 45.

136. Friend (ed.), *Yashpal Looks Back*, p. 100.

137. 'Warrior', NMML, OHT, p. 45. During the prosecution of the case an approver, Inderpal, suggested that Yashpal and Bhagwati Charan had proceeded with the action in order to prove themselves to the party, following doubts about their fidelity. 'Punjab Conspiracy Case Story', *Times of India*, 31 January 1931, p. 9. See also Harcourt, 'Revolutionary Networks', p. 343–4.

138. Friend (ed.), *Yashpal Looks Back*, p. 116.

139. Irwin to Viscount Halifax, 24 December 1930. Mss Eur C152/28.

140. Irwin to Viscount Halifax, 24 December 1930. Mss Eur C152/28.

141. Darling to Josie, 4 January 1931. CSAS, Darling Papers, 1:15, Envelope 1.

142. I have elaborated on this in 'The Art of Panicking Quietly: British-Indian Responses to "Terrorist Outrages", 1928–1933', in Harald Fischer-Tiné and Christine Whyte (eds), *Empires on the Verge of a Nervous Breakdown: Crisis, Panic and Anxiety in the Age of Imperialism, 1860–1940*, London: Palgrave (forthcoming).

143. Darling to Josie, 4 January 1931. CSAS, Darling Papers, 1:15, Envelope 1.

144. Brown, *Gandhi and Civil Disobedience*, p. 76.

145. First Day, Proceedings of the Forty-Fourth Session, in *EINC*, Vol. 9, p. 565.

146. Gandhi, Second Day, Proceedings of the Forty-Fourth Session, 31 December 1929. *EINC*, Vol. 9, p. 566.

147. Proceedings of the Forty-Fourth Session, Second Day, 31 December 1929. *EINC*, Vol. 9, pp. 566–8.

148. Kinnaid, 'Extract from a message from Correspondent at Congress Camp', Lahore, Christmas 1929, IOR/L/PJ/6/56, p. 89.

149. 117 voted for the resolution and 69 opposed it. AICC papers, 34/1929, Temporary File II, Lahore Congress, p. 12.

150. Brown, *Gandhi and Civil Disobedience*, p. 78.

151. Proceedings of the Forty-Fourth Session, 31 December 1929. *EINC*, Vol. 9, p. 568.

152. 'Question of the prosecution of Dr Kitchlew, Pt Jawaharlal Nehru, Mr Subhas Chandra Bose, and Baba Gurdit Singh'. NAI, HP, 65/1930, p. 23.

153. 'Brief note on the Alliance of Congress with Terrorism', 1932. IOR, L/PJ/12/391, p. 9.

154. 'The Philosophy of the Bomb', South Asia Microform Project, Reel 3, no. 28, p. 2.

155. Jain, CSAS, OHC, p. 6; DIB Report, 30 January 1930. IOR, L/PJ/12/389, p. 30.

156. Forbes (ed.), *An Indian Freedom Fighter Recalls Her Life*, p. 51. They were detained for two months and released when investigations failed to link them to the bombing.

157. Telegram P., from Lahore, 29 December 1929. NAI, HP, 98/1930.

158. Speech on 31 December 1929, in Zaidi (ed.), *Congress Presidential Addresses*, Vol. 9, p. 567; *CWMG*, Vol. XLII, p. 348.

159. Narain, NMML, OHT, p. 29.

160. Brown, *Gandhi and Civil Disobedience*, p. 80. Brown describes the dismay of the liberals and moderates for civil disobedience, pp. 82–9.

161. Letter from Emily Kinnaird, 8 January 1930, in IOR, L/PO/6/56 (i), pp. 101–2.

162. 'Presidential Address to the Lahore Congress', 29 December 1929. *SWJN*, vol. 4, p. 195.

163. Political situation in India and the Policy to be pursued in relation to the Situation created by the All-India National Congress Meeting at Lahore. IOR, L/PO/6/56 (i).

164. 'Message from Correspondent at Congress Camp, Lahore', 25 December 1929. IOR, PO/6/65 (i), p. 90.

165. Report on the political situation in Punjab for the fortnight ending 28 February 1931. NAI, HP, 18/1/31.

166. Bose, *Indian Struggle*, p. 173.

167. An 'appreciation' by Mr Ewart, Deputy Inspector-General of Police, CID. Report on the political situation in Punjab for the fortnight ending 31 December 1929. NAI, HP, 17/1929, December.

168. See 'The Hindustan Socialist Republican Association Manifesto', in Hale, *Political Trouble in India,* pp. 216–7. Yashpal, NMML, OHT, p. 14.

169. 'The Hindustan Socialist Republican Association Manifesto', in Hale, *Political Trouble*, p. 217.

170. Tabular Statement of Political Crimes and other Manifestations of the Revolutionary movement, from September 1929'. IOR, L/PJ/12/396, p. 13.

171. *Young India*, 2 January 1930. *CWMG*, Vol. XLII, pp. 361–4.

172. *Young India*, 2 January 1930. *CWMG*, Vol. XLII, p. 361.

173. Chaman Lal Azad, *Revolutionary Movement in India*, Delhi: All India Revolutionaries Conference, 1947, p. 36.

174. Editorial notes to 'Philosophy of the Bomb', in Verma (ed.), *Bhagat Singh*, p. 206.

175. 'Warrior', NMML, OHT, p. 36; Kapoor, NMML, OHT, pp. 230–1; S. Singh, NMML, OHT, p. 135.

176. DIB Report, 30 January 1930. IOR, L/PJ/12/389, p. 30.

177. Also noted were the HSRA plans to translate the document into regional languages, including Gujarati. DIB Report, 9 October 1930. IOR, L/PJ/12/389, p. 73.

178. 'The Philosophy of the Bomb' in Indian Proscribed Tracts, South Asia Mircoform Project, Reel 3, item 28 (unpaginated).

179. 'The Philosophy of the Bomb' in Indian Proscribed Tracts, South Asia Mircoform Project, Reel 3, item 28.

180. Potdar, CSAS, OHC, p. 7.

181. DIB Report, 22 May 1930. IOR, L/PJ/12/389, p. 48.

182. Officiating Chief Secretary to government of Bihar and Orissa, 30 July 1933. IOR, L/PJ/12/397, p. 17.

183. Khanna, NMML, OHT, p. 29.

184. Laushey notes that in Bengal, both Jugantar and Anushilan supported non-cooperation, the former actively, and the latter only by abstaining from violence. Laushey, *Bengal Terrorism and the Marxist Left*, p. 21.

185. DIB Report, 9 March 1933. IOR, L/PJ/12/425, p. 16.

186. 'Good if True', *Young India*, 3 March 1930. *CWMG*, Vol. XLVIII, p. 465. On the correspondence between Gandhi and revolutionaries including the HSRA, see Shankar, *Gandhi's Encounter with the Indian Revolutionaries*, Chapter 5.

187. DIB Report, 22 May 1930. IOR, L/PJ/12/389, p. 47.

188. Comrade Ram Chandra, oral history interview, in Sharma (ed.), *In Retrospect*, p. 45; Bhikshu Chaman Lal, CSAS, OHC, p. 21; 'Warrior', NMML, OHT, p. 22. From another interview, it appears that 'Warrior' had suggested to Azad that he join the Congress specifically to militarise it. 'Warrior', *In Retrospect*, p. 170.

189. Mukherjee, *Peasants in India's Non-Violent Revolution*, p. 80.

190. DIB Report, 17 May 1928. IOR, L/PJ/12/375, p. 12.

191. 'Naujawan Bharat Sabha: nine members arrested', *Times of India*, 18 April 1930, p. 15.

192. Singh, *Under the Shadow of the Gallows*, p. 64.

193. Tabular Statement of Political Crimes. IOR, L/PJ/12/396, pp. 16–17.

194. There was an attempt on the life of Jai Gopal in Jalegaon, where he had gone to give evidence on 21 February 1930. 'Alleged Rioting at Jalgaon', *Times of India*, 1 April 1930, p. 3.

195. Vohra, NMML, OHT, p. 21; 'List of Crimes'. IOR, L/PJ/12/396, p. 13.

196. Nigam, NMML, OHT, p. 5; Jain, CSAS, OHC, p. 9.

197. Nigam, NMML, OHT, p. 6.

198. Telegram from Viceroy to Secretary of State for India, 30 June 1930. IOR, L/PJ/12/375, p. 49.

199. Telegram from Viceroy, 25 June 1930. IOR, L/PO/6/65 (ii).

200. Khanna, NMML, OHT, p. 29.

201. NAI, HP, 498/1930, p. 17.

202. Report on the political situation in Punjab for the fortnight ending the 28th of February 1931. NAI, HP, 18/1/31.

203. *Tribune*, 14 October 1930, p, 9.

204. Jawaharlal Nehru, 'Eight Days Interlude'.

205. Bejoy Kumar Sinha, 'Sardar Bhagat Singh: His Last Moments', *Andhra Reporter*, 26 March 1966. NMML, Private Papers, Ajoy Kumar Sinha Collection. Acc. No. 1125.

206. Lajjawati, NMML, OHT, p. 118.

207. Lajjawati, NMML, OHT, p. 119.

208. Motilal to Purshottamdas Thakurdas, 29 May 1930. *SWMN*, Vol. 7, pp. 230–1.

209. Kapoor, NMML, OHT, pp. 326–7. See also Sanyal, *Sardar Bhagat Singh*, 1983, p. 92.

210. Sanyal, *Sardar Bhagat Singh*, 1983, p. 94.

211. Lajjawati, NMML, OHT, p. 120.

212. Lajjawati, NMML, OHT, p. 120.

213. Irwin to Benn, 9 February 1931. BL, Halifax Papers, Mss Eur C152/7.

214. Nehru, 'Karachi Congress', *Toward Freedom*, p. 261–2.

215. The American edition in question was edited by Sarvepalli Gopal and published by Beacon Press in 1958. One can only surmise that Gopal or perhaps even Nehru himself preferred to withhold this vignette revealing the Prime Minister's meeting with a wanted man from an American audience. This is consistent with Gopal's three-volume biography of Nehru (although curious, because Sarvepalli was the son of Dr Radhakrishnan, who was very favourably disposed to the revolutionaries), as well as with the Prime Minister's statements after independence, discussed in my Conclusion.

216. Friend (ed.), *Yashpal Looks Back*, p. 185.

217. Interview with Surendranath Pandey, in Sharma (ed.), *In Retrospect,* p. 134.

218. 'Notorious "Panditji" killed in Allahabad', *Civil and Military Gazette*, 1 March 1931, p. 1.

219. Friend (ed.), *Yashpal Looks Back*, p. 185.

220. 'Notes on Terrorism', 1932. IOR, L/PJ/12/404, p. 110.

221. 'Notes on Terrorism', 1932. IOR, L/PJ/12/404, p. 111.

222. Letter to Emerson, 19 March 1931. NAI, F/18/3/1931.

223. Letter to Emerson, 19 March 1931. NAI, F/18/3/1931.

224. This particular photograph also features in Roop Kishore Kapoor's *Azad Mandir*, beneath the focal image of Azad twirling his moustache (Fig. 34).

225. Superintendent of Police, Report on meeting in Delhi, 14 March 1931. NAI, HP, 159/1931.

226. A similar example can be found in *Hind Swaraj*, where Gandhi described Madanlal Dhingra, Curzon Wylie's assassin, as 'a patriot, but his love was blind'. Parel (ed.), *Hind Swaraj*, p. 78.

227. Bose, *Indian Struggle*, p. 168.

228. Ravinder Kumar, 'Motilal Nehru: Portrait of a Nationalist', in *The Making of a Nation: Essays on Indian History and Politics*, Delhi: Manohar, 1989, p. 131.

229. *Pioneer*, Allahabad (undated but mid-February 1931), quoted in U. C. Bhattacharya and Shovendu Sunder Chakravarty (eds), *Pandit Motilal Nehru: His Life and Work*, Calcutta: Modern Book Agency, 1931, p. 107.
230. Pandey, in Sharma (ed,), *In Retrospect*, p. 133.

7. THE KARACHI CONGRESS, 1931

1. Irwin to Secretary of State, 15 March 1931. BL, Halifax Papers, Mss. Eur. C152/16, p. 274.
2. Report on the political situation in the Punjab for the fortnight ending 15 March 1931. NAI, F/18/3/1931.
3. A small sample of this includes: Ashok S. Chousalkar, *Mahatma Gandhi and Sardar Bhagat Singh*, Mumbai: Mani Bhavan Gandhi Sangrahalaya, 2008; Amit Kumar Gupta, 'The Executions of March 1931, Gandhi and Irwin', *Bengal Past and Present*, January–June 1971, XC, part 1, no. 169; Meena Dutta and Jai Narain, 'Did Gandhi Fail to Save Bhagat Singh?', Punjab History Conference, Patiala: Panjab University, 30th Session, 10–12 March 1998; Chander Pal Singh, 'What Mahatma Gandhi did to save Bhagat Singh', *Gandhi Marg*, October–December 2010, 32(3); Preetha Nilesh, 'Gandhiji and the Trial and Execution of Bhagat Singh', *Indica*, 47(2), 2010, pp. 154–168.
4. See Noorani, *The Trial of Bhagat Singh*, and Datta, *Gandhi and Bhagat Singh*, 2008.
5. Bridge and Brasted, 'The British Labour Party "Nabobs" and Indian reform, 1924–31'; Sumit Sarkar, 'The Logic of Gandhian Nationalism: Civil Disobedience and the Gandhi-Irwin Pact', *Indian Historical Review*, 3, 1976, pp. 114–46; Muldoon, *Empire, Politics and the Creation of the 1935 India Act*.
6. Indeed, a poster commemorating the Pact by Prabhu Dayal, also published in Kanpur shows Bharat Mata in tears at the terms of the agreement, in *The Fate of India Sealed Up*, see Ramaswamy, *Goddess and the Nation*, p. 180.
7. 'Notes and Comments', *The Masses*, 15 April 1931, p. 2. R. E. Hawkins Papers, CSAS. *The Masses* was edited by Tayab Shaikh, a member of the (M. N.) Roy Group. Manjapra, *M. N. Roy*, p. 100.
8. Bulletin Seven, 12 February 1931, p. 14. R. E. Hawkins Papers, CSAS.
9. Lajjawati, NMML, OHT, p. 120; Bose, *Indian Struggle*, pp. 204–5.
10. 'Gandhi & Bhagat Singh's Conviction', *Hindustan Times*, 21 February 1931, p. 2; 'Mahatma Gandhi and Bhagat Singh: Dr Satya Pal Contradicted', *Tribune*, 22 February 1931, p. 4. Sachar, NMML, OHT, p. 103.
11. Chand, CSAS, OHC, pp. 66–7; Lal, NMML, NMML, OHT, p. 18; Narain, OHT, p. 43.
12. See letter from Bhagat Singh and B. K. Dutt to the Home Member, government of India, 28 January 1930. NAI, HP 137/1930; Horace Alexander, *Political Prisoners In India. A statement issued by direction of the Society of Friends*, January 1937, in IOR, L/PJ/12/314.
13. There are too many examples to list, but see 'Report on the political situation in the Punjab for the fortnight ending October 15, 1929'. IOR, L/PJ/12/694; Telegram from

Viceroy to Secretary of State, 15 March 1931, BL, Halifax Papers, Eur Mss C152/16, p. 277.

14. 'India and Party Politics', *Times* (London), 5 March 1931, p. 15.

15. 'Viceroy and Congress', *Times* (London), 19 January 1931, p. 12.

16. Irwin to the King-Emperor, 13 March 1931. BL, Halifax Papers, Eur Mss C152/2.

17. Lal, NMML, OHT, p. 18.

18. 'The Shade of Bhagat Singh at Karachi', *The People*, 22 March 1931, p. 191; *The Tribune*, 25 March 1931, p. 11. Two months later, the editor of the *People* claimed that 'Lord Irwin has taken on the responsibility of the executions on himself but it is universally believed that his hands were forced by the Punjab police and civilian officials.' *The People*, 3 May 1931, p. 280.

19. *The Searchlight's* correspondent in Karachi reported after the executions that 'Tactics of the civilians has succeeded' and 'Lord Irwin has yielded to the machinations of the civilians' were heard in the Congress camp following the commotion following the news of the executions. 'Karachi Astir', *The Searchlight*, 29 March 1931, p. 7.

20. Of Punjab civilians serving in the early 1930s, I have searched the papers of Penderel Moon, Malcolm Darling, John Perronet Thompson, and Frank Brayne; and of police, the papers of Jack Morton and Gordon Halland; all at some stage register the revolutionary movement in greater or lesser detail, but none a threat of the resignation of the Punjab Governor or Civil Service.

21. Telegram from Benn to Irwin, 17 April 1931. House of Lords Record Office, Stansgate Papers, ST/223/12.

22. Moon to Father, Easter Sunday 1931. Sir Penderel Moon Papers, BL, Eur Mss F230/3.

23. Cited in Anil Nauriya, 'Execution of Bhagat Singh', *Mainstream*, 6 April 1996, p. 32; see also Chander Pal Singh, *Bhagat Singh Revisited: Historiography, Biography and Ideology of the Great Martyr*, Delhi: Originals, 2011, p. 102, which traces the story to *Bhavishya*, 9 April 1931.

24. Carl Bridge, *Holding India to the Empire*, Delhi: Sterling, 1986, p. 64.

25. Lane-Fox to Baldwin, 13 March 1929, quoted in Muldoon, *Empire, Politics, and the Creation of the 1935 India Act*, p. 57.

26. *India Office List for 1931*, London: Harrison & Sons, 1932, p. 590.

27. Earl Halifax, *Fullness of Days*, New York: Dodd, Mead & Co., 1957, p. 105.

28. Clive Dewey, *Anglo-Indian Attitudes: The Mind of the Indian Civil Service*, London: Hambledon Press, p. 150.

29. The attacks were precisely one year apart; Irwin's on 23 December 1929, and de Montmorency's the following year. This 'curious coincidence' convinced Irwin of his earlier suspicion that the attacks were planned to commemorate the attack on Lord Hardinge. Irwin to Halifax, 24 December 1930. BL, Halifax Papers, Eur Mss C152/26.

30. De Montmorency to Irwin, 24 December 1930. BL, Halifax Papers, Eur Mss C152/27.

31. De Montmorency to Irwin, 1 January 1931. BL, Halifax Papers, Eur C152/26.

32. De Montmorency to Irwin, 1 January 1931. BL, Halifax Papers, Eur Mss C152/26. See also Irwin's rather apologetic letter to de Montmorency about the terms of the pact. Irwin to de Montmorency, 5 March 1931. BL, Halifax Papers, Eur Mss 152/27.

33. De Montmorency to Irwin, 24 January 1931; 27 January 1931. BL, Halifax Papers, Eur Mss C152/27.

34. De Montmorency to Irwin, 14 January 1931. BL, Halifax Papers, Eur Mss C152/27.

35. King's Birthday Honours list, de Montmorency to Cunningham, 9 February 1931. BL, Halifax Papers, Eur Mss C152/27.

36. De Montmorency to Irwin, 16 February 1931. BL, Halifax Papers, Eur Mss C152/27. By comparison, the Governor of Bengal, Sir Stanley Jackson, agreed to the cuts, although he demurred that 'my own inclination is to resist abolition of bodyguard on the ground that we are in transitional period'. Telegram from Jackson to Irwin, 16 March 1931. BL, Halifax Papers, Eur Mss C152/27. Jackson was right to be apprehensive; on 6 February 1932, he was shot at by Bina Das, who missed when the agile former cricketer ducked. Ghosh, 'Revolutionary Women and Nationalist Heroes in Bengal', p. 355.

37. NAI, HP, 4/21/31.

38. Irwin to Benn, 30 March 1931. BL, Halifax Papers, Eur Mss C152/7.

39. Indeed, this is a narrative that Gandhi himself wished to communicate, according to Irwin, asking: 'Would Your Excellency see any objection to my saying that I pleaded for the young man's life?' This was not known until the publication of Irwin's autobiography in 1957. Halifax, *Fullness of Days*, p. 149.

40. Philip Lutgendorf, *Hanuman's Tale*, New York: Oxford University Press, 2007, p. 156.

41. The title is given in the NMML Image Library's register only in English; we have no way of retrieving the original border information in Urdu or Hindi, or English. It has been suggested to me that the *Lone* in the title—given the misapplication of 'rendering' for 'rending' in Figure 40—might be productively interpreted as a *Loan*, in which Dutt is inviting Gandhi to borrow revolutionary sacrifice in the greater struggle. Philip Engblom, personal communication, 16 May 2013.

42. Vohra also appears posthumously in Figures 2 and 30; both are made by Lahore-based publishers, with Figures 2 and 53 made by the same publisher, Krishna Picture House. *Abhyudaya* carried a portrait of Vohra in demi-profile in its *Bhagat Singh Ank* (8 May 1931, p. 20), but Figures 2, 30 and 53 are based on a full-frontal portrait.

43. C. A. Bayly, 'Ideologies of the End of the Raj', in Ghosh and Kennedy (eds), *Decentering Empire*, p. 356.

44. Benn to Irwin, Enclosure to letter of 23 January 1931. BL, Halifax Papers, Eur Mss 152/6.

45. IOR, L/PJ/12/400, p. 74.

46. Telegram from Irwin to Benn, 25 July 1930. BL, Eur Mss, C152/16, p. 105.

47. Chief Secretary to GOI, United Provinces, 31 August 1933. IOR, L/PJ/12/397, p. 46.

48. 'Our Opportunity', in IOR, L/PJ/12/391, p. 49.

49. 'Effect of unrest on India's trade', *Civil and Military Gazette*, 2 March 1931, p. 6.

50. See 'Recent Outrages', *Civil and Military Gazette*, 28 December 1930, p. 2; 'The Shadow of Non-violence', *Civil and Military Gazette*, 16 January 1931, p. 2; 'A dastardly outrage', *Civil and Military Gazette*, 19 January 1931, p. 3.

51. 'Curtis Murder Case', *Civil and Military Gazette*, 23 January 1931, p. 3.

52. *Report on the political situation in the Punjab for the fortnight ending the 15th of January, 1931*; DIB Report, 22 January 1931. IOR, L/PJ/12/390, p. 22.

53. 'Curtis Murder Case', *Civil and Military Gazette*, 23 January 1931, p. 3.

54. 'Outrageous murder, Sikh slays mistress, Children at Death's door, Result of Labor's Laxity', *Cairns Post*, 15 January 1931.

55. Nigel Collett, 'Evidence Concerning Indian Attitudes and British Intelligence During the 1919 Punjab Disturbances', *Journal of the Royal Asiatic Society*, 21(4), 2011, p. 472.

56. 'Outrageous murder, Sikh slays mistress, Children at Death's door', *Cairns Post*, 15 January 1931.

57. F.W.C. 'Long Road to Justice', Editor's Post Box, *Civil and Military Gazette*, 21 January 1931, p. 3.

58. Craik, quoted in *Civil and Military Gazette*, 19 January 1931, p. 4.

59. 'Anarchical Crimes', *Times of India*, 17 January 1931, p. 11.

60. De Montmorency to Irwin, 18 January 1931. BL, Halifax Papers, Eur Mss 152/26.

61. 'The Lahore Outrage: Powers Against Punjab Terrorists', *The Times* (London), 19 January 1931, p. 11.

62. 'Justice for all', *Civil and Military Gazette*, 18 January 1931, p. 3.

63. 'Terrorist Outrages', *Civil and Military Gazette*, 1 January 1931, p. 3. In December 1928, the *Civil and Military Gazette* had formed a Saunders-Channan Singh Memorial Fund 'to make provision for the dependents of Punjabi policemen who are killed on duty'. 'The Lahore Murders', *Times* (London), 27 December 1928, p. 11.

64. De Montmorency to Irwin, 18 January 1931. BL, Halifax Papers, Eur Mss C152/26.

65. The investigation later revealed that he had been arrested in 1930 for picketing, and while in jail in Attack had 'acquired a murder complex', vowing to kill Europeans on his release. Statement of Political Crimes, IOR, L/PJ/12/396, p. 30.

66. See, for example, the poem 'The Cant of Non-violence', *Civil and Military Gazette*, 1 January 1931, p. 2.

67. DIB Report, 22 January 1931. IOR, L/PJ/12/390, p. 22.

68. 'Sikhs and Murder of Mrs Curtis', *Times of India*, 24 April 1931, p. 3.

69. *Civil and Military Gazette*, 18 January 1931, p. 1

70. 'Meanest and most cowardly act', *Times of India*, 9 February 1931.

71. 'Death Sentence confirmed', *Times of India*, 21 March 1931, p. 18.

72. De Montmorency to Irwin, 16 January 1931. BL, Halifax Papers, Eur Mss C152/26.

73. 'Justice for All', *Civil and Military Gazette*, 18 January 1931, p. 3.

74. 'Seventeen Outrages in Ten Weeks', *Civil and Military Gazette*, 19 January 1931, p. 4.

75. 'Our Opportunity', L/PJ/12/391, pp. 48–9.

76. 'Statement to the Press', 5 March 1931, *CWMG*, Vol. XLV, p. 255.

77. Emphasis in the original. Translation of a Bengali leaflet entitled 'Where is Peace?', from a version which appeared at Chandpur in March 1931. NAI, HP, 4/36 Part 1 1931.

78. Letter to Emerson, 19 March 1931. NAI, F/18/3/1931. Report on the political situation in the Punjab for the fortnight ending the 15th of March 1931.

79. Letter to Emerson, 19 March 1931. NAI, F/18/3/1931. Report on the political situation in the Punjab for the fortnight ending 15 March 1931. 'Speech at Public Meeting, Delhi', 7 March 1931, *CWMG*, Vol. XLV, pp. 271–2.

80. Bhikshu Chaman Lal, NMML, OHT, p. 18.

81. Letter to Emerson, 19 March 1931, NAI, F/18/3/1931. Report on the political situation in the Punjab for the fortnight ending 15 March 1931. IOR, L/PJ/12/694.
82. 'Speech at Public Meeting, Delhi', 7 March 1931, *CWMG*, Vol. XLV, pp. 271.
83. Viceroy to Secretary of State, 15 March 1931. BL, Mss. Eur. C 152/16, pp. 277–8.
84. Viceroy to Secretary of State, 15 March 1931. BL, Mss. Eur. C 152/16, pp. 277–8.
85. Emerson to Boyd, undated. NAI, HP 4/21/31.
86. Telegram, 17 March 1931. NAI, HP 4/21/31.
87. 'Bhagat Singh and the Karachi Congress: Rumours Current', *Tribune*, 25 March 1931, p. 8.
88. 'Commute those sentences', *Tribune*, 25 March 1931, p. 8.
89. De Montmorency to Irwin, 26 March 1931. BL, Halifax Papers, Eur Mss C152/26.
90. Report on the political situation in the Punjab for the fortnight ending 15 March 1931. NAI, F/18/3/1931.
91. Telegram from Secretary, Naujawan Bharat Sabha in Jhang to Secretary of Congress in Karachi. AICC Papers, NMML, G-13/1931, p. 7.
92. Fortnightly report for the second half of March 1931. NAI, F/18/3/1931.
93. R. E. Hawkins, Bulletin 13, 25 March 1931. R. E. Hawkins Papers, CSAS.
94. Quoted in 'Support from Unexpected Quarter', *Tribune*, 28 March 1931, p. 8.
95. 'Sworn enemies of Lord Irwin and Gandhiji', *Tribune*, 30 March 1931, p. 3.
96. Paliwal, NMML, OHT, p. 61.
97. Bhikshu Chaman Lal, NMML, OHT, p. 16.
98. *Tribune*, 24 March 1931, p. 1.
99. See the photographs in *Hindustan Times*, 2 April 1931, p. 3; *Tribune*, 3 April 1931, p. 5. Ram Chandra noted in his memoirs that this protest was orchestrated by the Kirti Kisan group, with whom the NJBS had been working for some time, and that it was part of a larger agenda to disrupt the Congress. Chandra, *Naujawan Bharat Sabha*, p. 170.
100. 'Interview to the Press', *CWMG*, Vol. XLV, p. 344; Bhikshu Chaman Lal, NMML, OHT, p. 16.
101. Bhikshu Chaman Lal, NMML, OHT, p. 16.
102. Jeet Mal Lunia, *Karachi ki Congress*, 1932. South Asia Microform Project, Reel 9, item 14, p. 9.
103. J. Gupta, NMML, OHT, p. 64.
104. Bhikshu Chaman Lal, NMML, OHT, p. 18.
105. Bhikshu Chaman Lal, NMML, OHT, p. 18.
106. Bhikshu Chaman Lal, NMML, OHT, p. 19.
107. Telegram from Commissioner, Sind to Home Department, 26 March 1931. NAI, HP 136/1931, p. 1.
108. Telegram from Viceroy to Secretary of State, 27 March 1931. NAI, HP 136/1931, p. 2.
109. Collins to Emerson, 1 April 1931, Fortnightly report for the second half of March 1931. NAI, F/18/3/1931.
110. Fortnightly Report, Punjab, 15 April 1931. NAI, F/18/4/1931.

111. Telegram From Commissioner, Sind to Home Department, 28 March 1931. NAI, HP, 136/1931, p. 6.

112. Brown, *Gandhi and Civil Disobedience*, p. 200.

113. 'Discussion with Red Shirts of Naujawan Bharat Sabha', 27 March 1931, *CWMG*, XLV, pp. 354–5.

114. Telegram From Commissioner, Sind to Home Department, 28 March 1931. NAI, HP, 136/1931, p. 6.

115. Bose, *Indian Struggle*, p. 206.

116. Telegram from Viceroy to Secretary of State for India, 2 April 1931. NAI, HP, 136/1931.

117. Bose, 'Speech at All India Naujawan Bharat Sabha', in Sisir K. Bose and Sugata Bose (eds), *The Essential Writings of Netaji Subhas Chandra Bose*, Delhi: Oxford University Press, 1997, p. 113.

118. Bose, 'Speech at All India Naujawan Bharat Sabha', pp. 118–9.

119. Bose, *Indian Struggle*, p. 160. 'Subhash Bose's statement', *Tribune*, 30 March 1931, p. 6.

120. Telegram from Commissioner Sind to Home Department, 29 March 1931, NAI HP, 136/1931. See also H. Williamson's assessment, 'Note on the Session of the Congress held at Karachi in March and April, 1931', 7 April 1931. NAI, H. NAI, HP, 136/1931, pp. 24–5.

121. *The Bombay Chronicle*, undated, p. 6. NAI, HP, 4/36 Part 1 1931, unpaginated.

122. 'Subhash Wants Socialist Republic', *Tribune*, 29 March 1931, p. 9; Chandra, *Naujawan Bharat Sabha*, pp. 170–3.

123. 'Bhagat Singh Day', *Tribune*, 25 March 1931, p. 4.

124. *Tribune*, 31 March 1931, p. 2; Chandra, *Naujawan Bharat Sabha*, p. 172; Chandra, oral history interview, in Sharma (ed.), *In Retrospect*, 1999, p. 47.

125. Bose, *Indian Struggle*, p. 161. The difficulty in tracing the narrative of events at the Karachi Congress is that, because the Congressites were all together, there was little need to write letters to each other of the event. The below analysis therefore relies on British sources and reportage.

126. *EINC*, vol. 10, p. 71.

127. Bulletin Fifteen, 8 April 1931. Hawkins Papers, CSAS.

128. Pandey, *Ascendancy of the Congress*, p. 112.

129. 'Report of the Commission of Enquiry into the Communal Outbreak at Cawnpore', June 1931, Cmd. 3891, p. 4.

130. Telegram R from Viceroy to Secretary of State, 27 March 1931. NAI, HP 136/1931.

131. *Tribune*, 29 March 1931, p. 8.

132. 'Foreword to a Biography of Ganesh Shankar Vidyarthi', *SWJN*, Vol. 5, p. 553.

133. Paliwal, NMML, OHT, p. 28–9.

134. Priya Agarwal, 'Forgetting the Violence, Remembering a Report: The Paradox of the 1931 Kanpur Riots', University of Pennsylvania Humanities Forum 2007–2008, at ScholarlyCommons, http://repository.upenn.edu/hist_honors/18/ (last accessed 3 December 2012), p. 8.

135. 'AICC Observes Five Minutes Silence', *Tribune*, 29 March 1931, p. 1.

136. 'Resolution on Bhagat Singh and Comrades', 29 March 1931. *CWMG*, XLV, p. 363. 'Indian National Congress', *The Indian Annual Register*, 1931, Vol. 1, pp. 266–7.

137. Nehru, 'On the Lahore Executions', pp. 505–6.

138. 'Indian National Congress', *The Indian Annual Register*, 1931, Vol. 1, p. 267.

139. Chandra, *Naujawan Bharat Sabha*, p. 164–5; Bose, *Indian Struggle*, p. 207.

140. *EINC*, Vol. 10, Proceedings of the 45th Session, p. 79.

141. 'Karachi Congress Proceedings, Resolution on BS passed', *Tribune*, 1 April 1931, p. 3.

142. 'Indian National Congress', *The Indian Annual Register*, 1931, Vol. 1, p. 268.

143. *EINC*, Vol. 10, p. 78.

144. *EINC*, Vol. 10, pp. 77–8.

145. 'Karachi Congress Proceedings, Conducted Expeditiously', *Tribune*, 1 April 1931, p. 3.

146. Telegram from Viceroy to Secretary of State, 2 April 1931. NAI, HP, 136/1931, p. 15.

147. Telegram from Commissioner of Sind to government of Bombay, 29 March 1931. NAI, HP, 136/1931, p. 10; Manjapra, *M. N. Roy*, p. 100; see also my discussion of the Fundamental Rights Resolution in the Conclusion.

148. DIB Report, 16 April 1931. IOR, L/PJ/12/390, p. 40.

149. *The Masses*, 15 April 1931, p. 1. Hawkins Papers, CSAS.

150. Chowduri, *Leftism in India*, p. 148.

151. H. Williamson, 'A Note on Terrorism in India (Excluding Bengal)', 1933. IOR, L/PJ/12/397, p. 84.

152. Brown, *Gandhi and Civil Disobedience*, p. 198.

153. Report on the political situation in the Punjab for the fortnight ending the 15th of April 1931. NAI, F/18/3/1931. A Bengali correspondent reported to Gandhi that 'interested politicians' in Bengal were saying that Gandhi expressed his 'admiration for Bhagat Singh and his comrades only being prevailed upon by the Navajuvanwallas, whose strong agitation you could not resist, and you wanted to please Pandit Jawaharlal'. *Young India*, 11 June 1931, in *CWMG*, Vol. XLVI, p. 358.

154. Bose, *Indian Struggle*, p. 207.

155. *Times of India*, 28 March 1931, p. 1.

156. Gandhi, *Young India*, 11 June 1931. *CWMG*, Vol. XLVI, p. 358.

157. DIB Report, 3 December 1931. IOR, L/PJ/12/375, p. 76.

158. Bose, *Indian Struggle*, p. 207. I will discuss this further in the conclusion.

159. Brown, *Gandhi and Civil Disobedience*, p. 203; Telegram from Viceroy to Secretary of State for India, 11 April 1931. NAI, HP, 136/1931, pp. 18–21.

160. As a community, the Sikhs had been neglected by several aspects of Congress policy, most recently in constitutional proposals such as the Nehru Report, and were subsequently isolated by the Gandhi-Irwin Pact and had been lobbying for representation in the Indian flag. Report on the political situation in the Punjab for the fortnight ending the 15th of March 1931. BL, IOR, L/PJ/12/717. Srirupa Roy, '"A Symbol of Freedom": The Indian Flag and the Transformations of Nationalism, 1906–2002', *Journal of Asian Studies*, 65(3), 2006, p. 504.

161. Note by Bhagwan Das, 9 April 1931, p. 21. NAI, HP, 143/1931, p. 21.

162. Note by Bhagwan Das, 9 April 1931, p. 21. NAI, HP, 143/1931, p. 21.

163. Dhian Singh, 10 April 1931. NAI, HP, 143/1931, p. 28.   ·

164. 'Lahore Terrorists' "Sacrifices Appreciated", Europeans Aroused', *Sydney Morning Herald*, 13 April 1931, p. 9.

165. *Times of India*, 16 April 1931, p. 16.

166. 'A note by Mr Emerson of an interview between himself and Mr Gandhi on the 13th, 14th and 15th of May, 1931'. NAI, HP, 33/9/1931.

167. See 'Violence and Praise of Murderers', in NAI, HP, 33/9/1931.

168. 'Circular instructions to Congress Workers', 22 April 1931. NAI, HP, 33/9/1931.

169. Low, *Britain and Indian Nationalism*, p. 129.

170. DIB Report, 11 June 1931. IOR, L/PJ/12/390, p. 58.

8. CONTROLLING POLITICAL VIOLENCE: THE GOVERNMENT, THE CONGRESS AND THE HSRA

1. Craik, quoted in 'Anarchical Crimes', *Times of India*, 19 January 1931, p. 11.

2. See, for example, the statement of V. B. Gogate, who cited the shootings of nonviolent protestors in Sholapur as one of the decisive factors compelling him to shoot the acting Governor of Bombay. Gogate, CSAS, OHC, p. 2.

3. This was not entirely true. A branch of the HSRA was formed in Madras in late 1931 'by a party of extremist Congress volunteers, who, while political prisoners, had imbibed revolutionary sentiments when in contact with Bengali detenus'. Government of Madras to GOI, 29 January 1934. IOR, L/PJ/12/398, p. 5. Several Madras newspapers, including the *Congress*, published eulogies to the executed trio, and the prosecution of a Madras Conspiracy Case in 1932–3 would suggest that the south was not quarantined from radicalism. See the digest of 'objectionable' newspaper articles from Madras in IOR, L/PJ/12/400, pp. 2–3.

4. S.K. Ghosh in the *Statesman*, 30 July 1936; quoted in Alexander, *Political Prisoners In India*, IOR, L/PJ/12/314, p. 13.

5. DIB Report, 30 July 1931. IOR, L/PJ/12/390, p. 78.

6. S. Das, NMML, OHT, p. 11.

7. See 'Statement showing the total number of officials and innocent victims killed and injured'. IOR, L/PJ/12/400, p. 85; DIB Report, 27 August 1931. IOR, L/PJ/12/390, p. 80.

8. Barrier, *Banned*, p. 114.

9. *The Gazette of India*, Extraordinary, 5 March 1931, p. 91.

10. 'Denigration in the Tone of the Press in the Punjab', NAI, HP, 13/XI & KW/1931.

11. See the Memo from Bamford, 16 April 1931. NAI, HP 4/22/1931.

12. Irwin to de Montmorency, 17 March 1931. BL, Halifax Papers, Mss Eur. C152/27.

13. Jawaharlal Nehru to Gandhi, 28 September 1931. *SWJN*, Vol. 5, p. 47. I am grateful to Graham Greenleaf for his interpretation of Section 302.

14. 'Congress Licence in Punjab: Governor's Warning', *Times* (London), 27 April 1931, p. 12.

15. Marquess of Reading, 29 April 1931. *House of Lords Debates*, vol. 80, cc. 990.
16. See Bridge, *Holding India to the Empire*, ch. 3.
17. Marbett to Emerson, 27 April 1931. NAI, HP 13/XI & KW/1931, p. 2.
18. 'Extract from Newspaper articles relating to the incitement to Terrorist Crime or to the Eulogy of those concerned in such crime', 1931, IOR, L/PJ/12/400, pp. 2–67.
19. See the full file of correspondence in NAI, HP 4/22/1931.
20. Memo from Emerson, 6 May 1931. NAI, HP 13/XI & KW/1931, p. 2.
21. The targets included District Magistrates, Commissioners, Governors, Judges, and the president of the European Association in Calcutta. See the figures in IOR, L/PJ/12/404, p. 105.
22. R. G. Casey, *An Australian in India*, London: Hollis & Carter, 1947, p. 9.
23. *Pioneer*, 30 July 1931. Cited in *SWJN*, Vol. 5, p. 290.
24. 'Terrorist Literature', 1932. IOR, L/PJ/12/404, p. 107.
25. DIB Report, 30 July 1931. IOR, L/PJ/12/390, p. 78
26. Statement of Crime, Punjab, IOR, L/PJ/12/400, p. 90.
27. DIB Report, 27 August 1931. IOR, L/PJ/12/369, pp. 8–9.
28. Statements of persons convicted or accused in recent terrorist conspiracy cases, IOR, L/PJ/12/400, p. 75.
29. Gogate, CSAS, OHC, p. 5.
30. Bose, 'Engendering the Armed Struggle', p. 160.
31. Forbes, 'Goddesses or Rebels?', p. 125.
32. 'Students', IOR, L/PJ/12/404, p. 111.
33. Gogate, CSAS, OHC, p. 7.
34. 'Students', IOR, L/PJ/12/404, p. 112.
35. Letter from Viceroy to Governors of all provinces, 30 September 1931. NAI, HP, 4/35/1931.
36. Letter from Viceroy to Governors of all provinces, 30 September 1931. NAI, HP, 4/35/1931.
37. 'Terrorism of Witnesses', IOR, L/PJ/12/404, pp. 106–7.
38. Ghosh and Jai Gopal were both shot at by an HSRA member, Bhagwan Das, while giving evidence in Jalgaon for the Bhusawal Bomb Case on 21 February. Jai Gopal was injured in the shoulder, but survived the attack. 'Attempt on life of Approver', *Times of India*, 26 February 1930, p. 12. Hearing of the attempt on the approvers, a crowd of 1,000 some of whom 'belonged to the local Congress Committee, some being office bearers', assembled outside the court, shouting 'Mahatma Gandhi ki Jai' and 'Bhagwan Das ki Jai'. Members of the crowd were charged with rioting and mischief under the rubric of the 'Jalegaon District Court Rioting Case'. *Times of India*, 1 April 1930, p. 3. After this incident, Jai Gopal appears to have gone into hiding.
39. N. K. Shukla (ed.), *The Trial of Baikunth Sukul: A Revolutionary Patriot*, Delhi: Har-Anand Publications, 1999, p. 23.
40. DIB Report, 3 October 1929. IOR, L/PJ/12/60, p. 36.
41. 'Notes in the DIBs office regarding speeches made in various places about the death of Chandra Shekhar Azad', 14 April 1931. NAI, HP, 159/1931, p. 8.

42. Proceedings of the civil and military conference held in Calcutta on July 2–4, 1934. IOR, L/PJ/12/400, p. 115.

43. Proceedings of the civil and military conference held in Calcutta on July 2–4, 1934. IOR, L/PJ/12/400, pp. 111–144.

44. Abbas, CSAS, OHC, p. 1–2.

45. 'A Note on Terrorism in India (excluding Bengal)', 19 August 1933. IOR, L/PJ/12/397, p. 90.

46. Lindsay to Henderson, 27 February 1931. IOR, L/PJ/12/434, p. 7.

47. 'DIB's review of the terrorist situation', August 1933, IOR, L/PJ/12/398, p. 69.

48. Letter from the Chief Secretary to government, Punjab, 2 September 1933. IOR, L/PJ/12/397, p. 90.

49. 'DIB's Review of the terrorist situation', 1934. IOR, L/PJ/12/400, pp. 14, 60.

50. *The United Provinces Political Who's Who*, no. 320.

51. 'Note by the Government of the Punjab', 19 August 1933. IOR, L/PJ/12/397, p. 90.

52. See, for example, Viscount Rothermere's *Daily Mail's Blue Book on the Indian Crisis*, April 1931, replete with text in bold and caps.

53. 'Note by the Government of the Punjab', 19 August 1933. IOR, L/PJ/12/397, p. 90.

54. 'Figures compiled for Parliament', 21 March 1934. IOR, L/PJ/12/398, p. 37.

55. 'The Punjab', IOR, L/PJ/12/400, pp. 33–4. Some pages from this list are missing, but the fact that the list concludes with outrage no. 43 is less indicative of a province under control than the India Office would have the House of Commons believe.

56. 'DIB's review of the terrorist situation in 1933', IOR, L/PJ/12/398, p. 69.

57. *The Indian Annual Register*, Vol. 2, July–December, p. 11. The reference to 'reliable sources' is to Kishan Singh.

58. 'Resolution on Public Violence', AICC, Bombay, 6 August 1931, in *EINC*, Vol. 10, p. 179.

59. Jawaharlal Nehru, 'On Political Violence', *Bombay Chronicle*, 7 August 1931, in *SWJN*, Vol. 5, p. 291.

60. 'Resolution on Public Violence', AICC, Bombay, 6 August 1931 in *EINC*, Vol. 10, p. 179.

61. DIB Report, 27 August 1931. IOR, L/PJ/12/369, p. 8.

62. See the intercepted letter from Gandhi to Anand Kishore, 22 June 1931. NAI, HP 4/12/31; and Comrade Ram Chandra's version of the events, *Naujawan Bharat Sabha*, pp. 164–5.

63. DIB Report, 27 August 1931. IOR, L/PJ/12/369, pp. 10–11.

64. DIB Report, 27 August 1931. IOR, L/PJ/12/369, p. 11.

65. CWC Resolution, 7–12 July 1931 in *EINC*, Vol. 10, pp. 190–1; Brown, *Gandhi and Civil Disobedience*, p. 264.

66. Circular to PCCs, Allahabad, 16 July 1931. *SWJN*, Vol. 5. p. 222.

67. CWC Resolution, Bombay 7–12 July 1931. In *EINC*, Vol. 10, pp. 191; CWC Resolution, 4–7 August 1931, pp. 199–200.

68. *EINC*, Vol. 10, p. 200.

69. Jawaharlal Nehru, 'On Terrorist Occurrences', *Pioneer*, 30 July 1931. *SWJN*, Vol. 5, p. 290.

70. *SWJN*, Vol. 5, p. 291.

71. *SWJN*, Vol. 5, p. 47.

72. 'Call to Eschew Violence', *Bombay Gazette*, 23 November 1931. *SWJN*, Vol. 5, p. 303.

73. Note by the Indian Political Intelligence unit, 30 August 1946. IOR, L/PJ/12/470, p. 95.

74. Chandrashekhar Azad narrowly escaped arrest on 1 December 1930 in Kanpur, when a meeting with Salig Ram Shukla was intercepted by police and the latter shot dead, and again on 6 December 1930 when he was spotted by a railway police constable at Delhi Railway station. Nigam, CSAS, OHC, p. 9; 'List of crimes', 1930, IOR, L/PJ/12/396, p. 18; Delhi Conspiracy Case Progress Report, week ending 13.12.1930. NAI, HP 4/13/30, p. 118.

75. Khanna, NMML, OHT, p. 28.

76. Ajoy Ghosh, *Bhagat Singh and his Comrades*, New Delhi: New Age Press, 1979, p. 46.

77. Nigam, CSAS, OHC, p. 11.

78. Friend (ed.), *Yashpal Looks Back*, p. 100.

79. 'To the young political workers', in which Bhagat Singh discussed the political situation in the lead up to the Round Table Conference, clarified that 'mere bomb throwing is not only useless but harmful'. This was first was published in Lahore's *The People*, IOR, L/PJ/12/400, p. 9, and subsequently republished in tracts, such as Svami, *Lahore ke shahid*, Jabalpur: Azad Granthmala, 1931. IOR, PP Hin B 355.

80. Sukhdev to 'Bhaiya', 9 October 1930. NAI, HP, 139/1931, p. 4.

81. 'Our opportunity', IOR, L/PJ/12/391, pp. 49–50.

82. H. Williamson, A note on subversive movements and organisations (other than terrorist) in India, Simla: Government of India, 1933, p. 157.

83. Friend (ed.), *Yashpal Looks Back*, p. 177; see also the interview with Pandey, in Sharma (ed.), *In Retrospect*, p. 130. Pandey, who was accused and acquitted in the Lahore Conspiracy Case, believed that it was Yashpal's marriage that set off this inter-party discord.

84. Khanna, NMML, OHT, p. 31–3.

85. 'A Note on Terrorism in the United Provinces', IOR, L/PJ/12/397, p. 4.

86. 'Khoon ka badla Khoon' (Blood for Blood)', IOR, PIB 27/22. Attempts were made on his life on 18 July in Kanpur, and again on 24 November 1931 when he was shot four times at close range in Jalaun. IOR, L/PJ/12/397, pp. 6–7.

87. 'Warrior', NMML, OHT, p. 82; 'Azad: the unsolved questions', *Times of India*, 28 February 2010.

88. Friend (ed.), *Yashpal Looks Back*, p. 195. This is corroborated in 'Notes on Terrorism', 1933. IOR, L/PJ/12/379, p. 9.

89. *The United Provinces Political Who's Who*, p. 362; 'Story of Widespread Terrorist Conspiracy', *Times of India*, 14 December 1933, p. 5.

90. DIB Report, 24 November 1932. IOR, L/PJ/12/369, p. 49.

91. 'The United Provinces, Punjab and Delhi', in Hale, *Political Trouble in India*, p. 68.

92. DIB Report, 26 January 1933. IOR, L/PJ/12/392, p. 8.

93. DIB Report, 23 March 1933. IOR, L/PJ/12/392, pp. 19, 32.

94. Sikka, CSAS, OHC, p. 3.

95. DIB Report, 18 May 1933. IOR, L/PJ/12/392, p. 33.

96. DIB Report, 24 August 1933. IOR, L/PJ/12/392, p. 52.

97. 'Memorandum on Terrorism', IOR, L/PJ/12/400, p. 47.

98. Yashpal, NMML, OHT, p. 16.

99. Sinha, *Memoirs of a Revolutionary*, p. 16. This of course is a reference to Lenin, who is said to have described prison as 'a university for communists'. See Raza, 'Meerut and Official Communism', p. 324.

100. Bhagat Singh, Prison Diary, NMML Private Papers, Acc. 716. On the broader influence of global leftist thought on Bhagat Singh, see Elam, 'The "Arch Priestess of Anarchy"', pp. 140–154.

101. Bharti, NMML, OHT, p. 67; Prasad, NMML, OHT, p. 84–5.

102. Sinha, *Memoirs of a Revolutionary*, p. 82–4.

103. Kapoor, NMML, OHT, p. 242.

104. 'Prisoners on Hunger Strike', *Times of India*, 3 February 1933, p. 5.

105. Kapoor, NMML, OHT, p. 242–3.

106. Kapoor, NMML, OHT, p. 245.

107. Kapoor, NMML, OHT, p. 249.

108. Kapoor, NMML, OHT, p. 248–251.

109. Sachar, NMML, OHT, p. 124.

110. Sachar, NMML, OHT, p. 125.

111. 'Punjab Release Orders', *Times of India*, 25 April 1946, p. 5.

112. Yaji, NMML, OHT, pp. 30–31; Sinha, *Memoirs of a Revolutionary*, p. 16.

113. DIB Report, 18 December 1936. IOR, L/PJ/12/394, p. 76.

114. Sinha, *Memoirs of a Revolutionary*, pp. 29–30.

115. Kapoor, NMML, OHT, p. 268.

116. Verma, NMML, OHT, p. 177.

117. Kapoor, NMML, OHT, p. 271; Verma, NMML, OHT, p. 184.

118. Kapoor, NMML, OHT, p. 275.

119. Williamson, quoted by Craik to Reid, 11 February 1936; and Reid to Craik, 28 February 1936, in IOR, L/PJ/12/394, p. 39, 44.

120. Ghosh, *Bhagat Singh and his Comrades*, p. 50.

121. M. Gupta, NMML, OHT, p. 63.

122. Nigam, CSAS, OHC, p. 14.

123. Nigam, CSAS, p. 15. Eventually, he moved to Nagpur and joined Subhas Chandra Bose's Forward Block, and in 1942 took part in the Quit India movement.

CONCLUSION: THE DYNAMICS OF ANTICOLONIAL VIOLENCE

1. Stephen Henningham, 'Quit India in Bihar and the Eastern United Provinces: The Dual Revolt', in Ranajit Guha (ed.), *Subaltern Studies II: Writings of South Asian History and Society*, Delhi: Oxford University Press, 1983, p. 136.

2. Chatterjee, 'Bombs and Nationalism in Bengal', p. 11.

3. Sinha, *Memoirs of a Revolutionary*, p. 22. Sinha was released in the late 1930s, roughly a decade earlier than his HSRA colleagues.
4. Chaman Lal, *Martyrs of India, War of Independence Centenary*, Kanpur; Kapur Publishing Press, 1957.
5. 'Khudiram Bose Memorial', *Times of India*, 3 April 1949, p. 9.
6. Khanna, NMML, OHT, p. 90.
7. Khanna, NMML, OHT, p. 90.
8. Robin Jeffrey, 'The Mahatma didn't like Movies and Why it Matters: Indian Broadcasting Policy, 1920s-1990s', *Global Media and Communication*, 2(2), 2006, p. 206.
9. Harcourt, 'Revolutionary Networks', p. 323.
10. As Jaidev Kapoor reminisced, 'he loved reading, writing, cinema and swimming. He was able to appreciate beauty and he sought it out. Whenever there was a meeting in Agra he would schedule it for the Taj Mahal, because he loved its beauty.' Kapoor, NMML, OHT, p. 311.
11. Nehru, *Toward Freedom*, p. 134.
12. Maclean and Elam, 'Who is a Revolutionary?', p. 120; Benjamin Zachariah, 'A Long, Strange Trip: the Lives in Exile of Har Dayal', *South Asian History and Culture*, 4 (4), 2013, p. 586. Simona Sawhney, for example, has pointed to religious and communal tropes in Bhagat Singh's early writings, in 'Bhagat Singh: A Politics of Death and Hope', in Anshu Malhotra and Farina Mir (eds), *Punjab Reconsidered: History, Culture, and Practice*, New Delhi: Oxford University Press, 2012, pp. 387–393.
13. In this particular incarnation, Mother India is devoid of the paraphernalia of a deity— a crown, effulgence and weaponry (as in Figures 2, 3, 18 and so on)—and owes more to Christian symbolism, but she nonetheless invokes a contemporary language of politics that was communally charged. See Charu Gupta, 'The Icon of Mother in Late Colonial North India', *Economic and Political Weekly*, 36 (45), 2001, pp. 4291–4299.
14. Chandra, 'Revolutionary Terrorists in North India', p. 242.
15. Chand, CSAS, OHC, p. 37.
16. Bhikshu Chaman Lal, CSAS, OHC, p. 6.
17. Muldoon, *Empire, Politics and the Creation of the 1935 India Act*, p. 52.
18. Letter to Jawahar, 10 April 1929, *SWMN*, Vol. 7, p. 37.
19. 'To English Friends', 23 January 1930. *CWMG*, XLII, p. 425; 'Answers to Questions', c. 11 March 1930, CWMG, XLIII, pp. 42–3.
20. Alexander, *Political Prisoners In India*, p. 8, IOR, L/PJ/12/314.
21. B. R. Dhurandhar, CSAS, OHC, p. 4.
22. See also Judith Brown, who notes that 'terrorist attacks were on the upsurge under cover of civil disobedience.' Brown, *Gandhi and Civil Disobedience*, p. 138. I draw on a Bengali example because, as noted in Chapter Six, according to Durga Das Khanna the HSRA's energies at the time of the Salt March were predominantly directed towards a plot to free Bhagat Singh and B.K. Dutt from jail, and there seems to have been an informal stay on actions against British targets. This is somewhat complicated, however, by N.K. Nigam's claim that Surya Sen and Ananta Singh were affiliated to the HSRA and

had conferred with Chandrashekhar Azad in Delhi prior to the raid in Chittagong. Nigam, CSAS, OHC, p. 18.

23. J. Gupta, NMML, OHT, p. 79. See also Michael Carritt's assessment of Peddie, who was shot in front of Carritt, *The Mole in the Crown: Memoirs of a British Official in India who worked with a Communist Underground in the 1930s*, Hove: Michael Carritt, 1985, p. 36. With thanks to Ben Zachariah for this reference.

24. Nehru, *Toward Freedom*, pp. 156–7.

25. I shall return to this below, but although a publicly divisive split was averted in Karachi, this fresh impetus in the Congress did alienate elements of the nationalist left in India.

26. Sohan Singh 'Josh' reports that he had this conversation with Bhagat Singh at the time of the Calcutta Congress, in 1928, just after the assassination of Saunders. 'Josh', 'My Meetings with Bhagat Singh', p. 26.

27. Quoted in Frank Moraes, *Jawaharlal Nehru: A Biography*, New York: Macmillan, 1958, p. 143.

28. This was a common refrain in the *Civil and Military Gazette*; see 23 December 1930, p. 1; 18 January 1931, p. 3.

29. Maria Misra, for example, after briefly describing the work of the HSRA, summarily concludes that 'all this activity came to nought when the leaders of the movement, including Bhagat Singh himself, were arrested and executed in 1931'. *Vishnu's Crowded Temple: India since the Great Rebellion*, New Haven and London: Yale University Press, 2007, p. 175.

30. Dennis Dalton, *Gandhi's Power: Nonviolence in Action*, New Delhi: Oxford University Press, 1993, p. 132. However, Shiv Verma remarks in his oral history interview that in 1930, while the Special Tribunal was in session, he was visited by a CID officer, Mumtaz Husain, who revealed to him that the government had intended to hang all of those revolutionaries present in Lahore on the day of the assassination (seven in total), but that some MPs in England intervened, pointing out that 'if so may persons were hanged, then the British justice in the international field would be defamed'. Verma, NMML, OHT, pp. 132–3.

31. Sarkar, 'The Logic of Gandhian Nationalism', p. 134.

32. Dewey, *Anglo-Indian Attitudes*, p. 223.

33. David C. Potter, 'Manpower Shortage and the End of Colonialism: The Case of the Indian Civil Service', *Modern Asian Studies*, 7(1), 1973, p. 55.

34. Casey, *An Australian in India*, p. 9.

35. Benjamin Zachariah, 'Rewriting Imperial Mythologies: the Strange Case of Penderel Moon', *South Asia*, 21 (2), 2001, p. 53.

36. Manchanda, interview with the author, 11 September 2010.

37. Reinhold Niebuhr, 'What Chance has Gandhi?', *The Christian Century*, Vol. 48, Issue 41, 1931, p. 1276.

38. DIB Report, 27 April 1935. IOR, L/PJ/12/394, p. 21.

39. 'Jawaharlal Nehru's note on Provisional Settlement', *CWMG*, XLV, p. 431.

40. 'Draft Resolution of Fundamental Rights for the Karachi Congress, 1931'. People's History Museum, Manchester, Bradley Papers, 6/9, pp. 1–2.

41. 'The Karachi Congress', *The Masses*, 15 April 1931, p. 2. Hawkins Papers, CSAS.

42. Nehru, *Toward Freedom*, p. 197. Chattopadhyay, NMML, OHT, p. 83.

43. 'Fundamental Rights Resolution', *CWMG*, Vol. XLV, p. 370.

44. Chattopadhyay, NMML, OHT, p. 83.

45. Chattopadhyay, NMML, OHT, p. 83.

46. Irfan Habib, 'The Envisioning of a Nation: A Defence of the Idea of India', *Social Scientist*, 27(9/10), 1999, p. 26; for an example of how it was deployed in the short term, see Papiya Ghosh, 'Articulating Community Rights: The Muslim League and Hindu Mahasabha in Congress Bihar, 1937–39', *South Asia*, 14(2), 1999, pp. 79–97.

47. Nehru, *Toward Freedom*, p. 197.

48. Viceroy to Secretary of State, 2 April 1931. NAI, HP, 136/1931, p. 15. The resolution has been interpreted widely as Nehru's reward for his submission to the Gandhi-Pact. Michael Edwardes, *Nehru: A Political Biography*, London: Allen Lane/Penguin Press, 1971, p. 94; Brown, 'Gandhi and Congress', p. 139. Sarvepalli Gopal saw it essentially as a Gandhian document, and therefore not Nehru's 'trade-off', although its clear genealogy from the Roy camp complicates this. *Jawaharlal Nehru: A Biography, Vol. 1, 1889–1947*, London: Jonathon Cape, 1975, p. 152.

49. Sapru, for example, felt that 'Gandhi had paid too high a price' for Nehru's allegiance. Brown, 'Gandhi and Congress', p. 139.

50. Chowdhuri, *Leftism in India*, p. 147.

51. Verma, NMML, OHT, p. 49.

52. Nigam, for example, cited 'indiscriminate firing in Delhi' in the early 1920s as the incident which made him anti-British; and Yashpal recounted his fury at having to pass by a grand statue of John Lawrence that taunted passers-by with its rhetorical inscription, 'Will you be governed by the sword or the pen?' Nigam, NMML, OHT, p. 4; Yashpal, *Singhavalokan*, p. 15.

53. Bombay Congress Bulletin, 16 May 1930, Hawkins Papers, CSAS.

54. Khanna, OHT, p. 70.

55. Verma, NMML, OHT, p. 86;

56. Nehru, *Toward Freedom*, p. 134.

57. Fanon, *The Wretched of the Earth*, p. 51. Nonviolent activist Barbara Deming challenged her readers to work through Fanon's book substituting the word 'violence' for 'radical and uncompromising action', contending that 'with the exception of a very few passages this substitution can be made, and that the action he calls for could just as well be nonviolent action'. Barbara Deming, 'On Revolution and Equilibrium', in Jane Myerdeng (ed.), *The We Are All Part of One Another: A Barbara Deming Reader*, New Society Publishers, 1984, p. 170.

58. 'If the masses ... take matters into their own hands and start burning and killing, it is not long before we see the "elite" and the leaders of the bourgeois nationalist parties turn to the colonial authorities and tell them: "This is terribly serious! Goodness knows how it will all end. We must find an answer, we must find a compromise."' Fanon, *The Wretched of the Earth*, p. 24.

59. It is important here to note the simultaneous shaping of radical politics through mech-

anisms such as the Meerut Conspiracy Case, which Roy and Zachariah argue was a maneuver to 'separate the antinational communists from the more palatable nationalists'. See 'Meerut and a Hanging', p. 361.

60. Chowdhuri, *Leftism in India*, p. 147; Sarkar, *Modern India*, p. 332.
61. J. Gupta, NMML, OHT, p. 55.
62. Partha Chatterjee, *A Princely Impostor? The Strange and Universal History of the Kumar of Bhawal*, Princeton: Princeton University Press, 2002, p. 378.
63. Jain, CSAS, OHC, pp. 18–19.
64. Bhagat Singh, 'Regarding Line of Defence in Hari Kishan's Case', in Verma (ed.), *Bhagat Singh: on the Path of Liberation*, p. 103.
65. 'Our Opportunity', in IOR, L/PJ/12/391, p. 49.
66. 'To the Young Political Workers', L/PJ/12/391, p. 64.
67. Parel (ed.), *Hind Swaraj*, p. 28.
68. Narayan, CSAS, OHC, p. 2.
69. Narain, NMML, OHT, p. 32.
70. Khanna, NMML, OHT, p. 37.
71. Sanjay Seth, 'Rewriting Histories of Nationalism: The Politics of "Moderate Nationalism" in India, 1870–1905', *American Historical Review*, 104(1), 1999, p. 104.
72. Saha, 'Everyday Violence in British India', p. 844; Shruti Kapila, 'A History of Violence', *Modern Intellectual History*, 7(2), 2010, p. 437.
73. Kolsky, *Colonial Justice in British India*, p. 1.
74. Sherman, *State Violence and Punishment in India*.
75. Amin, *Event, Metaphor, Memory, passim*.
76. This is not unique to South Asian studies. Rogers Brubaker and David D. Laitin, 'Ethnic and Nationalist Violence', *Annual Review of Sociology*, 24, 1998, pp. 423–52.
77. Slavoj Žižek, *Violence: Six Sideways Reflections*, New York: Picador, 2008, p. 213.
78. Pandey, *Construction of Communalism*, p. 243, fn 24.
79. Nehru, 'Communalism Rampant', in *Toward Freedom*, pp. 112–7.
80. Nehru, 'On the Lahore Executions', p. 505.
81. Nehru, 'On the Lahore Executions', p. 506.
82. Gopal, *Jawaharlal Nehru*, p. 150; Edwardes, *Nehru*, p. 90; Zachariah, *Nehru*, p. 72.
83. Irwin, 'Interview with the Viceroy', 19 March 1931, quoted in *CWMG* (Electronic Series), Vol. 50, p. 272.
84. Williamson, 'Note on the Session of the Congress'. NAI, HP, 136/1931, p. 21.
85. *Vir Bharat* (Lahore), 13 April 1931. NAI, HP, 13/XI & KW/1931, pp. 49–57. Sections that are underlined are done so in the original.

EPILOGUE: CONGRESS AND THE REVOLUTIONARIES, 1937–1946

1. Resolution on Ministerial Resignations, before 18 February 1938, in *CWMG*, Vol. LXVI, p. 376.
2. Cf. Sherman, *State Violence and Punishment in India*, pp. 102–110.
3. S. Das, NMML, OHT, p. 14.
4. Kapoor, NMML, OHT, p. 280.

5. Kapoor, NMML, OHT, p. 282.

6. Kapoor, NMML, OHT, p. 258.

7. Kapoor, NMML, OHT, p. 287.

8. 'Released Prisoners Active', *Times of India*, 6 December 1937, p. 9.

9. M. Gupta, CSAS, OHC, p. 19. In his prison writings, Nehru notes that he met Kapoor at the Ayodhya Uttar Pradesh Provincial Conference, but does not indicate how Kapoor came to be released from prison for the occasion. 5 March 1941. *SWJN*, Vol. 11, p. 227.

10. M. Gupta, *They Lived Dangerously*, p. 379.

11. Kapoor, NMML, OHT, p. 290.

12. 'More Active Policy in States Affairs: Congress Intention', *Times of India*, 23 November 1938, p. 12.

13. Kapoor, NMML, OHT, p. 291.

14. 'Jail Diary', 5 March 1941. *SWJN*, Vol. 11, pp. 556–9.

15. Kapoor, NMML, OHT, p. 295.

16. Verma, NMML, OHT, p. 187.

17. Verma, NMML, OHT, pp. 188–9.

18. Jawaharlal Nehru, 'Jail Diary', 5 March 1941. *SWJN*, Vol. 11, p. 557.

19. Kapoor, NMML, OHT, p. 299.

20. 'Punjab Release Orders', *Times of India*, 24 April 1946, p. 3.

21. 'U.P. Political Prisoners', *Times of India*, 15 May 1946, p. 1.

22. Friend (ed.), *Yashpal Looks Back*, p. 178.

23. Verma, NMML, OHT, p. 121, 201.

BIBLIOGRAPHY

Archives

National Archives of India (NAI), New Delhi

Home Political (HP), 1929–34

Private Papers

Proscribed Literature Collection

British Library, India Office Records, Asian and African Studies Collections

Public and Judicial Department
Proscribed Tracts Collection

British Library, European Manuscripts

Jack Morton Papers
Halifax Papers
Penderel Moon Papers
Frank Lugard Brayne Papers
John Perronet Thompson Papers

House of Lords Record Office

Stansgate Papers

Nehru Memorial Museum and Library

Private Papers
AICC Papers

Nehru Memorial Museum and Library, Oral History Transcripts (NMML, OHT)

Bharti, Desraj. Interviewed by S. L. Manchanda, 19 November 1977. Acc. No. 819.
Bedi, B.P.L. Interviewed by Hari Dev Sharma, 5 September 1965. Acc. No. 270.
Chattopadhyay, Kamaladevi. Interviewed by Hari Dev Sharma and K. P. Rungachary, 6 December 1978. Acc. No. 338.

BIBLIOGRAPHY

Das, Chhabil. Interviewed by S. L. Manchanda, 17 May 1971. Acc. No. 163.

Das, Durga. Interviewed by B. R. Nanda, 26 February 1969. Acc. No. 96.

Das, Shanti. Interviewed by Aparna Basu, 2 January 1969. Acc. No. 648.

Gupta, Jaidev. Interviewed by S.L. Manchanda, 10 May 1978. Acc. No. 346.

Gupta, Manmathnath. Interviewed by Hari Dev Sharma, 22 November 1969. Acc. No. 174.

Kapoor, Jaidev. Interviewed by S.L. Manchanda, 3 October 1974. Acc. No. 431.

Khan, Abdul Majid. Interviewed by Hari Dev Sharma, 16 June 1974. Acc. No. 348.

Khanna, Durga Das. Interviewed by S.L. Manchanda, 16 May 1976. Acc. No. 294.

Lajjawati, Kumari. Interviewed by S. L. Manchanda, 24 November 1981. Acc. No. 471.

Lal, Bhikshu Chaman. Interviewed by Hari Dev Sharma, 20 June 1969. Acc. No. 637.

Lal, Diwan Chaman. Interviewed by Hari Dev Sharma and K. P. Rungachary, 7 February 1967. Acc. No. 220.

Mehta, Pran Nath. Interviewed by S.L. Manchanda, 2 February 1980. Acc No. 374.

Musaddi, Sridevi. Interviewed by S.L. Manchanda, 4 February 1982. Acc. No. 585.

Narain, Lala Jagat. Interviewed by S.L. Manchanda, 16 May 1971. Acc. No. 373.

Nigam, N.K. Interviewed by S.L. Manchanda, 1 March 1968. Acc. No. 70.

Paliwal, C. L. Interviewed by S.L. Manchanda, 6 January 1978. Acc. No. 357.

Prasad, Gaya. Interviewed by S. L. Manchanda, 4 November 1973. Acc. No. 835.

Potdar, Gajanand Sadashiv. Interviewed by Usha Prasad, 21 November 1989. Acc. No. 583.

Rai, Ganpat. Interviewed by S. L. Manchanda, 7 July 1974. Acc. No. 330.

Ramchandra, Comrade. Interviewed by S. L. Manchanda, 20 January 1978. Acc. No. 356.

Sachar, Bhim Sen. Interviewed by Hari Dev Sharma, 16 December 1972. Acc. No. 182.

Sahai, Raghubir. Interviewed by Hari Dev Sharma, 12 April 1975. Acc. No. 178, Vols I and II.

Sahgal (Zutshi), Manmohini, interviewed by S.L. Manchanda, 4 June 1970. Acc. No. 65.

Sahgal, Durgadas, interviewed by S.L. Manchanda, Acc. No. 418. 5 May 1982.

Singh, Mangal. Interviewed by Hari Dev Sharma, 21 June 1973, Acc. No. 408.

Singh, Kultar. Interviewed by S.L. Manchanda, 15 May 1987. Acc. No. 798.

Verma, Shiv. Interviewed by Hari Dev Sharma and S.L. Manchanda, 16 February 1972. Acc. No 50.

Vohra, Durga Devi. Interviewed by S.L. Manchanda, 16 February 1972. Acc. No. 369.

Yaji, Shilabhadra. Interviewed by S. L. Manchanda, 18 January 1984. Acc. No. 740.

Yashpal. Interviewed by S. L. Manchanda, 10 February 1972. Acc. No. 467.

'Warrior', Rajendrapal Singh. Interviewed by S. L. Manchanda, 24 July 1986, Acc. No. 587.

Centre of South Asian Studies, Cambridge, Private Papers

H. A. N. Barlow Papers

Malcolm Darling Papers

A. Ewing Papers

G. A. Haig Papers

Gordon Halland Papers

E. W. Holland Papers

BIBLIOGRAPHY

R. E. Hawkins Papers
C. Tegart Papers

Centre of South Asian Studies, Cambridge—Oral History Collection (CSAS, OHC)
(Available online at http://www.s-asian.cam.ac.uk/audio.html)

Abbas, K. A. Interviewed by Uma Shanker, 1 February 1970. Interview no. 123.

Chand, L. F. Interviewed by Uma Shanker, 28 April 1972. Interview no. 205.

Dastur, Aloo Jehan. Interviewed by Uma Shanker, 5 September 1970. Interview no. 162.

Dhurandar, Bhalchandra. Interviewed by Uma Shanker, 17 June 1969. Interview no. 101.

Gogate, V.B. Interviewed by Uma Shanker, 24 April 1970. Interview no. 134.

Gupta, Manmathnath. Interviewed by Uma Shankar, 28 August 1974. Interview no. 204.

Jain, Bimal Prasad. Interviewed by Uma Shanker, 3 June 1987. Interview no. 221.

Jenkins, J. D. Interviewed by Uma Shanker, 12 December 1970. Interview no. 129.

Kabadi, W. Interviewed by Uma Shanker, 1 June 1970. Interview no. 142.

Khandwala, Navin. Interviewed by Uma Shanker, 16 May 1971. Interview no. 167.

Khanna, Jugal Kishore. Interviewed by Uma Shanker, 10 May 1975. Interview no. 207.

Kohli, K.D. Interviewed by Uma Shanker, 19 January 1989. Interview no. 225.

Kishan, Ram. Interviewed by Uma Shanker, 14 July 1987. Interview no. 222.

Lal, Bhikshu Chaman. Interviewed by Uma Shanker, 19 August 1976. Interview no. 210.

Narayan, J.P. Interviewed by Arun Gandhi, March 1969. Interview no. 235.

Nawalkar, G.B. Interviewed by Uma Shanker, 25 August 1970. Interview no. 158.

Nigam, N.K. Interviewed by Uma Shanker, 21 July 1974, Interview no. 199.

Paliwal, C. L. Interviewed by Uma Shanker, 5 April 1974. Interview no. 195.

Panchal, Kashidevi. Interviewed by Uma Shanker, 6 September 1970. Interview no. 253.

Potdar, G. S. Interviewed by Uma Shanker, 4 June 1970. Interview no. 135.

Sahni, J. N. Interviewed by Uma Shanker, 6 March 1987. Interview no. 203.

Sikka, Hans Raj. Interviewed by Uma Shanker, 23 March 1991. Interview no. 227.

Singh, Rana Jang Bahadur. Interviewed by Uma Shanker, 27 July 1975. Interview no. 208.

People's History Museum, Manchester

Bradley Papers

Newspapers

Abhyudaya (1931)
Bhavishya (1931)
Chand (Phansi Ank)
Civil and Military Gazette (1931)
Hindustan Times (1928–1931, 2007–2012)
The Searchlight (1928–1931)
The Statesman (1931)
Times of India (1928–1947; 2007–2012)
Tribune (Lahore 1928–1931; Chandigarh 2007–2012)

BIBLIOGRAPHY

Government Publications

Amar Shahid Bhagat Singh, Chandigarh: Suchna, Prachar and Paryatan Vibhag, Punjab, 1968.

Collected Works of Mahatma Gandhi, New Delhi: Publications Division, Ministry of Information and Broadcasting, Government of India. (All references to Gandhi's Collected Works are to the standard edition, published as 100 volumes with supplementary volumes to accommodate material as it came to light, as opposed to the newer edition, which has published all material chronologically but is currently only available electronically).

Fiftieth Anniversary of Martyrdom of Bhagat Singh, Rajguru and Sukhdev, Punjab Government Publication, 1981.

India in 1928–29: A Statement Prepared for Presentation to Parliament, New Delhi: Anmol Pubs, 1985 [1929].

India in 1930–31, New Delhi: Anmol Pubs, 1985 [1931].

India Office List, London: Harrison & Sons, 1928–1934.

Hale, H.W., *Political Trouble in India, 1917–1937*, Allahabad: Chugh Publications, 1974 [reprint].

Indian Annual Register: an Annual Digest of Public Affairs of India, Vols. 1 and 2, Calcutta: Annual Register Office, 1931.

Rajya Sabha Debates, http://rsdebate.nic.in (last accessed 22 October 2010).

Report of the Commission of Inquiry into the Communal Outbreak at Cawnpore, Cmd. 3891, June 1931.

The United Provinces Political Who's Who 1936, Second Edition, Allahabad: Superintendent of Printing and Stationary, 1936.

Published Materials

Alexander, H. G., *The Indian Ferment: A Traveller's Tale*, London: Williams and Norgate, 1929.

Alter, J. A., 'Celibacy, Sexuality, and the Transformation of Gender into Nationalism in North India', *Journal of Asian Studies*, 53(1), 1994.

Amin, Shahid, 'Gandhi as Mahatma: Gorakhpur District, Eastern UP, 1921–2', in Ranajit Guha (ed.), *Subaltern Studies III*, Delhi: Oxford University Press, 1984.

———, *Event, Metaphor, Memory: Chauri Chaura, 1922–1992*, Berkeley: University of California Press, 1995.

Anderson, Perry, 'Gandhi Centre Stage', *The London Review of Books*, 34(13), 2012.

Appadurai, Arjun, 'Patriotism and its Futures', *Public Culture*, 3(5), Spring 1993.

Arnold, David, 'Industrial Violence in Colonial India', *Comparative Studies in History and Society*, 22(2), 1980.

Arora, Subhash Chander, *Turmoil in Punjabi Politics*, Delhi: Mittal Publications, 1990.

Azad, Chaman Lal, *Revolutionary Movement in India*, Delhi: All India Revolutionaries Conference, 1947.

Bandyopadhyay, Sandip, 'Women in Bengal Revolutionary Movement (1902–35)', *Manushi*, July–August 1991.

BIBLIOGRAPHY

Bandyopadhyay, Sekhar (ed.), *Nationalist Movement in India*, New Delhi: Oxford University Press, 2009.

Banerjee, Roma, *Subhas Chandra Bose and the Bengal Revolutionaries*, New Delhi: Reference Press, 2006

Banks, Marcus and Jay Ruby (eds), *Made to be Seen: Historical Perspectives on Visual Anthropology*, Chicago: University of Chicago Press, 2011.

Banks, Marcus, 'Views of Jain History', in David J. Parkin, Wendy James and Paul Dresch (eds), *Anthropologists in a Wider World: Essays on Field Research*, New York: Berghnan, 2000.

———, *Visual Methods in Social Research*, London: Sage, 2001.

Barrier, N.G., *Banned: Controversial Literature and Political Control in British India, 1907–1947*, University of Missouri Press, 1974.

Barthes, Roland, *Camera Lucida: Reflections on Photography*, London: Vintage, 1993.

Basu, Aparna, 'Feminism and Nationalism in India, 1917–1947', *Journal of Women's History*, 7(4), 1995.

Bayly, C. A., *Empire and Information: Intelligence Gathering and Social Communication in India, 1780–1870*, Cambridge: Cambridge University Press, 1996.

Bhabha, Homi, 'Of Mimicry and Men', in *The Location of Culture*, Abingdon: Routledge, 1994.

Bhargava, M.L., *Ganesh Shankar Vidyarthi*, Delhi: Publications Division, Government of India, 1988.

Bhattacharya, U. C. and Shovendu Sunder Chakravarty (eds), *Pandit Motilal Nehru: His Life and Work*, Calcutta: Modern Book Agency, 1931.

Bolt, Neville, *The Violent Image: Insurgent Propaganda and the New Insurgent Revolutionaries*, London: Hurst & Co., 2012.

Bose, Purnima, 'Engendering the Armed Struggle: Women, Writing and the Bengali "Terrorist" Movement'. In T. Foster, C. Seigel and E.E. Barry (eds), *Bodies of Writing, Bodies in Performance*, New York: New York University Press, 1996.

Bose, Subhas Chandra, *The Indian Struggle: 1920–1942*, New York: Asia Publishing House, 1964.

Bose, Sugata and Ayesha Jalal, *Modern South Asia: History, Culture and Political Economy*, Delhi: Oxford University Press, 1997.

Bose, Sisir K. and Bose Sugata (eds), *The Essential Writings of Netaji Subhas Chandra Bose*, Delhi: Oxford University Press, 1997.

Bridge, Carl, *Holding India to Empire: The British Conservative Party and the 1935 Constitution*, Delhi: Sterling, 1986.

Bridge, Carl and Howard Brasted, 'The British Labour Party "Nabobs" and Indian Reform, 1924–31', *Journal of Imperial and Commonwealth History*, 17(3), 1989.

Brittlebank, Kate (ed.), *Tall Tales and True: India, Historiography and British Imperial Imaginings*, Melbourne: Monash Asia Institute, 2008.

Brown, Judith, *Gandhi's Rise to Power, Indian Politics 1915–1922*, Cambridge: Cambridge University Press, 1972.

BIBLIOGRAPHY

————, *Gandhi and Civil Disobedience: The Mahatma in Politics, 1928–34*, Cambridge: Cambridge University Press, 1977.

Brubaker, Rogers and David D. Laitin, 'Ethnic and Nationalist Violence', *Annual Review of Sociology*, 24, 1998.

Burton, Antoinette (ed.), *Archive Stories: Facts, Fictions, and the Writing of History*, Durham: Duke University Press, 2005.

Carbon, Claus-Christian, 'Famous faces as icons: The illusion of being an expert in the recognition of famous faces', *Perception*, 37, 2008.

Carritt, Michael, *The Mole in the Crown: Memoirs of a British Official in India who worked with a Communist Underground in the 1930s*, Hove: Michael Carritt, 1985.

Casey, R. G., *An Australian in India*, London: Hollis & Carter, 1947.

Chakrabarty, Dipesh, 'The Public Life of History: An Argument out of India', *Public Culture*, 20(1), 2008, pp. 143–168.

————, *Provincialising Europe: Postcolonial Thought and Historical Difference*, Princeton: Princeton University Press, 2000.

Chandra, Bipan, *Nationalism and Colonialism in Modern India*, Delhi: Orient Longman, 1979.

————, *Ideology and Politics in Modern India*, New Delhi: Har-Anand Publications, 1994.

————, 'Bhagat Singh and his Comrades', in Ravi Dayal (ed.), *We Fought Together for Freedom*, Delhi: Oxford University Press, 1995.

Chandra, Bipan et al., *India's Struggle for Independence, 1857–1947*, Delhi: Penguin Books, 1988.

Chandra, Comrade Ram, *Naujawan Bharat Sabha and Hindustan Socialist Republican Association/Army*, New Delhi: published by the author, 1986.

————, *Ideology and Battle Cries of Indian Revolutionaries*, New Delhi: published by the author, 1989.

Chatterjee, Manini, *Do and Die: The Chittagong Uprising, 1930–1934*, New Delhi: Penguin, 2010 [1999].

Chatterjee, Partha, *A Princely Impostor? The Strange and Universal History of the Kumar of Bhawal*, Princeton: Princeton University Press, 2002.

————, 'Critique of Popular Culture', *Public Culture*, 20(2), 2008.

Chaturvedi, Vinayak, 'A Revolutionary's Biography: the Case of V. D. Savarkar', *Postcolonial Studies*, 16(2), 2013.

Chopra, P. N. (ed.), *Who's Who of Indian Martyrs*, New Delhi: Government of India, 1969.

Chowdhuri, Satyabrata Ray, *Leftism in India, 1917–1947*, Basingstoke/New York: Palgrave Macmillan, 2007.

Chousalkar, Ashok S., *Mahatma Gandhi and Sardar Bhagat Singh*, Mumbai: Mani Bhavan Gandhi Sangrahalaya, 2008.

Collett, Nigel, 'Evidence Concerning Indian Attitudes and British Intelligence During the 1919 Punjab Disturbances', *Journal of the Royal Asiatic Society*, 3(21), 2011.

Copland, Ian, 'The Master and the Maharajas: The Sikh Princes and the East Punjab Massacres of 1947', *Modern Asian Studies*, 36(3), 2002.

BIBLIOGRAPHY

Coward, Harold (ed.), *Indian Critiques of Gandhi*, Albany: SUNY Press, 2003.

Craddock, Reginald, *The Dilemma in India*, London: Constable & Co., 1929.

Dalal, C. B., *Gandhi: 1915–1948, A Detailed Chronology*, New Delhi: Gandhi Peace Foundation, 1971.

Dalton, Dennis, *Gandhi's Power: Nonviolence in Action*, New Delhi: Oxford University Press, 1993.

Datta, V. N., *Gandhi and Bhagat Singh*, Delhi: Rupa, 2008.

Davis, Richard H. (ed.), *Picturing the Nation: Iconographies of Modern India*, Delhi: Orient Longman, 2007.

de Mel, Neloufer, *Militarising Sri Lanka: Popular Culture, Memory and Narrative in the Armed Conflict*, New Delhi: Sage, 2007.

Deming, Barbara, 'On Revolution and Equilibrium', in Jane Myerdeng (ed.), *We Are All Part of One Another: A Barbara Deming Reader*, New Society Publishers, 1984.

Deshpande, Sudhanva, 'A Tale of Two Bhagat Singhs', *Frontline*, 2 August 2002.

Devji, Faisal, *The Impossible Indian: Gandhi and the Temptation of Violence*, London: Hurst & Co., 2012.

Dewey, Clive, *Anglo-Indian Attitudes: The Mind of the Indian Civil Service*, London: Hambledon Press, 1993.

Dietze, Carola, 'Terror in the Nineteenth Century: Political Assassinations and Public Discourse in Europe and the United States, 1878–1901', *GHI Bulletin*, No. 40 (Spring), 2007.

Dublish, Kaushalya Devi, *Revolutionaries and their Activities in Northern India*, Delhi: B. R. Publishing Corporation, 1982.

Dutta, Meena and Jai Narain, 'Did Gandhi Fail to Save Bhagat Singh?', *Punjab History Conference*, Patiala: Panjab University, 30th Session, 10–12 March 1998.

Dwyer, Rachel, 'The Case of the Missing Mahatma: Gandhi and the Hindi Cinema', *Public Culture*, 23(2), 2011.

Edwardes, Michael, *Nehru: A Political Biography*, London: Allen Lane/Penguin Press, 1971.

Elam, J. Daniel, 'The "Arch Priestess of Anarchy" Visits Lahore: Violence, Love, and the Worldliness of Revolutionary Texts', *Postcolonial Studies*, 16(2), 2013.

Enloe, Cynthia, *Manoeuvres: The International Politics of Militarising Women's Lives*, Berkeley: University of California Press, 2000.

Fanon, Frantz, *The Wretched of the Earth*, translated by Richard Philcox, New York: Grove Press, 2004 [1963].

Fenech, Louis E., 'Contested Nationalisms, Negotiated Terrains: the Ways Sikhs Remember Udham Singh "Shahid"', *Modern Asian Studies*, 36(4), 2002.

Fischer-Tiné, Harald, *Shyamji Krishnavarma: Sanskrit, Sociology and Anti-Imperialism*, London: Routledge, 2014.

Forbes, Geraldine, (ed.), Manmohini Zutshi Sahgal, *An Indian Freedom Fighter Recalls Her Life*, London: M.E. Sharpe, 1994.

———, *Women in Modern India*, Cambridge: Cambridge University Press, 1996.

———, *Indian Women and the Freedom Movement: A Historian's Perspective*, Mumbai: Research Center for Women's Studies, 1997.

BIBLIOGRAPHY

Freitag, Sandria, 'More than Meets the (Hindu) Eye: the Public Arena as a Space for Alternative Visions', in Richard Davis (ed.), *Picturing the Nation: Iconographies of Modern India*, New Delhi: Orient Longman, 2007.

Friend, Corrine (ed.), *Yashpal Looks Back: Selections from an Autobiography*, Delhi: Vikas, 1981.

Gaur, Ishwar Dayal, *Martyr as a Bridegroom: A Folk Representation of Bhagat Singh*, Delhi: Anthem, 2008.

Gell, Simeran, 'L'Inde aux deux visages: Dalip Singh et le Mahatma Gandhi', *Terrain*, 31, September 1998.

Ghosh, Ajoy, *Bhagat Singh and his Comrades*, New Delhi: New Age Press, 1979.

Ghosh, Durba, 'Revolutionary Women and Nationalist Heroes in Bengal, 1930 to the 1980s', *Gender & History*, Vol. 25, No., 2, August 2013, pp. 355–375.

Ghosh, Durba and Dane Kennedy (eds), *Decentering Empire: Britain, India and the Transcolonial World*, Delhi: Orient Longman, 2006.

Ghosh, Papiya, 'Articulating Community Rights: The Muslim League and Hindu Mahasabha in Congress Bihar, 1937–39', *South Asia*, 14(2), 1999, pp. 79–97.

Gohain, Hiren, *The Contribution of the Revolutionists in India's Freedom Struggle*, translated by Amrit Jyoti Mahanta, New Delhi: National Book Trust, 2010.

Gopal, Sarvepalli (ed.), *Selected Works of Jawaharlal Nehru*, Delhi: Orient Longman, 1973.

———, *Jawaharlal Nehru: A Biography, Vol. 1, 1889–1947*, London: Jonathon Cape, 1975.

———, *Radhakrishnan: A Biography*, London: Unwin Hyman, 1989.

Gordon, Richard, 'The Hindu Mahasabha and the Indian National Congress, 1915 to 1926', *Modern Asian Studies*, 9(2), 1975.

Grewal, J. S. (ed.), *Bhagat Singh and his Legend*, Patiala: World Punjabi Centre, 2008.

Grover, D. R., *Civil Disobedience Movement in the Punjab, 1930–1934*, New Delhi: B.R. Corporation, 1987.

Guha, Ranajit, 'The Prose of Counter-Insurgency', *Subaltern Studies II: Writings on South Asian History and Society*, New Delhi: Oxford University Press, 2007 [1983].

Guha, Ramchandra, 'The Challenge of Contemporary History', *Economic and Political Weekly*, 28 June 2008.

Gupta, Amit Kumar, 'The Executions of March 1931, Gandhi and Irwin', *Bengal Past and Present*, January–June 1971, XC, part 1, no. 169.

———, 'Defying Death: Nationalist Revolutionism in India, 1897–1938', *Social Scientist*, 25(9/10), 1997.

Gupta, Charu, 'The Icon of Mother in Late Colonial North India', *Economic and Political Weekly*, 36 (45), 2001.

Gupta, Manmathnath, *They Lived Dangerously: Reminiscences of a Revolutionary*, Delhi: People's Publishing House, 1969.

———, *Bhagat Singh and His Times*, Delhi: Lipi Prakashan, 1977.

Habib, Irfan, 'Civil Disobedience, 1930–31', *Social Scientist*, 25(9/10), 1997.

———, 'The Envisioning of a Nation: A Defence of the Idea of India', *Social Scientist*, 27(9/10), 1999.

BIBLIOGRAPHY

Habib, S. Irfan, *To Make the Deaf Hear: Ideology and Programme of Bhagat Singh and His Comrades*, New Delhi: Three Essays Collective, 2007.

Halifax, Earl [Edward Frederick Lindley Wood], *Fullness of Days*, New York: Dodd, Mead & Co., 1957.

Hall, Stuart, 'Encoding/Decoding' in S. Hall, D. Hobson, A. Lowe, & P. Willis (eds), *Culture, Media, Language*, London: Hutchinson, 1980.

Hardas, Balshastri, *Armed Struggle for Freedom: Ninety Years of Indian Independence, from 1857 to Subhash*, translated by S. S. Apte, Poona: KAL Prakashan, 1958.

Hasan, Mushirul, 'Communalism in the Provinces: A Case Study of Bengal and Punjab, 1922–1926', *Economic and Political Weekly*, 15(33), 1980.

Heeger G., 'The Growth of the Congress Movement in Punjab, 1920–1940', *Journal of Asian Studies*, 32, 1, 1972.

Heehs, Peter. *The Bomb in Bengal: the Rise of Revolutionary Terrorism in India, 1900–1910*, Oxford: Oxford University Press, 1993.

———, 'Revolutionary Terrorism in British Bengal', in Elleke Boehmer and Stephen Morten (eds), *Terror and the Postcolonial*, Chichester: Blackwell, 2010.

Henningham, Stephen, 'Quit India in Bihar and the Eastern United Provinces: The Dual Revolt', in Ranajit Guha (ed.), *Subaltern Studies II: Writings of South Asian History and Society*, Delhi: Oxford University Press, 1983.

Homage to Martyrs, Delhi: All India Freedom Fighters Association, 1981.

Hooja, Bhupindra (ed.), *A Martyr's Notebook*, Jaipur, Indian Book Chronicle, 1994.

Jain, Jyotindra (ed.), *India's Popular Culture; Iconic Spaces and Fluid Images*, Mumbai: Marg Publications, 2007.

Jain, Kajri, *Gods in the Bazaar: The Economies of Indian Calendar Art*, Durham: Duke University Press, 2007.

Jeffrey, Robin. 'What the Statues Tell: The Politics of Choosing Symbols in Trivandrum', *Pacific Affairs*, LIII, 3, Fall, 1980.

———, 'The Mahatma didn't like Movies and Why it Matters: Indian Broadcasting Policy, 1920s-1990s', *Global Media and Communication*, Vol. 2, No. 2, 2006, pp. 204–224.

———, 'Mission, Money and Machinery: Indian Newspapers in the Twentieth Century', *ISAS Working Paper*, No. 117, 25 November 2010, pp. 26.

Juneja, M.M. (ed.), *Bhagat Singh par Chuninda Lekh*, Hisar: Modern Publishers, 2007.

Kapila, Shruti, 'A History of Violence', *Modern Intellectual History*, 7(2), 2010.

Kasturi, Leela, and Vina Mazumdar (eds), *Women and Indian Nationalism*, New Delhi, Vikas, 1994.

Kaur, Baljit, 'Pattern of Literacy in the Punjab, 1931', in *Punjab History Conference Proceedings*, 25th Session, 5–7 May 1992, Patiala: Department of Punjab Historical Studies, 188–192.

Kaur, Raminder, 'Martial Imagery in Western India: The Changing Face of Ganapati', *South Asia*, 25(1), 2002.

Kolsky, Elizabeth, *Colonial Justice in British India: White Violence and the Rule of Law*, Cambridge: Cambridge University Press, 2010.

Kooner, K.S. and G.S. Sindra, *Some Hidden Facts: Martyrdom of Shaheed Bhagat Singh*, Chandigarh: Unistar, 2005.

Kudaisya, Gyanesh, *Region, Nation, 'Heartland': Uttar Pradesh in India's Body Politic*, Delhi: Sage, 2006.

Kumar, Avinash, 'Nationalism as Bestseller: The Case of Chand's "Phansi Ank"', in Abhijit Gupta and Swapan Chakraborty (eds), *Moveable Type: Book History in India*, Delhi: Permanent Black, 2008.

Kumar, Kapil (ed.), *Congress and Classes: Nationalism, Workers and Peasants*, New Delhi: Manohar, 1988.

Kumar, Ravinder, *The Making of a Nation: Essays on Indian History and Politics*, Delhi: Manohar, 1989.

Kumar, Ravinder and Hari Dev Sharma (eds), *Selected Works of Motilal Nehru*, Vol. 7, New Delhi: Vikas, 1986.

Lal, Chaman, *The Vanishing Empire*, Tokyo: Kyodo Printing co., 1937.

———, *Martyrs of India, War of Independence Centenary*, Kanpur: Kanpur Publishing Press, 1957.

Lal, Chaman, (ed.), *The Jail Notebook and Other Writings*, Delhi: LeftWord Press, 2007.

———, 'Political Correspondence of Bhagat Singh', in *Mainstream*, Vol. XLVI, No. 14, 22 March 2008.

Lal, Kishan, *Revolutionary Activities in Delhi*, New Delhi: Agam Kala Prakashan, 1999.

Lal, Vinay, *The History of History*, Delhi: Oxford University Press, 2003.

Laushey, David M., *Bengal Terrorism and the Marxist Left: Aspects of Regional Nationalism in India, 1905–1942*, Calcutta: Firma K. L. Mukhopadhyay, 1975.

Leiten, G. K., 'When Communism Came to India', *South Asia*, 5(1), 1975.

Lidz, Victor, 'A Note on "Nonviolence is Two"', *Sociological Inquiry*, 38, Winter 1968.

Low, D.A. (ed.), *Soundings in Modern South Asian History*, Berkeley/Los Angeles: University of California Press, 1968.

———, *Britain and Indian Nationalism: The Imprint of Ambiguity, 1929–1942*, Cambridge: Cambridge University Press, 1997.

——— (ed.), *Congress and the Raj: Facets of the Indian Struggle, 1917–47*, Delhi: Oxford University Press, 2004.

Lutgendorf, Philip, *Hanuman's Tale*, New York: Oxford University Press, 2007.

Maclean, Kama, 'Hybrid nationalist or Hindu nationalist? The life of Madan Mohan Malaviya' in Kate Brittlebank (ed.), *Tall Tales and True: India, Historiography and British Imperial Imaginings*, Melbourne: Monash Asia Institute, 2008.

———, *Pilgrimage and Power: The Kumbh Mela in Allahabad, 1765–1954*, New York: Oxford University Press, 2008.

———, 'The Portrait's Journey: The Image, Social Communication and Martyr-Making in Colonial India', *Journal of Asian Studies*, 70(3), 2011.

———, 'The History of a Legend: Accounting for Popular Histories of Revolutionary Nationalism', *Modern Asian Studies*, 46(6), 2012.

———, 'Imagining the Nationalist Movement: Revolutionary Metaphors in Imagery of the Indian Freedom Struggle', *Journal of Material Culture*, December 2013.

————, 'What Durga Bhabhi Did Next: or, Was there a Gendered Agenda in Revolutionary Circles?' *South Asian History and Culture*, 4(2), 2013.

————, 'The Art of Panicking Quietly: British-Indian Responses to "Outrages", 1928–1933', in Harald Fischer-Tiné and Christine Whyte (eds), *Empires on the Verge of a Nervous Breakdown: Crisis, Panic and Anxiety in the Age of Imperialism, 1860–1940*, London: Palgrave (forthcoming).

Maclean, Kama and J. Daniel Elam, 'Who is a Revolutionary?', *Postcolonial Studies*, Special Issue, 16(2), 2013.

Manjapra, Kris, 'Communist Internationalism and Transcolonial Recognition', in Sugata Bose and Kris Manjapra (eds), *Cosmopolitan Thought Zones: South Asia and the Global Circulation of Ideas*, London: Palgrave/Macmillan, 2010.

————, *M. N. Roy: Marxism and Colonial Cosmopolitanism*, London: Routledge, 2010.

Masselos, Jim, *Indian Nationalism: A History*, New Delhi: New Dawn Press, 2005.

Mathur, L. P., *Bhagat Singh: the Prince of Martyrs*, Jaipur: Aavishkar Publications, 2001.

McLain, Karline, *India's Immortal Comic Books: Gods, Kings and other Heroes*, Bloomington: Indiana University Press, 2009.

McMurtrie, Beth, 'Secrets from Belfast', *Chronicle of Higher Education*, 26 January 2014.

Mehta, Nalin, 'The Amar Chitra Katha of 1857: The Nation in Comic', in Sharmistha Gooptu and Boria Majumdar (eds), *Representing 1857*, Delhi: Roli Books, 2007.

Misra, Maria, *Vishnu's Crowded Temple: India since the Great Rebellion*, New Haven & London: Yale University Press, 2007.

Mittal, S. K. and Irfan Habib, 'The Congress and the Revolutionaries in the 1920s', *Social Scientist*, 10(6), June 1982.

————, 'Towards Independence and Socialist Republic: Naujawan Bharat Sabha', Parts One and Two, *Social Scientist*, 8 (2 and 3), 1979, pp. 31–40; pp. 18–29.

Mitter, Partha, *Art and Nationalism in India, 1850–1922*, Cambridge: Cambridge University Press, 1994.

Mohan, Kamlesh, *Militant Nationalism in the Punjab, 1919–1935*, Delhi: Manohar, 1985.

Moore-Gilbert, Bart, *The Setting Sun: A Memoir of Empire and Family Secrets*, New York: Verso, 2014.

Mukherjee, Mridula, *Peasants in India's Non-Violent Revolution: Practice and Theory*, New Delhi: Sage, 2004.

Muldoon, Andrew, *Empire, Politics and the Creation of the 1935 India Act*, Farnham: Ashgate, 2009.

Moffat, Chris, 'Experiments in Political Truth', *Postcolonial Studies*, 16(2), 2013.

Moraes, Frank, *Jawaharlal Nehru: A Biography*, New York: Macmillan, 1958.

Naess, Arne, *The Selected Works of Arne Naess*, Vol. 1, Dordrecht: Springer, 2005.

Nair, L. R. (ed.), *Motilal Nehru: Birth Centenary Souvenir*, New Delhi: Motilal Nehru Centenary Committee, 1961.

Nair, Neeti, 'Bhagat Singh as "Satyagrahi": The Limits to Non-Violence in Late Colonial India', *Modern Asian Studies*, 43(3), 2009.

Nanda, B. R., 'Nehru and the British', *Modern Asian Studies*, 30(2), 1996.

————, *The Nehrus*, Chicago: University of Chicago Press, 1974.

BIBLIOGRAPHY

Nayar, Kuldip, *Without Fear: The Life and Trial of Bhagat Singh*, New Delhi: HarperCollins, 2007.

Nehru, Jawaharlal, *Toward Freedom: An Autobiography*, Boston: Beacon Press, 1936 [1958].

Niebuhr, Reinhold, 'What Chance has Gandhi?', *The Christian Century*, 48(41), 1931.

Nijhar, Milkha Singh, 'Bhagat Singh ki chori-chhipe khinche gaya chitra (Bhagat Singh's Secret Photograph)', in M. M. Juneja (ed.), *Bhagat Singh par Chuninda Lekh*, Hisar: Modern Publishers, 2007.

Nilesh, Preetha, 'Gandhiji and the Trial and Execution of Bhagat Singh', *Indica*, 47(2), 2010.

Noorani, A. G., *The Trial of Bhagat Singh: The Politics of Justice*, Delhi: Oxford University Press, [1996] 2008.

Orsini, Francesca, *The Hindi Public Sphere, 1920–1940: Language and Literature in the Age of Nationalism*, Oxford: Oxford University Press, 2002.

Pandey, Geetanjali, *Between Two Worlds: an Intellectual Biography of Premchand*, New Delhi: Manohar, 1989.

Pandey, Gyanendra, 'Mobilisation in a Mass Movement: Congress "Propaganda" in the United Provinces (India), 1930–1934', *Modern Asian Studies*, 9(2), 1975.

———, *The Ascendancy of the Congress in Uttar Pradesh, 1920–1940*, London: Anthem Press, 2002 [second edition].

———, *The Construction of Communalism in North India*, New Delhi: Oxford University Press, 2006.

———, 'Un-archived Histories: the "mad" and the "trifling"', *Economic and Political Weekly*, XLVII, 1, 2012.

Pandey, S.M., 'Ideological Conflict in the Kanpur Trade Union Movement, 1934–45', *Indian Journal of Industrial Relations*, 3(3), 1968.

Parel, Anthony J. (ed.), *Hind Swaraj and Other Writings*, Cambridge: Cambridge University Press, 1997.

Pavadya, Balram Singh, 'The Attitude of the Indian National Congress to Dominion Status, 1930–1947', *International Studies*, 6, 1964.

Pinney, Christopher, *Camera Indica: The Social Life of Indian Photographs*, London: Reaktion Books, 1997.

———, 'A secret of their own country: or, How Indian nationalism made itself irrefutable', in Sumathi Ramaswamy (ed.), *Beyond Appearances: Visual Practices and Ideologies in Modern India*, New Delhi: Sage Publications, 2003.

———, *'Photos of the Gods': The Printed Image and Political Struggle in India*, London: Reaktion Books, 2004.

———, 'The Body and the Bomb', in Richard H. Davis (ed.), *Picturing the Nation: Iconographies of Modern India*, Delhi: Orient Longman, 2007.

———, 'Visual history tells us about repressed histories', *Tehelka*, 5(37), 20 September 2008.

———, *The Coming of Photography in India*, New Delhi: Oxford University Press, 2008.

———, 'Iatrogenic Religion and Politics', in Raminder Kaur and William Mazzarella (eds),

BIBLIOGRAPHY

Censorship in South Asia: Cultural Regulation from Sedition to Seduction, Bloomington: Indiana University Press, 2009.

Potter, David C., 'Manpower shortage and the end of colonialism: the case of the Indian Civil Service', *Modern Asian Studies*, 7(1), 1973.

Rai, Rustom (ed.), *Pratibandhit Hindi Sahitya*, Part 1, Delhi: Radhakrishnan Prakashan, 1999.

Ramaswamy, Sumathi (ed). *Beyond Appearances: Visual Practices and Ideologies in Modern India*, New Delhi: Sage Publications, 2003.

Ramaswamy, Sumathi. 'Maps, Mother/Goddesses, and Martyrdom in Modern India', *Journal of Asian Studies*, 67(3), 2008.

————, *The Goddess and the Nation: Mapping Mother India*, Durham and London: Duke University Press, 2010.

Ramnath, Maia, *Haj to Utopia: How the Ghadar Movement Chartered Global Radicalism and Attempted to Overthrow the British Empire*, Berkeley: University of California Press, 2011.

Rao, Anupama, 'Problems of Violence, States of Terror: Torture in Colonial India', *Interventions: International Journal of Postcolonial Studies*, 3(2), 2010.

Raza, Ali, Franziska Roy and Benjamin Zachariah (eds), *The Internationalist Moment: South Asia, Worlds and World Views, 1917–39*, New Delhi: Sage, 2015.

Raza, Ali. 'Separating the Wheat from the Chaff: Meerut and the Creation of "Official" Communism in India', Comparative Studies of South Asia, Africa and the Middle East, 33 (3), 2013.

Roberts, Andrew, *'The Holy Fox': The Life of Lord Halifax*, London: Weidenfeld and Nicolson, 1991.

Rose, Gillian, *Visual Methodologies: An Introduction to the Interpretation of Visual Materials*, London: Sage, 2001.

Roy, Franziska and Benjamin Zachariah, 'Meerut and a Hanging: "Young India", Popular Socialism, and the Dynamics of Imperialism', *Comparative Studies of South Asia, Africa and the Middle East*, 33 (3), 2013, pp. 360–77.

Roy, Srirupa, '"A Symbol of Freedom": The Indian Flag and the Transformations of Nationalism, 1906–2002', *Journal of Asian Studies*, 65(3), 2006.

Saha, Jonathan, 'Everyday Violence in British India', *History Compass*, 9(11), 2011.

Sahni, J. N., *Truth about the Indian Press*, Delhi: Allied Publishers, 1974.

Sanyal, Jatinder Nath, *Sardar Bhagat Singh (A Short Life-sketch)*, Allahabad: J.N. Sanyal, 1931.

————, *Sardar Bhagat Singh*, revised edition, Nagpur: Vishva Bharati Prakashan, 1983.

Sarkar, Mahua, 'Between Craft and Method: Meaning and Inter-subjectivity in Oral History Analysis', *Journal of Historical Sociology*, 25 (4), 2012.

Sarkar, Sumit, 'The Logic of Gandhian Nationalism: Civil Disobedience and the Gandhi-Irwin Pact', *Indian Historical Review*, 3, 1976.

————, *Modern India, 1885–1947*, Delhi: Macmillan, 1983.

Sarkar, Tanika, 'Politics and Women in Bengal: the Conditions and Meaning of Participation', *Indian Economic and Social History Review*, 21(1), 1984.

Sawhney, Simona, 'Bhagat Singh: A Politics of Death and Hope', in Anshu Malhotra and Farina Mir (eds), *Punjab Reconsidered: History, Culture, and Practice*, New Delhi: Oxford University Press, 2012.

Seth, Sanjay, *Marxist Ideology and Nationalist Politics: the Case of Colonial India*, New Delhi: Sage, 1995.

———, 'Rewriting Histories of Nationalism: The Politics of "Moderate Nationalism" in India, 1870–1905', *American Historical Review*, 104(1), 1999.

Shankar, Rama Hari, *Gandhi's Encounter with the Indian Revolutionaries*, New Delhi: Siddharth Publications, 1996.

Sharma, I. Mallikarjuna (ed.), *In Retrospect: Sagas of Heroism and Sacrifice of Indian Revolutionaries*, Vol. 1, Hyderabad: Ravi Sai Enterprises, 1999.

Sharma, Shalini, 'Developing a Communist Identity: the Case of the Naujawan Bharat Sabha', *Journal of Punjab Studies*, 14(2), 2007.

———, *Radical Politics in Colonial Punjab: Governance and Sedition*, London: Routledge, 2009.

Shaw, G. and M. Lloyd (eds), *Publications Proscribed by the Government of India: A catalogue of the collections in the India Office Library and Records and the Department of Oriental Manuscripts and Printed Books, British Library Reference Division*, London: The British Library, 1985.

Sherlock, Steven, 'Berlin, Moscow and Bombay: The Marxism that India Inherited', *South Asia*, 21(1), 1998.

Sherman, Taylor C., 'State Practice, Nationalist Politics and the Hunger Strikes of the Lahore Conspiracy Case Prisoners, 1929–39', *Cultural and Social History*, 5(4), 2008.

———, *State Violence and Punishment in India*. London/New York: Routledge, 2010.

Shukla, N. K. (ed.), *The Trial of Baikunth Sukul: A Revolutionary Patriot*, Delhi: Har-Anand Publications, 1999.

Sidhu, Gurdev Singh (ed.), *The Hanging of Bhagat Singh, Vol. IV: The Banned Literature*, Chandigarh, Unistar, 2007.

Silvestri, Michael, '"The Sinn Fein of India": Irish Nationalism and the Policing of Revolutionary Terrorism in Bengal', *The Journal of British Studies*, 39(4), 2000.

Singh 'Josh', Sohan, 'My Meetings with Bhagat Singh', in *My Meetings with Bhagat Singh and on Other Early Revolutionaries*, New Delhi: Communist Party Publication, 1976.

Singh, Chander Pal, 'What Mahatma Gandhi did to save Bhagat Singh', *Gandhi Marg*, October–December 2010, 32(3).

———, *Bhagat Singh Revisited: Historiography, Biography and Ideology of the Great Martyr*, Delhi: Originals, 2011.

Singh, Gajendra, *The Testimonies of Indian Soldiers and the Two World Wars: Between Self and Sepoy*, London: Bloomsbury, 2014.

Singh, Gulab, *Under the Shadow of the Gallows*, Delhi: Rup Chand, 1963.

Singh, Jagmohan, 'Distorting Bhagat Singh's Legacy', *Alpjan*, April–June 2002.

Singh, Pritam, 'Review Article', *Journal of Punjab Studies*, 14(2), 2007.

Singh, Ujjwal Kumar, *Political Prisoners in India*, Delhi: Oxford University Press, 1998.

Sinha, Bejoy Kumar, *Memoirs of a Revolutionary: Andamans, the Indian Bastille*, Delhi: Mittal Publications, 1987 [1939].

BIBLIOGRAPHY

———, *Indian Revolutionary Movement*, Pune: Lokmanya Tilak Smarak Trust, 1994.

Sinha, Mrinalini, *Specters of Mother India: the Global Restructuring of an Empire*, Durham: Duke University Press, 2006.

Srivastava, Neelam, 'Bollywood as National(ist) Cinema: Violence, Patriotism and the National-Popular in Rang de Basanti', *Third Text*, 23(6), 2009.

Stiehm, Judith, 'Nonviolence is Two', *Sociological Inquiry*, 38, 1968.

Tan, Tai Yong, *The Garrison State: The Military, Government and Society in Colonial Punjab*, Delhi: Sage, 2005.

Tandon, Prakash, *Punjabi Century, 1857–1957*, Berkeley: University of California Press, 1961.

Tarlo, Emma, *Clothing Matters: Dress and Identity in India*, London: Hurst & Co., 1996.

Thapar-Bjorkert, Suruchi, 'Nationalist Memories: Interviewing Indian Middle Class Women', *Oral History*, 27 (2), 1999.

———, *Women in the Indian Nationalist Movement: Unseen Faces and Unheard Voices, 1930–1942*, Delhi: Sage, 2006.

Thomas, David A., 'Lucknow and Kanpur, 1880–1920: Stagnation and Development under the Raj', *South Asia*, 5(2), 1982.

Tomlinson, B. R., *The Indian National Congress and the Raj, 1929–1942: The Penultimate Phase*, Cambridge: Cambridge University Press, 1976.

Tripathi, S. D., 'Politics of a Multi-Union Plant: The Swadeshi Experience', *Indian Journal of Industrial Relations*, 3(4), 1968.

Vaidik, Aparna, 'History of a Renegade Revolutionary: Revolutionism and Betrayal in Colonial India', *Postcolonial Studies*, 16(2), 2013.

Venu, C. S., *Sirdar Bhagat Singh*, Madras, n.d. [c. 1931],

Verma, Shiv (ed.), *Bhagat Singh: on the Path of Liberation*, Chennai: Bharathi Puthakalaya, 2007.

Verma, Shiv, *Samsmritiyan: Krantikari Shahidon ke Samsmarnatmak Rekhichitra*, Lucknow: Rahul Foundation, 2006.

Vohra, K. Murty Ashok, *Radhakrishnan, His Life and Ideas*, New York: SUNY, 1990.

von Steitencron, Herman, *Hindu Myth, Hindu History: Religion, Art, and Politics*, Delhi: Permanent Black, 2005.

Wani, Aarti, 'Uses of History: *Rang De Basanti* and *Lage Raho Munnabhai*', *Monthly Review Magazine*, 12 February 2007.

Waraich, Malwinderjit Singh (ed.), *Bhagat Singh: The Eternal Rebel*, Government of India, Publications Division, 2007.

Waraich, Malwinderjit Singh and Gurdev Singh Sidhu (eds), *The Hanging of Bhagat Singh, Vol. I: Complete Judgement and other Documents*, Delhi: Unistar, 2005.

Waraich, Malwinderjit Singh and Harish Jain (eds), *The Hanging of Bhagat Singh, Vol. III: Confessions, Statements and Other Documents*, Chandigarh: Unistar, 2007.

Watt, Carey A., *Serving the Nation: Cultures of Service, Association, and Citizenship*, New Delhi: Oxford University Press, 2005.

Yadav K. C. and Babar Singh (eds), *Bhagat Singh: The Making of a Revolutionary: Contemporaries' Portrayals*, Delhi: Hope India Publications, 2006.

BIBLIOGRAPHY

———, *Bhagat Singh: Ideas on Freedom, Liberty and Revolution: Jail Notes of a Revolutionary*, Delhi: Hope India Publications, 2007.

Yashpal, *Singhavalokan (Sampurn)*, Allahabad: Lokbharati Prakashan, 2007.

Zachariah, Benjamin, 'Rewriting Imperial Mythologies: the Strange Case of Penderel Moon', *South Asia*, 21 (2), 2001.

———, *Nehru*, London/NY: Routledge, 2004.

———, *Developing India: An Intellectual and Social History*, New Delhi: Oxford University Press, 2005.

———, 'A Long, Strange Trip: the Lives in Exile of Har Dayal', *South Asian History and Culture*, 4 (4), 2013.

Zaidi, A. M. and Shaheda Zaidi (eds), *The Encyclopaedia of the Indian National Congress*, Vol. 9: 1925–1929, New Delhi: Chand & Co., 1980.

Zaidi, A.M. (ed.), *Congress Presidential Addresses*, Vols 9 and 10, Delhi: Indian Institute of Applied Political Research, 1988.

Žižek, Slavoj, *Violence: Six Sideways Reflections*, New York: Picador, 2008.

Online & Unpublished Sources

Agarwal, Priya, 'Forgetting the Violence, Remembering a Report: the Paradox of the 1931 Kanpur Riots', University of Pennsylvania, 2008, ScholarlyCommons, http://repository. upenn.edu/hist_honors/18/ (last accessed 3 December, 2012).

Banerjee, Himadri, 'Bhagat Singh in Bengali Writings', at http://bhagatsinghstudy.blogspot. com/2008/01/bhagat-singh-in-bengali-writings.html (last accessed 3 April 2010).

Chatterjee, Partha, 'Bombs and Nationalism in Bengal', paper presented at 'Subaltern Citizens and their Histories', 13–14 October 2006, Emory University. www.icis.emory. edu/subalterndocs/Chatterjee.pdf (last accessed 6 August, 2014).

Collected Works of Mahatma Gandhi (Online) http://www.gandhiserve.org/e/cwmg/cwmg. htm (last accessed 11 December, 2013).

Harcourt, Max, 'Revolutionary Networks in North Indian Politics, 1907–1935', D. Phil. dissertation, University of Sussex, 1974.

Laushey, David M., 'The Bengal Terrorists and their Conversion to Marxism: Aspects of Regional Nationalism in India, 1905–1942', PhD dissertation, University of Virginia, 1969.

Lutgendorf, Philip, 'Review of *The Legend of Bhagat Singh*', *Philip's Filums*, http://www. uiowa.edu/~incinema/LegendBhagat.html (last accessed 22 July, 2010).

INDEX

INDEX

INDEX

INDEX

INDEX